Reading and Writing Essays

THE IMAGINATIVE TASKS

Reading and Writing Essays

THE IMAGINATIVE TASKS

PAT C. HOY II
Harvard University

McGRAW-HILL, INC.

New York   St. Louis   San Francisco   Auckland   Bogotá
Caracas   Lisbon   London   Madrid   Mexico   Milan
Montreal   New Delhi   Paris   San Juan   Singapore
Sydney   Tokyo   Toronto

This book was developed by STEVEN PENSINGER, Inc.

READING AND WRITING ESSAYS: The Imaginative Tasks

Permissions Acknowledgments appear on pages xx–xxii, and on this page by reference.

1 2 3 4 5 6 7 8 9 0 DOH DOH 9 0 9 8 7 6 5 4 3 2 1

ISBN 0-07-030607-9

This book was set in Galliard by General Graphic Services, Inc. The editors were Steve Pensinger and Tom Holton; the designer was Joan Greenfield; the production supervisor was Leroy A. Young. R. R. Donnelley & Sons Company was printer and binder.

Library of Congress Cataloging-in-Publication Data

Hoy, Pat C.
    Reading and writing essays: the imaginative tasks / Pat C. Hoy.
        p.   cm.
    ISBN 0-07-030607-9
    1. English language—Rhetoric.   2. College readers.   3. Essays.
    I. Title.
    PE1408.H6855   1992
    808′.0427—dc20   91-22534

About the Author

Pat C. Hoy II, a former Professor of English and director of the Freshman Writing Program at the U.S. Military Academy, is now a Senior Preceptor in the Harvard Expository Writing Program. He has also taught at Bergen Community College in Paramus, New Jersey. He coedited *Prose Pieces* (with Robert DiYanni) and *Women's Voices* (with Robert DiYanni and Esther Schor). He has published articles, reviews, and familiar essays in a number of journals including *South Atlantic Review, Twentieth Century Literature, Sewanee Review, Agni,* and *Virginia Quarterly Review. Instinct for Survival,* a book of his familiar essays, will be published by the University of Georgia Press in 1992.

For
My Finest Teachers:

Agnes Etheridge
Herbert Howarth
David DeLaura
Tim Fox-Linton

Who, in Their Classrooms, Always Sought
to
Open Minds and Imaginations
to
Unexplored Possibilities

Contents

Contents

◊

Chapter 2

THE EXPLORATORY ESSAY
ENRICHMENT AND COMPLEXITY   62

Chapter 3

THE ANALYTICAL ESSAY
CRITICAL WRITING   104

Contents

◊

Chapter 4

THE SHORT RESEARCH ESSAY
ARGUMENT

Contents

◇

Appendix

MLA DOCUMENTATION
A SHORT GUIDE   227

*Student essays

Contents

*Student essays

Preface

Reading and Writing Essays is a different kind of writing book. As you know, traditional rhetorics and handbooks outline a writing process, explain rules for building and repairing sentences, and discuss the construction of paragraphs. But such books pay little attention to the essay's rich variety and complex development. Often they ignore the important relationship between reading and writing. This book aims at something educational rather than utilitarian. It aims to improve thinking, reading, and writing by showing students how to write three important forms of the essay: exploratory, analytical, and argumentative.

Experience has shown me that students who begin to master the essay begin to see more clearly the relationship between their mind's work and the work of the world. Essay writing fosters intellectual development, encourages students to make connections, and helps them understand the necessity for imposing order on experience.

I address this book to the students, responding directly to their needs as developing writers. What I say is no secret. I have been listening to my own students for years, trying to learn how to help them write better. They have taught me a valuable lesson: showing is far more effective than telling. So this book *shows* students how to write essays. There is, of course, much telling, much analysis. But my overriding purpose is to show students various writing processes, not a single process, and to encourage them to think as they write, to make discoveries in the act of developing essays.

The book's four chapters follow a developmental sequence that begins with the exploratory essay and ends with various argumentative essays. That sequence reflects a natural pattern of intellectual growth, a movement from experience to acquired knowledge, a movement from essays based on lived experience to those based on sources. Those first essays are exploratory, the latter exploratory, analytical, and argumentative. The exploratory essay gives the mind space to think on the page; the analytical and argumentative beg restraint, more formality. I think the latter are inherently harder for students to write, so I begin at what seems to me the beginning.

The exploratory essay encourages students to think at the keyboard or on paper. I want them to learn early the value of personal experience, but I don't emphasize expressive writing, or self-revelation per se. I begin with *images of experience,* showing students how their lives provide evidence they can use in their essays. Learning to shape that evidence, they also learn how experience shapes ideas and influences judgment. As they modify their views through reading and research, they begin to see that their own education influences their writing—what they say, how they say it, how they select appropriate forms to express what they know.

The exploratory essay gives students the latitude to ramble under control; it asks them to turn their experience into evidence, into ideas; it teaches them ultimately that their mind's work, besides

◊

being important, is almost always interesting if they learn to shape it for an audience. The most intriguing thing about the exploratory essay is its deceptive simplicity; students sense right away that they can write one, and they enter the act of writing unaware of the form's inherent complexity, its rich possibilities. They begin writing free from the restraints of formal argument. Because they produce texts they care about, texts they want to improve, they listen attentively to suggestions for improvement. Those suggestions, together with their own subsequent revisions, expose students to the limitless ways their work can be improved, the ways writers shape their essays. They begin to learn willingly about form.

After considering exploratory essays based solely on personal experience, I turn in Chapter 2 to the various ways of enriching those essays with evidence gleaned from reading and research. This chapter includes advice about integrating evidence and documenting sources within the text without interrupting the essay's movement. But students learn much more than technique. They begin to see clearly how reading yields its own fruit, how thoughts, ideas, and images gleaned from one text can be used in another. They learn how one writer's techniques can serve another writer's aims. In short, they learn the art of literary borrowing, a foundation for their education as readers, writers, and thinkers.

As students move gradually from exploration toward analysis and argument, they move with confidence in their ability to use language on their own terms, with a surer sense of how to use evidence from sources. They have learned how to draw conclusions, shape evidence, and influence an audience. The first two chapters of the book do more than teach a form of the essay; they provide the ground for the student's entire writing experience.

Chapter 3 shows students how to write analytical essays. They now look more closely at the form they've been working with in the earlier chapters, considering *how* professional essayists shape meaning. By examining how other writers create scenes, write dialogue, use images, and employ personae, students see that they, too, can handle such techniques to advantage. The essays they finally write about their discoveries require a more complex form of documentation and presentation than the exploratory ones did. These analytical essays move between exploration and argument, reaching back and pointing forward.

At the end of Chapter 3, I return to the notion of revision. I close with a consideration of what might happen if students go back to revise exploratory essays after they've done more reading, after they've analyzed the work of professional writers. The coda to this chapter aims to enlarge students' perceptions about revision.

Chapter 4 turns to argument. I consider how to discover controversies during preliminary research, how to develop questions that guide research, how to analyze evidence, how to form hypotheses about a controversy, how to develop argumentative strategies, how to write the essay. The final sections of the chapter show how exploration and analysis can serve in the development of short argumentative essays.

In each chapter of this book, I consider the development of different kinds of paragraphs: those that are essentially functional (beginnings and endings) and those that are substantive (middle), those well-suited for exploratory essays and those that serve analysis and argument. Students discover how paragraphs differ from essay to essay. They discover, too, how the demands of documentation change from one kind of essay to another. The Appendix gives guidelines for documentation and shows students how to become more persuasive by integrating sources into the texts of their essays.

Reading and Writing Essays encourages responsible experimentation. It shows students the flexibility of essay forms, and it encourages risk taking. Although this book cannot claim the final word on the essay and its many forms, it does have experience behind it, and its methods have been tested in various academic settings. Behind the book's expressed enthusiasms lies an informed sense that students enjoy experiments. They like to test new methods. Exploring feeds discovery, excites students. They ask only that we collaborate with them along the way, that we invest ourselves in discovering with them the rewards of writing.

Acknowledgments

Emily Barrosse, a former McGraw-Hill College Division editor, brought this book into existence; she found me, asked me to do it, and convinced the corporation to sponsor an experiment. Her successor, Sue Hurtt, continued the encouragement, as Charlotte Smith read and challenged my work and my assumptions. The three of them got me going. Leon Markowicz and his students at Lebanon Valley College read and used an early draft of this book; their enthusiasm spurred me on, and their critical assessments help shaped subsequent drafts, as did those of the early reviewers.

Steve Pensinger inherited the project when he joined McGraw-Hill. We had already worked together, and so it was a pleasure once again to have his wise counsel during the final stages. He brought to the project not only his own perfectly honed sense of a textbook but also a host of fine reviewers: Chris Anderson, University of Oregon; Kristine Hansen, Brigham Young University; Michael Hennessy, Southwest Texas State University; Barry Maid, University of Arkansas at Little Rock; and Jeffrey Sommers, Miami University—Middletown. I thank Steve and them for their generous contribution.

No one gave me more support than Nancy Sommers, who read the manuscript in three different stages, read it with loving care each time, raised pertinent questions, found gaps, found strengths, and always showed me how, in her words, "to make it better." That she made me want to make it better, even at the very end, is a tribute to her and her method. I could ask for no finer reader.

A number of my teaching colleagues helped shape this book in many ways, direct and indirect; they were friends who cared enough about their work and their students to invest themselves in the rigorous intellectual debate that most often accompanies spirited and informed teaching. All of them gave me ideas, pushed me in new directions, and roused me to thought: John Calabro, Mike Burke, Colin Dunn, Jake McFerren, Rick Kerin, Tim Hoffman, Janice Hudley, Gary Huested, Ray Kenny, Jerry Bolzak, Frank George, Sharan Daniel, Terry Blakely, Jose Vasquez, Ed Ruggero, Maxine Rodburg, Gordon Harvey, and Steven Donatelli. We learned together. Jack Capps, Peter Stromberg, and Richard Marius provided space and a community of writers; without them my work could not have been done.

As always, I thank my family—Ann, Patrick, Tim—for listening over the years to my obsessions, for tolerating my disappearances into the study, and for steadfast support. They seem to share my thrill when, finally, they hold the book itself in their hands.

Pat C. Hoy II

Permissions Acknowledgments

Chapter 1

THE
EXPLORATORY
ESSAY

—

SHAPING
AND
ORDERING
THE
FAMILIAR

A. *A Sense of this Book—Its Aims and Methods*

Reading and Writing Essays is a friendly book, a demonstration book that both *shows* and *tells* you how to write. It offers insight into an interesting and complex form of writing, a form all of us depend on from day to day. Whether you are writing a letter, a review, or a paper for one of your classes, you are writing something very much like an *essay*. So it makes sense that you should know about the essay. This book will help you understand the differences among essays as well as their common features. It should also give you your bearing in writing classes and keep you on course as you complete your education.

Writing is not easy for anyone, but it is exciting business. One of my good friends reminds me now and then that language is at times almost an enemy. We have to struggle with it, learn to use it, pay attention to the way it changes and slips out of control just when we think we have it reined in. But that's what makes writing fun. Even the best writers seldom get the words right the first time. They also struggle with language. That's why revision and collaboration are essential. In writing drafts, reading them to your friends, changing them, revising them, and seeking to say clearly and precisely what you need to say to get your point across, you will more than likely discover the magic of language by using it.

Focusing on the essay—its variety, its richness, its pleasures— you will begin by learning to transform the stuff of everyday life—your own experiences—into essays. That is to say, you will learn to make sense of the facts of your daily life as you create *exploratory* essays that permit you to make discoveries even as you write. Learning to use your own life as evidence, you should come to see how experience also shapes your ideas and influences your judgment.

Those exploratory essays will be followed by essays that analyze other essays. Your aim in the *analytical* essay will be to reveal the structural secrets in the work of professional writers; you'll actually learn how those writers transform experience, how they make sense of their lives, their observations, and their reading. The resulting essays will reveal something about technique, something about the way writers use language in their own special ways. Finally, you'll write short *research* essays, argumentative pieces, that will give you a chance to explore and analyze even as you develop your own arguments.

Reading is very important in this whole process of intellectual growth and development. The essays included within the chapters of this book and those in the section called Essays for Additional Reading should give you new ideas about yourself and about other writers who have used their own experience to create interesting, provocative essays. Looking at those writers' work, you should begin to *see* more clearly the relationship between your life and your writing. But there is even more to be gained from a consideration of those essays; you can learn how professional writers turn their own varied experiences into essays. Those writers, like the other students in your writing class, will become your teachers; they will collaborate with you, reading and commenting on your writing, helping you see, helping you understand the processes that all of us use to become better writers.

The various exercises in this book bring reading and writing together, showing you how these complementary experiences play off each other. But your reading in other courses will also help as you begin to discover how reading enriches your life and broadens your education. And, of course, education, the entire process of education, influences your writing—what you say, how you say it, how you select appropriate forms of the essay to express what you know and what you want to say to your readers.

Intellectual growth—the growth of your mind—follows a more crooked path than a textbook can follow. But this book does follow the logic of experience; it follows the logic of a mind awakening to new possibilities as it explores, accumulates knowledge, synthesizes, and draws conclusions. The book's *developmental sequence*—suggested by the order in which I present those three different but related forms of the essay (exploratory, analytical, argumentative)—follows the trail of the mind's awakening. Writing various kinds of essays, you will undoubtedly discover something exciting about the way your style evolves over time. Curiosity—intellectual curiosity—will lead you down the crooked path of learning, and as you learn, and as you read and write, you will undoubtedly find new ways to express yourself.

Naturally, as you begin to turn experience into text, you will write and then have to rewrite, reshaping your work, changing your words because someone in your class couldn't understand exactly what you meant or because you discovered gaps in your essays, places where even you couldn't remember what you had meant to say. And you will go on to rework those early drafts as you create the final version of the essay, trying to make it convey exactly what you mean. But you may also discover, as you move down that crooked path of the mind's journey, that no version of an essay need be final.

Education itself is an exploration, and as you read and broaden your experiences outside the writing classroom, you may change your mind and discover new ways to express your ideas. As you do, you may also find that essays written months or only weeks before need revising; they don't quite reflect what you know. Your essays may very well need to change shape as you add depth and variety to your thoughts. The kind of revision that follows such exploration points to the heart of your education. We learn, John Henry Newman reminds us, "not at a glance, but by piecemeal and accumulation." We learn over time as we awaken to new ways of seeing. Our explorations teach us.

This book will be an exploration, an inquiry into the very nature of essays, and it will also be an inquiry into imagination and order and meaning. Reading essays that are powerfully seductive, often provocative, and always interesting, you will learn to read yourself. You will learn to make sense of your experiences. Reading, exploring, and writing together, you and your fellow collaborators will become essayists.

B. *The Exploratory Essay—A Notion of Purpose and Shape*

We're going to begin our inquiry with the exploratory essay, a form that will give you a chance to stretch your mind a bit. Like all other essays, this personal, exploratory one has a *beginning, middle,* and *ending,* but unlike some other forms, it permits you a certain kind of leisurely reflection, an opportunity to meditate about an idea, chew on it, ruminate about it.

Other forms of the essay—those that we will consider later in this book—give you less latitude. They are tightly organized, streamlined, somewhat insistent about their conclusions. Those forms call for objectivity, a kind of logical, scientific certainty. The essayist seems to stand somewhat apart from the controversy under consideration, examining it from just the right distance to have the definitive word on the subject. Such an essay might begin this way:

Louis Agassiz, the greatest biologist of mid-nineteenth-century America, argued that God had created blacks and whites as separate species. The defenders of slavery took much comfort from this assertion, for biblical proscriptions of charity and equality did not have to extend across a species boundary. What could an abolitionist say? Science had shone its cold and dispassionate light upon the subject; Christian hope and sentimentality could not refute it.

Similar arguments, carrying the apparent sanction of science, have been continually invoked in attempts to equate egalitarianism with sentimental hope and emotional blindness. People who are unaware of this historical pattern tend to accept each recurrence at face value: that is, they assume that each statement arises from the "data" actually presented, rather than from the social conditions that truly inspire it.

The racist arguments of the nineteenth century were based primarily on craniometry, the measurement of human skulls. Today, these contentions stand totally discredited. What craniometry was to the nineteenth century, intelligence testing has been to the twentieth. The victory of the eugenics movement in the Immigration Restriction Act of 1924 signaled its first unfortunate effect—for the severe restrictions upon non-Europeans and upon southern and eastern Europeans gained much support from results of the first extensive and uniform application of intelligence tests in America—the Army Mental Tests of World War I. These tests were engineered and administered by psychologist Robert M. Yerkes, who concluded that "education alone will not place the negro [sic] race on a par with its Caucasian competitors." It is now clear that Yerkes and his colleagues knew no way to separate genetic from environmental components in postulating causes for different performances on the tests.

The latest episode of this recurring drama began in 1969, when Arthur Jensen published an article entitled, "How Much Can We Boost IQ and Scholastic Achievement?" in the *Harvard Educa-*

tional Review. Again, the claim went forward that new and uncomfortable information had come to light and that science had to speak the "truth" even if it refuted some cherished notions of a liberal philosophy. But again, I shall argue, Jensen had no new data; and what he did present was flawed beyond repair by inconsistencies and illogical claims.

This particular *argumentative* form of the essay serves a distinct purpose. We know where we are headed right from the beginning; we understand the terms of the argument. But there is an *exploratory* form of the essay that calls for something quite different. Instead of being direct and objective, you might begin in a more personal, more tentative mode. You might propose that you and your reader begin an exploration:

I used to have a cat, an old fighting tom, who would jump through the open window by my bed in the middle of the night and land on my chest. I'd half-awaken. He'd stick his skull under my nose and purr, stinking of urine and blood. Some nights he kneaded my bare chest with his front paws, powerfully, arching his back, as if sharpening his claws, or pummeling a mother for milk. And some mornings I'd wake in daylight to find my body covered with paw prints in blood; I looked as though I'd been painted with roses.

It was hot, so hot the mirror felt warm. I washed before the mirror in a daze, my twisted summer sleep still hung about me like sea kelp. What blood was this, and what roses? It could have been the rose of union, the blood of murder, or the rose of beauty bare and the blood of some unspeakable sacrifice or birth. The sign on my body could have been an emblem or a stain, the keys to the kingdom or the mark of Cain. I never knew. I never knew as I washed, and the blood streaked, faded, and finally disappeared, whether I'd purified myself or ruined the blood sign of the passover. We wake, if we ever wake at all, to mystery, rumors of death, beauty, violence. . . . "Seem like we're just set down here," a woman said to me recently, "and don't nobody know why."

ANALYZING *Reread those two very different beginnings. Before leaving them, jot down what you think are their major differences. Where is the writer in the first piece? Can you find him in and around his words? What do you think that essay will be about; that is, what contract do you think the writer has established with you as his reader? What has he promised to tell you in his essay? Now, speculate about the writer's aim in the second piece. Where do you think she's trying to lead you? Which piece makes you as a reader more sure about where you're headed? Explain.*

Here's the way those two beginnings strike me. The first one is a conventional *introduction* for an *argumentative* essay, a fairly streamlined, straightforward form of the essay that almost always begins with a general statement about the problem under consideration (pollution, birth control, world hunger, labor disputes, apathy, anything controversial) and then moves toward greater and greater specificity. Often the introduction ends with a thesis statement that represents the writer's conclusion about the controversial issue. The *body* of the essay defends that thesis in an objective, logical way. The *conclusion* usually begins with a reminder of the writer's thesis and ends with a meaningful generalization about the controversial problem. There is a certain predictability about this kind of essay. We may not know exactly what evidence the writer will use to establish his or her case and how the writer will use that evidence, but we know from the promise in the beginning—from the thesis and the organizational suggestions—what general form the essay will take.

In this particular essay about race and IQ, we know that in the *body* of the essay, Stephen Jay Gould, a geologist and winner of a National Book Award, will refute Arthur Jensen's claims about IQ and scholastic achievement. That is the promise we find in the last sentence of Gould's introduction: "But again, I shall argue, Jensen had no new data; and what he did present was flawed beyond repair by inconsistencies and illogical claims." Gould's burden of proof is there in that last sentence. Jensen presents no new data, and the data he presents is flawed—inconsistent and illogical. We cannot predict exactly how Gould will organize the body of his essay, but we do know from this last sentence what to expect. Gould must focus on Jensen's inconsistencies. He must undercut Jensen's conclusions about race and IQ just as he has already undercut Agassiz's and Yerkes' conclusions; that's what we learn inferentially from watching Gould work in his introduction. Agassiz and Yerkes had their work exposed by other scientists; Gould will expose Jensen. That is his contract; that will be his contribution to the ongoing debate about the relationship between race and IQ.

The beginning for the second essay—personal, perhaps even shocking to some readers—*teases us into thought.* The story about the old tomcat is so interesting, and it evokes such strong visual images, that we are likely to get lost in the story; we are likely, if we are not attentive, to pay too little attention to the details of the story. Yet those details suggest to us why the writer might be telling the story in the first place. We know that as an essayist, she wants to get our attention, wants to arrest our imagination. We know, too, that in an exploratory essay of this sort, she is not going to say straight out what this essay will be about. She has an *idea* that she wants us to mull over, but she doesn't want to give the whole show away at the outset. She wants us to follow her mind's crooked journey as she develops that idea. So we have to be alert; we can't expect her to be as predictable as the first essayist, even though both writers are bound by the same general *beginning-middle-end* structure that holds all good essays together, whatever their nature.

In the *beginning* of this particular essay, Annie Dillard, a Pulitzer prize–winning essayist, asks us to think about the strange, perhaps mysterious relationship between her and that old tomcat who walks all over her "bare chest" and leaves her body "covered with paw prints in blood." Dillard makes us wonder what this morning ritual is all about. Under Dillard's skillful guidance, where will this cat-story introduction lead us? What might the paw prints have to do with "the mark of Cain"? What does the essay's idea have to do with the woman's statement that Dillard uses at the very end of that beginning? Those are some of the questions her details ask us to ponder.

Clearly, we can't know the answers to those questions until we read Dillard's essay. We can't guess exactly. But she makes us *wonder*, makes us want to see where her mind will take us. As experienced readers, we know that after we have read Dillard's essay—any exploratory essay—we can return to the beginning and see much more than we could at the outset. Having a coherent beginning is a part of her writer's contract, part of what she's obligated to do for us. But in the exploratory essay, her purpose is different from Gould's, and she need not lay out a predictable argument at the outset. She wants to pique our curiosity, wants to interest us in her subject without revealing her game plan.

In this essay, Dillard's going to conduct a fairly complex inquiry about God and mankind: Did God create us in earnest or in jest? That's not a question Dillard can treat the way we treat the relationship between race and IQ. The idea, Dillard's idea, needs a bit more breathing room to work itself out than Gould's case against Jensen needs. Hers is an exploratory rather than argumentative mode; hers is an inquiry rather than a tightly reasoned conclusion. At the beginning of her exploration, Dillard asks nothing more than that we get excited about following her mind's journey and that we be alert.

Dillard is there in her essay. What she says comes from the experience of her own personal life, but she's using her experience as a way of presenting an idea. She uses the personal as a means to something universal, something that belongs to all of us. Her experience reconstructed reminds us of our own. We begin to see our life in hers. Scott Sanders, another essayist, clarifies this important point in an essay called "The Singular First Person": "I write about my experience not because it is mine, but because it seems to me a door through which others might pass." He sees the exploratory essay as "a private experiment carried out in public."

Sanders also tells us what it's like to write one of these exploratory pieces. He says that writing such an essay "is like finding my way through a forest without being quite sure what game I am chasing, what landmark I am seeking. I sniff down one path until some heady smell tugs me in a new direction, and then off I go, dodging and circling. . . . The pleasure in writing an essay—and, when the writing is any good, the pleasure in reading it—comes from this dodging and leaping, this movement of the mind." But Sanders issues an interesting note of caution. "It must not be idle movement, however, if the essay is to hold up; it must yield a pattern, draw a map of experience, be driven by deep concerns."

We will consider patterns later in this chapter and in others, but for now, remember that the "dodging and circling" is a way of enlarging an *idea;* it is a way of bringing more and more pertinent *evidence* into your essays. Sanders encourages you to follow the odd scent, to dart about in the forests of your mind and your experience, seeking connections. The search should lead you to the "deep concerns."

The exploratory essay lets your mind play over almost any subject. Your essay will be a record of your mind discovering connections, clarifying, and rendering judgments; the more interesting your mind, the more interesting your essay. Your readers should sense your excitement, should know something of the fun you're having making discoveries as you write. Joan Didion, an accomplished essayist, says, "I write entirely to find out what I'm thinking, what I'm looking at, what I see and what it means." She writes to clarify her thinking. So can you.

ANALYZING   *Look at these beginnings for two student essays. See if you can classify each as either* argumentative *or* exploratory.

A Confused Idealist
by Jay Varma

With the dispassionate power of a camera, Annie Dillard's "The Deer at Providencia" presents the death and consumption of a deer as a poignant commentary on suffering—how one woman and, on a larger level, all humans confront violence. To that end, her images, and the pain they convey, penetrate our consciousness with stunning skill. Described with the vivid clarity of immediate narratives, these potent visions expose the randomness and pain of suffering—a brutal continuum permitted by God and ignored by humanity. She argues that the agony of a deer's exhausted, wracked limbs and of a man's charred flesh, are part of our daily baggage; we feed off their misery, never acknowledging its existence or our own moral cannibalism. Charging all humans with insensitivity, Dillard draws portraits of brutality, savagery, and despair for us to explore and understand—to bring into our hearts—and then admonishes our empathy with moral indignance.

It is this philosophical exposition, however, that eventually undermines Dillard's effectiveness as a social commentator. Retreating to moral higher ground, Dillard grows sententious and self-righteous at the end of "The Deer of Providencia"—"This is the Big Time here, every minute of it," she warns, reproving both the reader and the "gentlemen of the city" for allegedly ignoring the inevitability of suffering (559). But, as a result, the reader is dragged from self-reflection, ostensibly Dillard's goal, into defensive posturing: Dillard becomes a hypocritical whiner, feeding off the pain of the burnt man and decrying, not accepting, the immutability of misery—the same failings she condemns so forthrightly. In "The Deer at Providencia," Dillard guides us into suffering with compelling images but, eventually, leaves us disoriented, mired in her own idealistic confusion.

11

Onamaewa
(What is your name?)
by Leon Yen

A person's name is a person's identity. I lost mine when I immigrated to this foreign land; I have been searching for it ever since. Throughout the years I have adopted other names to use as my own, only to find myself enmeshed with their reality and going around in a circle, gradually returning to the starting point, a point where I should always have been. I never thought I would be able to find myself again.

When I first entered elementary school in the States, I went by many names. One day I might call myself John, another day Steve, Devin, so on, and so on. My teacher didn't care, really. She just thought I was kind of queer and liked to play this identity game that kids like to play sometimes. To her I was number eleven in her roll book, and so I called myself Eleven. My classmates never got used to that. One day this bully cornered me during recess and demanded to know my name.

"Eleven," I answered him.

"No, stupid! You can't have a number for a name," he yelled at me. "What is your REAL name?"

I told him I didn't have one. He badgered me and twisted my arm. Finally, I relented and said that I had had a name before, but that it was dead, and so it didn't matter anymore.

"What is your old name then," he insisted.

"Shih-Wei," I said flatly, unconvinced that the name belonged to me.

Hearing my gibberish, he burst out, "What kind of a name is that? That's not a name; I've never heard of it. Why can't you have a normal name like the rest of us. Get a real name! Will ya?"

I did.

◊

ANALYZING AND WRITING *What do you think Jay's contract is with his readers; what must he do? Can you guess from his introduction how he might go about making his case against Dillard? What about Leon's contract and his plan of development? What do you imagine that he will do in his essay? Make detailed notes about each essay, and then turn to the Essays for Additional Reading section (pp. 249–259) to check your assessment. How well does each beginning prepare you for the rest of the essay? Explain.*

C. *Beginnings, Middles, and Endings—How They Work Together*

I have suggested that all essays are built on a three-part structure— *beginning, middle,* and *ending*—but we have seen from just four beginnings that those structural units can differ significantly from one kind of essay to another. There are other interesting differences even within the same form of the essay. You need only be aware of the general function of each part and the relationship of one part to the others.

In the first two chapters, we're going to focus on the exploratory essay, developing as we go along a sense of the characteristics of that particular form. We'll turn later in this chapter to a method that will help you get started, help you turn your own experiences into essays, but here at the beginning, we want to uncover general principles that will give you an understanding of the kind of essay you will be writing. We want to discover what makes these essays hang together, what makes all the parts fit together so that the entire essay makes sense, each part contributing to the whole.

As you may have already surmised, the *beginning* of an exploratory essay gives your readers a sense of the intellectual and emotional journey they are about to take; it invites them to consider an idea, but it need not lay out any fixed plan. Instead, it ought to entice your readers, introduce them to the idea under consideration, coax them into the *middle* of the essay, where development, analysis, and revelation take place. There, in the middle of the essay, you, as a writer, consider your topic, examine it from your personal perspective, try to make your readers see as you see. In the middle, you unfold your mind's logic; you make your reader aware of your unique way of thinking about the idea under consideration. The *ending* reminds your readers where they've been and gives them, as well, a final perspective on the idea you have been exploring in the essay. That ending is not simply a restatement of what has already been said; rather, it is an artful closure to the exploration, a subtle movement back through the essay that reminds your readers of the value of the intellectual journey they have just taken. Going back to the beginning, readers know more; they go back pleased and enlightened, if you have done a good job leading them down that crooked path that must always turn back on itself.

Looking in detail at one exploratory essay, we can see just how closely the structural parts work together to express the writer's point of view, his evolving judgment about his subject. Roy Reed's "Spring Comes to Hogeye"—the first essay we're going to read together in this book—seems, on the surface, to be no more than a story about Ira Solenberger, an aging farmer who lives near Reed in the Ozark mountains of Arkansas. But if we look closely at the beginning, middle, and ending to see how they contribute to the story Reed is telling, we begin to get a clearer sense of how tightly bound this exploratory form of the essay is.

In the act of revealing Solenberger's life to us, Reed reveals an idea. It might be more accurate to say that Reed, examining Solenberger's life, discovers meaning, meaning that probably no one else would detect. Having found that meaning, Reed presents Solenberger in a way that lets us see and understand what he has discovered. Therein lies *the most basic principle of essay writing.* You, as a writer, impose order on the materials that you bring together; you make them make sense. That's why every essay you write becomes your own. No one else can write it the same way.

Pause now and think about that obligation. You impose order; you create meaning. How? By your discoveries, by the connections you make, by the way your mind plays over your subject, by the way you tell whatever stories you have to tell within your essay, by the way you bring your experiences together to express your idea.

Reed's *idea* doesn't seem very complex if we strip it out of the context of his essay: he sees an interesting relationship between Solenberger's life and the seasons of the year. The idea behind that relationship binds Reed's whole essay together, but he does not attempt to prove the relationship in a direct and forceful way; rather, he introduces us to the notion through suggestion; he proceeds by indirection. Reed wants to interest us in Solenberger even as he uses the old farmer as the embodiment of an idea. Reed's idea, like Dillard's, resists objective, logical proof; it begs for leisurely exploration. Reed, on his own terms, at his own pace, creates Solenberger; he chooses what to put into this portrait, what to leave out.

As we determine how Reed's beginning, middle, and ending work together to create an idea, we'll be looking for general principles about writing. Seeing how Reed works, we will get a sense of how other writers work. Indeed, we will get a sense of interesting possibilities for ourselves. Virginia Woolf and a number of other writers have suggested that we might profit from reading a book, a poem, or an essay two ways at once. We can and should read to see what's going on: where the story or the plot is taking us, what the poem is telling us, what the essay is about; at the same time, we might also *become attentive to the way the writer writes*. Reading two ways at once, we discover something about method, something about how to write our own essays.

Here for your consideration is "Spring Comes to Hogeye."

Spring Comes to Hogeye
by Roy Reed

1   Spring was late in the Ozark Mountains. The first week of April had passed, and the oaks and maples were only then risking a few pale green shoots, tentative little leaves that would not constitute much of a loss if another frost stole in at night on the villainous northwest air.

2   Ira Solenberger was also late. Practically everybody else in Hogeye had braved the hazard of frost and had planted corn, onions, English peas and Irish potatoes. A few, emulating the bold dogwood and redbud trees, which for more than a week had been blooming bright white and purple against the dark hills, had gone so far as to put out beans, squash and even tender tomato plants.

3   But Mr. Solenberger, who was regarded as the best gardener in Washington County, had not plowed a furrow or planted a seed. Like the craggy maple in front of his house (itself one of the oldest things in Hogeye, a relic of the Butterfield Stage era), he found that his sap was slow to rise that spring. It had not occurred to him to blame it on his eighty-six years.

4   "It's that old flu," he said. "Got it back in the winter and can't get rid of it. First time I've had it since 19 and 18."

5   He opened the door of his heating stove and threw another chunk of wood on the fire. He closed it a little sharply and glanced out the window toward his empty garden.

6   Every April, the main thing going on in the rural South is vegetable gardening. A farmer might take an hour to talk politics or help a cow give birth, but the really urgent business for him, his wife and all of the children who are old enough to keep their feet off the onion sets is getting seeds and plants in the ground to take advantage of the warming days. With a little luck, the sweet corn planted in early April will have roasting ears ("roashnears," they are called) by the middle of June.

7   This is a pursuit that seeks every year to outwit the awful force that pushes the shoots from the oak's branches, and that turns Seth Timmons's meadow from brown to green, and impels swallows to build nests in weathered barns.

8   It was the same force, that spring, that pushed Ira Solenberger out the door in a hat and coat, hunched against the biting bright air blowing up from the Illinois River, to kick the dirt and study the sky, and then retreat to the house to throw another chunk of wood on the fire.

9   There is still a poet up the road at Fayetteville who, in those days, drove into the hills every April to study the hills and watch for Robert Frost's signs—the gold that is nature's first evidence, "her hardest hue to hold"—and for private signs of his own that stirred his spirit.

10   Ira Solenberger's mind ran less to poetry than to science. He was an amateur magician, and he performed magic with plants as well as cards.

11   "Summer before last, I grafted some tomatoes on some poke stalks."

12   Why?

13   "Just to see if they would grow."

14   But when he talked of nature and growth, he used words that Frost might have used, or Thoreau.

15   "Plow deep. There's one acre right under another acre. I plow both of them."

16   "Phosphorous makes things grow roots. If you get roots, you're going to get something else."

17   "I farm with a tractor. But when it gets rowed up and a-growing, I use a roan horse."

18   He was now in the April sun, away from the stove. His eye scanned the three and a half acres where, just a year earlier—unencumbered by the flu—he had planted rhubarb, corn, tomatoes, squash, sweet potatoes, Irish potatoes, okra, green beans, cantaloupes, radishes, onions, cucumbers and strawberries. He

had harvested a bumper crop of everything. He had eaten what he wanted and sold the rest at the farmers' market on the square at Fayetteville.

19   He pointed to a fallow patch and said, "That's where I had my watermelons last year." He spoke in a loud, professorial voice, as if addressing the cows at the top of the hill.

20   "They told me I raised the biggest watermelons in Northwest Arkansas. One of them weighed eighty-three pounds.

21   "I've had people ask me, 'What's your secret for raising watermelons?' I tell them, 'I ain't got no secret.' "

22   Then, still addressing the cows, he proceeded to tell the secret. Plow the ground deep. Watermelons need more air than water, and deep plowing lets in air.

23   "I plow turrible deep. Eight or ten inches." He grinned with private satisfaction and moved on to a strawberry patch.

24   Mr. Solenberger believed in humus. He produced it by placing mulch between the rows. I once knew a Mississippi liberal who enjoyed a minor reputation as a gardener by mulching old copies of *The New York Times.* Mr. Solenberger did not take the *Times.* He used dead crab grass.

25   "Make sure it's rotten," he said, jabbing the air with an open pocket knife. "If you plow under something that ain't rotten, it's a detriment to you for the first season."

26   Many of his neighbors planted by the moon, and still do. Mr. Solenberger did not.

27   "I don't pay any attention to the moon, and I'll tell you why. I've got a neighbor that plants by the moon, and I asked him a question one day that he couldn't answer. I said, 'You plant a seed in dry ground, when the moon is right, and it won't come up. Then ten days later it comes a rain and that seed sprouts and comes up. But by then the sign of the moon is wrong. How do you account for that?' He couldn't answer that. I don't plant by the moon. I plant by the ground."

28   He was troubled, though, by another phenomenon, and he was a little reluctant to talk about it. He said the frosts seemed to come later each spring, just as the force that drove him to the plow seemed to have arrived late that year.

29   "The timber's awful slow a-leafing out." He cast a blue eye toward the hill across the road. "When I was a boy, we weren't bothered with frost. When spring come, it come. Our spring's almost a month later than it used to be."

30   I asked him what he thought the reason was. He glanced at my face to see whether I was ready to accept what he had to say. He decided to risk it.

31   "Well, sir, I believe the world twists a little bit. You know, everything that grows twists around to the right. Follows the sun. Even our storms that come out of the Gulf, they twist to the right. It's just nature."

32   Why was a man of eighty-six still involved every April with the earth's greening, as if it were his own? He passed the question off quickly. He indicated that it was merely the same motive that led him to do card tricks and tell jokes and graft tomatoes to poke weed.

33   "I just like to be doing things."

34   He returned to the question later, however, sidling up to it so as not to sound too serious. He began by confessing that spring was his favorite season. I asked him why, and he said, "Life is at a high ebb in the spring."

35   He leaned his chair back against the porch wall and hooked his shoe heels over the lower rung. He studied the trees on the hill across the road, and then he said, "People who are getting up in years, more of them die in the winter when the days are short, and in the hours after midnight. Life is at a low ebb after midnight and in the short days. Did you know that? And the shorter the days, the lower the ebb."

36   Thus it was the lengthening days that sent Ira Solenberger to the garden, and he could no more resist than the hapless oak bud could resist becoming a leaf.

37   He was also right about the other. He thrived for one more season of the high ebb. He made one more garden. Then he died in the winter, during the short days.

Reed's first five paragraphs constitute the *beginning* of his essay. The first announces the general notion about spring's lateness; the second introduces Ira Solenberger and shows how he is different from "practically everybody else in Hogeye." Like the spring that year, Ira is late coming out. The third, fourth, and fifth paragraphs make more explicit the relationship between the man and the season, the man who, "like the craggy maple in front of his house . . . found that his sap was slow to rise that spring." We sense Ira's impatience with spring's lateness. He is ready to get on with planting but wise enough to wait for the right signs.

At the end of the beginning, we know only that Reed wants us to associate Ira with spring. But as we read on, we discover that those five initial paragraphs *foreshadow* the rest of the essay, prepare us for it. Like all good beginnings, this one entices us, teases our imaginations into thought. It puts an idea before us that will be the basis for the essay: "Ira Solenberger was also late." There you have economy. One word, "also," sends us back to the first sentence of the essay: "Spring was late in the Ozark Mountains." Spring was late; Ira was late also. Our first hint. The foundation for all that will follow. We know by the end of this five-paragraph introduction that Reed will explore this curious and special relationship between Solenberger and the seasons.

In the *middle* of the essay, Reed becomes a storyteller, an interviewer, and an explainer. In other words, he uses different ways to present his material about Solenberger. Reed is not just a storyteller, not just an interviewer, not just an explainer. He is all of those and more. He tells us about Solenberger, talks to him, and suggests directly and indirectly that Solenberger enjoys a very special relationship with the seasons, a relationship developed and enhanced over a long life. He lets us know that even Solenberger has a keen sense of that relationship. The old man is so close to nature that they seem magically in harmony with one another. Reed is so good at revealing this relationship that he moves us very close to Solenberger; he makes us believe that the old man is indeed a special creature, that he can read nature's signs, and that reading them, he lives by them, wisely and well. We'll return to the middle of the essay later to see just *how* Reed does all of this so economically.

The last two paragraphs of the essay—the *ending*—reinforce the harmonious relationship and send us right back to the essay's beginning, making us see what we might have missed on the first reading. Reed's final paragraph is a masterpiece of control, suggesting as it does something about the natural relationship between life and death, something about the rewards of living in harmony with the earth's rhythms. It focuses precisely on Ira, yet it moves beyond the confines of a single life in Hogeye and gives us a sense of life in general, our life as well as Solenberger's. The final, moving sentences match Reed's attitude about Solenberger's death. They reflect his sense of loss, stopping short of sentimentality: "He thrived for one more season of the high ebb. He made one more garden. Then he died in the winter, during the short days." Just as he was supposed to do, Reed suggests. When spring returns, so will Ira . . . at least in our imaginations. We leave the essay with both a sense of loss and a sense of promise. We know that Reed has rendered a judgment, that he has given us his personal perspective on a very special man. But he has not just told a story about Solenberger; *he has written an essay using Solenberger's life as evidence.* That life serves as the embodiment of an idea.

Let's consider that idea before we go on to look more closely at various techniques that Reed uses to develop it. We can reduce a thesis to a simple declarative sentence: "Water pollution in Albany must be brought under control" or "Final examinations should be abolished" or "Abortion laws in New York State are unfair." But a good idea loses much of its appeal and power if we limit it: "Ira Solenberger lived his life in accordance with the seasons." A thesis seems to call for "proof"; it demands something akin to a hearing in court, something reasonable, direct, and persuasive; it calls for scientific certitude. An idea calls for a different kind of hearing, a different way of expressing itself.

Reed begins by mere suggestion, by pinning Ira to a particular spring day, and as he develops his essay, the relationship between the two becomes more and more interesting. We begin to find out how a man's personality can be affected by the seasons, how a man's gardening philosophy matches his philosophy about life, how a man can still believe in magic at 86, how man and nature can live in harmony—and all of this accumulation and amplification is a part of the exploration that takes place in the essay; the idea becomes more complex, more interesting, more enticing as we see the essayist's mind play over and shape his material. An idea doesn't call for proof; it asks for a hearing in the front porch swing instead of in a courtroom; it wants only a receptive mind, an unhurried reader who has time to watch the idea evolve by piecemeal and accumulation at a fairly leisurely pace.

Now that we have gained some sense of how the structural parts of an essay work together to help develop an idea, let's turn to a consideration of Reed's techniques, *to the way he turns evidence into essay.* Our aim will be to uncover those techniques (other structural secrets) that we can use in our own essays.

D. *Shaping the Evidence—Imposing Order*

Annie Dillard says that the "writer of any work, and particularly any nonfiction work, must decide two crucial points: what to put in and what to leave out." Dillard is right, but there is another problem, perhaps a more complex problem: how to shape the experiences that go into the text, how to turn the raw material of everyday life into useful evidence. Dillard calls the whole process fashioning a text. It's all a matter of learning to tell truth, I think, a matter of learning that

———————————————— ◊ ————————————————

exploratory essays depend on the imaginative reconstruction of experience to make their *ideas* come to life.

Again, Reed's essay yields valuable insights into this transformation process. What he did, shaping his own experience to create "Spring," you will have to do time and again as you write your own essays.

Reed, who lives in Hogeye, Arkansas, was once a full-time correspondent for *The New York Times*. "Spring" developed as a result of a phone call he got one day from David R. Jones, who was the national editor of the *Times*. It was a spring day, and Jones called Reed in Hogeye to ask his usual question: "What's going on down there?" "Spring" was Reed's answer; he put it together in just two days.

When Reed began his field work, he had heard about Solenberger's reputation as a gardener but had not met him. So Reed had some work to do. Tom Wolfe, another experienced journalist turned essayist, calls that work the "damnable locker-room digging" every good writer has to do to gather his material. Reed's work began with a series of visits; he talked two or three times at "Mr. Solenberger's place" and once during an unexpected visit when Solenberger dropped by Reed's house to carry on a conversation they had started earlier in the day. Over those two days of conversations, Reed assembled his evidence, got to know Solenberger face-to-face, wrote his drafts, and polished the piece—what Reed calls "adding shine to it."

When Reed sat down after collecting his evidence about Solenberger, he did not simply record all that he had learned and send it off to the *Times*. Instead, the essay developed out of Reed's reconstruction and reordering of experience. To create an essay from his notebooks and his conversations with Solenberger, Reed had to make important decisions about what to put in, what to leave out. He also had to shape his evidence, presenting Solenberger's life so that he could make us understand the *idea* he had discovered about that life.

An outline of the *middle* of "Spring" reveals the general *pattern* that Reed used to develop that idea; that pattern gives us a sense of how he began to impose order on the raw materials he had collected. There are three sections in the middle of the essay; in each of those sections, Reed develops an important aspect of his idea about Solenberger.

♦ In the first section (paragraphs 6–8), Reed explains "the awful force that pushes the shoots from the oak's branches." Those three paragraphs establish Ira's relationship with that force.

♦ Section two (paragraphs 9–27) focuses on magic, the magic that Ira Solenberger practices every spring in his garden.

♦ Section three (paragraphs 28–35) moves beyond Ira's garden to Ira's consideration of nature—the late frosts, the lateness of spring, the earth itself, storms out of the Gulf, Ira's relationship with life's high and low ebbs. Section three, playing on the idea of magic, suggests Ira's penetrating insight into nature's mysteries, his certain knowledge of that "awful force" Reed identified in section one. Although section three turns to larger considerations that might involve all of us, it is grounded on everything that precedes it in the essay. Reed moves from the *particular* to the *general*, from Ira and his garden to Ira and nature. That general pattern reveals Reed's movement from a particular life to the way all of our lives might be lived in harmony with nature; that pattern yields what Scott Sanders might call Reed's "deep concerns."

That brief description of the three sections from the *middle* of the essay suggests something of the way writers make essays cohere. But the description says too little. Reed does more than organize his presentation into three functional sections within the middle; he uses other techniques that will also stand you in good stead when you begin to write stories and convert them into essays, "adding shine" to your own work.

We have already considered how, in his *beginning*, Reed presents a paragraph about spring and then one about Ira, paragraphs so

◊

similar in form that they beg us to consider their relationship. Besides that internal pattern, Reed uses another interesting technique. In paragraph 4, he lets Ira talk. So Ira actually comes into the essay as a character in his own right; he comes alive. In paragraph 5, Reed shows us how to reveal character through gestures. We see that Ira "threw another chunk of wood on the fire"; that he closed the door of his stove a "little sharply"; that he "glanced out the window toward his empty garden." Those gestures—throwing, closing, glancing—reveal Ira's impatience. Reed doesn't have to tell us what they mean; he need only *show* us Ira expressing his impatience. We can make the connection between spring's lateness and Ira's impatience. Reed simply teases us into thought by letting us watch Ira. As an added bonus, we get to hear Ira talk.

Reed's technique for linking various parts of his essay together shows us how to make things cohere. We want to consider how he weaves things together, moving back and forth. Let's watch him work in paragraphs 9 through 17 as he establishes Solenberger's status as a magician:

9   There is still a poet up the road at Fayetteville who, in those days, drove into the hills every April to study the hills and watch for Robert Frost's signs—the gold that is nature's first evidence, "her hardest hue to hold"—and for private signs of his own that stirred his spirit.

This paragraph serves as a transition between section one—the meditation on spring's "awful force"—and section two—on magic. As a transitional paragraph it points backward and forward, linking the two sections together.

How exactly does Reed do his weaving? Notice first how he makes use of Robert Frost; those words between quotation marks are, of course, Frost's words. We'll see now what Reed does with the material in this next paragraph, how he comes back to it and makes use of it to tie his thoughts together.

25

10   Ira Solenberger's mind ran less to poetry than to science. He was
an amateur magician, and he performed magic with plants as well
as cards.

In this paragraph, Reed returns to Ira, distinguishing him from the
poet mentioned in paragraph 9, establishing him as a scientific magician. Note how Reed keeps weaving things together, still going back
and forth, as he lets Ira talk and then links Ira and Frost.

11   "Summer before last, I grafted some tomatoes on some poke
stalks."
12   Why?
13   "Just to see if they would grow."
14   But when he talked of nature and growth, he used words that
Frost might have used, or Thoreau.

In these short paragraphs Reed brings Ira back into the essay as a
character, lets us eavesdrop on a conversation between the two of
them, and then in paragraph 14 Reed turns to explanation again. He
picks up the notion of the poet from paragraphs 9 and 10 and asks us
indirectly not to rule out the possibility that Ira might also be a poet;
he talks like one, Reed suggests.

As evidence to support his suggestion about Ira's poetic bent,
Reed offers three more short paragraphs—Ira delivering his hard-
earned poetic wisdom, wisdom culled from all those years of gardening . . . of living with his ear to the ground. Here are Ira's maxims.

15   "Plow deep. There's one acre right under another acre. I plow
both of them."
16   "Phosphorous makes things grow roots. If you get roots, you're
going to get something else."
17   "I farm with a tractor. But when it gets rowed up and a-growing,
I use a roan horse."

By letting Ira speak, Reed puts us in touch with the old man, creates immediacy. But Reed never lets Ira talk too long and never lets him talk about anything that does not keep before us the relationship between Ira and nature. To make sure that we do not lose track of the essay's idea, Reed intervenes occasionally by offering a short paragraph of explanation or by asking a pertinent question. Less experienced writers might be overwhelmed by a character as strong as Ira; they might surrender to the storytelling (the *narration*) and forget to make the story serve the idea. But Reed focuses our attention, keeps our mind on his idea. That's the sign of a writer in control of his work.

IMAGINING AND ANALYZING   *Why might a writer create patterns in an essay? What does Reed gain by the patterns we identified? As you ponder these questions, think about patterns in general. What are some patterns that impose order or regularity on your life? Do they contribute in any way to your enjoyment or understanding of life? Do those patterns from life help you detect other patterns in "Spring"? If so, note them.*

WRITING   *Identify in Reed's essay gestures (other than throwing, closing, and glancing) that reveal Ira's character. Select one of those gestures that Reed reveals through action, and replace it with an explanation of what Ira was doing. In other words, instead of showing us what Ira does, tell us. Which version do you prefer? Explain.*

ANALYZING   *Often, writers less experienced than Reed tell their stories and then offer a paragraph or two of explanation (exposition) at the end to tell us what the story means. Reed, as we have seen, integrates explanation with his storytelling. What do you see as the advantages and disadvantages of Reed's method?*

EDITING AND ANALYZING   *Why, do you suppose Reed sets off Ira's bits of wisdom in separate paragraphs (15–17)? The conventional rules for paragraphing do not call for that. Put those sayings all together in one typed paragraph, and see what you think. Which way is more effective? Why?*

REVISING AND ANALYZING   *Take any occasion where Reed uses dialogue, and rewrite that section of the essay without the dialogue, explaining in your new paragraph what the dialogue had suggested. Which version do you prefer? Explain.*

Now that we have discovered in Reed's essay a number of general structural principles, as well as techniques that writers use to create effective essays, let's begin to look at the writing process from your point of view. Let's look at the generative process, the one that helps you get started, and then let's see how to go on to develop interesting essays out of your experience that will take full advantage of the lessons you've learned from reading.

E. *Personal Experience—Journals, Memory, and Imagination*

The kind of digging Reed did to assemble his evidence can take place in the library, on the street, in the courtroom—anywhere where there is evidence to collect. We will consider other kinds of digging later in the book. As we turn now to your own essays, let's stick to experiences that you have already had, experiences that may seem commonplace to you but might very well turn out to be the stuff that good essays are made of. Some of the writing assignments will send you out to do research on a character like Ira Solenberger, but for now let's concentrate on making essays out of your life's experiences. Like Reed, you have the background to write certain kinds of essays; you carry with you knowledge that you can convert into interesting pieces.

A personal journal is a good place to record special moments in your life. When you sit down to write your essays, a good journal will help you sort through memories; it will be a source of evidence for your essays. Joan Didion claims that in her notebook she records not what happens but how she feels about what happens. In your notebook, try doing what Didion does. Keep an abbreviated record of moments that linger in your mind at the end of a day. You need not worry about format. In the journal, you're writing for yourself.

These entries from a journal I kept during a wilderness excursion in Wyoming give you the flavor of such writing:

> Visual metaphors are very interesting to me as I ride my horse. I find myself skiing my way up and down mountains as I ride.
>
> Find my male imagination turning to organization, teamwork, friendly games: putting up tents well, riding well, doing things cleanly without wasting energy. Want to cook too, especially breakfast, want more perfection on the camp stove: a more caring sense of preparation. The food's not just good because I'm hungry. To hell with too much easiness. Why is Hemingway playing in my head now? He came second, after the desire for everything to be cleanly perfect.
>
> I love the horses, the whole idea of TRUST.
>
> My favorite person: Press. Fine, warm, competent man. Finest leadership characteristic: he praises involvement. Gives verbal rewards for future work, gives them naturally without guile. Second best characteristic as a leader: he is magnificently *competent* & it's a caring competence. He loads for the horses' comfort. Likes tight, clean, balanced loads. No flapping canvas. There's a kind of spirituality in the perfection. No end to the investment's return. Work, good, hard, competent work yields satisfaction—not self-satisfaction but communal satisfaction.

When I read these notes, they take me back to Wyoming, and they remind me of things I'd like to write about. They also remind me of other experiences I've had since the trip, experiences that seem to be related to those in Wyoming. Rereading my notes, I begin to remember much more than I actually put in the notebook. The notes activate my imagination, and I begin to pull things out of memory.

Journal entries will help you make sense of your experiences, and they might very well make your writing more convincing, especially if you have taken time to record important details about things that interest you—the way a man walks; the shape of a woman's face; the furniture in a room; the succulent, ever-changing taste of a mango; the smells in the neighborhood; the feel of an autumn day. You need not try to make sense of events as they occur; begin by recording only those experiences that jolt you into awareness, moments that interrupt the humdrum routine of daily life. Those experiences last; they have sticking power.

After you have developed the good habit of keeping up with those special moments, you might begin to be a bit more expansive as you write in your journal. Start to reflect. Connect moments across time. Look back at my last two entries. The next-to-last is not reflective at all, so I've forgotten much of what was on my mind when I wrote that entry about trust. The last entry will be much more useful to me when I begin to write. I see now that it connects nicely with the entry about my male imagination. Looking at the two entries together, I see possibilities.

Whether you are searching your journal or your memory, you will eventually have to rely on imagination to help you reconstruct the evidence that you are amassing for your essay. Do not be dismayed if you cannot remember all the details about a recalled event before you begin to write. Chances are that your imagination in conjunction with memory (and your journal) will supply the missing details as you begin to write and develop your ideas. While writing, you will undoubtedly discover what you thought you had forgotten.

F.   *Images—A Source of Ideas*

Many professional writers, including Didion, begin with an image, a recollected picture of experience recalled from memory. Didion claims that such images—the good ones, the ones worth writing about—"shimmer." They have life in them; they have energy. She even claims that they contain a "grammar" of their own, an inherent form that helps the writer record the story represented by the image. Loren Eiseley insists that the writer does not have to impose a story on these pictures that are stored in memory; the story is in the picture, waiting for the writer to discover it, to turn it into words.

Your own images of experience can get you started, and those images always lead to imaginative possibilities, to ways that will help you discover your own ideas, ideas that you actually care about.

Look again at that last journal entry of mine, the one about Press, who was the leader of the wilderness excursion:

My favorite person: Press. Fine, warm, competent man. Finest leadership characteristic: he praises involvement. Gives verbal rewards for future work, gives them naturally without guile. Second best characteristic as a leader: he is magnificently *competent* & it's a caring competence. He loads for the horses' comfort. Likes tight, clean, balanced loads. No flapping canvas. There's a kind of spirituality in the perfection. No end to the investment's return. Work, good, hard, competent work yields satisfaction—not self-satisfaction but communal satisfaction.

These notes call to mind a stunning image of experience; they rouse my memory, make me see something I had sent to the attic of my brain. I'll try now to let you see what I saw months ago, relying on *explanation* and *description* as little as possible. I'll try to re-create the image *dramatically*. My aim is to take you to Wyoming, where I'll let you see Press in action:

We had gotten to the first camping spot the evening before, at the end of a long, disorienting day. Despite our claims to the contrary, we were all rookies—all out of our element.

The flight from Newark through Denver had been annoying: bad food, missed connection, indifferent agents at the Continental counter, late arrival in Jackson Hole. Smoke everywhere.

Yellowstone was burning. No visibility. The only mountains we saw appeared at wingtip as we came down below the smoke into the tiny airport.

Gretel drove the four of us in a pickup to a spot between Jackson Hole and Dubois. The horses were waiting. So were Press and his helpers. Others were waiting too, so we ate our sack lunches in a hurry, watched someone else load our gear, mounted the horses, listened to words of wisdom—"Ride your stirrups long" "Give Minny the reins, trust her"—and began our trek to the campsite, crossing what we thought was the most rugged terrain we would ever see: straight up, straight down, nine of us strung out in a line with nine other packhorses, up and down for three hours on dusty little trails more narrow at the bottom than our horses' bodies a few hands higher up. On flat land, the brush and trees seemed to vee up and out from the trail. I felt suspended in a triangular wedge of space as I looked down trying to help Minny put one foot in front of the other, deliberately, gracefully.

As we started a steep descent, I recalled the cowboy's words, "Give her the reins, trust her." The left side of the triangular wedge I had been watching disappeared straight down to a creek bed two football fields away; the other side of the vee shot straight up the mountain. Minny and I were suspended on an inclined plane, held there by her four hooves . . . yet we were moving down, straight down without much sliding. One foot in front of the other, two by two. I started skiing down the winding path in time with her rhythm, weight on the downhill stirrup.

I remember little about that first evening, only the rushing, shallow streams that surrounded our campsite, the red disk of the sun's reflection I drank from the icy water . . . my sore body. I helped unload the horses, but paid no attention. Press, our guide, asked the men in the group to put up tents. We did. Sleep came just after the Milky Way appeared. We were beyond the smoke.

By the time we woke up, the wrangler was coming back with the horses. Press had his collapsible stove blazing and was ready to pour the pancakes on an old cast-iron griddle he kept rotating with a pair of channel lock pliers. "Got a cold spot on the stove," he said.

Press hadn't done much talking the day before. I had watched him set things in motion, but hadn't gotten to hear much of what he said. I could see that he said very little. When he spoke, men moved. He looked like a cowboy on his horse, more at home there in the saddle than he would have ever been back in Atlanta, I suspected. His accent was too flat to be southern. And he didn't look like an art history major, but I knew from Gretel's essays that he was.

I began to like him when he put me to work after breakfast. He started talking about packhorses and Custer and Indians and thousands of soldiers with hundreds of horses. We were a miniature Army; that was his point. We had loading to do, and he had a loading plan. We still called them loading plans in the Army I was in.

Press's plan called for nine loads, split into eighteen stacks. Each pair of stacks would be balanced for the horses' comfort (he had scales when he didn't trust his own feel). We placed the stacks on the ground, split far enough apart for Jickey Jack (the wrangler) to lead the horses through. Press and Jack put this plan in motion; the rest of us were expected to be alert, join in where we thought we could help. I was on the opposite side of a horse from Press before anyone had issued a word of instructions.

"Okay," Jickey Jack, "You get another horse." I was holding up a load of three bedrolls, three bags of tent poles, and filler. I don't know how I got there leaning the load into the side of the horse, pressing it against the loading saddle. "Pat, I'm gonna tie em high and tight. You take the rope from under the belly, bring it under the corner of the load like this and pass it back over the top to me." He had gotten around to my side somehow. "Keep it tight. I'll take up the slack, you lift up the load and keep the canvas cover straight." He disappeared back to the other side of the horse. I couldn't see over the load.

"I don't hire many short packers," I heard him say from the other side as we began the back and forth motion that finally turned into a rhythm as we moved down the line of horses. He talked, half to himself, half to me during the hour or so we spent across horses from one another. Mostly I learned to respond to grunts and "Yo's" that had to do with lifting, taking up slack, smoothing canvas. He tied all the knots, made all the decisions about weight distribution, and warned me about each horse's personality.

"Don't get behind this one. She's mean. Jickey Jack, come up here and stare her in the eye. Hold her steady." And then he'd tell a story about how she came to be so skittish.

After every tying operation, I'd hear him. "Good. Good job. Okay, you ready?" And he'd help me arrange and steady the load on my side of the next horse before he disappeared again, scale in hand, to finish his side alone, pulling and hauling on the rope harness he had laid out before I could even get oriented. I know now, as I think about it, that he was also giving other people jobs, praising them, and keeping his horses happy. Unflappable.

During that week, I watched him move us around, giving us as much work as he knew we could stand, keeping each of us involved somehow in the survival of the whole lot. Watching Press I began to think about leadership again and remembered what someone years ago had told me in a class at West Point: Good leaders know how to get soldiers to do willingly and cheerfully what needs to be done to survive. Watching Press, I began to think again about heroism, and I began to see quite clearly that heroism and soldiering had more to do with preservation and survival than with destruction and death.

When you set your memory and your imagination to work on an image of experience, that image almost always causes you to start telling someone a story. You have to work with the image, as I have done in this fragment, play with it in your mind, let it take shape in words. One of my friends calls it image-work.

You might ask yourself now what it is that I just produced, and that's a good question. Like all stories and essays, that fragment has a beginning, middle, and ending, but it's not a finished story, and it's surely not an essay. But there in that last paragraph, an idea starts to take shape, an idea about heroism. So this story might turn out to be the *beginning* for an essay. On the other hand, it seems a little long for a beginning. But I like it, nevertheless, and I know that when I use it, I'll have to reshape it, change it here and there to make it suit my purpose. In writing it—creating that image in words—I found something I want to go back to, something I want to turn into an essay. I know that eventually I'll use it in an essay about heroism.

Perhaps the most important thing you need to know as you begin to write is this: write about nothing unless it interests you. Search those images in the attic of your mind, and let your imagination go to work re-creating an experience in words. Focus on an experience that compels you. If you don't care about it, discard it. As you begin to write, don't fret about an idea. Work on the idea after you do your image-work. The idea is always embedded in the image. Count on it.

WRITING *Begin keeping a journal of significant events that occur in your life. Record only those images of experience that seem to have some sticking power; they keep compelling you to remember them. Try to record how you felt as the event occurred. A chance encounter with someone you haven't seen might set off a chain of recollections; record the recollections. The loss of a game of some kind might have left you with a sinking feeling in your stomach; note the way the loss affected you. Why was it so important? What does your reaction tell you about your own values?*

WRITING AND SHAPING *After a few days, perhaps a week or two, look back in your journal; select the image of experience that seems most significant to you. See if you can re-create that experience for your readers. Limit yourself to about three typed pages (double-spaced).*

G. *Student Renditions of Experience—Images and Ideas*

PRELIMINARY IMAGE-WORK

Let's look now at some images reconstructed by students who had talked briefly in class about images and the reconstruction of experience. Their requirement was to recall two moments from past experience: the earliest and the most profound. They were asked to reconstruct those two moments in a visual picture created with words. Here are two short responses, both from the same student:

Standing in a classroom learning to skip is as far as my memory reaches. The room was oddly shaped not resembling the typical rectangular shape of most classrooms. A large white circle took up a major portion of the room. I stood with my classmates around this circle and learned how to skip. We went around and around this circle many times. I skipped home because I was so proud of myself for learning this new mode of travel.

My sister and I walked to school together very often at my early age of 7. This one day she must have learned the art of getting dizzy and decided to test this newly learned trick on me. She started to twirl me around and around in front of the neighbor's house. I began to laugh and told her to stop, but her desire to see what would happen overcame her. She laughed then lost control of me, and I had lost control of me long before she did. I fell and hit my head on the curb which didn't take half the damage I did. I didn't get stitches but I did get a headache.

After this student read these short accounts in class, he saw no relationship between them, saw no idea that might connect them. As it turned out, he was comfortable recording—telling the story—but uncomfortable thinking about ideas. In the classroom, other students talked about what the images suggested to them, and after awhile, he began to make his own connections. He eventually wrote a coherent essay, exploring the idea that "practice is the most important part of learning." That essay developed out of the two memories, but he made direct use of neither as evidence; here is the best paragraph from his essay:

> The hardest part of learning is practicing. I am a kayaker, and one of the most [pleasant]—and most dangerous—things about kayaking is the eskimo roll. The eskimo roll is an exercise where you flip upside down under water and then roll back up while in your kayak. The first time I did this roll, I saw my life flash before my eyes as water filled my nostrils. Even though I was scared to do it, I practiced more and more until I mastered the eskimo roll. My cousin knew this and took me to a whitewater river where we dedicated a whole day to whitewater kayaking. I flipped over once and easily flipped back up because I had practiced so much.

This paragraph about kayaking was the final one in the *middle* of an essay that focused on the relationship between practice and learning. The writing exercise showed him that his early image-work could lead to an idea and to other moments in his personal life that he could bring out of memory into his essay. The circular images—the skipping and the spinning—led him to the eskimo roll, that other, related experience. Recalling that incident, he began to use his imagination to explore and order his experiences. He also began to have fun with ideas and to discover their sources.

THINKING *Return for a moment to this student's two initial images. What other ideas seem to be embedded in them? To answer that question, you will have to think of that student's experiences in terms of your own, asking yourself what those experiences remind you of, what they suggest to you. Ask yourself, finally, What do those experiences mean, to me? Would they necessarily mean the same thing to that student? Explain.*

IDEAS—SUPPLE AND ENTICING

Let's go back to the distinction we considered earlier, the distinction between a thesis and an idea. If image-work is going to lead you to an idea, you need a good sense of what an idea is before you consider the entire writing process.

We said that a thesis can often be reduced to a declarative sentence or two ("But again, I shall argue, Jensen had no new data; and what he did present was flawed beyond repair by inconsistencies and illogical claims") and that judgment seems to call for proof, seems to call for a hearing in court. It wants a reasonable, direct, and persuasive defense. An idea, on the other hand, begs an inquiry, an exploration. An idea is more supple than a thesis; it gains appeal and power in the hands of an essayist who is willing to take us round that idea, make us see it as he or she sees it.

These opening and closing paragraphs from a student essay called "Lucky Icarus" should give you a sense of the suppleness of a good idea. The body of this essay consists of an artful presentation of what happened to young Icarus when he momentarily threw caution to the wind and found himself facing death; these two paragraphs (the beginning and ending) frame the story of his exploits.

The snow had been growing wet and heavy in the warm sunshine of the past week. From the ascending cable car I saw that at lower altitudes the melt had exposed patches of damp earth and strawlike grass. Spring was climbing out of the valley. All week I had taken no risks, always skiing or surfing with at least one friend, but today I was alone. I felt that winter's end called for memorable bravado. Although I could not ride a snowboard exceptionally well, I was helplessly addicted to the sensate rush one feels when tearing down a powdery slope on this modern relative of the ski.

Surfing into the valley was easy enough after that. Rather more difficult was the task of coming to grips with my experience. I ordered a beer at a cafe and sat down to think. Would my little tryst with fear mean that I would never again be afraid of dying? Clearly not, for I was shivering. I could no more rationalize away the innate dread of death than I could become blind to the redness which affrights in the blood. Perhaps people who face danger daily, like soldiers, completely lose their fear of death, as paramedics learn to master their inborn aversion to gore; but I had not seen nearly enough to count myself so brave. Yet I was less afraid of death now than I had ever been. Some of the awful mystery of dying was gone: I now had an inkling of what it must be like to face imminent death; I now had some reason to hope that I might greet my passing with dignity. I was frightened, but my fear was the quieter and more reasoned fear of one who has come to know himself better.

We cannot find in these two paragraphs anything that resembles a thesis; there is no declaration of truth. Nevertheless, the paragraphs are enticing; they make us want to read the entire essay. We want to know what happened to young Icarus; we want to know what made him so meditative about his brush with death. We want to know how he handled the catastrophe, whatever it may have been.

It is clear from these two paragraphs that he has had an experience that has shaken him to his foundations; he knows now what it's like to reckon with death, what it's like to face it and move past it. And while our young hero has moved past it, he has moved respectfully, learning something in the process about himself. He adds depth to his story with these two sentences, near the middle of his account: "I was a lucky Icarus. A clear pocket in the cloud enabled me to see the three-meter dropoff just as I came upon it." That allusion to Icarus puts his story in the context of an older story, suggests a mythic dimension that makes his story our story. We're all prone to get our egos inflated on occasion and try to fly too high. This is the old story of derring-do. Yet this is not any Icarus we're reading about; this is a "lucky Icarus," lucky because he came to his senses there in the face of death. He had a choice, and in making that choice he learned something about fear and recovery. He became conscious in the face of death.

Jadran Lee begins his essay by mere suggestion, by setting us up for a bit of "memorable bravado," by letting us into his frame of mind as he rides the cable car to the top of the mountain for an excursion on his snowboard. As he develops his essay, we watch the bravado turn to fear and then resolve; we watch him respond to his luck, watch him move crablike down the mountain to recover his snowboard from a crevasse, watch him survive. We also watch his meditative, reflecting mind play over the experience even as he re-creates it for our edification. You can follow his whole excursion in the Essays for Additional Reading section (p. 358).

By the time we consider Jadran's *ending,* the second of the two paragraphs printed above, we can see that there is *distance* between Jadran Lee, the writer of the essay, and that young Icarus (a more daring, more naive Jadran) who is the essay's focal point. In the time interval between the experience and the writing—or, more precisely, between his initial reconstruction of that image of experience and the revision that created an essay—an idea evolved. The older Jadran began to reflect on the younger Jadran; that reflection let the older writer make sense of an experience. Jadran makes his idea more enticing and seductive by the way he explores his own reaction to his younger self. The idea—Jadran's judgment about death—doesn't call for proof; it asks instead for that hearing on the front porch in a rocking chair. The idea wants only a receptive mind, an unhurried reader (listener) who has time to let the idea evolve by piecemeal and accumulation at a fairly leisurely pace.

Jadran's essay develops around a single experience; at its core is a central image about snowsurfing. The idea Jadran found in that image was about death, about facing it, learning to respect it, moving past it respectfully. The idea is bound to a reflective self, recollecting experience, thinking about that experience, making sense of it.

H.   *Student Essays—From Image to Meaning to Essay*

Writing essays, as you're beginning to see, involves more than recording memories or typing out notes from a notebook. It is not enough just to tell an interesting story. Retrieving powerful moments, turning them into words, making imaginative connections—these are necessary aspects of the writing process, but there is yet another aspect that shows your reader that you are indeed a master craftsman or craftswoman, that you know how to tell your stories in such a way that they highlight the idea that holds your essay together. You should be getting some sense of how necessary it is to *reconstruct* experience, to *shape* your memories so that they serve your purpose as an essayist.

Let's consider the evolution of two student essays so that you can see more clearly this process of turning raw experience into coherent essays.

CHINA FORBES'S "NAKED" — A STUDENT ESSAY FROM START TO FINISH

China Forbes was asked first to respond to this writing exercise:

Reclaim an Experience

Think about experiences that have become permanent parts of your memory, experiences you cannot forget.

Your task in this initial writing exercise is to retrieve one of those embedded moments from your memory and reconstruct it. Re-create the experience, not by describing it but by rendering it in such a way that those of us in the class can participate in it. Put us on the scene; arrest us with vivid details. We want to get some sense of why traces of that profound experience linger in your memory.

That requirement led China to write this short narrative:

Bus Stop

1   In the summer I was naked, stumbling over cold flat stones, and cool, dew-laced grass until I tumbled giggling into my mother's arms. On the patio, she sat with a book, sheltered by the weave of wisteria that perfumed the air. With the book left open, face down on the flat white table that wobbled with the burden of summer drinks, my mother looked down to me with violet eyes and straight black eyelashes and smiled. We would chat a while, and I needed to stand on my favorite rock while I talked. My rock came right up out of the patio floor, and it had an iron pole beside it, holding it in place. And when I stood on my rock, I held the pole tightly with one hand, one outstretched arm, a locked elbow, and my other hand fell on my waist in such a way that with hip cocked to the side, I became Marilyn Monroe until I tired of it. Usually when I assumed that position, I was bathing suit clad, but not always. For in the summer, I was mostly freely, happily, obliviously naked.

2   Our house was long and flat-roofed. It meandered down a sloping hill that was our front lawn. The lawn stretched on in every direction until it met with several different barriers: a wall of trees, a gravel drive, an apple orchard. We were entirely secluded, and I thought, self-sufficient. We rarely met with the outside world— save trips to the dump via Dairy Queen with Dad, or buying shoes at the brown-rugged, rubber smelling store. I was, therefore, totally immodest, and associated summer, early fall, and spring with a marked absence of clothing. Sometimes, however, when the summer deepened my fast-browning legs, I would stretch a pair of tights

over them, and up to my chest as far as they would go. I hated the look of tan legs.

3   In the fall, my older sister would go to school. She would wear her hair in two braids and put on dresses, and carry a lunch box. And when she got home she carried all the paintings she'd made at school, and stories to tell our mother. And while I played with my toys, she would sit in a corner with a big book, and read.

4   I was fascinated by the idea of school, of a place where my sister would go, and always come home with new things. When she left in the morning, she would walk importantly down the drive to Plympton Rd. where the school bus would pick her up. And on this particular morning, I was outside when she marched off to school. As she disappeared between the leaves, I slowly started to follow. My bare, soft feet pressed into the gravel, and I was slightly chilled with goose bumps. It was a long drive and I walked it without the air of determination my sister always had. I was curious. With my stomach poking out, I reached the mouth of the drive where the bus was just stopping. My sister turned and saw me standing there, mute and bashful, and cackled. I looked into the bus, through the windows that reflected the turning leaves, and saw the huge, open mouths of the students, climbing over each other to get to the window, their bodies shaking, their faces pressed to the glass. As the door opened, there was a burst of sound which had been trapped in the closed bus, escaping suddenly like steam from a kettle. I stood still, and cold as the bus pulled away, with the pounding of their noises still surrounding me, and turned to walk back up the drive.

There was a short note to China on the cover sheet: "Promising! Let's explore ways to pull this one together." China had read "Bus Stop" in class, so when she came to her conference to discuss her plans for an essay, she had thought about my comments written within the story and about the comments her fellow students had made in class. My comments had to do with style; the comments in class came mostly in the form of laughter or sighs when she read about nakedness within the frame of her story.

By the time China arrived at the conference, she had decided to write about nakedness. So she had a *subject* for her essay, but she did not have an *idea*. Nevertheless, her judgment about nakedness was already implicit in "Bus Stop"; she was concerned about the strange reaction she got from her sister's friends when she showed up at the bus stop. Even that early sketch of her experience reflects her concern about what happens when we walk from a safe haven such as her backyard to a critical world outside. She had a notion about the way society looks upon nakedness, and she wanted to explore that notion, react to it.

Before the conference, China had also thought about other scenes from her life that had to do with her subject, so she had a cluster of images to work with. She decided to retain the patio scene and the bus scene and to reshape them so they would tell her reader something about the way she feels about nakedness, but she also wanted to create additional scenes based on an encounter with a boyfriend and an encounter with one of her roommates.

In her final essay, China uses what Tom Wolfe calls "scene-by-scene construction." The scenes move us along through a time sequence, commenting on each other, suggesting how the writer feels about her subject. Very little explanation within the scenes or between them is required if the writer constructs those scenes effectively. They speak for themselves, dramatically. Let's take a look at the final product, the essay itself.

Naked

by China Forbes

1   In the spring I was born naked. I was stuffed into a chamois cloth and presented to my mother.

2   In the summer I was naked, stumbling over cold flat stones and cool, dew-laced grass until I tumbled giggling into my mother's

arms. On the patio she sat with a book, sheltered by the weave of wisteria that perfumed the air. Leaving the book open, face down on the white table that wobbled with the burden of lemonades, my mother looked down to me with violet eyes and smiled. We would chat while I stood on my favorite rock that came right up out of the patio floor. I held the iron pole beside it with one outstretched arm, and my other hand on my waist so with hip cocked to the side, I became Marilyn Monroe until I tired of it. Usually when I played Monroe I was in my suit, but not always. For in the summer I was mostly, freely, happily, obliviously naked.

3   Our house was long and flat-roofed. It meandered down a sloping hill that was our front lawn. The lawn stretched on in every direction until it met with several different barriers: a wall of trees, a gravel drive, an apple orchard. My parents, sister, and I were entirely secluded, and I thought, self-sufficient. We rarely met with the outside world—save trips to the dump via Dairy Queen with Dad. I was, therefore, immodest, and associated summer, early fall, and spring with nudity.

4   In the fall, my older sister would go to school. She should wear her hair in two braids, put on dresses, and carry a lunch box. In the afternoons she came home with bright paintings under her arm, and stories about apple seeds. I would play in my toy box while she'd sit in the rocker and read.

5   I was fascinated by the idea of school, of a place where my sister would go and always return with new things. When she left in the morning, she would walk importantly down the drive to Plympton Rd. where the school bus would pick her up. And on this particular morning, I was outside when she marched off to school. As she disappeared between the leaves, I started to follow, slowly keeping my distance. My bare, soft feet pressed into the gravel, and I was slightly chilled with goose bumps. It was a long drive, and I walked it without the air of determination my sister always had. I was curious. With my stomach poking out, I reached the mouth of the drive where the bus was just stopping. My sister turned and saw me

standing there, mute and bashful, and cackled. I looked into the bus, through the windows that reflected the turning leaves, and saw the huge, open mouths of the students, climbing over each other to get to the window, their bodies shaking, their faces pressed to the glass. As the door folded open, there was a burst of sound escaping suddenly like the whistle of steam from a kettle. Once my sister had stepped up into the bus, and the door had closed off the noise, it pulled away. I hurried back up the drive, just until I was between the trees, just so long as I was inside the barrier.

6   That was fourteen years ago. But last summer, I was naked. At eighteen I stepped out of hiding, on purpose.

7   I had a boyfriend. As far as boyfriends go he was all right. He said a lot of nice things, made a lot of stupid mistakes, and was usually there when I wanted him to be. I suppose I loved him, though that's hard to say now. I used to say it all the time. It was an easy thing for me to yell after him as he left my doorstep. I never understood why my friends couldn't tell it to their boyfriends when they wanted to. It was a "stupid mistake" to speak the truth at the wrong time. I always stripped down as soon as I could. I just said it one day, he said it too, and we were happy.

8   Then summer came. We were separated by vacation plans. He was a counselor at a tennis camp, and I was living with my sister. For weeks we accepted our parting with optimism, like two children before Christmas, knowing it wouldn't be too long. I tried to hurry it along by taking a bus up to Vermont to see my Grandparents, who live near the camp. I told him I was coming, to take two days off. But when I got there, he couldn't get away. He had no transportation. He had no time off. We spoke on the phone from a distance of thirty miles.

9   "I think we should break up," he said.

10   "What?"

11   "It's ridiculous to keep this up. I never see you."

12   "That's your fault."

13   "Maybe."

14   "I can't believe you're saying this. Over the phone."

15   "How else could I? I never see you. . . . I can't love someone I
      never see."

16   "Right."

17   "I'm going to be in California for four years, we'll never be
      together for more than three or four days again. Do you want that?"

18   I was crying.

19   "Look, I've gotta go, it's 6:30. Dinner."

20   "Uh huh."

21   "I'm gonna go."

22   After two days I wrote a letter. I mailed it the day I left for Europe.
      It was eight pages of words I had never been able to say to him;
      more than "I love you." They explained things, told him exactly
      how I felt. They were soft words, and so honest that I surprised
      myself. They remembered times we spent in high school, waiting to
      graduate together. They were sad words, admitting the loss I felt.
      They told him he was right. And they told him I still loved him.

23   In three weeks I got back from Europe. There was no letter.

24   This fall, sitting between the pillows on the futon, my room-
      mates discussed art. We were hanging posters and I tacked up
      Matisse postcards on my bulletin board: a woman reclines on a
      chaise lounge in red harem pants, naked from the waist up. The
      walls of the room are orange and yellow flowers, and a blue and
      white patterned screen surrounds her. Her hands are behind her
      head and she is resting, calm. One roommate caught sight of a
      bared breast, and stopped.

25   "What is that?"

26   "What?"

27   "That's naked!"

28   "I know it's naked. Haven't you seen a nude before?"

29   "Not in a painting. I've seen myself."

30   "You've never seen nude painting? Aren't there museums in
      Newfoundland?"

31   "Yes, but they don't exhibit that."

32 "But it's important, it's beautiful."

33 "That's not beautiful, it's disgusting."

34 "It's art."

35 "It's disgusting."

36 I wondered if I had unconsciously taped the centerfold on my wall.

37 I see others carefully covering up their tracks like criminals, spreading the dust thin over the unique grooves they refuse to leave behind. They twist words into measured speeches, keeping silent the taboo feelings. They do it out of fear. They do it out of habit. They learn it young on school buses. They create barriers and never cross them. Because when we see nudity, when we hear nudity, we turn away, close the door to the dressing room in awkward haste or simple ridicule. So I keep reminding myself: I was born naked. I was born naked.

China uses a number of interesting techniques in this essay that might help you when you begin to weave your reconstructed memories into a coherent whole. "Scene-by-scene construction" works well because she constructs the scenes with economy: they are compressed and full of energy; she mixes storytelling and explanation very well within a scene or paragraph without overdoing her explanations— look carefully at paragraph 5 to see how she merely suggests what happens when a naked, curious, carefree child dares walk outside the barriers of her own yard into the company of older children; she creates other scenes that depend on dialogue (paragraphs 8–21 and 24–35), giving us variety; throughout the essay she also makes good use of her own images—the Marilyn Monroe pose, the child with the stomach poking out, the breast on the Matisse postcard.

One of the most striking aspects of the essay is the way China varies the length of paragraphs. The two-sentence opening paragraph that indeed constitutes the *beginning* of her essay says very little but suggests a great deal. Like one of Roy Reed's paragraphs, it is so perfect in its simplicity that to tamper with it by adding explanation might be to ruin it. Her longer *ending* is reflective and explanatory yet still restrained and suggestive.

What is most interesting about this essay is that we see several versions of the writer in this piece; she appears twice as a child, once as a high school student, and once as a college freshman. Outside all of these scenes is the writer, China—reflecting, shaping evidence, making sense of the materials of her life.

That shaping of evidence is very important. Essayists do not merely tell stories. Neither do they write confessions. The essayist tells just enough of her story to keep her readers interested and to get her point across. Good judgment is crucial. It takes restraint to turn personal, private experience into an essay for a general audience.

IMAGINING, ANALYZING, AND WRITING   *Go through China's essay and separate the scenes. Try to give a short title to each one. Write down what you think China accomplishes in the scene. What aspect of her main idea does she develop? As you are thinking about the scenes, be sure to take into account what they suggest. After you have studied each scene, see if you can pinpoint China's idea, the one that makes the entire essay cohere. Can you reduce it to a single sentence, or does it demand more space? Explain. Actually write down all the things she suggests to you about nakedness in this essay.*

ANALYZING   *Look at the construction of the boyfriend scene (paragraphs 6–23), perhaps the longest and most involved scene in the essay. What are the signs of restraint in that long scene? How does China keep that scene from becoming confessional?*

REVISING AND ANALYZING   *Try to rewrite the last scene of the essay (paragraphs 24–35) without the use of dialogue. Which version do you think is more effective, yours or China's? Take her ending and recast it slightly so that it can serve as a* beginning; write a new *ending. Exchange your new paragraphs with those created by another student. Comment on their relative merits. Which version(s) do you like best?*

Essays such as "Naked" give us the deceptive sense that they were written easily, without difficulty. Reading them, you think they must have fallen in place effortlessly. Rarely, if ever, is that the case. Although China came to her writing class with a love of language and a good sense of how to create scenes (she acts in campus theatrical productions), she nevertheless spent a great deal of time writing this essay, making parts of her life come together. She listened to peer evaluations in the classroom, exchanged her work out of class with another student, and discussed (during a teacher conference) the scenes that were beginning to interest her. The essay developed over two weeks of give-and-take. It evolved slowly from a single moment of recollected experience, from that piece she called "Bus Stop."

ANDY McLAUGHLIN'S "IN CONTROL" — A STUDENT ESSAY FROM START TO FINISH

Let's consider the evolution of another student essay. Remember, as we turn to this very different essay, what John Henry Newman said about the way we learn: not at a glance but by piecemeal and accumulation. Different writers have different styles of working and different ways of coming to terms with themselves and their discoveries. Some writers begin with penciled drafts, fragments, and they keep putting those fragments together, trying out combinations until an idea starts to take shape. These writers actually think with pencils in hand, looking for connections as they write. Other writers tend to put those fragments together in their heads, letting them sit in suspension for days playing off each other. Those writers wait until the playing gets so exciting that they have to seek relief, finally, at the keyboard. You can imagine that the initial drafts for these two groups of writers would be very different, no matter what their particular writing task might be.

For each of us the writing process is different. This next student's work gives yet another sense of how we might move from experience to essay. Do not be overly concerned because the process changes from writer to writer. Over time, you'll discover the pleasures of your own process. Part of the excitement of writing comes from making discoveries, not only about ideas but also about the best way for you to work. As you gain experience, you will see that techniques that work in one essay will not work in another. Each idea and each set of experiences create new possibilities and new demands. Each time you sit down to write, you have an interesting new puzzle to solve. In short, you have to find an idea you care about, and then you have to figure out how to get that idea across to a reader. Let's see *how* this student does it.

The starting point for this essay was again an early, profound memory. Here is Andy McLaughlin's preliminary sketch of the recollected moment:

> At the age of three, I remember myself trapped in a hospital. Teams of medical staff were continually taking my anal temperature. I was in need of surgery; my tonsils needed removal. I knew little of the procedure so I just did as I was told. And soon [they] were cutting my throat. Throughout this early episode my parents never felt I had a "need to know" on what was happening. I didn't care. I was young and the young aren't supposed to know or make decisions.

When Andy read this sketch to the class, we asked him if he saw an idea embedded in this early memory, an idea that only he could see in its sketchy, rudimentary form. He did. He saw himself, at that early age, subject to the whims of a lot of people who were doing things to him, taking his temperature, cutting his throat, trapping him. Someone in class asked if that idea helped him understand other experiences in his life, asked him, in short, if he thought he could record one or two other related memories. This is what he wrote:

1   At the age of three, I remember myself trapped in a hospital. My tonsils needed removal and this meant surgery. I knew little of the procedure so I just did as I was told. Teams of medical staff were

continually taking my anal temperature and soon were cutting my throat. Throughout this early episode my parents never felt I had a "need to know" on what was happening. I didn't care. I was young and the young aren't supposed to make decisions.

2   Later in life when I first began to make my own decisions, I found the hand of guidance still holding me with a tight grip. Limited to what I could and could not do, I disobeyed my parents. While living in Hawaii, I took a swim in the ocean without supervision. I soon found myself lost in an undertow, unable to return to shore. By remaining calm I was able to find an underwater reef and climb back to safety—no longer lost. The control of my destiny was gradually belonging to me.

3   Eventually, I would find myself standing alone. Placed in front of a few thousand eyes sealed in my tux, I soon conquered Moussorgsky's "Great Gate" with a sound and echo. The strength of personal accomplishment was great. No longer would I be a parents' pawn or find myself lost in misadventure. I now would seek greater control for myself.

Keep in mind that these are still student notes, unexamined by anyone else. They are leading Andy to discoveries. When he discussed them in class, it seemed clear to him and most of the class that his idea would have something to do with his personal development; it would have something to do with being free of parental control, with growing up and making his own decisions. The precise idea is still fuzzy; he's still exploring as he writes, but the idea is beginning to come into focus.

Comments from several students in class led to further development. Everyone wanted to know more about the various experiences. Each experience was significant to Andy, but other students couldn't tell why. The recollected moments were too sketchy and asked too much of the reader. There were too many gaps and holes that needed filling. The class suggested that Andy had written a preliminary sketch that might serve well as a working outline, but there was no essay yet. Asked if he could identify in that outline the beginning and ending for his essay, he said that he could see a beginning in his first episode but couldn't find an ending, couldn't yet tell the class how he thought he might bring the essay to a close. He was caught up in the storytelling and didn't want to think yet about how he was using the stories to write an essay. At that moment in the process, his was a good response. He was still exploring, trying to find a more precise idea.

We asked Andy to try to get outside the storytelling to think about why he was telling the stories in the first place. We asked him to think of the sketches he had written as the middle of the essay and to think about how to frame that middle with a beginning and an ending. These questions begged him to think clearly about what he was trying to do with his stories. He needed to discover the idea that would pull them all together into a coherent essay.

What follows is his first version of a complete essay. The italicized sections are explanatory passages, comments that make Andy's *idea* more or less explicit. I have italicized those sections to show you how Andy made various sections of the essay cohere. Think of those words as the glue that holds the pieces of this composition together.

In Control
by Andy McLaughlin

1   At the age of three, I remember myself trapped in a hospital. My tonsils needed removal and this meant surgery. When my mother first told me I had tonsilitis I simply smiled and felt good that I had something my younger brother didn't. While at the hospital I was treated much like a playdough doll. Teams of medical staff were continually stabbing me and taking my anal temperature. Even in the bath my mother found the need to scrub, wash, and dry me off as I stood in front of her naked. I never really understood how the doctors were going to get at my throat. The week prior, I had attempted to take my cat Charlie's tonsils out with a playtell screwdriver, but to no avail. I never knew what I was looking for down his throat. The big day soon arrived and I was off to

Frankensteins' table awaiting his assistant to lower a mask of painless sleep and begin cutting at my neck. Throughout this early episode my parents never felt I had a "need to know" on what was happening. I didn't care. *I was young, and the young aren't supposed to understand or make decisions.*

2   *Later in life when I first began to make my own decisions, I found the hand of guidance still holding me with a tight grip.* As an adventurous nine year old, living in Hawaii was ideal. The weather was always great for playing outside along the shorefront, especially at my great palm. Limited to what I could and could not do, I often frequented my favorite palm to increase my 'ape climbing' dexterity. Amasing great numbers of coconuts from the tallest branches one day, I decided to take a rewarding swim. Disobeying my parent's warnings of swimming without supervision, I soon found myself lost in an undertow, unable to return to shore. I just knew my dad was going to beat my ass when I got home—if I was going to get home. Swimming frantically, I only grew tired. The best I could do was hold my place for a few seconds. My great palm was now only a blurred vision growing smaller in the distance, as were my hopes. *The control of my destiny, which I had so eagerly wanted, definitely now belonged to me; however, I wasn't in control.* The ocean's dominance was increasing as my strength grew faint. Moreover, the branding I had foreseen earlier by my father began to look appealing. As a last hope I prayed with anxiety, *realizing that there was much to learn about standing alone.* Then almost miraculously, I came upon an underwater reef and was able to climb back to shore—*no longer lost.*

3   *Eventually, I would find myself standing alone again, this time in control.* Placed in front of a few thousand eyes sealed in my tux, I was seated on stage in Atlanta's Symphony Hall anticipating the thunderous recapitulation of Modest Moussorgsky's final episode of *Pictures at an Exhibition,* the "Great Gate of Kiev." Moussorgsky, a nineteenth century Russian composer, had transformed a local art exhibit of the time into paintings of sound, highlighting

his work with the ominous and powerful depiction of the Great Gate of Kiev, a historic Russian southern fortress. The orchestra was currently bowing at a whisper as the conductor motioned a smooth transition. I then erupted into my savored solo. Using every ounce of breath I struck the audience with my bass trombone as a hammer pounding an anvil. Capturing everyone's attention, especially the wide eyes of the maestro, *I was in control,* filling the hall with a wall of sound and echo. *No longer a parents' pawn or lost in misadventure, I had found the strength of personal control and accomplishment in a flood of pedal E flat.*

4   The playdough doll years were over. Mom finally lets me bathe myself. My great palm, once lost in a blur, now remains in sight and the corpulent tone of my solo exemplifies a *new found confidence—my destiny in my control.*

Andy McLaughlin's is a promising essay. It shows that he is learning to turn stories into effective evidence, that he knows how to make an essay cohere. Those italicized sentences are important ones; they show a writer learning how to shape and control his stories. His idea is still not as clearly formed as it might be. He seems to have discovered that standing alone is a more complex matter than he might have imagined when he set out to be independent; he never says that directly, but it is implicit in the essay. We, as readers, want to know more about what Andy means by control. The exploration isn't over. But in this initial effort, he shows that he knows something about making an essay stick together. He has not only an idea worthy of exploration but also a good sense of the difference between stories and coherent essays.

ANALYZING *Notice that there are only four paragraphs in Andy's essay. Two are essentially functional (beginning and ending); they get the essay started and end it. Two are substantive (2–3); they develop the idea, providing evidence and explanation. What do you think about that balance between functional and substantive paragraphs? Explain. Do you consider the short ending effective? Why?*

ANALYZING *Make a photocopy of Andy's essay. Try your hand at commenting on the essay. The first time through look only for places where you do not understand what he is trying to tell you. Underline those instances, and put a question mark in the margin to indicate confusion. Do not give him the benefit of the doubt, but be reasonable. If you are confused, let him know so that he can clarify matters for your benefit. If he has included details that seem to have nothing to do with the idea he's trying to develop, write a question in the margin asking him why he includes such details. If you think he needs more details, indicate where. Mark obvious spelling or grammar errors, but do not clutter the paper. If Andy does something you like, indicate your pleasure in the margin with a check mark or a short comment. Encourage him where he deserves to be encouraged.*

THINKING, ANALYZING, AND WRITING *Think about various ways Andy might improve his essay. At the end of the paper or on a separate page, make two or three specific suggestions, brief notes that will help him when he sits down to revise. What does he make you wonder about? What else would you like Andy to tell you in this essay that you do not know? You're not trying to wring a confession out of him; you're trying to get him to tell you what you need to know to understand his idea. Keep him focused on the development of the idea. Try to help him improve his effort.*

COMPARING AND REVISING *Consider Andy McLaughlin's essay in light of China Forbes's. He chooses to make his essay one continuous story, linking each of his experiences with explanatory sentences—the italicized ones. We leave his essay with a sense of continuity, a sense that we have watched him develop over time into a more independent young man. China moves from one scene to another without comment. Growth and development have much less to do with her essay. She's trying to present a different kind of idea in a different way. Rewrite one of China's scenes as a paragraph. Rewrite one of Andy's paragraphs as a scene. Which method is more effective and why? Can you put either of the revised versions into the original essay without making other modifications to the original piece? Explain. Speculate about the way the form and shape of these essays may have been dictated by the ideas themselves. To what extent do you think these two writers have found the right form to express their very different ideas?*

I.   *Summing Up—A Closing Perspective on Exploration*

We have seen how professional essayists can tell us a great deal indirectly about writing essays. We read Reed two ways at once, looking for his idea and for his technique, and we began to use that same reading method when we looked at student essays. It served us well; it helped us discover techniques and principles that should help us write better, more interesting essays.

Besides reading techniques out of those essays, we also found that some writers are quite open about principles that guide them as they write. Recall Didion and Eiseley; each had something important to tell us about images. Scott Sanders reminded us about our personal relationship to the essays we write. Sanders likes writing essays because he can "speak without disguise of what moves and worries and excites" him; he can be honest and direct without having to displace himself. Yet he senses that he writes in "a personal voice about the impersonal, the not-me, for the world is a larger and more interesting place than my ego." That last thought is a complex one, but at bottom it suggests that Sanders tells his personal stories because they turn out to be everyone's stories. They're not merely personal; they reach out to embrace the world.

As important as those remarks are, Sanders' remarks about how an exploratory essay develops, how it accumulates meaning, are even more cogent to our discussion. They're worth repeating on the way out of this chapter. He tells us that writing an essay (an exploratory one) "is like finding my way through a forest without being quite sure what game I am chasing, what landmark I am seeking. I sniff down one path until some heady smell tugs me in a new direction, and then off I go, dodging and circling. . . . The pleasure in writing an essay—and, when the writing is any good, the pleasure in reading it—comes from this dodging and leaping, this movement of the mind." But Sanders issues an interesting note of caution. "It must not be idle movement, however, if the essay is to hold up; it must yield a pattern, draw a map of experience, be driven by deep concerns."

We will consider other patterns in greater detail in later chapters, but for now, remember that the "dodging and circling" is a way of enlarging an idea; it is a way of bringing more and more pertinent evidence into your essays. Sanders encourages you to follow the odd scent, to dart about in the forests of your mind and your experience, seeking connections. The search should lead to the "deep concerns," those worth writing about.

J. Practice—Thinking and Writing

THINKING

1.   Read Leon Yen's essay, "*Onamaewa* (What is your name?)" (Essays for Additional Reading section, p. 255). Identify the essay's most effective images. Explain why they are effective. What do those images have to do with Leon's main idea?

2.   Turn to the *beginning* (paragraphs 1–9) of Scott Sanders' essay, "The Men We Carry in Our Minds" (Essays for Additional Reading section, p. 263). See if you can guess from that beginning what point of view—what idea—Sanders might develop in his essay. As you speculate, think too about his title and about the kind of sensibility he displays toward his friend Anneke in those beginning paragraphs. Can you get a clue about his attitude toward women by examining the .

relationship he has with her? Characterize that attitude in a few sentences; jot down your evidence. Before reading the body of the essay, turn to the *ending* (the last two paragraphs). How do those two paragraphs change your speculations? Finally, turn back to the beginning, and read the entire essay. What do you think is Sanders' deepest concern? What makes you think so? What does Sanders' personal "map of experience" (the map you see depicted in the *middle* of his essay) have to do with his deepest concern? In what ways does Sanders surprise you in this essay?

3.   In its first version—the one for *The New York Times*—"Spring Comes to Hogeye" ended with paragraph 36. When Reed revised the essay to put it in *Looking for Hogeye,* a collection of his work, he added paragraph 37. Mr. Solenberger had died between the time the piece appeared in the *Times* and the time of the revision. Reed added paragraph 37 to account for Mr. Solenberger's death. How does that paragraph change the way you perceive the essay? Explain.

4.   Go to the microfilm room in the library. Find *The New York Times* for April 12, 1976. On page 31 you will find "An Ozark Gardener, 86, Awaits Coming of the Greening Season," the newspaper version of "Spring Comes to Hogeye." Make a paragraph-by-paragraph comparison of the two versions, keeping track of what you think are the most important changes. Make a list of the five most important things Reed did to "put shine on" the final version of the essay. In class, discuss with other members of your work group what you think Reed accomplished by making those five changes.

5.   Reread Roy Reed's essay. As you reread it, perhaps the third time, underline what you think are the sentences and phrases that make it cohere. Do those underlined parts seem to be as sparse and as separated as those in Andy McLaughlin's essay? If not, why do you suppose they aren't? Why does Reed tell us so much about what Solenberger believes in and what he doesn't believe in? What might

Solenberger's beliefs have to do with the *idea* Reed is trying to develop in his essay?

WRITING

1. Recall a memory, and reconstruct it in words. Turn it into a story. Try simple narration first without dialogue. After you have the account of what happened down on paper, try to make it more immediate. If people are included, let them talk to each other. Try to let your reader know what they are thinking even if they are not talking to each other. Add details that might put the reader on the scene: details about the place or the room where the action takes place; details about the people—the way they look, walk, talk. At the same time you're adding things, see what you can take away that is not important. Do this revising over at least a two-day period. Work with another student, someone who will read and react to your piece.

2. Recall a person from your past. Write down your fondest memory of that person. Instead of explaining that memory, as if from a distance, see if you can re-create the moment itself. Put us there, inside the experience, by rendering a dramatic scene, one we might very well enact on the stage. Try to link that scene with another that occurred at a different time. Bring together two aspects of that person's life that will give us a fuller sense of the individual you're trying to bring to life.

3. Try an assignment like the one David Jones gave Roy Reed. You might think first of Jones's question, "What's going on down there?" Think about something that is going on in your community or in the college you attend. Find a colorful character who might be caught up in the event, someone who might, by your artful rendition, serve as the embodiment of an idea. If starting with an idea leads you nowhere, reverse the process. Seek out a colorful character you've heard others talk about. Get to know that person. Do your "locker room digging." Convert the raw material you gather into an essay. Take lessons from Reed.

4. Turn back to Section H, and reread the assignment that led to China Forbes's essay. Recount one of your own memories, getting it down on paper so that someone who knows nothing about it can experience it through your account. Meet outside of class with two other students who have also responded to the requirement. Exchange papers, comment on them, and help each other discover ideas that are embedded in your accounts. Then without help, perhaps back in the quiet of your room, see how many of your experiences will cluster around one of those ideas, experiences that you can turn into evidence when you develop an essay. Go on and develop that essay, borrowing appropriate techniques from Reed, China, and Andy.

5. Read Scott Sanders' essay, "The Men We Carry In Our Minds" (Essays for Additional Reading section, p. 263). Write an exploratory essay of your own that develops a different perspective on the idea Scott Sanders examines in his essay. After you have written your essay, compare your "map of experience" with Sanders'.

6. Recall a profound event from your life, *or* focus on some aspect of your personality that others just do not understand. Write an exploratory essay that develops out of your consideration of either of these topics. Remember that your main task is to explore an idea. Start with images—one that recalls a profound moment, another that recalls an aspect of your personality. The two images should serve as starting points for an essay. Let your mind's exploration lead you from topic to image of experience to essay.

Chapter 2

THE
EXPLORATORY
ESSAY

—

ENRICHMENT
AND
COMPLEXITY

A. *Enriching Experience—Reading: Searching for Ideas,
Making Connections*

In the last chapter, you learned about an essay's beginning, middle,
and ending; you also learned how to turn your personal experience
into essays. The chapter closed on a note from Scott Sanders, an
essayist who urges writers to let their minds dodge and leap as they
write. He claims that the writer's pleasure and the reader's come from
"this dodging and leaping, this movement of the mind." In this
chapter, we will consider how your mind, dodging and leaping, might
create richer, more diverse essays. We'll be seeking ways to include in
those essays *evidence* from books, articles, pictures, songs, poems—
other sources—that will help you develop your *ideas* in more interesting and more persuasive ways.

As you learn to write more complex, more interesting exploratory essays, you will still use images of experience; they will continue to provide the foundation for your essays, but you will be learning to connect those images with other kinds of evidence. You might decide to shed light on an important personal experience by relating it to a poem you have read, or you might use a movie or a painting or a song to clarify a particular idea that you are developing. Your aim—as you make connections, select evidence, and integrate that evidence into your essays—will be to write exploratory essays that are more persuasive and more interesting than those that rely solely on images of experience. You want your readers to have a clear sense of your mind's play as it dodges and leaps, but, of course, dodging and leaping is not your primary business. Enlarging your readers' sense of your idea is.

In "Being Familiar," Sam Pickering reminds us that a familiar essay (the kind we're calling exploratory) "saunters, letting the writer follow the vagaries of his own willful curiosity. Instead of reaching conclusions, the essay ruminates and wonders." E. B. White, like Pickering, acknowledges that the essay is a "relaxed form," but White also reminds us that an essay "imposes its own disciplines." Pickering evokes the freewheeling, meditative spirit of the essay. White calls for discipline, for artistic control.

As a good essayist, you will have to ruminate and wonder even as you meet the demands of discipline. Rambling for its own sake will not do. But rambling for the purpose of enlarging your subject, of extending the range of your inquiry, is another matter. Such rambling, done under the demands of discipline, is the essence of good exploratory essays. It is your way of reaching out, of making sure that you include in your exploration everything that is pertinent. Such rambling brings enrichment and diversity to your essays. It keeps you from falling victim to a narrowly defined thesis that might limit inquiry.

Aiming to extend the range of your exploration—pushing deeper and deeper into the idea under consideration—you will actually learn how to make essays more coherent. An enlarging that is also a pulling together: that's what we're going to be attempting. How to make the exploration more interesting, the subject more enticing; how to explore without losing control—those will be our main interests.

As the essayist's meditative, playful spirit starts to attract you, as you begin to read more, you will more than likely begin to make important connections as you think about your life in relation to the pieces you are reading or as you think about one book in terms of another book. The life of your mind and the life of action will more than likely come together in exciting ways, providing fresh insights. You'll begin to have more interesting conversations with yourself.

Some of the connections you begin to make may come from classroom work, but they might just as well be the result of your imagination's play over the various books you read, the movies you see, the art galleries you visit. Reading and observing, you can begin to see what was once hidden to you. Annie Dillard claims that one kind of "seeing" depends on knowledge, what she calls love for your subject. She suggests that you can't see some things clearly until you know enough about them to know what to look for. She suggests, too, that another kind of seeing results from your being open to new possibilities, awake and alive to what might happen to you at any given moment. Both modes of awareness are important to you as you begin to study and to prepare yourself as an essayist. Seeing and connecting, you may very well begin to formulate new ideas as you gather different kinds of evidence for your essays.

If you glance back at that last paragraph (or at the first and third paragraphs of this chapter), you can see how you might bring another writer's thoughts into your own discussion to help you clarify a point. In the preceding paragraph, as I began to develop my notion about learning to see what is often hidden, I remembered Annie Dillard's essay "Seeing," remembered ideas of hers that clarify and extend points I wanted to make. So I brought her ideas to the service of my own. That paragraph and many others in this chapter will be developed with the help of other writers. My aim will be to show you in a variety of ways how your mind might reach out to what you have read and remembered, to show you how to use those connections to clarify points in your own essays.

As you enlarge your own notion of evidence, you might want to turn back to the previous chapter (pp. 28ff.) to think again about the importance of keeping a journal. Much of your reading and many of your important observations—those moments when you "see" things as if for the first time—will slip away from you if you do not write them down somewhere—in a journal, in a notebook, in your computer's memory. There is no need to try to organize such notes; they're a permanent record of thoughts and memories and connections. Yet those journal entries can nudge you toward an idea. Writing them, you begin having conversations with yourself about other books and characters that your memory releases, about related ideas. Those entries, those memories, and those ideas can serve you later as you sit down to write your essay and to remember again.

An essayist's mind wonders as it wanders, looking for the jewel in the commonplace, seeking the excitement that Virginia Woolf mentions, the excitement that comes from putting the severed parts of experience together. In an effort to form new wholes, an essayist records intellectual journeys, gives the reader a sense of the bends and crooks in the mind's journey. The essay becomes a track record of the significant connections that have led to insight and ideas.

The trick, the essayist's trick, is to give the reader the pleasure of thinking about an idea in a new way. As Pickering reminds us, the familiar essayist's aim is not to be right, not to reach hard-edged conclusions, but to be thoughtful. And evidence of thoughtfulness comes in many guises. The surest way to add depth and variety to your essays is to read often and to read with willful curiosity. Reading, thinking, reflecting, and writing, you begin to make those connections that can enrich your essays. This chapter will show you how.

B. *Using Someone Else's Ideas—Connecting and Integrating Evidence*

A STUDENT ESSAYIST AT WORK—MAKING CONNECTIONS

Let's turn first to a paragraph from a student essay that illustrates this business of making connections; it illustrates as well how to turn those interesting connections into evidence, how to make use of them in an essay.

Gian Neffinger's essay is called "House of Cards." Later in this chapter, we'll consider his entire essay. For now, let's focus on a paragraph. Gian's main idea has something to do with the way an object's beauty can be revealed in its own destruction. His uncle builds houses out of playing cards, and Gian and his cousin always vie for the opportunity to pick the card that, when pulled, will topple the house his uncle has built; it is in the toppling that Gian discovers the beauty of the structure.

When Gian was writing his essay, his mind played over a couple of images that helped him settle on the house of cards as his subject. As he thought about the house of cards and about the notion that beauty can be revealed in the collapse of a structure, his memory came into play; when he was writing a draft, he remembered a poem by A. E. Housman that (in his own imagination) had something to do with his main idea about beauty and destruction. At a conference, Gian asked if he could bring the poem into his essay. What he was asking was fundamental and quite important: Do the rules for writing an essay permit me to tell my readers about something that seems important to me, something that I can recall from my reading that, at the time I read it, had absolutely nothing to do with a house of cards?

Gian was making connections and needed nothing more than confirmation that he was on the right track. Here is how he used Housman's poem:

Whatever the meaning hidden in that final moment of splendor, one thing is sure: a sudden demise grants a certain timelessness. A. E. Housman, in his poem "To An Athlete Dying Young," tells of a champion who died in his prime, before his reknown faded. He took his championship crown to his grave, where he could never be dethroned. Thus went the Titanic. It met its end as the pinnacle of naval technology, and now, whenever anyone thinks of the mightiest ship ever to cruise the open sea, none think of Old Ironsides, bobbing in its secure harbor with its heavy cargo of tourists; none think of the newest, most massive cruise liners or battleships, for the Titanic owns the title of mightiest—has owned it since that fateful night, and will own it forever.

Gian's main idea for his essay has to do with the revelation of beauty in a moment of destruction. This particular paragraph adds an interesting dimension to that idea. Gian seems to be telling us that we not only detect beauty in the moment of destruction but also discover that the act of destruction can grant the destroyed object a certain permanence. Gian uses Housman's poem to highlight and reinforce this sense of permanence, to extend his own notion of timelessness to the human dimension.

He could have used Housman a number of ways within the essay. He could have *quoted* lines from the poem—"Smart lad, to slip betimes away/From fields where glory does not stay"—but citing those lines, he would have been obligated to explain them in the context of Housman's poem. That might have taken too much space, might have diverted too much attention to the poem and the language of the poem. Instead, Gian chose to *summarize* Housman's poem, to give us its essence in two sentences: "A. E. Housman, in his poem 'To an Athlete Dying Young,' tells of a champion who died in his prime, before his reknown faded. He took his championship crown to his grave, where he could never be dethroned." There is a wonderful economy in the way Gian uses his source. He identifies that source (Housman and the particular poem), and he gives us the idea from the poem that is important to his own paragraph; he actually gives us that idea twice, once in each sentence, making it difficult for us to miss his and Housman's paradoxical point: that by dying young, the young man achieved lasting fame.

Let's look now at the way Gian develops this notion about permanence, considering as we do the paragraph that precedes and the paragraph that follows the one we've just been examining. Notice how Gian weaves his notion about permanence *from* the house of cards *to* the Titanic *to* Housman and then *back to* the Titanic and *back*, finally, *to* the house of cards:

> When the house [of cards] fell, when the invisible hand of physics let go and the cards fell in chaos, something very powerful happened. Having that power between thumb and forefinger was a grand feeling indeed. After all of the care that had gone into its assembly, it seemed ironic that it must all end with the tiniest of movements. Perhaps it was irony that made the moment magic. It would certainly seem equal to the task; it was irony that made the Titanic legend great. Had it not been billed as the Unsinkable Ship, its sinking would not have been so remarkable, and the world would never have had cause to learn that eight ninths of an iceberg's mass lies concealed below the water's surface.
>
> Whatever the meaning hidden in that final moment of splendor, one thing is sure: a sudden demise grants a certain timelessness. A. E. Housman, in his poem "To an Athlete Dying Young," tells of a champion who died in his prime, before his reknown faded. He took his championship crown to his grave, where he could never be dethroned. Thus went the Titanic. It met its end as the pinnacle of naval technology, and now, whenever anyone thinks of the mightiest ship ever to cruise the open sea, none think of Old Ironsides, bobbing in its secure harbor with its heavy cargo of tourists; none think of the newest, most massive cruise liners or battleships, for the Titanic owns the title of mightiest—has owned it since that fateful night, and will own it forever.

So goes the house of cards—quickly, gloriously. No such house ever lasted long enough to suffer the indignities of time and fortune. Most great monuments are not nearly as lucky. Their features are worn away by time, or tourists; their reknown is drowned in the wake of Progress. No one actually apprehends their beauty; it just slowly fades away with time.

These three paragraphs from the middle of Gian's essay give you a sense of how you might bring into your own essays what you have read in history books (Titanic) or poetry books (Housman) or your own life (house of cards). Even more important, they show you how you might take evidence from a variety of sources and turn it to the service of an *idea* of your own, an idea as interesting as Gian's about beauty and destruction and timelessness.

These paragraphs show you how you can make the connections, how you can reach out with your mind and pull together the evidence that will illuminate your idea and make it interesting for your readers. You can let your mind follow the vagaries of your own willful curiosity, and in so doing, in making those connections, you can put your stamp on the essay you are writing; you can make it your very own.

CONNECTING *Go back to some of your earlier journal entries. Reread them, and see if they make you think of anything that has happened to you, ever. Do they remind you of a movie you've seen? A book or an essay you've read? Another experience? Make a new journal entry, jotting down your trail of connections. If you haven't made journal entries before, start now. Begin the practice of rereading those entries occasionally and making new notes as appropriate.*

A PROFESSIONAL ESSAYIST AT WORK— CONNECTING THOUGHTS, INTEGRATING EVIDENCE

Essays by professional writers—like that essay of Gian Neffinger's— can also teach you a great deal about the use of evidence—how to introduce it, how to cite it in your essays, how to develop it within the context of your own paragraphs. Looking at other essayists' work, you actually get to see how they make connections, how they make use of evidence.

Loren Eiseley's essays almost always illustrate the nature of a connecting mind. He was an anthropologist who wrote what he called "concealed" essays in which "personal anecdote [is] allowed gently to bring under observation thoughts of a more purely scientific nature." Eiseley delighted in making use of his experiences. Most of his essays, whether about the evolution of the universe or some fascinating idea about a primitive, are grounded in his own experiences as an anthropologist and a curious wanderer. In his essays, the higher thoughts—the ideas themselves—are revealed through the personal anecdotes that add depth and variety to his exploration. But Eiseley quite often calls on other thinkers to clarify his own ideas, and we can learn a great deal about how to write richer essays by considering how Eiseley incorporates borrowed material into his own pieces.

Connecting

Before turning to Eiseley's "The Illusion of the Two Cultures" to see how he incorporates evidence from other sources, let's look briefly into his notebooks to see how he kept track of some of the connections that interested him. These entries—selected from the period 1947–1966 in *The Lost Notebooks of Loren Eiseley*—provide insight into Eiseley's imagination and his reading habits; they show us as well how he recorded ideas for his own essays long before he was ready to make use of those ideas in his essays. Most important of all, they show us how Eiseley made natural and meaningful connections among a wide variety of experiences. Here are some of his notebook entries:

For a personal essay: Archaeological findings of how people went away in past time. Their doors closed for a last time. Their belongings hidden. There is a hidden pathos of departure here which properly handled could be turned into a good essay.

An archaeologist is a man who knows where last year's lace valentines are.

I would never again make a profession of time. My walls are lined with books expounding its mysteries. My hands have been split and raw with grubbing into its waste bins and hidden crevices. I have stared so much at death that I can recognize the lingering personalities in the faces of skulls and feel accompanying affinities and revulsions. I am the last in an Ice Age leaf fall.

Paraphrasing for my fire paper: The campfire is more real than the hydrogen bomb, we must have fire at first hand, the fire of leaves in autumn, the simple homeliness of things.

Man's ego suffered three great blows. Loss of the center of the stage—Copernicus. Loss of directed evolution—Darwin. Loss of the moral mind—Freud.

Reading in Thoreau's journals today. It strikes me that Thoreau's writing is like his own landscape—a vast expanse of weeds, brush, thickets, and just occasionally a singing bird with a soft note hidden in some unexceptional underbrush. Thoreau, in other words, is as chaotic as the real world of nature and just as full of trivia, with here and there some remarkable observational nugget.

Idea: "Diary of a Suicide Year." Saw in New York a few days ago two pigeons persistently mating on the corner of a tall building. They kept falling off and recovering in midflight. Living dangerously!

Fog. See Thoreau's *A Week on the Concord and Merrimack Rivers.* "Always the laws of light are the same, but the modes and degrees of seeing vary. . . . There was but the sun and the eye from the first." (p. 134) Use this for start of nature book.

The writer's creativity is to open man's eyes to the human meaning of science, to find his path in the open society, to prevent his relapse into "aloneness in the universe."

"It is always one world that generates another."

—Santayana

Here in these entries, we see Eiseley snipping ideas from thought, experience, and reading as he went along. His is a mind concerned with imagination, longevity, evolution, life—a mind seeking to understand how we came to be where we are in place and time. Eiseley seems comfortable in the world of action and in the world of ideas.

Perhaps your mind will not focus itself on your life's work for a number of years, but as you learn to write essays, as you learn to think and make connections and put things in perspective, you will begin to discover hidden meanings. Then the provocative quotations you have recorded or remembered, the observations you have made about nature, and your creative thoughts will all begin to come together in your imagination as you sit down to write. Those chunks of evidence provide the interesting stuff of your essays, but they cannot just be copied directly from notebook to essay. You will have to bring them together effectively, just as Eiseley does in his essays, giving us the essentials, culling out the rest. You want to enrich your own essay, not make it appear as a copybook into which you have merely transcribed raw material from your journal.

Integrating the Evidence

Let's see how Eiseley puts his imagination to work in an essay called "The Illusion of the Two Cultures" (Essays for Additional Reading section, p. 279). In this essay, written, perhaps, to his peers, he focuses on a problem that plagues the modern mind and lies at the heart of our educational system. In a very general sense, Eiseley is concerned about a split between scientists and humanists that causes each group to retreat into its own dogmatic way of thinking, thereby closing out other possibilities. In specific ways, Eiseley's essay explores the nature of the split, considers its implications, and, in the end, raises a vexing question about our future. You can read the entire essay later, at your leisure. For the moment, let's concentrate on ways that Eiseley enriches this important essay about education, keeping in mind that this is a sophisticated example, one that takes us beyond Gian's use of Housman and beyond my own development of the journal entries about Press. Yet Eiseley's is still an exploratory essay, scholarly but compelling, the kind of essay all of us might like to write someday.

In the first nineteen paragraphs (an extended, leisurely introduction), Eiseley cites Ashby, Santayana, Snow, Bacon, Thoreau, Huxley, Lamarck, Chambers, Burroughs, Hudson, Tolkien, Andersen, Dunsany, Verne, and Petrie. Later in the essay, he cites or mentions Mauriac, Mumford, Donne, Lyell, Leonardo, Darwin, Einstein, Newton, Hobbes, Bacon (again), Shakespeare, and Bergson. These are all names important to the history of ideas and the development of our culture. Eiseley calls on them not to display the range of his own reading but to make specific points about the evolving split between science and the humanities.

Let's consider how Eiseley uses one or two of these men's ideas to help him develop his own, how he integrates their ideas into his essay. We can get a glimpse of Eiseley's technique if we look at only the first four paragraphs of "The Illusion of the Two Cultures":

1   Not long ago an English scientist, Sir Eric Ashby, remarked that "to train young people in the dialectic between orthodoxy and dissent is the unique contribution which universities make to society." I am sure that Sir Eric meant by this remark that nowhere but in universities are the young given the opportunity to absorb past tradition and at the same time to experience the impact of new ideas—in the sense of a constant dialogue between past and present—lived in every hour of the student's existence. This dialogue, ideally, should lead to a great winnowing and sifting of experience and to a heightened consciousness of self which, in turn, should lead on to greater sensitivity and perception on the part of the individual.

2   Our lives are the creation of memory and the accompanying power to extend ourselves outward into ideas and relive them. The finest intellect is that which employs an invisible web of gossamer running into the past as well as across the minds of living men and which constantly responds to the vibrations transmitted through these tenuous lines of sympathy. It would be contrary to fact, however, to assume that our universities always perform this unique function of which Sir Eric speaks, with either grace or perfection; in fact our investment in man, it has been justly remarked, is deteriorating even as the financial investment in science grows.

3   More than thirty years ago, George Santayana had already sensed this trend. He commented, in a now-forgotten essay, that one of the strangest consequences of modern science was that as the visible wealth of nature was more and more transferred and abstracted, the mind seemed to lose courage and to become ashamed of its own fertility. "The hard-pressed natural man will not indulge his imagination," continued Santayana, "unless it poses for truth; and being half-aware of this imposition, he is more troubled at the thought of being deceived than at the fact of being mechanized or being bored; and he would wish to escape imagination altogether."

4   "Man would wish to escape imagination altogether." I repeat
that last phrase, for it defines a peculiar aberration of the human
mind found on both sides of that bipolar division between the
humanities and the sciences, which C. P. Snow has popularized
under the title of *The Two Cultures.* The idea is not solely a product
of this age. It was already emerging with the science of the
seventeenth century; one finds it in Bacon. One finds the fear of it
faintly foreshadowed in Thoreau. Thomas Huxley lent it weight
when he referred contemptuously to the "caterwauling of poets."

In the first sentence of his essay, Eiseley cites Sir Eric Ashby's
remarks on the proper nature of a university education so that he can,
in turn, establish a counterclaim, but Eiseley's in no hurry to establish
that claim. First things first. He uses Ashby to set up his own
argument. Look carefully at how he does it. Ashby says a university
ought to set up a "dialectic" in students' minds, a dialectic—or
dialogue—"between orthodoxy and dissent." To make sure that we
know what Ashby meant, Eiseley explains the quotation that he has
selected from Ashby's work. Eiseley wants us to know that a university
education ought to teach students to enter into the dialogue between
past and present, between orthodoxy and dissent, and that students, as
they enter into that ongoing debate, ought to heighten their awareness and begin to sift through experience, making sense of things as
they are. In the second paragraph, Eiseley shifts his emphasis to
"memory and the accompanying power to extend ourselves outward
into ideas and relive them." He shifts his emphasis to the imagination.

Eiseley spends the greater part of those first two paragraphs
showing us that, in large measure, he agrees with Ashby about a
university's chief function, but near the end of the second paragraph,
Eiseley suggests that it would be "contrary to fact . . . to assume that
our universities always perform this unique function . . . with either
grace or perfection." In addition, Eiseley enlarges the terms of his own
argument by making another claim, a claim that the universities are
investing more in the development of science than in the development

of man. Overemphasis on science devalues the humanities, which devalues the importance of the imagination.

To substantiate his claim, Eiseley looks back thirty years through Santayana's thoughts to find an early trace of "deterioration." Santayana had sensed it; Snow had "popularized" the split between science and the humanities; Thoreau had feared it. Even Bacon, in the seventeenth century, recorded it. In the nineteenth century, Thomas Huxley "lent it weight." To this history of ideas that he is tracing, Eiseley will add his own ideas, ideas that evolved out of that history he is sketching. Eiseley's will be an inquiry into the illusion of two separate cultures, an exploration into the nature of the split itself; his will be a plea for enlightened awareness of new possibilities for rejoining the severed parts.

Looking carefully at just those four paragraphs, you can begin to see how you as an essayist might make use of someone else's ideas to develop your own. You can see as well that the essayist uses such evidence in differing ways for different purposes. Eiseley develops Ashby's and Santayana's ideas as a way of expressing his own and as a way of establishing the terms of his own argument. He uses Snow, Bacon, Thoreau, and Huxley only as touchstones to lend weight to his own authority and insight. It's as if Eiseley asks us, "If I have all these great thinkers on my side, how can you doubt the reliability of my own argument?" As an essayist, you can learn much from Eiseley as you take note of how he *quotes* these men on the one hand and how he *paraphrases* or *summarizes* their thoughts on the other. How much he quotes and how he explains what he quotes depends on how he's trying to use these other thinkers to influence his readers.

In "The Illusion of the Two Cultures," you will find no *block quotations*—quotations so long they need to be set off within the paragraph and indented. Eiseley has chosen to cite only the most telling phrases and sentences; he has identified those phrases and sentences with quotation marks and has integrated them into his own paragraphs, being very careful always to distinguish his ideas from those of the men he is citing. We have no difficulty finding Eiseley's thoughts in his essay; neither do we have trouble identifying thoughts belonging to other writers.

In essays of this kind, in exploratory essays, there are *usually* no traditional footnotes, and there is no parenthetical documentation within the paragraphs. But you will notice that the writers are, nevertheless, identified within the text of Eiseley's essay just as they are within this chapter. When I cite Didion's ideas or Sanders' or Dillard's, I let you know that I am borrowing. More formal techniques for documentation are appropriate for analytical and scholarly essays (Chapters 3 and 4).

Because you, as a writer of exploratory essays, have a responsibility not to pass someone else's ideas off as your own—*a responsibility not to plagiarize, not to steal someone else's work*—you should look carefully at how Eiseley identifies each of the writers within the text of his essay: how he puts their words in quotation marks and how he makes it clear that he is summarizing or paraphrasing another writer. He is very mindful of his responsibility because he is writing, after all, to express his own ideas, ideas that he has developed by "forming new wholes." The essay is his vehicle for revealing his own thoughts. So Eiseley wants us to be able to distinguish his work from that of the other thinkers.

CONNECTING AND INTEGRATING *Select from your journal or your memory an image of experience that is connected in some way with a book you have read, a movie you have seen, or a song you've heard. Write a few paragraphs that give your reader a clear sense of the connection you've made.*

REVISION *Reconsider an exploratory essay you've already written. Select a paragraph or an image of experience from the essay that calls to mind a connection with other evidence. Rewrite the selected passage to include the new evidence.*

ANALYSIS *As you study Eiseley's methods in "Illusion," you might ask yourself a question or two about Eiseley's intended audience. Does he assume that his audience will know the writers he cites? If he couldn't make that assumption, would he make his essay more interesting and persuasive if he identified each writer more clearly within the text of his essay, identified them briefly in a way that would establish their authority? In the first sentence, he tells us that Sir Eric Ashby was an "English scientist," but in paragraph 3, he doesn't identify George Santayana. Would it help you to know that Santayana was a modern philosopher, or can you guess that from what Eiseley tells us about Santayana's ideas? To what extent do you think Eiseley does establish the identity of his sources in the essay?*

IMAGINING *Consider your readers for just a moment. If you plan to cite evidence to enrich your essay—whether that evidence be a quotation from a book, an allusion to a song, or a reference to a work of art—what must you do to help your reader understand your use of that evidence? Make a short list of considerations, and discuss them with someone else in the class. Compare your list with lists compiled by other students.*

C. *A Sense of Personal Style—Ruminating, Not Disappearing in the Evidence*

LOREN EISELEY'S STONE

There is one more writing lesson worth learning from "The Illusion of the Two Cultures." Eiseley does not lose his personal touch even when he cites so many authorities. We have no trouble distinguishing his thoughts from those of the other writers he cites, no trouble separating Eiseley from his sources. And in an essay that argues for imagination, we get revealing glimpses into Eiseley's. In paragraphs 11 through 19—the final paragraphs of his extended beginning— Eiseley develops an imaginative meditation on a "stone" that he picks up from his desk. His turning to that stone is a very personal gesture after he has outlined the history of ideas that led him to his own version of truth about the illusion of the two cultures. He turns to the stone to objectify and clarify his idea; when he does so, we see him at his very best. We see Eiseley's mind working in a fresh, meditative way.

11   It may now reasonably be asked why one who has similarly, if less dramatically, spent his life among the stones and broken shards of the remote past should be writing here about matters involving literature and science. While I was considering this with humility and trepidation, my eye fell upon a stone in my office. I am sure that professional journalists must recall times when an approaching deadline has keyed all their senses and led them to glance wildly around in the hope that something might leap out at them from the most prosaic surroundings. At all events my eyes fell upon this stone.

12   Now the stone antedated anything that the historians would call art; it had been shaped many hundreds of thousands of years ago by men whose faces would frighten us if they sat among us today. Out of old habit, since I like the feel of worked flint, I picked it up and hefted it as I groped for words over this difficult matter of the growing rift between science and art. Certainly the stone was of no help to me; it was a utilitarian thing which had cracked marrow bones, if not heads, in the remote dim morning of the human species. It was nothing if not practical. It was, in fact, an extremely early example of the empirical tradition which has led on to modern science.

13   The mind which had shaped this artifact knew its precise purpose. It had found out by experimental observation that the stone was tougher, sharper, more enduring than the hand which wielded it. The creature's mind had solved the question of the best form of the implement and how it could be manipulated most effectively. In its day and time this hand ax was as grand an intellectual achievement as a rocket.

14   As a scientist my admiration went out to that unidentified workman. How he must have labored to understand the forces involved in the fracturing of flint, and all that involved practical survival in his world. My uncalloused twentieth-century hand caressed the yellow stone lovingly. It was then that I made a remarkable discovery.

15   In the mind of this gross-featured early exponent of the practical approach to nature—the technician, the no-nonsense practitioner of survival—two forces had met and merged. There had not been room in his short and desperate life for the delicate and supercilious separation of the arts from the sciences. There did not exist then the refined distinctions set up between the scholarly percipience of reality and what has sometimes been called the vaporings of the artistic imagination.

16   As I clasped and unclasped the stone, running my fingers down its edges, I began to perceive the ghostly emanations from a long-vanished mind, the kind of mind which, once having shaped an object of any sort, leaves an individual trace behind it which speaks to others across the barriers of time and language. It was not the practical experimental aspect of this mind that startled me, but rather that the fellow had wasted time.

17   In an incalculably brutish and dangerous world he had both shaped an instrument of practical application and then, with a virtuoso's elegance, proceeded to embellish his product. He had not been content to produce a plain, utilitarian implement. In some wistful, inarticulate way, in the grip of the dim aesthetic feelings which are one of the marks of man—or perhaps I should say, some men—this archaic creature had lingered over his handiwork.

18   One could still feel him crouching among the stones on a long-vanished river bar, turning the thing over in his hands, feeling its polished surface, striking, here and there, just one more blow that no longer had usefulness as its criterion. He had, like myself, enjoyed the texture of the stone. With skills lost to me, he had gone on flaking the implement with an eye to beauty until it had become

a kind of rough jewel, equivalent in its day to the carved and gold-inlaid pommel of the iron dagger placed in Tutankhamen's tomb.

19   All the later history of man contains these impractical exertions expended upon a great diversity of objects, and, with literacy, breaking even into printed dreams. Today's secular disruption between the creative aspect of art and that of science is a barbarism that would have brought lifted eyebrows in a Cro-Magnon cave. It is a product of high technical specialization, the deliberate blunting of wonder, and the equally deliberate suppression of a phase of our humanity in the name of an authoritarian institution, science, which has taken on, in our time, curious puritanical overtones. Many scientists seem unaware of the historical reasons for this development or the fact that the creative aspect of art is not so remote from that of science as may seem, at first glance, to be the case.

The image that Eiseley creates of the polished stone—the "hand ax [that] was as grand an intellectual achievement as a rocket"—took shape in his imagination. Pondering the stone he picked up from his desk, he saw through it back to the past and forward into the future. The stone itself was a mere fact, something he could pick up and hold in his hand. But the stone means little to us *without Eiseley's thoughts attached to it.* Like all other evidence, the stone had to be turned toward the writer's end, toward the essay's purpose. In that stone, Eiseley spied an idea. He would say the idea was there in the first place, waiting for him to discover it and write it down. From that stone and his thoughts about it, Eiseley *created an image* with words, an image that eventually makes his essay cohere. It also clarifies his idea and makes his essay more interesting.

ANALYZING   *Look at paragraph 19 of Eiseley's essay. How does it differ from the paragraphs that precede it? Think of a general rule about citing evidence: introduce the evidence or the authority; cite the evidence (experience, quotation, anecdote); explain it in the context of your argument. Consider paragraphs 11–19 in light of this general rule. Does Eiseley follow it? As a way of comparing his technique with the general rule, look back at paragraph 4 (cited above). What is the relationship between paragraphs 4 and 19; that is, what similar rhetorical purpose do those two paragraphs serve?*

IMAGINING *Turn to the Essays for Additional Reading section (p. 292), and look at the last three paragraphs of the essay, where Eiseley speaks of another stone, a "heavy stone of power." What is the relationship between the two stones? Why do you think Eiseley chooses to end his essay by returning to that early image and enlarging our sense of it? How effective is his final plea for us to make better use of our "artistic imagination"? What does that plea entail for those of us who live and write at the very end of the twentieth century?*

REVISING AND ANALYZING *What do you think would have been the effect on the essay if Eiseley had deleted paragraphs 11–18 and modified paragraph 19 just a bit to make it serve as the final paragraph of his scholarly introduction? Read through the rest of the essay, and see if anything would be lost by leaving out the personal anecdote.*

ANNIE DILLARD'S WEASEL

Eiseley created his image by meditating on a stone he picked up from his desk. But images just as powerful can come from books, from the reading you do to improve your education. Let's consider an image from an essay by Annie Dillard, another professional essayist. Although she borrows the image from another writer, she makes it her own, uses it to give power and dimension to a personal experience. The central event in "Living Like Weasels" (Essays for Additional Reading section, p. 292) is Dillard's encounter with a weasel near Tinker Creek:

He had two black eyes I didn't see, any more than you see a window.

The weasel was stunned into stillness as he was emerging from beneath an enormous shaggy wild rose bush four feet away. I was stunned into stillness twisted backward on the tree trunk. Our eyes locked, and someone threw away the key.

Our look was as if two lovers, or deadly enemies, met unexpectedly on an overgrown path when each had been thinking of something else: a clearing blow to the gut. It was also a bright blow to the brain, or a sudden beating of brains, with all the charge and intimate grate of rubbed balloons. It emptied our lungs. It felled the forest, moved the fields, and drained the pond; the world dismantled and tumbled into that black hole of eyes.

Dillard's personal experience with the weasel—the locking of eyes—must certainly have provided the occasion for this essay. That look seized her imagination, and she developed the idea she found embedded in the "black hole of eyes." What she learned about weasels *through additional reading* she used to elaborate and enhance her own ideas. She is not as careful as Eiseley about identifying her sources, but in the introduction to this essay, she tells us that Ernest Thompson Seton gave her one story about an eagle that was shot out of the sky; she says, too, right after her introductory paragraphs, that she has been "reading about weasels because I saw one last week." Clearly, she turns from a primary experience of her own to secondary sources. She reads to enrich and clarify her experience so that she can create an essay.

In the introduction to "Living Like Weasels," Dillard gives us two short accounts of weasels in action. A weasel bit a naturalist, "socketed into his hand deeply as a rattlesnake"; the man could not pry him off; "he had to walk half a mile to water, the weasel dangling from his palm, and soak him off like a stubborn label." Another weasel, the one she read about in Seton's book, was found as "a dry skull . . . fixed by the jaws to [an eagle's] throat." Dillard wonders about that weasel before his death, carried aloft as it was by the eagle. She wonders whether she could have seen the "whole weasel still attached to his feathered throat, a fur pendant" or whether the eagle gutted "the living weasel with his talons before his breast, bending his beak, cleaning the beautiful airborne bones." She is obviously fascinated with this *socketing image*—with the weasel's instinctive action and his tenacity even in the face of death. Later in the essay, when she regrets not going for the weasel's throat under the wild rose bush, we know what she has in mind. We understand more clearly the idea she is developing, the idea that we, like the weasel, ought to yield "at every moment to the perfect freedom of single necessity" and hold on for a "dearer life."

Returning again and again to the socketing image through allusion as well as explanation, Dillard finally concludes her essay by reminding us of the metaphoric nature of her image: "I think it would be well, and proper, and obedient, and pure, to grasp your one necessity and not let it go, to dangle from it limp wherever it takes you." Combining aspects of the initial images from her introduction (the weasel dangling from the naturalist's hand and the one fastened to the throat of an eagle in flight), Dillard makes one last effort to put image and idea together, asking us to imagine ourselves overcoming death even in the act of dying, being carried "aloft," our eyes burning, our flesh falling off in "shreds" as our "very bones unhinge and scatter, loosened over fields, over fields and woods, lightly, thoughtless, from any height at all, from as high as eagles." So from a very personal experience, Dillard develops an idea that goes far beyond a mere exchange of glances with a weasel. She exhorts us to be weasels, "to stalk [our] calling in a certain skilled and supple way, to locate the most tender and live spot and plug into that pulse."

Dillard, a naturalist who goes out to live in the wilderness alone to stalk her calling, and Eiseley, the digger, the brooding anthropologist, show us that good essays can indeed take shape from personal experiences and that those experiences and the ideas we glean from them can be enriched and amplified by the reading we do. The evidence we borrow and cite from other sources becomes our own as we use it and credit others. But we ought to use it only when it gives expression to our own ideas, when it clarifies those ideas for our readers.

D. *A Review—Guidelines for Incorporating Evidence*

Gian Neffinger, Loren Eiseley, and Annie Dillard show us how to bring both lived experience and gleaned experience into our own work. We see how to make use of imaginative connections, how to enrich our essays. We see, too, that integrating evidence into our essays is not just a matter of sticking in a quotation here and there to dress up an idea.

We bring evidence into our essays to illuminate our ideas; we bring it there to add depth and variety to what we have to say. No single rule tells us just how to integrate that evidence. It makes good sense always to introduce our evidence, to cite it, and to explain it in the context of the paragraph in which it appears. But we can follow that sensible advice and still be short of our objective. Consider this draft paragraph from a student essay about Richard Selzer's "Four Appointments with the Discus Thrower." In Selzer's essay, a doctor visits a patient on four different occasions—watches him, thinks about him, tries to imagine what's going on inside the man's head as he lies there on his bed in the aftermath of amputation. This student believes that there is an intriguing relationship between the doctor and his patient:

> The doctor is in love with this patient in room 542. Selzer shows this through descriptive language. He compares the legless man to "an ornamental tree, roots and branches pruned to the purpose that the thing should suggest a great tree but be the dwarfed facsimile thereof." The doctor obviously admires this man. He is attracted to him and must watch him, actually "spy on [him]." He notices that

there is nothing in the old man's room; no "get-well cards, [no] small private caches of food, [no] day-old flowers, [no] slippers." Instead of being callous to the situation, Selzer compares this desolate room to. . . .

This is a promising paragraph. The student has an idea. She believes that the doctor is in love with the patient, and she wants to make her case by looking at the way Selzer describes the patient, by considering the way he uses language. Even the evidence (the quoted material) she selects is quite good, but her explanation of that evidence seems scant, undeveloped. Why, we want to know, is it so obvious that the doctor admires the man? What is there in the quoted material that makes her suspect the doctor's love for the patient? As readers, we want to know what she sees and what Selzer the writer sees. We want a fuller account of what the evidence means to her.

Here is a revised version:

The doctor is in love with this patient in room 542. Selzer suggests that love when he compares the legless man to "an ornamental tree, roots and branches pruned to . . . suggest a great tree," but a tree that remains a "dwarfed facsimile thereof." The doctor seems to see the potential in that ornamental tree; he sees the inherent power, something residual in the form itself. But surely, he also sees himself. He is after all the pruner; he is the one who has done the dwarfing.

So the doctor is a culpable admirer of a form he has created. Like a lover who has been destructive, he's trying to preserve something in the form of things and to suggest in the form how very compli-cated that doctor-patient relationship actually is. Getting past the imagined form to the patient himself is difficult; neither man seems able to talk directly to the other. Nevertheless, Selzer's language, his images, tell us how the doctor feels. He is so attracted to the patient that he must watch him, actually "spy" on him. Looking around, trying to understand, he notices that there is nothing in the man's room: no "get-well cards, [no] small private caches of food, [no] day-old flowers, [no] slippers." Noticing, he signals his concern, his love for his patient. Noticing, he makes us notice, makes us see that even if no one else sends the traditional tokens of concern, the doctor himself cares. And in noticing, the doctor never fails to suggest his own culpability—no slippers, no slippers for the legless man. It's as if the doctor's love arises out of desolation, out of failure, failure to be able to save the man's legs, failure to be able to talk to him, failure to be able to reach out and touch him. He can do little more than watch and wish and love and be sorry that he can't do more, much more than preserve the relationship in words and images.

ANALYZING   *In the first version, underline the sentences that actually interpret the evidence. Do the same in the revised version. What do you see as the major differences between the two versions? Which version do you prefer and why? Where is the student essayist in these two versions? Is she more clearly present in one version than in the other? Explain.*

The Selzer example suggests that one of the essayist's primary tasks is to explain the evidence that she cites. It is seldom sufficient just to make an assertion ("The doctor is in love with this patient in room 542"), cite a few lines of evidence ("He notices that there is nothing in the old man's room; no 'get-well cards, [no] small private caches of food, [no] day-old flowers, [no] slippers' "), and conclude that the case has been made. Your task, when you write an essay, is to make the evidence you cite come to life in the essay. You want to let your readers know what you know. Often it takes a number of tries to get your paragraphs just right. Sometimes you don't know everything you need to say about your evidence until you actually begin to write out your explanation. After all, you're still making discoveries as you write. The connection comes to you out of memory, and then you begin to develop that connection; you begin to discover how you might show your readers why that evidence is so appropriate.

Much of your success will depend on your figuring out just how much explaining you have to do. Part of the answer lies in the assumptions you make about your audience. Part of it lies in how efficiently you can get your point across while keeping your readers sufficiently informed so that they can follow your mind through its twists and turns. Let's look at a paragraph I had a great deal of trouble working out.

I was trying to come to terms with the *idea* of a woman that I carry around in my head. Some writers think of that woman as a muse, an inspiration. I saw her in a larger context and wanted to explain just what she meant to me, why she was important, why she was so hard to deal with. To introduce that woman to my readers, I decided to refer to a song Willie Nelson sings called "Black Rose"; the song seems to say something significant about an imaginary woman who can disrupt a man's life. The character in this song is troubled by such a woman; she haunts his imagination and affects his real life. Every woman he meets seems to be just another manifestation of Rose.

Here are two early versions of my introduction where I try to get the words right, try to say just enough about the song so that my readers can understand my idea and my reason for citing the song:

Version 1

I had been listening to Willie Nelson as another antidote to confinement, and he had given me some insight into my soul's restlessness. "Black Rose" was no surprise to me; I knew about her. But I hadn't made up my mind yet whether she was there in my imagination to hold me in tormenting limbo or to show me the way. Even Carl Jung saw her in one guise as a nixie, siren, lamia, succubus—the mad woman of fairy tale "who infatuates young men and sucks the life out of them." But Jung would also see her as anima, as a way into the life behind consciousness, the feminine aspect of the male, his guide. Somehow, on this journey of mine, I had to make up my own mind, find out about my relationship with the complex woman in my head.

Version 2

I had been listening to Willie Nelson as another antidote to confinement, and one of his songs had given me insight into my soul's restlessness. "Black Rose" was no surprise to me. I was not the "cain-raising" man Nelson sings about, but I understood how that man could turn from woman to woman for salvation and be left with "trembling hand and a bottle of gin," with nothing more to claim time after time than "a Rose of a different name." All his women turned out to be mere variations of the woman who made him first "feel lightening," and she, even she, was no more than a projection—the woman inside his head transfiguring the ones outside.

In our heads that woman often wreaks havoc, and I hadn't been able to figure out whether she was there in mine to hold me in tormenting limbo or to show me the way. Even C. G. Jung saw her in one guise as nixie, siren, lamia, succubus—the mad woman of fairy tale "who infatuates young men and sucks the life out of them." But Jung would also see her as a way into the life behind consciousness, as *anima,* the feminine aspect of the male, his guide. Somehow, on this journey of mine, I had to come to terms with her.

ANALYZING AND WRITING   *Comment on the differences between these two versions. Was it necessary for the single paragraph to become two, or could the two paragraphs in Version 2 just as easily be combined? Explain. Consider the two allusions to "Black Rose." Which development of the allusion do you prefer and why? Given the treatment of "Black Rose" in the first version, what implicit assumption do you think I make about your knowledge of the song itself? Is that a wise assumption?*

*Explain. Who is C. G. Jung? Should I tell you, or would that depend
again on the assumption I make about you and other readers? Explain.*

Consider yet a third version of these paragraphs. In my final
essay, these three paragraphs constitute my *beginning:*

Version 3

In my early forties I was seized by a compelling urge to escape—
not to run away from it all forever, but to escape once in a while.
Responsibly, mind you. The sleek, bright orange MG that I bought
to wind round and round the roads outside the back gate of the
Army post took me nowhere, but I got there fast. I also bought the
Klipsch speakers I'd been wanting since high school, bought them
so I could hear Beethoven's "Hymn to Joy" as if I were inside
Beethoven's own head. I wanted to be transformed.

I'd been inside Willie Nelson's head, or he in mine, for a long
time. "Black Rose" was no surprise to me. I understood how a
"cain-raising man" could turn from woman to woman for salvation
and be left with nothing more to claim time after time than "a Rose
of a different name"—a man duped by a mere projection, the
woman inside his head wreaking havoc, transfiguring the ones
outside.

Whether the woman in my head was there to hold me in limbo
or show me the way, I didn't know. Even C. G. Jung saw her in one
guise as nixie, siren, lamia, succubus—the mad woman of fairy
tale "who infatuates young men and sucks the life out of them." But
Jung would also see her as a way into the life behind consciousness,
as *anima,* the feminine aspect of the male, his guide. Somehow, I
had to come to terms with her.

ANALYZING AND WRITING *Comment on the relationship between the three paragraphs. Does the first paragraph help you understand the second and third? Explain. Which of the paragraphs about*

————————————————— ◊ —————————————————

"Black Rose" do you prefer? Explain your preference. Do I tell you enough in Version 3 to keep you interested, or do you need to know more? Would you read on after this beginning, or would you stop? Explain.

Citing evidence and developing that evidence, accounting for its place in your essay, is not a mechanical process. You cannot follow one or two easy rules. There are no easy rules, but there are guidelines, suggestions that can lead you to think about your readers and about how best to bring your evidence to life within the context of your essay. The most important of those guidelines is to keep trying to please that imagined reader; think about what he or she needs to know to understand and stay interested in your idea.

When you incorporate evidence into your exploratory essays, remember to represent borrowed sources accurately and to make that evidence blend into your paragraphs. Evidence and text should seem inseparable. When they do not, you interrupt your reader's train of thought. Consider this awkward version of the "Black Rose" citation:

I'd been thinking about a Willie Nelson song for a long time. In that song he sings about a woman named "Black Rose." We don't know whether Black Rose is real or not, but she causes a lot of trouble for the man in the song. He tells us: "First time I felt lightening,/I was standing in the drizzling rain,/Trembling hand and a bottle of gin,/And a Rose of a different name." He tells us in the song that he needs help to "leave this Black Rose alone." I wasn't in quite such dire straits as this man, but the song itself reminded me how powerful a woman in a man's head can be, and I turned to Carl Jung for clarification and help.

In this version, I spend too much time on the song and too little on my own idea. Evidence and text do not seem inseparable. I cite too much of the song and say too little about Jung. I fail to strike the proper balance between the need to illustrate my idea with the song and the need to develop my own idea.

Include only evidence that clarifies your thinking and enriches your essay; it should add depth and variety to your exploration but should not take the place of your own thinking and analysis.

E. *Student Essays—Images, Ideas, and Explorations*

GIAN NEFFINGER'S "HOUSE OF CARDS"

Let's look now at a piece of student writing that will help us review the various enterprises we have been considering in the first two chapters. We want to see how reading, thinking, and reflecting can produce interesting prose.

Recall Gian Neffinger's paragraphs that we looked at earlier in this chapter (pp. 67–69). We saw how Gian used a poem by A. E. Housman to clarify an idea of his own about beauty and destruction and permanence. He showed us how to integrate evidence economically and effectively in that single instance within his essay. We turn now to Gian's entire essay as a way of reviewing the process of developing a complex, exploratory essay—from start to finish.

Gian came to class first with an image that was largely fictive; he seemed to have made it up out of whole cloth. It was about a man who designed cars, perfect cars. The man had not smiled since the day he produced the first perfect car. After that day, he supervised the assembly operation and the testing. But he wasn't happy. Then one day, on the test track, the car coming toward him out of the fifth curve exploded in midair. The design engineer smiled. He smiled, the draft tells us, because he saw beauty in the destruction.

I read the draft, or what we were calling an image of experience; I read the image to the class and asked for comments. The other students wanted to know only one thing. "What does that man have to do with you?" they asked Gian. In response, he leaned back in his chair; he seemed actually to scoot back into the corner of it, looking out under his baseball cap with the brightest eyes, smiling. No other answer.

Gian came to the next class with a second image, one about a house of cards his uncle built. At a subsequent conference, we talked about the possibility of making those two images work together in an essay. He was excited, and I was excited about his imagination. As he was leaving, he asked if he could bring a poem into his essay. Several days later, he said he just couldn't make the car image work; he wanted to know if he could use other images that had come to him as he worked on the essay. We talked about how he might use those other images if he let the story about the house of cards serve as the basis for the whole essay.

Here is what he wrote:

House of Cards
by Gian Neffinger

1   My uncle is an artist, a master craftsman. He does not paint or sculpt or write or draw, at least not particularly well; these things are not his speciality. My uncle Pete is a master builder of the House of Cards. He says he built his first such house when he was four, and although grandmother tends to doubt this claim, it is certain that he has worked at his skill for some time.

2   At family gatherings he would build the most magnificent structures imaginable, anything from a cottage complete with windows to a modern skyscraper eight stories tall. No high-rise was ever more of a feat to construct than one of uncle Pete's master-pieces. At the crucial moment, when all of the family cringed and looked away, his hand was steady, his movements effortlessly precise. And when the occasional indoor breeze did drift through and fell his fragile giant, he simply sighed and sipped his coffee.

3   When at last he had finished, resisting the inexorable temptation to add just one more wing, he stood back to witness the sum of all the whims that went into its creation. Having duly admired it, he

then turned his attention to another matter, that of choosing The Card. After careful analysis he rendered his decision: "That's the one." At this cue my cousin Andy and I began to salivate with anticipation. Who would get to pull out *the* card?

4   The Pulling of the Card was always saved as an after-dinner treat, but well before the appointed hour, Andy and I would examine the card in question and envision the fateful event like a child adoring a package under the tree on Christmas Eve. Surely it was great fun, watching Uncle Pete enlist each card into his conspiracy to defy the universal law of gravitation, but what made all of his efforts worthwhile to us was not the spectacle of completion but the spectacle of destruction. For upon the pulling of that one card, all of the delicate relationships that held the structure aloft dissolved, and that brilliant conspiracy was reduced to a scattered pile of playing cards, each as ordinary as the next. It was amazing just how little disturbance it took; just to bump it would suffice. The only good way to get a sense of the delicate precision involved in creating it was to touch it gently, to try to alter it ever so slightly, and have it crumple to nothing. Andy and I used to promise each other the most outrageous things we could think of in exchange for the other's turn to tinker with The Card.

5   It was an altogether unique phenomenon, the fall of the house of cards. Having not actually witnessed it, you might guess it would be fun to watch, but for all the wrong reasons. Mother never understood at all; she thought we were just being beastly, destroying the card house just like we destroyed our Lego airplanes and our Matchbox cars and our new Sunday slacks. It was not anything malicious at all. "Malicious" is laughing at the blood dribbling from Tyler Evans' nose after my friend Pete clocked him. I hated that kid. But Andy and I never had anything against Uncle Pete's houses; in fact we quite liked them. Maliciousness had nothing to do with it.

6   Part of the appeal of getting to pull The Card was the sense of power—that's the part Andy and I fought over. Of course, we

fought over everything that even vaguely resembled a privilege. But I remember, when no one was around, I used to go into the china cabinet, carefully bring out the beautiful, rose-colored heirloom teapot and hold it out at arm's length over the hardwood floor. The first time I tried this I was nervous—after all, what if I slipped? That would require some wild explaining—even if I did tell the truth, no one would believe me, and they would suspect something far more treacherous instead. That first time I got scared; I clutched the teapot against me and proceeded to carefully return it to its proper place. But something drew me back, until, after several visits, I would grandly swing my arm out to its full extension, as if presenting a trophy of war, and I would admire the finely crafted treasure, pausing only to glance at the unforgiving oak surface below. And I would think to myself, "I could, of course. I could just drop it, and no amount of surgery and no amount of prayer could ever bring it back." And oh, how I smiled!

7   When the house fell, when the invisible hand of physics let go and the cards fell in chaos, something very powerful happened. Having that power between thumb and forefinger was a grand feeling indeed. After all of the care that had gone into its assembly, it seemed ironic that it must all end with the tiniest of movements. Perhaps it was irony that made the moment magic. It would certainly seem equal to the task; it was irony that made the Titanic legend great. Had it not been billed as the Unsinkable Ship, its sinking would not have been so remarkable, and the world would never have had cause to learn that eight ninths of an iceberg's mass lies concealed below the water's surface.

8   Whatever the meaning hidden in that final moment of splendor, one thing is sure: a sudden demise grants a certain timelessness. A. E. Housman, in his poem "To an Athlete Dying Young," tells of a champion who died in his prime, before his reknown faded. He took his championship crown to his grave, where he could never be dethroned. Thus went the Titanic. It met its end as the pinnacle of naval technology, and now, whenever anyone thinks of the

mightiest ship ever to cruise the open sea, none think of Old Ironsides, bobbing in its secure harbor with its heavy cargo of tourists; none think of the newest, most massive cruise liners or battleships, for the Titanic owns the title of mightiest—has owned it since that fateful night, and will own it forever.

9   So goes the house of cards—quickly, gloriously. No such house ever lasted long enough to suffer the indignities of time and fortune. Most great monuments are not nearly as lucky. Their features are worn away by time, or tourists; their reknown is drowned in the wake of Progress. No one actually apprehends their beauty; it just slowly fades away with time.

10   When I first came across the tragic hero in literature, I felt as if I had met him somewhere before. Here was a man, arguably a great man, who reached the pinnacle of his greatness in his own destruction. In his ruin, he proves himself, revealing, to the swift, the moral: "What a piece of work is man!" and leaving even the stupid with a sense of wonder at the spectacle they have witnessed. The exceptional character placed in an unnatural circumstance makes for an extraordinary event, stretching the boundaries of our comprehension.

11   My uncle Peter builds tragic heroes as a hobby; my cousin and I stage the plays: we circle, examine, touch gently, then grasp The Card, pause for a moment, and pull.

12   To this day I've never met anyone who could build a house of cards as well as Uncle Pete. To this day Andy and I take turns performing the after-dinner ritual; we have long since retired our Legos and our Matchbox cars, but I don't know if we'll ever surrender our childhood rights to The Card. After all, better us than the breeze. What does a breeze know about beauty?

ANALYZING AND REVISING   *If Gian Neffinger's main idea has something to do with the notion of beauty in destruction, what other, subordinate ideas does he introduce along the way of his exploration? Why do you suppose he includes the discussion about maliciousness? The episode about the teapot? The allusion to the Titanic? The paragraph on the tragic hero in literature? Why does he alternate these various subordinate notions with his continuing story about the house of cards? What if he gave us the entire story about the house of cards and then gave us the subordinate notions in a separate section? How would that change your reaction to the essay? Explain.*

Gian Neffinger was attentive to his controlling image (the house of cards); he had the courage of his imagination, and that made all the difference. He made his connections, and he teaches us something about beauty. He doesn't prove anything about beauty, doesn't have to. Instead, he lets us see his mind moving around an idea that he enlarges as he proceeds; he explores an idea he cares about, enriching it with evidence gleaned from reading and imagining.

DEIRDRE McMULLEN'S "ALONE AT LAST"

The next student essay developed out of a different exercise. Instead of asking students to begin with an image of experience, I asked them to select one of their favorite paintings, one they had become attached to in some special way. Initially they brought to class only a word picture of the painting; their initial task was to re-create the picture for students who might never have seen it.

Deirdre McMullen's essay evolved from a painting that hangs in her aunt's dining room. That painting is not the focus of the essay; the painting led her to an idea about the pleasures of loneliness. It is that idea that makes the essay cohere. Shifting her focus away from the painting itself, she gives her imagination free play over the idea. The painting becomes part of her evidence; she uses it to illuminate the idea she is exploring. She uses as well thoughts she had gleaned from reading essays by E. B. White and Loren Eiseley. The painting, White, and Eiseley add depth and variety to her essay.

Alone at Last
by Deirdre McMullen

1   A pressing urgency in my bladder is what disturbed my sleep, and I knew the chilled night journey to the outhouse could not wait until morning. My warm bare feet hit the cool linoleum and reluctantly tip-toed in the darkness through the screen door onto the cold wooden porch. Even though the nature of this night trek was an emergency, I stood motionless on the porch waiting for the sleep to clear from my eyes. The strong smell of stagnant mud met my nostrils, and there was no need for my eyes to clear to know that it was low tide. I could hear the screeching of the sea gulls from the point, and I wondered if they were this noisy every night. Everything was so different out here alone; so peaceful, that I had forgotten what I came outside for. It was only a moment before I was again reminded of the pressure in my side, ending my sojourn, and my feet continued along the long boards in the sand to the outhouse.

2   On the way back to the porch I could hear little field mice scurrying in the brush, away from the large, lumbering shadow my body cast over the sand, and I was acutely aware that I was a trespasser in this world, the world of night sounds and creatures. The small mechanical bodily function which had awakened me, oddly enough, was now the key which opened the door to a world I had never consciously been aware of; therefore the loss of an hour of sleep seemed a small sacrifice, so I nestled down on the porch steps alone.

3   A lot can be said about being alone, and it is all not so antisocial or pathetically empty as the word may sound. Greta Garbo had the right idea; all she "vanted" was to be left alone. She probably had great insight to the world around her. So, there I sat on the steps, feeling much like Greta and glad to be alone.

4   Sitting in the pale glow of the half-full moon, I thought about insight and about what Loren Eiseley speaks of in "The Judgment of

the Birds." Eiseley feels that in order for man to gain insight, he must go apart from the rest and live for a time in the wilderness. Not everyone can afford the time to become a hermit, and therefore, must take small sabbatical moments wherever possible. That night, my bed and the muddy beach left uncovered, was my moment, and the porch was to be my hermitage.

5   The moon was high in the sky, and it played hide and seek with everything below as dark clouds drifted by her crescent grin. It reminded me a lot of a charcoal painting hanging in my aunt's dining room. I'd always loved that painting and the way it made me feel. The painting is of the moon shining down upon an inlet of water. The land on the right side of the canvas cuts down sharply to the water's edge, and on the left side of the canvas, no land can be seen because of the dark foggy clouds that roll across the moon and out to sea. What little you can see of the moon though, shines bright white through the charcoal mist straight down to the middle of the canvas on the bottom. Little ripples of water can be seen at the bottom suggesting that the water is shallow there, possibly nearing the shore or a reef. The entire canvas is mostly all in dark shadow with very little highlighting, but it makes me feel peaceful, ethereal, a child of the night, just as I was feeling that night.

6   I sat real still. I became part of the night and was able to take in all the sights and sounds of the seething life that went on around me while the others slept inside. The gulls on the point were calling to their young, and flew back and forth from shore to brush indubitably frenzied over the feeding grounds that the ebbing tide had exposed. The silhouette of their wings against the clouds made their presence more prominent than in the daylight, as they folded them back, and shaped like an arrow, dove downward toward the small crustaceans that lived on the mud bed below. This was a repetitive routine for the gulls which I know I'd seen before, but could never truly devote my full attention to until that night when I was alone. Their ebullience made me want to jump up and return

their screeches, but I did not want to intrude; they were already kind enough to allow me to observe, alone.

7   From the moored sailboats out on the water, I could hear the clanging of the rigging against the masts as the waves gently rolled them side to side. This resonant, metallic sound echoed inland, a call to worship, and there I sat in my pew in the sanctuary of night. E. B. White once said that "the richness of the scene was in its plainness, its natural condition." Surely what I had just been witness to was a natural condition, one I would have missed had I not been alone, and it left me bonded with nature, inextricable and unforgettable.

8   The gulls' cries were soon calmed, and I heard the returning tide lapping against the sea wall. The sparrows were out on their early morning errands, and the moon disappeared with the breaking of dawn. I could not believe the time had passed so quickly. For the first time I became aware of the dew that had settled on my hair, and I stood up and shook myself free of morning's moist greeting. I hurried back through the screen door across the floor to my bed, but climbed back in reluctantly, just as I had left. The urgency that had aroused my slumber was nothing compared to the urgency that now filled me. I gently rolled from side to side trying to resume my lost hours of rest, but the moon smile on my lips and the metallic sound echoing in my heart told me I would not sleep. My impatience for the rest to awaken to my day, a day so enlightened by the night, was overpowering. No one else knew, but I did. I had been alone with my vision. No need for sleep.

Both Deirdre's and Gian's essays show us in innumerable ways that adding depth and variety to our essays does not mean going out to look for quotations or images to decorate our pieces. Good essays grow naturally out of our lived experiences and out of the imaginative and reflective experiences of our mind. As we develop good reading habits and begin to make connections—as we begin to make sense of life because of those connections—we begin to discover interesting ideas. We become capable of rendering judgments. When we begin to bring quotations, images, and ideas together within our essays, we become capable of giving our readers the distinct pleasure of thinking in a new way about an idea of our choosing. We become writers worth our salt.

F. *Practice—Thinking and Writing*

THINKING

1. Reread Deirdre McMullen's final paragraph, her *ending*. Among the many fine sentences in that paragraph, this one stands out: "I gently rolled from side to side trying to resume my lost hours of rest, but the moon smile on my lips and the metallic sound echoing in my heart told me I would not sleep." How is that sentence related to other parts of the essay? Be very specific. Find other sentences in the essay that "glue" the piece together. Find words or images that serve the same purpose. Highlight them.

2. Look at paragraphs 4 and 7 in Deirdre's essay. Take out the references to Eiseley and White; take away the paragraphs themselves if nothing much is left. What effect do these changes have on the essay?

3. Gian Neffinger's essay is "held together" by the story about the house of cards, Deirdre's by the story of a night journey to the outhouse. What else holds these two essays together? What else makes them cohere? Explain.

WRITING—SHORT PIECES

1. Have you had an experience similar to Deirdre McMullen's? If so, jot down ideas from your reading that might enrich Deirdre's essay. See if you can integrate a paragraph of your own (based on your reading experience) into Deirdre's essay. What difficulties do you encounter?

2. Turn to the Essays for Additional Reading section, and read "Living Like Weasels" (p. 292). Read carefully the first two paragraphs, the *beginning*. Jot down the most telling details from Dillard's description of the two weasels. Go through the entire essay, and highlight every instance when she refers to one of those details. Explain her purpose on each occasion. Write a short paragraph in which you explain how her ending depends on her beginning.

3. Reread the third paragraph of this chapter. See if you can rewrite that paragraph by eliminating the quotations. Which version seems more effective? Why? Compare the opening sections in Chapters 1 and 2. What differences do you note in the development of those two sections? Explain.

4. Select a paragraph from this chapter, and examine the way I use evidence to support and clarify the ideas I am developing. To what extent do I follow the general guidelines for incorporating evidence? Find an instance where you think the quoted material creates confusion. Rewrite the paragraph, eliminating the quotation. Summarize, but give the other writer credit within the paragraph.

WRITING—ESSAYS

1. Begin with an image of experience just as you did for the essays in Chapter 1. After you develop your image of an important memory, locate in that reconstructed image an *idea*. Let the idea serve as a lodestone; let it call in other images of experience, items from your reading, and perhaps a song or a painting. Develop an exploratory essay about your idea, letting the images of experience and the other evidence help you. Let your readers see how your mind can play over all of this evidence, make sense of it, and use it to enrich the idea.

2. You might follow these steps as a way to an essay. *Step 1:* Find

your special painting, and create a word picture of it to share with others in your class. *Step 2:* Write out your reaction to the painting in an effort to discover your special relationship with it, or develop a scene that will convey your relationship to the painting. *Step 3:* Try to identify an idea embedded in what you did for Steps 1 and 2. *Step 4:* Write an essay in which you explore that idea, using the painting and other evidence to enrich it.

3. Go to the library and find a collection of essays by Loren Eiseley. Read "The Running Man" or "The Judgment of the Birds." Assume that Eiseley is still alive, and write him a letter about the essay of your choice. Discuss with him some controversial point that you uncover in the essay or some section of the essay that seems unclear to you. See what you can discover about using evidence from his essay in your letter. Your letter should actually be an *epistolary* essay with a beginning, middle, and ending.

4. Select for revision an exploratory essay that you wrote in response to a requirement in Chapter 1. Rethink your idea. Give your imagination a freer rein; let it go out in search of new connections. Try to bring your reading into play. Prepare notes that outline your plan for revision; mark spots in the text where you want to add new material. Develop your new essay.

Chapter 3

A. *The Analytical Essay—Writing about Writing: A More Direct Approach*

Writing the exploratory essay, you learned to be a disciplined rambler, guided by Sam Pickering's contention that the "essay saunters, letting the writer follow the vagaries of his own willful curiosity" and E. B. White's suggestion that "the essayist's escape from discipline is only a partial escape." Having written exploratory essays of your own, you have probably learned that good writing, even when it seems to follow the interesting twists and turns of a writer's mind, is shaped and crafted by disciplined revision. You know, too, that the easy, rambling nature of good exploratory essays conceals a great deal of hard work and that much of the reader's pleasure comes from the uncluttered richness of those essays. As an essayist, you must work hard to make the reading pleasurable.

In this chapter, we will consider various techniques that an essayist might use to give such pleasure. We will focus on the close reading of exploratory essays written by professionals so that we can gain a better understanding of how they create their essays, how they make sense of their various experiences. Analysis of those professional essays will be our initial business. You will eventually write an essay about one of the essays you read, but you will not be able to write that essay without first attending to reading and to thinking analytically about what you have read.

The exploratory essay, as you began to see in the last chapter and as you began to discover as you wrote, is an essay rich in pattern and complexity. Its evocative images suggest levels of meaning below the surface; its scenes create intimacy while giving insight. Most of those essays are so rich that we cannot exhaust them in one reading; there are pleasures below the surface, and there are pleasures in the form and in the images. Sometimes those pleasures are hidden from readers unaware of techniques. But, of course, writers—all writers—have to know about those techniques, have to use them in their own essays.

As a way of helping you become better writers, we will uncover some of those techniques and consider how the professional essayist uses them. We'll do that first and then concern ourselves with telling interested readers what we have learned. You'll actually write an analytical essay about what you discovered as you analyzed an exploratory essay written by a professional essayist.

Your analytical essay will aim to convince your readers that you have discovered something important about the way the exploratory essay conveys its idea to the reader. You'll be trying to persuade readers that you know *how* the other essayist used selected techniques to develop an idea. Although your analytical writing will be a bit more direct, a bit more streamlined, perhaps a bit more scholarly, than exploratory writing, it, too, should give pleasure to your readers.

Sometimes when students first begin to write an analytical essay, they tend to turn stiff and scholarly, forgetting how clear, forceful everyday language can serve them well even in this more formal type of essay. Russell Baker—whose syndicated columns often give us a sense of our own foibles—translated "Little Red Riding Hood" "into the modern American language" a few years ago; he did so to "make the classics accessible to contemporary readers." In Baker's modern version of the story, his narrator writes the way some scholars write: "At this point in time the wolf moderated his rhetoric and proceeded to grandmother's residence. The elderly person was then subjected to the disadvantages of total consumption and transferred to residence in the perpetrator's stomach." Little Red Riding Hood, finding the wolf in grandmother's bed, talks the same way: "Grandmother," she said, "your ocular implements are of an extraordinary order of magnitude."

As we move from the exploratory essay to the analytical one, you may be tempted to inflate your language, trying to sound distinguished, authoritative, and fancy. If you catch yourself getting carried away, think of Baker and think, too, of this delightful example Lord Noel G. Annan gave during a commencement address at the University of Pennsylvania. Annan, the vice-chancellor of the University of London, had been outlining the virtues of the spoken American language, but he turned from praise to warning. He warned the graduating class about the universities' failure to teach students "how to convey their conclusions lucidly, logically, elegantly." Instead, he insisted, students learn to "write a language full of jargon and clichés, and we pretend they are scholarly technical terms." Annan continued:

Why write, "The doubtful validity assigned by this individual to different role behavior stances may lead one to doubt his ability to distinguish between the total life situation and its interaction with the ongoing immediate situation which he should define selectively"—why write this when the living American language taught to me 44 years ago by my cousins in Lebanon, Pennsylvania, is, "He doesn't know his ass from a hot rock"?

The living scholarly language, the language of analysis, ought to lean closer to that of Lord Annan's cousins' than that of the scholar he quotes. The writer who wants the audience to understand needs to learn again to say quite simply, "The wolf ate grandmother." Little Red Riding Hood to say, "My . . . grandmother, what large eyes you have." You to convey your conclusions "lucidly, logically, elegantly."

When writing your analytical essays, try to keep Baker and Annan before your mind's eye. Your analytical task will be to discover how someone else's essay works, to answer the question, How do professional essayists make meaning? The simplest response to the question is this: They say lucidly, logically, and elegantly what is on their minds. But the probing question still remains. How do essayists say logically and elegantly what they mean? To answer that question and to write the essay about your discoveries, you will have to perform two distinct, pleasurable tasks.

First, you'll have to do some locker-room digging. Reading critically and analytically will be your first task. The evidence for your analytical essay will not come directly from your personal experience; it will come from someone else's essay. Reading that essay critically, you will have to discover technique, and what you discover in that essay will depend on the knowledge you bring to your critical reading. You will be making discoveries; you will be interpreting the evidence; and you will be the one writing about your discoveries.

Writing about your discoveries will be your second task. The essay you write will bear the stamp of your mind just as the exploratory one did, but the evidence for this one will come from the essay you analyzed rather than from your lived experiences. In your essay, you will want to reveal conclusions that you have reached through careful, systematic study of that other essay. Even though your work in this essay will be *interpretive,* you will be writing closer to the hard edge of argument than you were when writing exploratory essays. You will be contending with a reader who is anxious to know about your interpretations, a reader who might be impatient if you choose to ramble and digest. You want to help the reader of your analytical essay become a better reader of the essay you have investigated. That reader wants a payoff—one that is lucid, logical, elegant, and direct, more direct than in the exploratory essay.

To help you deliver that payoff, we want to turn now to techniques. What you learn will prepare you for the rigorous reading you must do in preparation for writing your analytical essay. And the techniques you discover professionals using in their exploratory essays may also serve you later in indirect ways when you write other exploratory essays of your own.

B. *Image, Scene, Persona, Pattern—How Professional Essayists Make Meaning*

In order to write your analytical essay, you will have to know a great deal about the way other writers put their essays together. As you begin thinking about structure (those organizational elements that shape an essay and help make it cohere), you should not be misled into thinking that essayists sit down with a preconceived building plan and make essays the way construction engineers put up a building. Your own writing should have convinced you that the writing process is more complex than that. Some essayists do work from a fixed plan, but most begin with explorations, without a clear, definitive sense of how the essay will take shape; often they discover order as they write. But good writers certainly do know about techniques they can use to develop their essays. They are familiar not only with basic sentence patterns but also with ways to vary and combine those patterns, ways to use them as playgrounds for their active imaginations. They know a great deal about words—the way words combine to make sounds, the way words take on new meaning in different contexts. They know, too, about image, scene, persona, pattern, and many other techniques available to writers. They have learned much of what they know by reading, by paying careful attention to the way other writers write.

When they read, they look not only for meaning but also for the techniques that all good writers use. We will look closely at just four of those techniques: image, scene, persona, and pattern.

IMAGE

Roy Reed

In Chapter 1 we considered how images help writers get started, how they lead to ideas and interesting essays. In the context of that chapter, we thought of an image as a picture of experience recollected from memory. As you begin to discover how other essayists develop their ideas, you can learn even more about images by considering how writers actually use images to make their essays cohere. Recall Ira Solenberger in Roy Reed's "Spring Comes to Hogeye" (p. 16). Two of Reed's images in that essay are arresting, and they work together to give us a sense of his idea about Mr. Solenberger. Near the beginning of the essay, Reed let's us *see* Ira inside the house:

> He opened the door of his heating stove and threw another chunk of wood on the fire. He closed it a little sharply and glanced out the window toward his empty garden.

Reed gets a great deal out of that simple paragraph and that single picture of his central character. We know from the opening section of the essay that it's spring in the Ozarks. We should know, too, that in Arkansas in late spring, there ought to be no need for a fire in the heating stove. So it should come as no surprise to us that a man might close the door of his stove "a little sharply" just before he glances "out the window toward his empty garden." Very economically, Reed conveys Ira's frustration, his longing to be outdoors, his exasperation about having to wait for spring.

Three paragraphs later, Reed has the "awful force" of spring push

Ira Solenberger out the door in a hat and coat, hunched against the biting bright air blowing up from the Illinois River, to kick the dirt and study the sky, and then retreat to the house to throw another chunk of wood on the fire.

This second, more intense image of frustration takes us back to the earlier image and leaves us with a haunting picture of the old man kicking and studying, unable to do anything but go back inside and wait. Ira "throws" yet another "chunk" of wood on the fire to ward off the cold from the biting, bright, blowing air outside. These two images show us Ira under Nature's charge, waiting for his chance to turn Her to his good use, waiting to plant his crops. We learn that other farmers in the hills plant early, defy Nature; Ira waits Her out. We discover later that Ira knows Her secrets, knows how to raise the crops that baffle others. In short, those two pictures show us both Ira's frustration and his wisdom. They are doubly charged. Reed uses them to enhance his idea.

But as powerful as those images are, the essay does not depend entirely on them. They are secondary pictures that Reed uses to enhance his presentation. The same might be said of the circular image in the student essay about kayaking in Chapter 1; that was primarily an image of motion, an image the student discovered when he was recalling pictures from childhood. We know that those childhood images of circular motion—going round and round with his sister and skipping around in his classroom—gave him an idea about repetition that he associated with the notion of practicing. But he did not use those earlier images in his essay. So the image of the eskimo roll in the paragraph about kayaking is not central to the essay's meaning; it is central only to our understanding of how the essay came into being. We would probably not want to write an analytical essay about that image in the student essay because the essay's meaning does not depend very much on that image of circularity. The paragraph and the image are interesting if we're studying the process that led the student to write the essay, but they are not very interesting if we're trying to figure out how the essay actually works. On the other hand, we could certainly write an important essay about how Reed's secondary pictures of Ira (the two we've examined and others) enhance the presentation of the central idea in "Spring Comes to Hogeye."

As you read, mark striking images that make you sit up and take notice. When you go back to analyze the essay, you will more than likely discover that those images convey meaning, that they are very central to your understanding of the essay's idea.

A single image might hold an entire essay together. Think of Eiseley's stone and the way it reverberates throughout "The Illusion of the Two Cultures" and of Dillard's socketing image in "Living like Weasels." Our discussion in Chapter 2 about those central images sets the stage for your understanding of how an entire essay can depend so much on a single image.

June Jordan

Let's consider a scene from "Many Rivers to Cross" (Essays for Additional Reading section, p. 297) and see how a central image carries the meaning of the entire essay. Before June Jordan develops this important image, she tells us about the dire circumstances that have caused her to move back into the "brownstone of her childhood" with her parents. With her child, she moves back, seeking temporary shelter until she can earn money from her writing projects. Her mother takes the two of them into the house against her father's angry protests. Here is the scene:

> From my first memory of him, my father had always worked at the post office. His favorite was the night shift, which brought him home usually between three and four o'clock in the morning.
>
> It was hot. I finally fell asleep that night, a few nights after the argument between my mother and myself. She seemed to be rallying; that afternoon, she and my son had spent a long time in the backyard, oblivious to the heat and the mosquitoes. They were

both tired but peaceful when they noisily re-entered the house, holding hands awkwardly.

But someone was knocking at the door to my room. Why should I wake up? It would be impossible to fall asleep again. It was so hot. The knocking continued. I switched on the light by the bed: 3:30 a.m. It must be my father. Furious, I pulled on a pair of shorts and a t-shirt. "What do you want? What's the matter?" I asked him, through the door. Had he gone berserk? What could he have to talk about at that ridiculous hour?

"OK, all right," I said, rubbing my eyes awake as I stepped to the door and opened it. "What?"

To my surprise, my father stood there looking very uncertain.

"It's your mother," he told me, in a burly, formal voice. "I think she's dead, but I'm not sure." He was avoiding my eyes.

"What do you mean," I answered.

"I want you to go downstairs and figure it out."

I could not believe what he was saying to me. "You want me to figure out if my mother is dead or alive?"

"I can't tell! I don't know!!" he shouted angrily.

"Jesus Christ," I muttered, angry and beside myself.

I turned and glanced about my room, wondering if I could find anything to carry with me on this mission; what do you use to determine a life or a death? I couldn't see anything obvious that might be useful.

"I'll wait up here," my father said. "You call up and let me know."

I could not believe it; a man married to a woman more than forty years and he can't tell if she's alive or dead and he wakes up his kid and tells her, "You figure it out."

I was at the bottom of the stairs. I halted just outside the dining room where my mother slept. Suppose she really was dead? Suppose my father was not just being crazy and hateful? "Naw," I shook my head and confidently entered the room.

"Momma?!" I called, aloud. At the edge of the cot, my mother was leaning forward, one arm braced to hoist her body up. She was trying to stand up! I rushed over. "Wait. Here, I'll help you!" I said.

And I reached out my hands to give her a lift. The body of my mother was stiff. She was not yet cold, but she was stiff. Maybe I had come downstairs just in time! I tried to loosen her arms, to change her position, to ease her into lying down.

"Momma!" I kept saying. "Momma, listen to me! It's OK! I'm here and everything. Just relax. Relax! Give me a hand, now. I'm trying to help you lie down!"

Her body did not relax. She did not answer me. But she was not cold. Her eyes were not shut.

From upstairs my father was yelling, "Is she dead? Is she dead?"

"No!" I screamed at him. "No! She's not dead!"

At this, my father tore down the stairs and into the room. Then he braked.

"Milly?" he called out, tentative. Then he shouted at me and banged around the walls. "You damn fool. Don't you see now she's gone. Now she's gone!" We began to argue.

"She's alive! Call the doctor!"

"No!"

"Yes!"

At last my father left the room to call the doctor.

I straightened up. I felt completely exhausted from trying to gain a response from my mother. Then she was, stiff on the edge of her bed, just about to stand up. Her lips were set, determined. She would manage it, but by herself. I could not help. Her eyes fixed on some point below the floor.

"Momma!" I shook her hard as I could to rouse her into focus. Now she fell back on the cot, but frozen and in the wrong position. It hit me that she might be dead. She might be dead.

This scene presents a rout of images: the father knocking on Jordan's door; Jordan rushing downstairs; Jordan confronting her mother; her mother trying to get up from the bed; the father helpless, upstairs, waiting; the father tearing down the stairs and into the room; the confrontation between father and daughter. Each image could be developed by a good writer, but Jordan chooses only one—the image of her mother trying to stand up—to unify her entire essay. She uses it there in the middle of her essay, and she returns to it for her ending. In that ending, we see Jordan herself lying flat on her back in Harlem Hospital, thinking about what has happened to her. There on that bed, Jordan decides what she will do about her own life:

> I wanted to be strong. I never wanted to be weak again as long as I lived. I thought about my mother and her suicide and I thought about how my father could not tell whether she was dead or alive.
>
> I wanted to get well and what I wanted to do as soon as I was strong again, actually, what I wanted to do was I wanted to live my life so that people would know unmistakably that I am alive, so that when I finally die people will know the difference for sure between my living and my death.
>
> And I thought about the idea of my mother as a good woman and I rejected that, because I don't see why it's a good thing when you give up, or when you cooperate with those who hate you or when you polish and iron and mend and endlessly mollify for the sake of the people who love the way that you kill yourself day by day silently.
>
> And I think all of this is really about women and work. Certainly this is all about me as a woman and my life work. I mean I am not sure my mother's suicide was something extraordinary. Perhaps most women must deal with a similar inheritance, the legacy of a woman whose death you cannot possibly pinpoint because she died so many, many times and because, even before she became your mother, the life of that woman was taken; I say it was taken away.
>
> And really it was to honor my mother that I did fight with my father, that man who could not tell the living from the dead.

And really it is to honor Mrs. Hazel Griffin and my cousin Valerie and all the women I love, including myself, that I am working for the courage to admit the truth that Bertolt Brecht has written; he says, "It takes courage to say that the good were defeated not because they were good, but because they were weak."

I cherish the mercy and the grace of women's work. But I know there is new work that we must undertake as well: that new work will make defeat detestable to us. That new women's work will mean we will not die trying to stand up: we will live that way: standing up.

I came too late to help my mother to her feet.

By way of everlasting thanks to all of the women who have helped me to stay alive I am working never to be late again.

This essay's power depends on the way Jordan brings the image of her mother back into the closing section of the essay. The following short analysis explains to another person, perhaps a person who hasn't studied "Rivers," *how* Jordan makes use of that single image of her mother:

In her essay "Many Rivers to Cross," June Jordan makes good use of a stunning image of her dying mother. Jordan wants to let us know how she will live her life to make it radically different from her mother's. She uses the first three pages of her essay to give us a relatively straightforward account of the circumstances in her life that have caused her to move back into a brownstone with her parents. Because her husband abandons her, because she has a child and too little money to support him, and because she is pregnant with another child, she desperately needs help. Jordan lets us know that she can get more help from her women friends than from her father, lets us know that her mother, over her father's protest, allows her to bring her son back home until they have money enough to go out on their own again.

Jordan's narrative account—her chronological, causal explanation during those first three pages—sets the stage for an important, fully-developed confrontation between her and her father. Within that protracted scene of confrontation, we have an opportunity to witness her father's helplessness in the face of her mother's death. We see him unable to determine if his wife is living or dead. Helpless, he turns to his daughter, insists that she go downstairs to find out whether her mother is alive. Here is what Jordan found: "At the edge of the cot, my mother was leaning forward, one arm braced to hoist her body up. She was trying to stand up! I rushed over. 'Wait. Here, I'll help you!' I said" (23). But even though her mother's body is not yet cold, it is stiff. Jordan tries to help but eventually discovers that she has come too late. After this scene, which ends with a fight between her and her father, Jordan leaves the house and eventually ends up in Harlem Hospital with a miscarriage. She lies there angry at her father, of course, but far more angry at her mother and the circumstances that contributed to her mother's suicide.

As Jordan recreates that anger for us in the closing section of her essay, we begin to see how that very anger begins to redirect her life and refocus her energies. What began as a simple narrative essay ends as a stirring political protest proclaiming Jordan's resolve to live her life without surrendering to circumstances. It is a clarion call to all women to follow suit. The power of Jordan's appeal and its lasting effect on her readers depends heavily on the image of her mother trying to stand up from her cot, the cot that is her death bed. Jordan uses that image again at the very end of her essay when she praises strength.

Jordan resolves to be strong, never to be so weak and confused that people will be unable to tell whether she is alive or dead, never to let her life be "taken away" by circumstance, never to be defeated because she is weak (26). Finally, she takes us back to the image, leaves us with it as a reminder of all that went wrong in her mother's life—and by extension what is still going wrong in the lives of far too many women:

> I cherish the mercy and the grace of women's work. But I know there is new work that we must undertake as well: that new work will make defeat detestable to us. That new women's work will mean we will not die trying to stand up: we will live that way: standing up.

> I came too late to help my mother to her feet.

> By way of everlasting thanks to all of the women who have helped me to stay alive I am working never to be late again. (26)

Jordan's is a stirring emotional appeal, an appeal that depends on that picture she has placed in our minds of an older woman, defeated, unable to stand up from her own cot, unable under the circumstance to continue with her life. That image focuses our attention on what Jordan thinks is the plight of too many women.

We know from Jordan's own account, that when she headed back to her mother's house, she headed back to defeat. The confrontation with death broke the deadlock of circumstance, freed her body of its burden, and cleared her mind. Lying on her back thinking in Harlem Hospital, Jordan ends her essay on her feet, calling all of the oppressed to stand and join her—before it's too late. Jordan's power comes from her mother's image, from her mother's failure to stand up and be counted. Time is critical she tells us; women must not be caught late again. They must get up and get on with their business. That's Jordan's message, and she uses that central image to convey it.

Work Cited

Jordan, June. "Many Rivers to Cross." *On Call: Political Essays.* Boston: South End Press, 1985. 19–26.

Writing an analytical essay of this kind depends very much on your being thoroughly familiar with the skills that we considered in Chapters 1 and 2. You have to read Jordan's essay critically to get to know how it works; as you read, you will be exploring, trying to identify Jordan's writing techniques even as you come to terms with her idea. That *exploratory* analysis actually takes place before you start writing, and it depends on your knowing about the way essayists use images and other techniques to help them develop ideas. Your analysis leads you finally to the interpretative conclusion that you want to present in your own essay—your main idea about the essay you're analyzing. By the time you actually begin to write your essay, you should know Jordan's essay inside out, and you should have been selecting evidence from that essay as you read so that you can cite it in your own essay to support your interpretation. The general guidelines for incorporating evidence that we considered in Chapter 2 (p. 66) apply here as well, and each piece of analytical writing in this chapter will serve as an example of how to integrate and document evidence within the text of your essay.

REVISING *Certainly, Jordan could have ended her essay without bringing that picture of her mother back to our mind, but consider how its absence might affect the last section of the essay. Rewrite the ending of Jordan's essay, leaving out the references to that picture of her mother trying to stand up. In the revised ending, just explain what Jordan means in her essay; bring the essay to a close in a single paragraph that reminds us what the essay was about. Which version do you prefer? Why?*

ANALYZING AND WRITING *Select an image from an essay of your choice, and write a short, preliminary analysis of why you think that image is important to the essay's meaning. Think about what your readers will need to know to understand your analysis. You cannot assume that readers will know the essay well enough to remember details or even what the essay's idea is. Look back at my analysis of Jordan's image. Mark those passages where I provide background; mark other passages where I'm actually analyzing, trying to make sense of what Jordan does with her image. Is there a place where I tell you what I think Jordan's essay means, what I think is its central idea?*

SCENE

Our discussion of image in the preceding section necessarily included mention of scene. In Jordan's essay, we found her central image embedded in a fairly long scene of confrontation. Think of *scene* as an episode that we might see enacted on the stage—a charged moment rendered dramatically. If you look back at Jordan's entire essay, you will discover that the confrontation scene is located in the middle of the essay; it is central. In the first third of the essay, she sets the stage with that causal narrative we have already mentioned; the scene itself constitutes roughly the second third of the essay; the final third gives us Jordan's explanation of the aftermath of the confrontation, as well as her resolution.

The scene is the centerpiece. It differs from the narrative account of her past that precedes it and the explanation of the consequences of her mother's death that comes after it. It presents directly to us the action, the confrontation between her, her father, and her infirm mother. The scene itself is dramatic; it doesn't tell us about something that happened; it does not explain. We get to *see* things happen. We, as readers, have the privilege of witnessing the action as if we were there in the living theater of her parents' home. Never mind that Jordan, the writer, controls the scene, determines what she wants us to see—that is a complication of a different order, one that might be important to a more thorough analysis of this essay. What concerns us for the moment is the distinction between a causal narrative and the dramatic scene itself, the moment of direct action.

Tom Wolfe, one of the most successful of the modern essayists, has long been a spokesperson for the so-called New Journalists who laid claim in the 1960s to the techniques of the novelists. They wanted to put readers on the spot, to let them experience the event as if they had been there. One of the techniques these journalists used was what Wolfe called "scene-by-scene construction." The idea behind such construction was to minimize narrative and draw the reader into the action. By linking scenes without intervening narrative or explanation, writers create a sense of immediacy, just as China Forbes did in "Naked" (p. 44). By putting the reader directly into the action, a writer becomes more convincing. Often the scenes, placed side by side without comment or explanation, move the reader through a time sequence. They also stimulate thought, raise questions, and develop an idea in an interesting, subtle way.

In "Los Angeles Notebook" (Essays for Additional Reading section, p. 319), Joan Didion devotes the first half of her essay to an explanation of the relationship between California's Santa Ana winds and human behavior. Didion's idea is deceptively simple: "To live with the Santa Ana is to accept, consciously or unconsciously, a deeply mechanistic view of human behavior." She wants to demonstrate that motion and matter are related in some very significant way, that people and weather are part of a mechanistic system, that when the winds blow, they affect behavior in strange ways. She believes that "Los Angeles weather is the weather of catastrophe, of apocalypse, and. . . . The wind shows us how close to the edge we are." The second half of the essay consists of four scenes set side by side; they do not move us through a time sequence. They simply give us glimpses of behavior in Los Angeles when the winds are blowing. Here are two of those scenes:

3

It is three o'clock on a Sunday afternoon and 105° and the air so thick with smog that the dusty palm trees loom up with a sudden and rather attractive mystery. I have been playing in the sprinklers with the baby and I get in the car and go to Ralph's Market on the corner of Sunset and Fuller wearing an old bikini bathing suit. That is not a very good thing to wear to the market but neither is it, at Ralph's on the corner of Sunset and Fuller, an unusual costume.

Nonetheless a large woman in a cotton muumuu jams her cart into mine at the butcher counter. *"What a thing to wear to the market,"* she says in a loud but strangled voice. Everyone looks the other way and I study a plastic package of rib lamb chops and she repeats it. She follows me all over the store, to the Junior Food, to the Dairy Products, to the Mexican Delicacies, jamming my cart whenever she can. Her husband plucks at her sleeve. As I leave the check-out counter she raises her voice one last time: *What a thing to wear to Ralph's,"* she says.

4

A party at someone's house in Beverly Hills: a pink tent, two orchestras, a couple of French Communist directors in Cardin evening jackets, chili and hamburgers from Chasen's. The wife of an English actor sits at a table alone; she visits California rarely although her husband works here a good deal. An American who knows her slightly comes over to the table.

"Marvelous to see you here," he says.

"Is it," she says.

"How long have you been here?"

"Too long."

She takes a fresh drink from a passing waiter and smiles at her husband, who is dancing.

The American tries again. He mentions her husband.

"I hear he's marvelous in this picture."

She looks at the American for the first time. When she finally speaks she enunciates every word very clearly. "He . . . is . . . also . . . a . . . fag," she says pleasantly.

The first scene is not rendered dramatically, but Didion tells us what happened to her in the supermarket in such a way that we can experience her humiliation. She renders the scene in the present, and so we follow her around the supermarket. In the second scene, after a short explanation to set the stage, Didion gives us dialogue. We get to eavesdrop; we get to witness the action as if we were at a play. If we read these scenes out of the context of this essay, neither would make much sense. We would be able to conclude something about the people in the scenes, but we certainly wouldn't be able to link their unusual behavior to the Santa Ana winds. In the context of Didion's essay, however, these scenes serve as very concise illustrations of her controlling idea. Didion expects us to connect odd behavior and the prevailing winds; she expects us to know that she is developing her idea and persuading us without offering explanations.

ANALYZING *Think of yourself as a critic. Do Didion's scenes effectively put you on the spot, where the action is? Would the four scenes together make sense without the first half of the essay? What does Didion gain by moving from explanation to scene-by-scene construction? Do you think the final scene is effective as a closing for the essay?*

WRITING *After studying carefully Didion's entire essay, discuss your answers to the "Analyzing" questions with other members of your work group. After this preliminary discussion with others in your group, complete this homework assignment: Write your own short analysis of "Los Angeles Notebook," accounting for your reaction to Didion's use of scenes. Use as a model the analysis of Jordan's essay in the "Image" section. Bring your analysis to class, and compare it with other responses from your group. Work together again to draft a composite response that includes the most significant judgments rendered by members of your group.*

WRITING *Turn to Sam Pickering's "Being Familiar" (Essays for Additional Reading section, p. 269), and read the entire essay so that you can identify Pickering's main idea. Then reread the scene where Edward gets a raisin stuck in his nose (p. 273). Write a short analysis of why you think Pickering included that scene in his essay. What does the scene have to do with his main idea?*

PERSONA

"Persona" literally means "mask." By extension, we think of the characters in a play as personae; they are people pretending to be other people in the context of the play. We think, too, of the "I" in a poem as a persona, a character the poet has created for specific purposes. The same may be said of the narrator in certain novels. Often, readers confuse the poet with the persona or the novelist with the narrator. They fail to see that the writer creates other characters for specific artistic and rhetorical purposes. A character is someone different from the writer, even if the character is called "I."

The persona in an exploratory essay is a bit more complex. We assume that the essayist is in fact the "I" of the composition, that he or she is trying to reveal an idea, trying to render a judgment. But even in the essay, things are not always as simple as they might seem. An essayist often creates a persona for a particular rhetorical purpose. That persona may reveal only one aspect of the essayist's many-sided personality. On the other hand, the persona may be complex, multidimensional. Let's see how China Forbes and June Jordan make use of the "I" in their essays.

China Forbes

In "Naked," China seems to be unchanging in her attitude toward nudity, even as she grows up. No matter what her age, no matter what her experiences, she sticks to her belief. She was born naked; she continues to champion nakedness even when the world demands another standard. Yet we know that China is not naive; she has tested her idea against experience. Because we see her as a mere babe, as a child at the family swimming pool, as a young lover, as a maturing young woman in college, we get to see how her idea about nakedness is tested by experience. China grows up, but she holds fast to her principle even when she gets burned by experience. Holding fast under trial, she gives us a sense of how important, how powerful her conviction is about nudity.

That conviction leads us to an important consideration about a writer's persona in a particular essay. In effect, China the writer creates a character called "I" who conveys China's attitude about both nakedness and her earlier experiences; that "I" becomes China's mouthpiece, her voice in the essay. We cannot be certain about what China thought as a child or as a teenager; we know only that when China finally sat down to write about nudity, she reconstructed those earlier experiences so that they would convey her idea about nakedness. She chose what to put in and what to leave out of the essay, and it is her attitude toward those earlier experiences that establishes the tone of the essay. Her persona conveys that tone, that attitude, to us.

To gain a clearer sense of the distinction between China herself and the "I" of the essay, you need only consider how the essay might have changed if China had reconstructed any one of those scenes so that it conveyed dismay and prolonged pain. What if she showed us a young child at the bus stop embittered, wounded (perhaps for life) by that rejection? What if, in addition to the early rejection, China showed us an eighteen-year-old's life turned upside down by her boyfriend's rejection? What if we saw that sixteen-year-old China in a scene of despair following the rejection? How might those modifications change our sense of the "I" in the essay? How might those changes begin to affect the tone, and perhaps the meaning, of the whole essay? How might the "I" who eventually emerges from that new piece differ from the "I" in "Naked"?

IMAGINING   *What would be the effect on China's essay if she presented an evolving persona, one whose first thought of nakedness was revulsion and whose later thoughts and experiences gave her a more positive sense of nakedness? How might such a different persona change our reaction to the essay's main idea? Do you think a steadfast China makes a more effective case for nakedness than an evolving China? Explain.*

June Jordan

June Jordan's persona in "Many Rivers to Cross" seems to change within the essay. At the beginning, she is down and out; at the end, she is strong, even when flat on her back in Harlem Hospital. That evolving "I" seems to be important to Jordan's idea, central to her clarion call to other women to evolve, to stand up finally and be counted.

ANALYZING *Read through "Rivers" (Essays for Additional Reading section, p. 297), tracing as you go Jordan's reasonable but tired voice. Where does the tone of that voice begin to change? How is the change of tone reflected in Jordan's sentences and in the way she relates her story?*

IMAGINING *What would be the effect on this essay if June Jordan walked into her mother's house and then tore down the barricades and chastised her mother for putting up with an intolerant father? Would her final appeal be as powerful? Explain. What (or who) actually determines which persona of June Jordan we see at the beginning of the essay?*

Consider another "I" from a different essay by June Jordan, the "I" from the opening paragraph of "Report from the Bahamas":

> I am staying in a hotel that calls itself the The Sheraton British Colonial. One of the photographs advertising the place displays a middle-aged Black man in a waiter's tuxedo, smiling. What intrigues me most about the picture is just this: while the Black man bears a tray full of "colorful" drinks above his left shoulder, both of his feet, shoes and trouserlegs, up to ten inches above his ankles, stand in the also "colorful" Caribbean salt water. He is so delighted to serve you he will wade into the water to bring you Banana Daquiris while you float! More precisely, he will wade into the water, fully clothed, oblivious to the ruin of his shoes, his trousers, his health, and he will do it with a smile.
>
> I am in the Bahamas. . . .

Now, the immediate question you might ask yourself, right at the outset, is this: Who is this "I"? One answer to that question—the simple, direct answer, the one you can get by looking at the cover of the collection of essays (*On Call: Political Essays*)—is simply June Jordan. And who is June Jordan? The answer to that question is more complicated. If you've read "Many Rivers to Cross," as you have, you may think you already know June Jordan. If you haven't read "Rivers" or anything else by Jordan, you can turn to the inside of the back cover of the collection for a tentative answer: "The political writer June Jordan is a leading poet of international acclaim. To date she has published sixteen books and her poems, articles, essays. . . ." That simple and direct answer from the inside of the back cover points to the public June Jordan, who writes and wins awards. But what about the "I" in this particular essay? Does it help us to know what's on the inside of the back cover? Does it help us to know that Jordan is black? Does it help us to have read other essays or poems by Jordan? Perhaps. But what we really need to know is this: How is Jordan making use of the "I" in her essay? How does that "I" help Jordan develop her idea?

If we know that Jordan is black and that she is a woman, we might suspect that the "I" will speak out finally in a voice of political outrage about this black man serving drinks while ankle-deep in water, trying to please the tourists. But if we take the "I" at face value as she appears in the essay and let that "I" evolve, we begin to sense what we need to know to understand the essay's idea.

This particular "I" tells us at the outset about the black man; tells us, too, that "I am in the Bahamas"; tells us in the second paragraph of the beginning something about "New World History"; tells us how that history includes Bahamian history—how black and white, British, Bahamian, and American interests might coalesce down there in the Bahamas; suggests to us, finally, in the first sentence of the third paragraph, that all of this national and international and racial business has something to do with "my consciousness of race as I unpack my bathing suit in the Sheraton British Colonial." Just when we think we're about to figure out that this "I" might be winding up into a fit of outrage, she glances back at the black man, complicating our view of her and of the essay's central idea:

> And every time I look at the photograph of that fool standing in the water with his shoes on I'm about to have a West Indian fit, even though I know he's no fool; he's a middle-aged Black man who needs a job and this is his job—pretending himself a servile ancillary to the pleasures of the rich. (Compared to his options in life, I am a rich woman. Compared to most of the Black Americans arriving for this Easter weekend on a three nights four days' deal of bargain rates, the middle-aged waiter is a poor Black man.)
>
> We will jostle along with the other (white) visitors and join them in the tee shirt shops or, laughing together, learn ruthless rules of negotiation as we, Black Americans as well as white, argue down the price of handwoven goods at the nearby straw market while the merchants, frequently toothless Black women seated on the concrete in their only presentable dress, humble themselves to our careless games:
>
> "Yes? You like it? Eight dollar."
>
> "Five."
>
> "I give it to you. Seven."
>
> And so it continues, this weird succession of crude intruders that, now, includes me and my brothers and my sisters from the North.

The "I" of this essay will go on to worry about "Olive," the black woman who cleans her hotel room; she will worry about the Jews she reads about, and about the Jewish boy who loaned her the novel about the other Jews; she will worry about Women's Studies, about Black History, about Easter in her parents' home, and about a young South African woman back in Brooklyn who is the victim of abuse. In essence, the "I" of this essay will worry about her own "consciousness of class." That "I" will consider the ironies associated with finding herself—a black woman—in the Bahamas, complicating her relationship with others in the world. Jordan could have created an angry "I"; she could have created an outraged "I" who would have railed against the indignities perpetrated against the "fool standing in the water with his shoes on," but she chose instead to create an "I" who is down there in the Bahamas jostling along with all the other tourists, taking advantage of someone else's disadvantages.

IMAGINING   *Why do you suppose Jordan chose to create that guilty "I" rather than an outraged one? How might one "I" be more effective in an essay than the other "I"?*

Masking for a Purpose

As you can see, a writer's persona can change from essay to essay, from subject to subject. Part of the excitement of reading a number of essays by the same writer is to discover that writer's complexity, to see how he or she might put on different masks at different times to achieve particular rhetorical effects.

In the following exercises, we'll consider other ways that writers create a persona for a specific purpose.

ANALYZING   *Most us wear masks, literally several masks. Consider your interaction with three or four people during the last week. Make notes about the way you presented yourself during those interactions with different people. Were you consistent in each of those conversations, or did you treat your professor one way, your friends another, and your parents or spouse yet another? Looking back over that same week, make notes about the way you acted around your closest acquaintance. Were you consistent, and if not, can you see why you acted one way at one time and another at another? Perhaps you are the sum total of those actors, and your writing is likely to reflect one of those actors at one time and another at a different time. As a writer, you should be aware of the persona you create in your essay and consider the way your persona performs before a particular audience. As a critical reader, you want to be ever alert to the way essayists present themselves to you. Think about them; think about what they are asking you to believe; think about their imagination and their values. Think most clearly about whether you think they are effective and why.*

ANALYZING *Consider the first two paragraphs of "Cocksure Women and Hensure Men," an essay by D. H. Lawrence (Essays for Additional Reading section, p. 325):*

1   It seems to me there are two aspects to women. There is the demure and the dauntless. Men have loved to dwell, in fiction at least, on the demure maiden whose inevitable reply is: Oh, yes, if you please, kind sir! The demure maiden, the demure spouse, the demure mother—this is still the ideal. A few maidens, mistresses and mothers *are* demure. A few pretend to be. But the vast majority are not. And they don't pretend to be. We don't expect a girl skillfully driving her car to be demure, we expect her to be dauntless. What good would demure and maidenly Members of Parliament be, inevitably responding: Oh, yes, if you please, kind sir!—Though of course there are masculine members of that kidney.—And a demure telephone girl? Or even a demure stenographer? Demureness, to be sure, is outwardly becoming, it is an outward mark of femininity, like bobbed hair. But it goes with inward dauntlessness. The girl who has got to make her way in life has got to be dauntless, and if she has a pretty, demure manner with it, then lucky girl. She kills two birds with two stones.

2   With the two kinds of femininity go two kinds of confidence: There are the women who are cocksure, and the women who are hensure. A really up-to-date woman is a cocksure woman. She doesn't have a doubt nor a qualm. She is the modern type. Whereas the old-fashioned demure woman was sure as a hen is sure, that is, without knowing anything about it. She went quietly and busily clucking around, laying the eggs and mothering the chickens in a kind of anxious dream that still was full of sureness. But not mental

sureness. Her sureness was a physical condition, very soothing, but a condition out of which, she could easily be startled or frightened.

Jot down ways that Lawrence creates the persona of a man who is trying to be fair in what he says about the types of women he identifies. Discuss your reactions to this persona with others in class. Base your reaction on only the first two paragraphs. As a follow-up exercise, turn to the Essays for Additional Reading section (p. 325) and read the rest of the essay. Make notes so that you can explain to other members of your discussion group how Lawrence tries to use that "reasonable" persona created in paragraphs 1 and 2 to develop his idea in the rest of the essay. Your first step in that assessment will be to come to terms with the idea itself. What is Lawrence's point about women? When, if at all, does Lawrence start to seem unreasonable? Does the persona take on a new dimension later in the essay? During your group discussion, consider whether Lawrence remains fair throughout the essay. Do the men in your discussion group react differently than the women? See if you can reach a consensus within the group about whether Lawrence is ultimately convincing.

ANALYZING *Sam Pickering is a critic as well as a writer of familiar essays. Here are his assessments of books written by Paul Hemphill and Robin Magowan:*

Paradoxically honesty itself is often false, merely a device used to manipulate readers into believing they are seeing the inner workings of a real human being, not a literary construct. Such insight, so intention goes, leads first to sympathy, then to understanding, and finally to noncritical reading. Paul Hemphill is a gifted writer, and *Me and the Boy,* the account of his attempt to hike the Appalachian Trail with his nineteen-year-old son, is powerful. It is also irritating. In the name of honesty Hemphill paints himself as sincere and suffering, a man like other men, something he does not for a moment believe. Again and again Hemphill ostensibly bares his heart and his weaknesses, problems with cigarettes, drink, and women. Supposedly to get closer to the boy from whom he has been estranged, but in fact to snuggle intimately up to the reader, he talks to his son about sleeping with the boy's mother. He recounts holding a fellowship at Harvard and implies he felt inferior. In truth one suspects he felt aggressively superior. Several times he mentions being the son of a truck driver from Birmingham. Hemphill is a snob, proud of being born with a crankshaft in his craw and certain that a background like his, dripping gritty black oil, makes a person a better writer and a better man. Yet, despite the self-serving posturing, *Me and the Boy* is a strong book. When Hemphill forgets himself and the boy and describes the Appalachian Trail and the characters he meets while hiking, the book has magnetic power. Strangely enough one grows to admire Hemphill, though not to like him, as he struggles to complete the hike before his gimpy knees give way.

At times Hemphill's prose smacks of the Good Old School of Strutting, consciously rough-hewn and cloyingly exuberant. In general, though, Hemphill writes well; and, emotions aside, he describes things clearly. Not only does he make one see and smell the Appalachian Trail, but he makes the reader feel it under foot. In contrast to Hemphill's concrete world Robin Magowan's *And Other Voyages* is poetic. Reality for Magowan is spongy and mood is truth. In describing trips to Persia, Nepal, and Zambia among others, Magowan attempts to get at the empurpled essence of things, in the process obscuring place and event and writing a silly book. Of an encounter with a prostitute in Zambia, he writes: "I roll into bed first, and there things are unaccountably warm, even passionate, and as such, incomprehensible. So from sword to star I rise, sucked up by pleasure, not knowing anything and not wishing to: because self-knowledge, whatever the long term results, pulls me up short, stuttering on the ice? Because I'd rather live and breathe by obsession, 'I need this, therefore I'm here,' this being the offered heavy sweetness, these hips that I dig my nails into, rise along, a kingfisher poised in air, rattling his colors."

Magowan is well-connected. On the back of his book are long puffs written by James Merrill, Elizabeth Hardwick, and Richard Howard. Their strenuous puffing aside, however, *And Other Voyages* remains earthbound, rattling not so much of the kingfisher as of that lumpy, generally flightless, hatchery-bred bird with which Americans puff themselves on Thanksgiving.

To what extent does Pickering's judgment of these two books depend on his sense of the personae that the two writers create? Explain. What about this persona of Pickering's who seems rather cranky about men who are "proud of being born with a crankshaft in their craw" or about men who puff themselves up with lumpy quotes from their well-connected friends? Could you guess that "Being Familiar" (p. 269) and the critical assessments were written by the same writer? Explain.

WRITING *Read June Jordan's "Report from the Bahamas" (Essays for Additional Reading section, p. 306). Assume that you want to teach a group of students in another writing class what you have learned about the persona a writer creates in an essay. Use Jordan's essay as the source of evidence. Write a short analysis showing how Jordan uses her persona to good advantage. In your analysis, show the other students how Jordan might have created yet another "I"; let the students hear what that other persona might sound like. Remember, she's got to sound like Jordan, not like you. So you'll have to put on one of Jordan's masks as you write, and to be able to do that, you may have to read a few more of Jordan's essays. You should be able to find them in the library.*

PATTERN

Every essay has what we might consider an external organizational pattern—a beginning, a middle, and an ending. But the external pattern of an essay often reveals less than the internal patterns. In

Aspects of the Novel, E. M. Forster suggests that a novel is often stitched together by something from the inside. Forster prefers to think of this internal stitching in terms of a musical analogy. What he has in mind is "repetition plus variation," something within a novel like a musical phrase that repeats itself throughout the composition, but each time it reappears, it is slightly altered. As listeners we hear the phrase, recognize it, and take pleasure in that recognition; we take pleasure, too, in the variation and the pattern it creates.

We also find "repetition plus variation" in essays. We can easily count the number of paragraphs in an essay's beginning, its middle, and its ending and claim to have a sense of what the essay is like externally, a sense of its overall organizational pattern. But as you have seen from the outset, the shape within those three basic structural units varies considerably from essay to essay, whether the essay be exploratory, analytical, or argumentative. Those internal variations often point toward meaning. As we recognize them, as we look for repetition plus variation rather than a single, fixed notion that we can apply to every essay like a template, we begin to discover an essay's structural richness.

As a way of clarifying our sense of this richness, let's turn to Alice Walker's essay "Beauty: When the Other Dancer Is the Self" (Essays for Additional Reading section, p. 329) and look at the way its surface simplicity belies a fairly complex organizational pattern. This analysis of Walker's essay will be the first of two tasks we must complete before writing an essay of our own. After reading Walker's essay several times, I discovered two internal patterns: one we can detect in the essay's scene-by-scene construction and the other in an important image; both patterns are central to the essay's main idea.

Walker moves her essay along in a time sequence by rendering side by side a number of scenes. She takes us from a moment in childhood when she was the apple of everyone's eye to the moment when her brother shot her in the eye with a BB and then to later moments that allow us to see how she suffered. There is a pattern in this movement through time, a pattern that shows us what happened to Walker physically and what happened to her psychologically. Each of Walker's scenes depends on her storytelling ability; each of the stories she tells is rendered in the present, and each contains dialogue to make it more immediate. Walker draws us into the action, much the way that Didion does, and she does this to some extent so that we can experience what she experienced. She also does it to render two worlds: her inner world, which has been torn asunder by the accident, and the outer world, which seems unaffected by Walker's suffering. Although each of the scenes has a dramatic quality, not a single scene is rendered in the direct, dramatic way that Jordan renders the central, confrontational scene in "Many Rivers to Cross."

Besides the scene-by-scene construction, Walker relies on a very important image that does not appear until paragraph 13 in the essay: that image in the beginning is "a glob of whitish scar tissue, a hideous cataract," on her eye. That "glob" appears on her eye after her brother shoots her, and it is that "glob" that Walker uses—repeating it and varying it—throughout her essay to achieve certain effects. She transforms the "glob" at the end of the essay into an image of joy. That transformation and the scene construction point to internal patterns of the essay that are quite different from the external components we've thought about until now—the beginning, middle, and ending, which give a shape to every essay.

Those are the internal patterns I discovered when I read and studied Walker's essay; those discoveries came from my preliminary work—the close reading, the reflecting, the exploring. But those discoveries, as I just gave them to you, do not constitute an essay; we will get to that essay momentarily. That summary of my discoveries is just a way of getting started, a way of outlining for myself what I learned about the way Walker's essay works. I was trying to enter Walker's imagination to find out what the essay means, and I was trying to pinpoint her techniques. I was also trying to find out exactly how those techniques helped her develop her idea. I wanted very much to try to discover how she manages to capture my imagination every single time I reread the essay.

The second task, the task of turning those discoveries into an essay, requires more analysis. My first order of business is to find an idea that will account for all of that evidence, an idea that will make my essay cohere and will interest my readers. Eventually, I will have to think about how to present those discoveries to my readers, how to shape them into a coherent explanation of how Walker's internal patterns help convey her idea.

ANALYZING   *Consider the first section of Joan Didion's "Los Angeles Notebook" (p. 319). It seems to serve as the* beginning *of her essay; section 5, given its position, ought to be her* ending. *That would leave sections 2, 3, and 4 as the* middle. *That external pattern seems oddly proportioned; it seems even odder if we consider what Didion does in each of those five sections: the first offers an* explanation *of the scientific and unscientific effects of the Santa Ana winds on human behavior; sections 2, 3, 4, and 5 are* scenes. *Can we tell from the external patterns whether this is actually an essay? Or do these five sections simply constitute a notebook, as the title suggests? Explain.*

WRITING   *Look carefully at the first section of "Los Angeles Notebook." Didion is interested in conscious and unconscious effects of the winds; she is interested, too, in scientific explanations for the odd effects of the winds, the way the winds seem to affect human behavior. In that first section of the essay, see if you can determine exactly how Didion makes her case for science and for mystery. What is the* internal order *in that first section? Write a short analysis, explaining to the class whether Didion convinces you in that section that there is a causal connection between the winds and human behavior; consider both the way she makes her case (the pattern, the way she presents her information) and the quality and sufficiency of the evidence she presents. Is there enough evidence, and do you believe it? Why?*

C. *Turning Discoveries into Essays—Idea, Order, Evidence, Documentation*

IDEA AND ORDER

You know by now that the techniques we have been considering do not pop out of a text and announce themselves to a reader. Scene, image, persona, and pattern are inherent parts of good essays; they are there holding the essays together, giving them richness and variety. But when the writing is good, we hardly notice how the writer uses those techniques. So we have to be attentive readers, reading the text two ways at once, following its idea while also observing its method. Such reading, we have seen, leads to the discovery of how the essay coheres and what it means.

Let's turn now to the task of writing about our discoveries. As we saw earlier in this chapter, the analytical essay is more direct than the exploratory one, and its main purpose is to reveal conclusions that you have reached through exploratory reading and careful, systematic study of someone else's writing. Your analytical essay may not have the hard edge of argument, but you do want to persuade your reader that your interpretations and discoveries have merit. Your reader will expect you to get to your point in the beginning, so your essay will be a bit more streamlined and scholarly than the exploratory one. Nevertheless, your language should be lively and free of jargon and clichés.

As you can recall from my summary of discoveries in the preceding section, I found two internal patterns in Walker's essay that interested me: a pattern that had to do with time and a pattern that had to do with an image. The pattern related to time traced changes in Walker's life that resulted from the accident; the image pattern gave me a sense of the transformation that actually took place in that damaged eye and in Walker's imagination as she learned to live with her disfigurement.

Before I can write an essay about "Beauty," I have to figure out why Walker uses those two patterns, what they tell me about the meaning of her essay. When I figure out the relationship between technique and meaning, I will more than likely have the *idea* for my own essay; that relationship, the one I figure out, constitutes my *interpretation.*

Looking back through my notes and back through the essay, I begin to see that Walker keeps changing my perspective. She's trying to make me see what it's like to be disfigured, what it's like to be pretty one day and ugly the next, what such a change might do to one's perspective on life. Walker's essay tells me that beauty is not necessarily an external thing but is something that's in the eye of the beholder. I begin to understand how she's trying to make me see, how important sight and insight are both to those patterns and to her meaning. The patterns point to Walker's meaning, and I realize that I will have to show my reader how they work together to reveal something about beauty and insight.

Later in this chapter, we'll look at two analytical student essays. For now, though, let's look at my essay as a way of gaining insight into "Beauty" and as a way of gaining insight into the organization of an analytical essay. General principles, applicable to all analytical essays, will be outlined in *comments* offered at significant points throughout my essay.

Double Vision in Alice Walker's "Beauty: When the Other Dancer Is the Self"

1   Alice Walker's essay "Beauty: When the Other Dancer Is the Self" recalls folk wisdom my Mom used to pass on to me. Grounded in experience, her old injunctions still ring true. Two of them—one about enduring and another about beauty—seem to provide the foundation for Walker's essay. Hit in the eye by a BB from one of her brothers' guns, Walker learned early in life that *What can't be cured must be endured.* But that is not the point of her essay, not the explicit point anyway. Walker brings new life to the other notion, the notion that *Beauty is in the eye of the*

beholder. She shows us how she rediscovered her own beauty after that BB left her blind in one eye—disfigured and psychically maimed.

2   To convince us about the power of inner perception, Walker creates a series of scenes, grouped in intricate patterns to move us along in time, yet presented in such a way that we occasionally double back, halt the forward movement to retrace and recapture Walker's trauma. These scenes keep changing our perspective, turning us outside in, inside out, moving us backward and forward in time. Privy to Walker's suffering, we begin to share it, begin too to understand how she overcame it. Within that intricate pattern associated with suffering, there is another simpler, more subtle pattern associated directly with sight and insight. A scar, a white blob, becomes a bluish crater, becomes a world swirling in space and time, a world of joy that finally reunites Walker with her other self. That imaginal transfiguration leads to insight—ours as well as Walker's.

COMMENT   *Three important features of this introduction might guide you as you write your own analytical essays. First, the tone is personal, but slightly more formal than in the exploratory essay. The anecdote about my Mom conveys a sense of my feelings about Walker's essay. I am close to the essay and want you to know that; this is to be no dry, distanced analysis. I want you to see what I see. Because I have important business to conduct, I move directly from the anecdote to my analytical obligations. Second, I tell you straight out what idea I think Walker develops in her essay, the idea about beauty and the eye of the beholder. I cannot render that important judgment about meaning without coming to terms with the whole essay, and I cannot possibly go on to analyze how Walker creates that meaning until I make that judgment. After rendering that judgment, I can spend the rest of my introduction and my essay analyzing how I think Walker develops her idea. That obligation— your obligation as an analytical essayist to explain how Walker develops her idea—leads to the third important aspect of this introduction. I must let you know in the* beginning *exactly what features of Walker's essay I will analyze, and so I identify those two patterns within the essay that interested me—one a time pattern, the other an image pattern—and I establish my contract with my audience. The entire second paragraph of my essay is an elaboration of that contract; in that paragraph, I outline my own idea about the two patterns, letting my readers know that I will account for* how *Walker uses those patterns within her essay to convey her idea about beauty and perception. That's my purpose in writing the essay. Let's continue now with the* middle *of the essay, considering how I organize and how I try to keep you aware of the relationship between Walker's idea and her technique.*

3   In the first two scenes (Paragraphs 1–3, 4–6) of the essay, we see a "cute," perky little two and a half year old who is the apple of her father's eye (386). If three of his eight children get picked to go to the fair, young Alice never doubts that she will be among the chosen. Dressed and ready to go, she whirls, shows off her clothes, knows assuredly that she is "the prettiest" (385). Again at six, performing in church in the limelight, she is the chosen one, "a little *mess*," everybody's "*cutest* thing!" (385, 386). These two glimpses of Walker come out of a period of childhood innocence when her inner world and the outer world are in coincidence: the sassy little girl (womanish, proud, whole) draws strength from the adoring outside world. She needs approval and gets it. Walker, the essayist, develops these two scenes to show us what she was like as a young girl before the accident.

4   When the idyllic period ends, when the BB strikes her eye and leaves "a glob of whitish scar tissue, a hideous cataract," her life changes, but no one seems to notice what goes on *inside* (387); people see perfectly well what goes on *outside*. They see the disfigurement, see her drop her head, unable to face the world. But when they do not understand, young Alice feels isolated and alone. To give us a sense of her agony, the older Walker (the one writing the essay and reflecting) creates three scenes, sets them side by side

and connects them with a simple refrain: " 'You did not change,' they say" (389–90). The point of these scenes, of course, is to reveal how much she did change and to suggest that others didn't seem to notice her inner struggle. Walker's aim is to involve us in her personal struggle. To do so she gives us glimpses of that struggle over time, tries to let us experience it.

COMMENT *Paragraphs 3 and 4 serve as a preface for my analysis of the time pattern. Even as I begin my analysis of the first two scenes of the essay, I begin to prepare you for further analysis, and I render additional judgments about the two worlds Walker must deal with: the one inside her head and the one outside. I summarize only enough of Walker's essay to keep you oriented. My most important task is to interpret what's going on in the two scenes, to show you what I think Walker is showing us about the inside and the outside of her life. I also have to keep reminding my readers what my interpretations have to do with Walker's technique and her idea. Notice particularly the concluding sentences of paragraph 4, where I judge, summarize, and point to the analysis that will follow in paragraphs 5–9. Compare those concluding sentences with the ones in paragraph 3. In what similar ways do they help me make my point; in what way do they help you keep track of my analysis? Back to the* middle.

5   The first scene (Paragraphs 16–25) recalls the period just before and just after the accident. The family moves to a new community. Walker's school is a former "state penitentiary" (388). In that building, she feels tortured by her classmates who want to know about her eye. Outside world and inside world again have much in common. But neither is satisfying. She is a prisoner in her own body and a prisoner as well in the place where she goes to study, to learn. Because she suffers so much humiliation among her peers, she goes back to her old community to stay with her grandparents, yet in going, must leave behind her cat and her mother. Relief involves loss. Being a " 'one-eyed bitch,' " she learns, costs her dearly (388). She can't raise her head.

6   In the poignant second scene (Paragraphs 28–30), we see Walker at 12, isolated, either in her room on her bed or in the bathroom before the mirror ranting, abusing her eye . . . or praying for "beauty" (389). In this scene, a visiting cousin intrudes, breaks into the isolation to ask about the eye. The glob, still visible, shows up in the school picture, and the cousin can't restrain herself, must ask about it. We sense Walker's misery, view the struggle within the room, share her frustration, resent the cousin's intrusion.

7   The last of the three scenes (Paragraph 32) recounts a visit to her brother's home in Boston, tells of the surgical removal of the "glob." But we learn too that "a small bluish crater" remains after "the ugly white stuff is gone" (389–90). Nevertheless, Walker raises her head and wins boyfriend, praise, and prizes. She responds and so does the world. But she does not win lasting inner peace. Outside and inside worlds are not in coincidence. The inner psychic wound remains, clouds her thinking, continues to undermine her confidence. The scene ends with an ironic twist. The girl voted "most beautiful" is not Walker. But that winner, the beauty, is later shot in the chest by a "male companion, using a 'real' gun," and we're asked to wonder if hers is not Walker's story told again (390). These three scenes give us a sense of how little people around Walker understand her suffering. They show us that Walker cannot regain her sense of her own beauty even after the operation.

8   The final four scenes of the essay (Paragraphs 34–40, 42, 44, and 46–49) again move us forward and then backward in time. But mirroring the earlier scenes, they reverse our sense of consequences. They begin 30 years ahead during a moment of suffering and then move back in time to recover joy. In a curious way they seem to reflect what must be Walker's alternating sense of herself, her movement in and out of pain, in and out of joy. Nevertheless, our final glimpse is a glimpse into an inner world of joy.

9   The first two scenes among the final four give us a deeper as well as a broader sense of Walker's suffering. Thirty years after the accident, she agonizes over a cover photo for a magazine, worries

about whether her bad eye will wander, worries about the "beautiful journalist" who will come to interview her (390). But chastised by her lover, Walker remembers that she has made peace with herself, that she shouldn't be tentative or self-conscious. The next two scenes reconstruct her recovery, show us how she rediscovered her own beauty. Initially, her brother helped her see that her father had not abandoned her on the day of her accident; the white man who would not stop to pick them up abandoned her; her father did not. Later, in the desert, overwhelmed by the world's beauty, Walker drops to her knees grateful for the years of sight, for all the accumulated images she had been able to store in her memory. Grateful, she begins to write, to create her own images. But the final healing, the inner healing, occurs later when her little girl discovers a world of beauty within her mother's eye.

COMMENT, QUESTIONS   *Look back over paragraphs 5–9 to see how I integrate Walker's evidence (her words) into my sentences. Is that evidence sufficient to convince you that my judgments about Walker's essay are sound? Explain. Identify a place where you think more evidence could be included. As you look back over those paragraphs, notice, too, how I include information about the "glob" but do not comment on the image pattern that I have promised to analyze in the essay. In what way do you think I prepare you for the analysis that will follow in paragraph 10 of my essay?*

10   The last scene (the ending to the essay) gives us a clearer sense of the pattern that orders this fine essay. At the beginning of the scene, Walker is thinking about what her daughter's reaction might be to her eye. She anticipates something bad, thinks that Rebecca will one day react cruelly as children often do. But the scene that begins inside Walker's mind moves quickly outside, to the child, to the child's world, to the television show that Rebecca watches—"Big Blue Marble." The show is important to Walker's method as well as to the revelation that comes from the image that opens the show: "It

begins with a picture of the earth as it appears from the moon. It is bluish, a little battered-looking, but full of light, with whitish clouds swirling around it" (392). Notice the perspective: a picture of the earth as it appears from the moon. To heighten our own sense of perspective and to complicate it, Walker tells us that the image reminds her of her grandmother's house. When she sees it, it makes her "weep with love." The house (full of light, with whitish clouds swirling around it) is an inner image, a private, healing image. For her daughter, who studies Walker's face ("her inside and me outside her crib"), the Big Blue Marble is a "*world*" in her Mommy's eye (392–93). It fascinates Rebecca and sends her Mommy to the mirror to look into her own beauty, to find there in the bad eye the beauty that her daughter can see from outside. Looking into that eye, Walker finally confirms her two selves, the apprehending one and the one who has suffered. Whirling and joyous in Walker's imagination, those two selves unite in dance. Walker finally sees that the other dancer is "beautiful, whole and free. And she is also me" (393).

11   Walker discovers what my Mom tried to teach me so many years ago; she discovers that beauty is indeed in the eye of the beholder, whether that beholder be looking in from the outside or looking out from the inside . . . or simply looking within. Moving us back and forth from outside to inside, taking us concurrently from innocence through the bitterness of experience to insight, Walker offers not mere chronological accounting but a deep, broad look at the psychic effects of physical disfigurement, at what it means to be put at odds with oneself and the world one lives in, what it means to be different. She shows us that reconciliation is difficult, terribly difficult, but certainly not impossible. She shows us as well that even a child can be mother to the woman. Walker gives us *in*sight, doubles (at least) our capacity for seeing, teaches us about endurance.

Work Cited

Walker, Alice. "Beauty: When the Other Dancer Is the Self." *In Search of Our Mothers' Gardens*. New York: Harvest-Harcourt, 1983. 384–393.

ANALYZING *Paragraph 11 constitutes the ending for this analytical essay. I remind you about "the eye of the beholder," about moving "from outside to inside," about going from innocence to insight, and about reconciliation. Have I left anything of significance out of the ending? Why do you suppose I end the essay with the word "endurance"? What echoes of the beginning do you find in the ending? In what ways have your ideas about beauty and endurance and insight been changed by this analysis of Walker's essay? Explain.*

ANALYZING *Paragraphs 3–10 constitute the middle of this essay. Outline those eight paragraphs in an effort to see how they are organized. Is there a discernible pattern?*

DOCUMENTING *Throughout this essay, numbers appear in parentheses after the evidence (quotations) included from Walker's essay. These page numbers correspond to pages in the collection of Walker's essays listed under "Work Cited." The essay is reprinted for your consideration in Essays for Additional Reading (p. 329). Why are the page numbers included in parentheses within the text of "Double Vision"?*

EVALUATING *Does this essay make you want to reread Walker's essay? What do you think of the language in this essay? Have I made terms such as "pattern" and "image" clear to you? What about the quality of the evidence I cite? What do you understand about Walker's essay from this analysis that you did not understand before? Do you understand more about how Walker makes her essay cohere?*

WRITING *Select either Sam Pickering's "Being Familiar" or Annie Dillard's "Living Like Weasels" (Essays for Additional Reading section, pp. 269 and 292), and look for internal patterns within the essay that help either Pickering or Dillard develop the main idea. Make notes about those patterns, and begin to write your preliminary analysis, explaining how the patterns enhance the presentation of the idea.*

EVIDENCE AND DOCUMENTATION

Because your analytical essays always depend on interpretation, readers will expect you to support your ideas and conclusions with evidence taken from the essay you're analyzing. Evidence in this case means two things. Your explanation of what you see in the essay—its patterns, its images, its language—constitutes one kind of evidence, and such evidence appears in your essay as a summary or paraphrase of what you have discovered. Another kind of evidence that is very important in analytical essays is the essayist's own words. Look back at my essay on "Beauty" to see how often I use Walker's words to help make my case. When you use an essayist's words, when you use anyone's words, they must be in quotation marks, and they must be documented within the text of your essay. We'll consider such documentation in subsequent paragraphs.

As you present your interpretation, you will have to decide how much evidence you need to cite to be convincing, how to cite that evidence (paraphrase, summary, or direct quotation) in your essay, and how to establish a context that will let your reader understand the evidence itself and the point you are trying to make as you cite that evidence. Turn back, if necessary, to Chapter 2 for a review of the general principles that govern the integration of evidence (p. 66). Other suggestions appear in the Appendix (p. 240).

Long block quotations, traditionally set off from the rest of your text, are not nearly as effective as selected words, phrases, and sentences quoted within your paragraphs. Those more selective bits of evidence illustrate the truth of what you are saying, and they have the additional advantage of being short and easy to understand in the context of your own explanations. Those explanations—your own analysis of the evidence—distinguish your work from someone else's; they put the stamp of your mind on your essay.

Documentation of evidence for the analytical essay is quite simple. Because you will normally be citing evidence from only one essay and because you will not normally be going to the library to read what other critics have said about the essay you're analyzing, there should be a single entry in your bibliography; it is there so that an interested reader can consult your source and compare your citations with the text you're analyzing.

When you cite evidence from that essay within the text of your own essay, include page numbers in parentheses, usually at the end of the sentence that contains the evidence. Let's turn back to the third paragraph of my essay on "Beauty" to see how I select evidence and how I document it:

> In the first two scenes (Paragraphs 1–3, 4–6) of the essay, we see a "cute," perky little two and a half year old who is the apple of her father's eye (386). If three of his eight children get picked to go to the fair, young Alice never doubts that she will be among the chosen. Dressed and ready to go, she whirls, shows off her clothes, knows assuredly that she is "the prettiest" (385). Again at six, performing in church in the limelight, she is the chosen one, "a little *mess*," everybody's "*cutest* thing!" (385, 386). These two glimpses of Walker come out of a period of childhood innocence when her inner world and the outer world are in coincidence: the sassy little girl (womanish, proud, whole) draws strength from the adoring outside world. She needs approval and gets it. Walker, the essayist, develops these two scenes to show us what she was like as a young girl before the accident.

The quoted evidence is sparse; I quote only when Walker's words will make my case more economically than I can make it with my own words. I try to choose telling words and phrases: "cute," "the prettiest," "a little *mess*, everybody's *cutest* thing." Those words and phrases make it quite clear that as a child, Walker was indeed the chosen one, that she was a performer whom people admired. Those words and phrases tell you exactly what I want you to know about how Walker saw herself before the accident; they keep me from having to write out longer explanations. I use Walker's words and phrases within my own sentences to give weight to my explanations; those sentences—my words and Walker's words—come together to reveal what I want you to understand. But I also summarize some other things from Walker's essay, and I do that in my own words. Those summaries establish a context for understanding; they tell you enough about what's going on in Walker's essay so that you can understand my analysis. I have yet a third obligation in that paragraph. Besides explaining the selected evidence or using it in a way that is clear enough without explanation, I must also explain what the evidence has to do with the main point I'm trying to make in my essay. I try to do that in the *last three sentences* of this paragraph. That's where I clarify, where I try to make you see what I see. That's where I try to keep you oriented.

This example should remind you of the general guidelines for incorporating evidence that we considered in Chapter 2 (p. 66): introduce the evidence, cite it, and explain it in the context of the paragraph where it is being cited. Add one other guideline: Include in parentheses, within the text of your own analytical essay, the page numbers for the pages on which the quoted material appears in the essay you are analyzing. If, for example, that essay appears in an anthology, a page number in parentheses in your essay would correspond to the page in the anthology from which you have taken the material you are quoting.

More detailed rules governing documentation are included in the Appendix (p. 227), should you want to look ahead. For the analytical essays we will consider in this chapter, you need not be concerned about other procedures.

D. *Student Essays—Variations*

The two student essays that follow give you a sense of how to combine analysis, explanation, and evidence. There is no template, no approved solution. What you are trying to do is find an effective way to reveal your discoveries to an interested reader. Because those discoveries are your own, because they reflect the perspective that only you bring to the essay you're analyzing, you will have to figure out a logical way to bring evidence to the service of idea. The guidelines from the previous section will point the way. So will these student essays.

Each of your essays will have its own internal pattern based both on what you have discovered and on the way you decide to reveal your discoveries. These student essays about Dillard and Eiseley should give you a sense of the various ways you might turn your own discoveries into interesting essays, ways you might organize your work and ways to cite evidence and document it.

The analytical essays that follow rest on a few simple but very important assumptions about *audience:* your readers are interested in essays and how those essays reveal meaning; they have not studied Dillard's essay or Eiseley's; they may have read them, but they will not remember every detail; they are educated, literate, and bright, but they do not necessarily understand what you may mean by "image," "scene," "persona," or "pattern." They want to know what you know about the other writers' essays, and they want your language to be lucid, logical, elegant, and direct. Those readers will be pleased with a jargon-free essay that establishes the context for all of your remarks. They want to be able to follow your essay without having to refer to the essay you are analyzing. Your analysis ought to stand on its own.

Your essay might very well compel your readers to read or reread the essay you're analyzing. If they go back, they'll go back to see what they had not or would not have seen; they'll go back surprised because you have given them a new way of seeing.

SIMON POLE'S "PAINFUL (IN)JUSTICE?"—
AN ANALYSIS OF "THE DEER AT PROVIDENCIA"

Let's look first at an analysis of Annie Dillard's "The Deer at Providencia." Before reading Simon Pole's essay, you might want to read "Deer" (Essays for Additional Reading section, p. 338). Simon examines the relationship between justice and suffering in that essay. He seems to be intrigued with the paradoxes inherent in Dillard's own exploration. To come to terms with those paradoxes, Simon shows us *how* Dillard creates them in her own essay, *how* she makes us think about their inherent complications.

Painful (in)Justice?
by Simon Pole

1   Annie Dillard's essay, *The Deer at Providencia,* is about suffering—about those who must bear it and those who inflict it. In Dillard's vision of ever-present pain, there is no pity to be had for victims. Instead, there is in their suffering, dignity. Dillard also suggests that neither the victims nor those who are the cause of the victims' pain understand the justice of this suffering, whether its source is Dillard, or God himself. The essay revolves around two suffering creatures—a fragile deer and a burned man—who are both forced to bear their pain. There is also a third figure, the one who is causing them to suffer. This figure is Dillard, the narrator detached from the agony before her. She does not pity the victims. She sees in them dignity, even though they can do nothing to remedy a state of suffering they do not understand. Finally, Dillard makes the most intriguing move of her essay and raises a question about God and the justice of suffering, linking her own detached self to the person of God. This question about suffering is the ultimate question that Dillard confronts us with. One wonders if we are courageous enough to provide the answer.

2   Pain is the first thing that strikes us upon reading *The Deer at Providencia,* the intense pain of the deer and the burned man. Much of the essay is a prolonged description of their suffering, and we are left without doubt, that yes, they are really in pain. The convulsions of the deer are described in detail: "Its hip jerked; its spine shook. Its eyes rolled; its tongue, thick with spittle, pushed in and out" (62). Furthermore, our idea of the intensity of the pain is influenced by the fragile body Dillard has given her deer. The deer's skin is "almost translucent, like a membrane" and its neck is very thin (61). The deer is vulnerable and the suffering seems much more cruel when this frail body is pierced and the skin rubbed raw to make it tender for eating.

3   The power of the pain of the burned man is also obvious. In a single, short paragraph Dillard gives us all we need to know about the agony of burn victims. "Medicine cannot ease their pain. . . . The people just lie there and weep. Later they kill themselves" (65). Very little could be more painful than that. The burned man suffers in this way. He remembers the torment of being burned as a child. He remembers it and so tries to kill himself. Unfortunately, he was prevented and now must live in agony forever. He is a man who is experiencing the most pain possible in his terrible state, perhaps as much pain as any human being can bear, for as Dillard tells us "people who survive bad burns tend to go crazy" (65).

4   For there to be victims, there must be those who have hurt them. The deer is a victim. Its suffering is the fault of not only the hunters who captured it, but of Dillard as well. Though it is not Dillard herself who has roped the deer to the tree, she still makes it evident that she is also responsible indirectly for its suffering. "I eat meat," she says, thus drawing herself into the circle of conspirators who plan to slaughter the deer for food (64). In addition, Dillard also shows us she does have the power to put an end to the deer's pain. The North American men she is travelling with expect her to insist that the deer's torment be eased and not stop insisting on it until it has been done. Nevertheless, she does not exercise this privilege,

which convention has allowed women. She lets the deer continue to suffer. The burned man is also a victim, except in his case, Dillard has fingered God as the culprit. "Why does God hate me?" he asks after being burned for the second time (64). In despair, he says, "No, God couldn't do this to me again." God is responsible for all of this pain (65).

5   Something very interesting happens as the essay moves from the description of the deer to the description of the burned man. A link has been made between Dillard, the source of the deer's suffering, and God, the source of the burned man's suffering. Dillard's relationship to the deer is the same as God's relationship to the burned man. Dillard's relationship to the deer is a detached one. She is not sobbing over the dying deer as her men friends have anticipated. Instead, she eats deer meat as she watches the deer writhing and bleeding in front of her, without even the faintest tinge of nausea. Dillard cannot be much more detached than that. She feels "very old and energetic" as she considers what is happening (64). This is more the detachment of a serene, old wise woman who has experienced and relished many things in her lifetime than a lack of emotion or empathy.

6   The burned man takes the place of the deer as the central, suffering figure and God assumes Dillard's role as tormentor. A connection is made between God and Dillard. When Dillard is watching the deer she feels more than just unemotional detachment. She describes herself like a serene, old wise woman—much as one would imagine God to be after eons of existence—a serene, old wise man. Furthermore, as Dillard eats deer meat in full view of the suffering deer she says, "It was good" (63). This statement has biblical connotations, "good" in the biblical sense meaning sanctioned by God. Dillard is sanctioning her act of eating deer meat right in front of a dying deer. Dillard has given herself the same powers of proclamation that God has throughout the Bible. There is a connection between the two and once this link is made,

all comments that Dillard makes about herself are made about God as well.

7   In speaking both for herself and God, Dillard says that no pity is felt for those who suffer. Instead dignity is seen in their agony. She makes this obvious in the end when she describes the burned man "in his dignity" and the "the deer . . . in his dignity" (66). The deer has a quiet dignity as it tries unsuccessfully to free itself from the rope, straining desperately, but only entangling itself further. Dillard does not pour out pity in sympathy with its predicament. In the conclusion of the essay when she says "poor little thing" about the deer, her pity is not real for she says, "I knew at the time it was a ridiculous thing to say" (66). She sees only dignity in the deer's struggles. There is also dignity in the condition of the burned man as well. He does not moan or cry out. He is facing his pain with a stiff upper lip, a resolution to die without complaint. The newspaper article also gives the burned man dignity because it sanctions the burning as Dillard sanctions the suffering of the deer. On paper, his pain becomes official, in fact, set out free from question. In this way the burned man's story acquires dignity, the dignity of books and archives. Dillard's essay serves the same function; it sanctifies McDonald's suffering.

8   Nevertheless, though there may be dignity in suffering, it does not follow that the victims understand the justice of their pain. Certainly the deer and the burned man may be bearing their pain with dignity, but neither of them understands the justice of their suffering. The deer, obviously, is incapable of understanding why it is in pain. When it is freed by the native boys from the rope it does not comprehend the nature of its trap and simply gets itself tangled up again, starting the cycle of pain one more time. The burned man understands what is causing his pain, but he does not know why he has been served such an injustice as to be burned twice. He wonders why God has done this to him a second time. "Man, it just isn't fair," his wife says (65). It isn't. There is no justice here to be

found, no reason why one man should feel so much pain. For the victim of vicious chance, there is never a good enough reason.

9   However, as interesting as this point may be in itself, Dillard goes beyond it and asks a disturbing question. Do those who cause pain really understand what they're doing? When Dillard examines the fact that she is a carnivore and thus responsible for the pain of the deer tied to the tree she reveals she has thought about it for a long time. However, she still does not understand it for such things "are not issues; they are mysteries" (64). They are not issues to be debated in which there is a right or wrong answer to be reached. Suffering is a mystery to which there are no answers. There is no justice in it, for that suggests there is a right and wrong. Suffering just *is*. Dillard also suggests that suffering is beyond the comprehension of God, one who is also a source of it. The link she sets up between God and herself shows that if Dillard does not comprehend the agony of the deer then God must not comprehend the agony of the burned man. The ramifications of this conclusion are terrifying. If God does not understand suffering, then there is no justice in it, for is God not the force that controls the events of the world as they unfold. Annie Dillard thinks so. It is not fair or unfair that the man was burned a second time, since no one, not even God, can decide that. He simply *was* burned a second time. The justness of pain is still a mystery.

Work Cited

Dillard, Annie. "The Deer at Providencia." *Teaching a Stone to Talk*. New York: Colophon-Harper, 1983. 60–66.

ANALYZING   *Simon Pole uses none of the technical terms ("scene," "image," "persona," "pattern") that we considered earlier in this chapter. Can you, nevertheless, find places within his essay where he demonstrates a clear understanding of the concepts we associated with those terms? In other words, does he show some awareness of persona without referring to the "I" of Dillard's essay as a persona? Or awareness of scene or image or pattern? What other of Dillard's writing techniques or strategies does Simon identify that we have not considered formally in this chapter?*

WRITING AND ANALYZING *Simon uses the* passive voice *on a number of occasions in his essay. Paragraph 5: "A link has been made between Dillard, the source of the deer's suffering, and God, the source of the burned man's suffering."Paragraph 6: "A connection is made between God and Dillard." Paragraph 7: "Instead dignity is seen in their agony." These sentences are* passive *because we cannot tell from the sentences who causes things to happen. If we rewrite these sentences in the* active voice, *we identify the causal agent. For example, the sentence from paragraph 6 becomes "Dillard makes a connection between God and herself." The sentence in paragraph 7 could become either "Dillard sees dignity in their agony" or "I see dignity in their agony." Cast the sentence from paragraph 5 in the active voice. Try these revised sentences in Simon's paragraphs. Which versions do you prefer? Why? Is there a pattern associated with Simon's use of the* passive voice*? That is, does he use it only on certain occasions?*

ANALYZING *In paragraph 7 of his essay, Simon does not tell us about how Dillard reacts to the burned man's suffering. Is there evidence in "Deer" about that reaction? Would her reaction match God's? How do you think Simon would feel about that comparative reaction?*

WRITING AND ANALYZING *Read "Deer" in its entirety (Essays for Additional Reading section, p. 338). What is your assessment of Dillard's persona? How does she help Dillard develop her idea? What if the persona were a man? How might that change the way you react to the essay? Taking these questions into consideration, write a short analysis explaining how the "I" in the essay helps Dillard develop her idea.*

Simon's essay is virtually free of the technical language of analysis, free of words that might confuse the common reader. He does not talk about persona or scene or pattern, but he clearly sees how Dillard's essay works. And he has an interesting idea about the way Dillard becomes godlike in her essay so that we can understand something about the nature of suffering, the dignity that resides there in the pain of it all.

BARBARA PETERS' "ANOTHER LIGHT" — AN ANALYSIS OF "THE DANCE OF THE FROGS"

Our second analytical essay was written by Barbara Peters. This essay about Loren Eiseley's "The Dance of the Frogs" (Essays for Additional Reading section, p. 343) investigates Eiseley's use of light images. It shows us how we might enrich our analysis of essays by bringing in evidence from secondary sources—from our reading— just as we did in Chapter 2 when we began enriching our exploratory essays. We get to see Barbara making connections, shedding light of her own on a complex subject.

Another Light
by Barbara Peters

1   "And God said, Let there be light: and there was light. And God saw the light, that it was good: and God divided the light from the darkness. . . . And the evening and the morning were the first day" (Genesis 1:3–5). "I form the light and create darkness: I make peace, and create evil. I the Lord do all these things" (Isaiah 45:7). "The path of the just is as the shining light . . . the way of the wicked is as darkness: they know not at what they stumble" (Proverbs 4:18–19). From the dawn of creation, light has been associated with goodness and the absence of it with evil. Light is a positive force that encourages growth, understanding, and peace. Darkness symbolizes loneliness, wickedness, and death. Loren Eiseley uses these basic truths as he unfolds his mysterious tale of "The Dance of the Frogs."

2   In that tale, Eiseley [the mature essayist] draws two scientists together in understanding: Eiseley, young and self-assured; and Dreyer, aged, experienced, and retired. "There were just two men under a lamp, and around them a great waiting silence" (109). They realized their common ground; they could be comfortable, communicate, and be receptive to one another as they sat in the warmth of the fire. I would suspect that at some level the young Eiseley realized there was so much to learn, and he was in the presence of a real man of science. He said, "One has to huddle in, there [was] so little light and so much space" and so he listened to what Dreyer had to say (109).

3   Light is used to make the transition from this fireside chat to a tale of intrigue: it sets the stage for the story to follow. Describing the road he walked often at midnight while waiting the result of an experiment, Dreyer, the aged scientist, said, "It was a strange road. Wild all right, but paved and close enough to the city that there were occasional street lamps. . . . A place to be alone. A place to walk and think. A place for shadows to stretch ahead of you from one dim lamp to another and spring back as you reached the next" (110). A dark and lonely place where most people would never venture, yet a lone scientist comfortable with solitude and nature dared to frequent it.

4   As he recounted the events of that night for Eiseley, Dreyer remembered that there was "No moon, [and it was] secretive and dark, with just those street lamps wandered out from the town" (110–11). He felt the "forces of mighty and archaic life welling up from the very ground" (112). The street lamps dimly illuminated the damp night and gave just enough light to give one the sense of what was going on around, but not enough light to give one warm and peaceful feelings. "All around, under the street lamps, [Dreyer] saw little frogs and big frogs hopping steadily toward the river" (112). They did not need the light to make their way. A force was driving them. Caught up in the passion, he joined them in their hopping in the darkness through the shadows toward the river.

5   Again the street lamps shed more light on Dreyer, but this time not only did they create his own shadow but they also revealed "another great, leaping grotesquerie [one] that had an uncanny suggestion of the frog world about it" (113). This shadow seemed to be a manifestation of a terrifying but intriguing force that drove Dreyer uncontrollably through the darkness toward the river.

6   The Bible tells us that light is good and can break through darkness—the force of evil. When Dreyer's evil closed in with a "frenzy of terror," his eyes beheld the light on the wharf and "the beam that made a cross" (114). He cried out from somewhere within to the ultimate source of all light. "Help! In the name of God, help me! In the name of Jesus, stop!" (114). This cry to the Father of all light saved him from an unknown fate, from possible destruction. Eiseley used the light not only to show Dreyer's salvation, but also to conclude the event. Dreyer "looked down in the circle of the arc light, and there by [his] feet hopped feebly some tiny froglets of the great migration" (114). He was safe, and the great leaping grotesque frog-like creatures of the shadows were exposed by the light. All that was left were Dreyer and those tiny froglets.

7   Once again, we might conclude that light had conquered the darkness of evil. But in yet another sense, it had conquered a self-indulgent young scientist, pulled him into an intimate circle of light with Dreyer where he could see both good and evil: the light as well as the shadows within the circle. Dreyer's light allowed young Eiseley to grow and develop understanding and tolerance for other people and ideas: seeing things in another light.

Work Cited

Eiseley, Loren. "The Dance of the Frogs." *The Star Thrower*. New York: Harvest-Harcourt, 1978. 106–115.

Barbara's essay examines yet another of those interesting patterns that writers create as they develop their essays. This one—the pattern of light imagery—reminds us of Forster's suggestive definition of pattern: "repetition plus variation." Barbara helps us see the pattern by isolating it and by showing us *how* Eiseley, the essayist, uses it to develop an idea. She, under Eiseley's influence, asks us to see how light might actually shine out of darkness.

IMAGINING   *Read Eiseley's "The Dance of the Frogs" (Essays for Additional Reading section, p. 343), paying particular attention to the play of light and dark throughout. As you do, think about what Dreyer says at the end of the essay: "Perhaps I should have trusted them and hopped onward. Who knows? They were gay enough, at least." After reading "Dance," think of Barbara Peters' essay, which tells us about the effect of light and dark on the maturation of a young Eiseley. If you wrote an analytical essay about the pattern of light imagery in "Dance" and you concentrated on the effect of light and dark on Dreyer rather than on the young Eiseley, how might that change the way you think about the meaning of "Dance"? Would things be so black and white from Dreyer's point of view? From the mature Eiseley's? Explain.*

REVISING, ANALYZING, AND WRITING   *Here is a revised version of paragraph 5, from the middle of Barbara Peters' essay:*

Again the street lamps shed more light on Dreyer, but this time not only did they create his own shadow but they also revealed "another great, leaping grotesquerie that had an uncanny suggestion of the frog world about it" (113). This shadow seemed to be a manifestation of a terrifying but intriguing force that drove Dreyer uncontrollably through the darkness toward the river. At this particular point in Dreyer's experience, light seems to be playing the devil with him, showing him another world, creating shapes and shadows, and sending him as well toward a new destiny. Without the light, there would be no shadow; without the darkness, there might be no force.

◊

Think of the first two sentences of this paragraph as a summary of a particular moment in "Dance." Barbara is telling us what happened, telling us something we need to know to understand the rest of her essay. Think of the last two sentences of this revised paragraph as analysis. She is explaining the significance of what happened in terms of the idea she is developing in her essay. What effect, if any, do those added sentences have on the paragraph or on your understanding of Barbara's essay? Consider other paragraphs in the middle (paragraphs 2–6) of Barbara Peters' essay. Select one, and see if you can make it and the essay more coherent by providing a bit more analysis. Bring that paragraph to class.

TRANSITIONAL THOUGHTS

Barbara Peters' use of the Bible to open her essay and establish the ground for her analysis reminds us that analytical essays, like exploratory ones, need not depend entirely on a close reading of a single essay. We can enhance our analysis by making meaningful connections with other texts, with ideas we have gained over a lifetime of reading. When we turn to the short research essay in the next chapter, we will again be interested in the way the essay changes shape as we consider the formal properties of argument. But we will not be leaving exploration or analysis behind as we consider yet another variation of the essay.

Although our focus in this chapter has been on a close analytical reading of an exploratory essay written by a professional, we should not overlook the fact that this is primarily a chapter that concerns itself with learning to read, write, and think analytically. The familiar essay—the one we've called exploratory to suggest its method—is an essay rich in pattern and complexity. Its evocative images suggest levels of meaning below the surface; its scenes create intimacy while giving us insight. We cannot read these essays once and claim to have exhausted them. They repay our rereading and our close study. They continue to delight and instruct us over time. So the skills that we have been considering in this chapter are skills that carry over into our reading of other texts, whether they be literary or critical. And the analytical essay that we have been considering is an essay that should serve you well in other classes. It is a transitional essay, one that develops out of close reading and one that points to the more complex, more tightly organized argumentative essay that we write often in every academic discipline, the kind of essay we will consider in the next chapter.

E. *A Coda—Thoughts on Revision*

But the analytical essay is also a transitional essay that points back to what we did in the first two chapters of the book; it points back to the personal, exploratory essay. Perhaps as you studied—preparing to write the analytical essay—you began to discover and understand the complexity of the exploratory essay. If so, you might want to reread one of your own early exploratory essays. You might discover that you could enhance that essay, make it better, because of what you have learned. Some of the techniques you have studied in this chapter might very well give you new ideas about how to revise one of those early essays.

In Chapters 1 and 2 we learned about writing sequences, a fairly complex step-by-step process that leads from experience to idea to text. Recall again China Forbes's "Naked." That essay began to take shape from an *image of experience* that China called "Bus Stop." Within that short piece, China discovered an idea about nakedness that she wanted to develop into an essay. As she thought about her idea and talked to her friends and to her instructor about it, she began to recall other images of experience, other stories, that would illustrate and give substance to her idea about nakedness. When she actually sat down to write her essay, she went back to *revise* "Bus Stop." She modified it, rewrote parts of it, so that it would serve her idea. She added to her revised version of "Bus Stop" other stories in the form of scenes; together those scenes (with an introduction and an ending) make up her essay.

The kind of revision that China did as she rewrote her initial *image of experience* is an integral part of the writing process. Typically, we move from drafts by way of revision to a product that we often consider the final version of an essay. During those composing periods, writing and revising go on concurrently as we move backward and forward over drafts toward the final essay. But there is another kind of revision that takes place over time. Often such revision results in more extensive changes than those we made as we worked intently to finish our essays. I'm referring to the kind of revision that we might do weeks or months after we have written an essay, after we have come across new evidence that would enhance our original version, or after we have learned something about technique that we didn't know when we wrote the essay the first time. Often when we go back to revise under these circumstances, we change our initial product significantly; the early essay takes on a new shape, a new complexity. It becomes clearer and more interesting.

Here are two different versions of the first three paragraphs of Jadran Lee's exploratory essay "Lucky Icarus." We looked at the beginning and ending of the second version of this essay in Chapter 1 (p. 38) so that we could get a better sense of the suppleness of a good *idea*. We want to look now at the two versions together to get a sense of how a writer might reshape his or her material over time. Jadran wrote the first version at the beginning of the course; he completed the second about two months later, after he had written an analytical essay and had begun studying George Orwell's essays for a short research project. As you read, think about the way the two versions differ and about your reaction to the differences.

Version 1

The snow had been growing wet and heavy in the warm weather of the past week. The lower reaches of the mountain had bare patches of damp earth and strawlike grass. Higher up the Swiss had posted emphatic warnings against skiing outside of marked slopes, for wet snow is prone to avalanches. I felt that the prospect of not skiing or snowsurfing again until Christmas called for some memorable bravado. Although not an exceptionally good snowsurfer, I was hopelessly addicted to the sensate rush one experiences when tearing down a powder field upon this modern relative of the ski.

I took the cable car up to the highest point I could reach far above the treeline. All of that week I had taken no risks, never skiing or surfing without a friend. The view from the top station of the cable car was one of the most imposing I had ever seen. The sky was of a strong blue unknown at lower altitudes; the snow was obviously dying yet it retained a brilliance that almost hurt the eyes. This was a landscape that wanted a story. I was a deity atop Mount Olympus; the dingy, settled valleys were in a different plane of existence, separated from me by white clouds that mingled with the snow.

I followed the slope until the first bend. There I had the option of branching off onto forbidden ground which looked fairly easy from the cable car but which now was covered in cloud. Temptation carried the day, and I found myself pushing into the little-known. I was surfing full tilt when I hit a cloud. It was exceptionally beautiful to be utterly engulfed in white. I could barely see a meter in front of me, as the snow I raised on my snowboard mingled with the crisp white mist.

Version 2

The snow had been growing wet and heavy in the warm sunshine of the past week. From the ascending cable car I saw that at lower altitudes the melt had exposed patches of damp earth and strawlike grass. Spring was climbing out of the valley. All week I had taken no risks, always skiing or surfing with at least one friend, but today I was alone. I felt that winter's end called for memorable bravado. Although I could not ride a snowboard exceptionally well, I was helplessly addicted to the sensate rush one feels when tearing down a powdery slope on this modern relative of the ski.

I rode the cable car to its highest station, far above the treeline. At the exit from the cable car the Swiss had posted emphatic warnings against skiing outside of marked slopes, for wet snow is prone to avalanches. The warnings did not hold my attention nearly as long as did the view of the Alps. I took a long time to strap on my snowboard, savouring the beauty of a landscape that I would soon be rushing through. Wet snow reflected the April sun with unmerciful brilliance. The sky was of a strong blue seldom seen from below the clouds; a blue without hazy paleness; vigorous and beautiful, like a woman with character. It offset frozen peaks: regal, jagged, perhaps impregnable; relics of geological violence in epochs so ancient as to make men seem transient as the snow. Brown valleys far below were obscured by clouds merging into the snow of the slopes. Up there I felt god-like, with the Mont Fort my Olympus. I stood up, lingered for an instant like a projectile at the apex of its flight, then pushed downhill.

I followed the slope until its first bend. There I had the option of branching off onto forbidden ground, which had looked fairly easy from the cable car but was now partly covered in cloud. Temptation won. I was surfing full tilt when I hit the cloud and was utterly engulfed in white. The snow and mist seemed to form a single medium through which I floated, so that I felt briefly an exhilarating sense of being free from the ground. I could hardly see a meter ahead of me, and did not especially care to.

ANALYZING *Compare each paragraph in Version 1 with the corresponding paragraph in Version 2. Make general notes about changes that you consider especially important; compare notes within your discussion group. Consider the two versions as versions written by two different writers. Which writer is more aware of audience? How can you tell? Think about what you have learned about persona. Which persona is more appealing? Why? Turn to the two complete versions of the essay in*

*the Essays for Additional Reading section (pp. 358 and 361). Follow the
different personae through the two versions. Which essay is more interesting? Why? In what way does the persona in each piece affect the way you
react to the main idea about death? Which persona seems more self-
aware? Which more reflective? Explain your preference for one essay or
the other.*

Perhaps these two versions of just one student essay will suggest
to you something about the ongoing nature of revision. As long as you
are learning new things about techniques and as long as an essay's idea
remains interesting to you, there may be reasons for revision. Professional essayists will tell you that some pieces take shape very fast and
change little over the course of the writing. But other pieces take shape
slowly. They start out in one form and then change over time to a
version that is radically different from the first. There is no set process,
no formula, but there is always the likelihood that reading and study
will create new possibilities, set in motion new revisions.

F. *Practice—Thinking and Writing*

THINKING

1. Consider these opening paragraphs from Jay Varma's analytical
essay about Annie Dillard's "The Deer at Providencia":

A Confused Idealist

With the dispassionate power of a camera, Annie Dillard's "The
Deer at Providencia" presents the death and consumption of a deer
as a poignant commentary on suffering—how one woman and, on
a larger level, all humans confront violence. To that end, her
images, and the pain they convey, penetrate our consciousness
with stunning skill. Described with the vivid clarity of immediate
narratives, these potent visions expose the randomness and pain of

suffering—a brutal continuum permitted by God and ignored by humanity. She argues that the agony of a deer's exhausted, wracked limbs and of a man's charred flesh, are part of our daily baggage; we feed off their misery, never acknowledging its existence or our own moral cannibalism. Charging all humans with insensitivity, Dillard draws portraits of brutality, savagery, and despair for us to explore and understand—to bring into our hearts—and then admonishes our empathy with moral indignance.

It is this philosophical exposition, however, that eventually undermines Dillard's effectiveness as a social commentator. Retreating to moral higher ground, Dillard grows sententious and self-righteous at the end of "The Deer at Providencia"—"This is the Big Time here, every minute of it," she warns, reproving both the reader and the "gentlemen of the city" for allegedly ignoring the inevitability of suffering (559). But, as a result, the reader is dragged from self-reflection, ostensibly Dillard's goal, into defensive posturing: Dillard becomes a hypocritical whiner, feeding off the pain of the burnt man and decrying, not accepting, the immutability of misery—the same failings she condemns so forthrightly. In "The Deer at Providencia," Dillard guides us into suffering with compelling images but, eventually, leaves us disoriented, mired in her own idealistic confusion.

As you recall from Chapter 1, a *beginning* should establish the terms of the essay, draw us into the world that the essayist will explore, and give us a sense of the main idea. What is your reaction to these paragraphs? Can you understand enough about Dillard's essay to be able to follow the train of thought in these paragraphs? What do you suppose the student essay will be about? Jot down your guesses, and compare them with those of two other students.

2. Turn now to "A Confused Idealist" (Essays for Additional Reading section, p. 249). Check your guesses against the essay. Look

at the way Jay incorporates evidence from Dillard's essay into his own. Are there any instances where you are confused by the evidence? If so, make a note of them. Note any instances in the essay where you do not know enough about Dillard's essay to understand what Jay is trying to tell you. Before you fault him, make sure that you have read carefully what he has told you. Read between the lines, imaginatively. Note remaining problems if there are any. Now, read "The Deer at Providencia," and make editorial suggestions to Jay about how he can improve his essay. Make those suggestions within the text and in the margins on a photocopy of his essay as if you were his copy editor, helping him prepare his essay for publication.

WRITING

1. Earlier in this chapter we looked at the personae in "Cocksure Women and Hensure Men" and "Report from the Bahamas." Select one of those two essays, and see how Lawrence's or Jordan's use of scene or pattern or image might inform our reading of the essay. Write a few paragraphs about the technique or techniques you consider most important in one of the essays. Do not hesitate to consider the effectiveness of one technique in terms of another: Persona is less important than image in "Cocksure," *or* Jordan achieves a powerful effect in "Report" by the skillful use of persona and scene.

2. Turn to Virginia Woolf's essay "Old Mrs. Grey" in the Essays for Additional Reading section (p. 353). Write an analytical paragraph in which you explain the effectiveness of the rook image in the last paragraph of the essay: "So we—humanity—insist that the body shall still cling to the wire. We put out the eyes and the ears; but we pinion it there, with a bottle of medicine, a cup of tea, a dying fire, like a rook on a barn door; but a rook that still lives, even with a nail through it."

3. See if you can detect in "Old Mrs. Grey" some internal organizing pattern that makes the essay or a part of the essay cohere. If you find no interesting pattern, see if you can discover some other techniques that Woolf uses to develop her idea. In a short essay, explain to a class of your peers what you discover about the way Woolf makes her point concerning Mrs. Grey. Explain to them *how* Woolf develops her idea. You might follow these steps: (1) State Woolf's central idea in no more than two sentences; (2) make detailed notes about the technique that you will write about, paying particular attention to the way Woolf makes use of that technique in her essay; (3) determine exactly how Woolf uses that technique to develop her idea; (4) write your essay.

4. In "Spring Comes to Hogeye" (Essays for Additional Reading section, p. 259), Roy Reed uses dialogue on a number of occasions. Consider each of those occasions. Think about what Reed gains by letting his characters speak. Write a short analytical essay about how Reed uses dialogue to enhance his essay and develop his idea.

5. Trace Samuel Pickering's rambling mind in "Being Familiar" (Essays for Additional Reading section, p. 269). Write an outline of the movement of that mind. See if that movement suggests a meaningful pattern. See if you can break down the movement into sections or minichapters that you can title. Figure out why Pickering moves from subject to subject as he does; see if there is a method behind his rambling. Write a short essay about your discoveries. Write a short paragraph explaining what you discovered about writing as a result of your investigation.

6. Gretel Ehrlich once told an audience of teachers that "Looking for a Lost Dog" (Essays for Additional Reading section, p. 355) is about writing. Test that assertion by thinking about the process of looking for a lost dog as if it were the process of looking for an idea. Think about the simile X is like Y. Considering what you have learned about the exploratory essay, investigate the possibilities inherent in that comparison. Think, too, about Pickering's "Being Familiar" and what that essay says about rambling. Write a short analytical essay that presents your conclusions to an interested but skeptical reader.

Chapter 4

THE
SHORT
RESEARCH
ESSAY
—
ARGUMENT

A. *Research—Exploration and Analysis*

Turning now to the short research essay, we will draw on the preliminary work done in the three preceding chapters of this book, work that had to do with exploration, enrichment, and analysis. As we took up the analytical essay, we saw that our first task was to read carefully and thoughtfully someone else's essay. As we read, we explored; we looked for techniques and searched for connections within the text, for clues that pointed to meaning. We were trying to understand someone else's essay. Exploration and analysis led to that understanding.

That same kind of careful, exploratory reading is the foundation for good research. As a researcher, you will be examining a variety of texts. Some of those texts will be *primary,* like the essays you have been studying. Other texts will be *secondary*—critical articles or books written by scholars about someone's primary work. In reading those different texts, you will be trying to learn all you can about a given subject. Your aim will be to create a text of your own, an argument in the form of a short research essay that will present your point of view about a controversial topic.

B. *The Argumentative Essay—Focusing on Controversy*

The research essay—whether long or short, whether written for a science course or for a humanities course—requires that you become knowledgeable about a given topic and that you reach a conclusion that you want to present to someone. But at the outset, while you are exploring, you should be alert to *controversy,* something that stirs you a bit and rouses you to debate. Your topic need not be global in scope. Good research topics are always close at hand. They need not come to you by way of international news or scholarly journals. If you are alert to what is going on around you, you may very well discover a topic worthy of research.

Consider this possibility. During a trip to the nursing home to visit your grandmother, you notice that there are only three nurses each evening to care for fifty elderly people. Many of the older, infirm patients require a great deal of attention; often, they seem neglected. You begin to think that the nursing home needs more nurses on the staff, but you are not sure. Stirred to action, you begin an informal investigation that turns finally to scheduled interviews with supervisors, visits to other nursing homes, and visits to the library to read about the operation of such facilities. Even though you are inclined from the beginning to think that the home needs more nurses, you remain open-minded as you investigate so that you will not overlook reasonable evidence that could influence your decision.

Having conducted a thorough investigation, you have to decide what the evidence means, what it tells you about the particular nursing home where your grandmother lives. If you find the staff-to-patient ratio in keeping with federal guidelines and in accord with the ratios for other nursing homes in the area, you might consider the case closed. But you might also begin to wonder whether the guidelines are reasonable. That question requires a much larger research effort. That is grist for another paper.

However, if during your initial investigation you find that conditions in your grandmother's nursing home are far out of line with established standards, you have to decide what to do with your findings. Will you write a letter to the director of the home, or will you make an appeal to a regulatory agency, or will this project turn into a larger case study for a sociology class? Think about the way your presentation might differ in each of those cases. Think, too, about the controversial nature of what you must present. Think of resistance, of opposition. How will those who hold different views affect the way you shape your letter or paper? You will be making a logical appeal to them, asking them perhaps to change their attitude about the adequacy of the nursing home staff. Whatever form your response takes, you must ultimately render your best judgment on the basis of your research and analysis. You must try to resolve the controversy.

The argumentative essay—the short research paper—that we will consider in this chapter focuses on such controversy. That essay differs from the exploratory essay in two important ways. Your own persona is more objective, less personal than it is in the exploratory essay, and that persona goes about its business more directly. Streamlined and logical, the argumentative essay claims a kind of scientific objectivity; it satisfies the call for academic rigor. Its most distinguishing characteristic is the enlightened way it presents and defends its conclusion. Although this essay can and should be entertaining, entertainment and rambling exploration are not its primary business; persuasion is, lively persuasion.

Think of argument not as a heated, emotional outburst between two people but as a reasoned exchange that might take place between a prosecutor and a defense lawyer in a judge's private chambers, with the judge serving as arbiter; between one scholar and another with yet a third listening, interjecting, keeping the discussion on track; between a corporate executive and a staff researcher with a project director serving as go-between. These educated, experienced people must solve day in, day out the complex, controversial problems common to their particular line of work. Should officers on active duty in the armed forces of the United States be allowed to hold positions of responsibility in the National Security Council? Is Samuel Hynes, a distinguished literary critic, correct when he claims that the characters in E. M. Forster's novels are incapable of love? What can we do to make Medicare more effective for the elderly? What seems most central to Roy Reed's imagination in *Looking for Hogeye*? What was the most decisive influence on the outcome of the American Civil War? To what extent have American psychologists abandoned their three great teachers: Freud, Adler, and Jung? Should Stephen W. Hawking's *A Brief History of Time: From the Big Bang to Black Holes* be required reading in undergraduate physics courses? Should undergraduate mathematics courses put primary emphasis on teaching students to solve representative and routine problems, leaving creative problem solving for engineering courses? The answer to any one of these questions—or to some restricted aspect of one of these questions— might very well serve as the controlling idea for some form of argumentative essay: a treatise, a book, a decision memorandum, or a research essay.

Controversy is at the heart of argumentative writing. But controversy need not be focused on such large issues. Research papers, as we have seen, do not have to solve global problems associated with nuclear armaments, abortion, trade deficits, and hunger. Indeed, later in this chapter, we will consider controversies no more earthshaking than the interpretation of a writer's body of work. Those interpretative papers differ little from the analytical essays we discussed in Chapter 3. We add only evidence gathered from outside sources, and we make the presentations more direct, more forceful. Like the exploratory and analytical essays, the argumentative one also aims to persuade. But the first two have the latitude to ramble and tease the mind into thought. The argumentative essay calls for disciplined directness.

Writers of argumentative essays invariably want to influence the way others think. After they have sat down with colleagues to debate controversial issues, they inevitably take pen in hand to straighten out their thinking. As a way of reaching their conclusions, they will certainly *explore* as they write; they will be *analytical* as they consider the various points of view they have heard expressed or have read about. They will call on their own experiences. They will draw tentative conclusions about a number of related issues as they think their way to a solution. But their aim is to present the reasoned conclusion they have drawn after the discussions with other experts have ended, after all the research has been done, after the experiments have been conducted, after the exploratory (and, in this case, preliminary) writing has led them to what they consider the best answer.

The argumentative essay presents that "best answer" (the paper's *thesis*) and provides sufficient supporting evidence so that other interested parties will be swayed. Effective argumentative essays counter other arguments and present the most compelling, most persuasive version of the truth that logic and available evidence will permit. Yet they never, in their most persuasive forms, ignore other versions of the truth.

C. *Preliminary Research—Reading to Find a Controversial Issue*

KEEPING AN OPEN MIND

Good researchers, like good readers, begin with an open mind. Perhaps the best advice I received from a high school English teacher was to let the writer of the novel I was reading have his say. I cannot remember the novelist or the novel; I can only remember the admonition that turned my attention to a world outside my own. I became painfully aware that the world I had been shaping inside my head was more limited than I had imagined. My teacher wanted me to keep my mind open to whatever possibilities the writer might raise in the novel, to consider the legitimacy of the fictive world the novelist had created. She was telling me not to impose my values, not to close my mind to someone else's version of truth.

Her advice was sound. Reading with an open mind, you can detect nuances and points of view that differ from your own. Being open-minded does not preclude being critical. An open-minded, critical reader reads actively, remaining receptive to new ideas and new ways of seeing things. But that reader is not passive, not unwilling to question. Active readers generate questions, discover connections, uncover gaps, make notes in the margins of texts, read with a highlighter in hand. They perform preliminary research every time they read, whether they are reading novels, scholarly texts, or articles in periodicals.

EXPLORATION, TOPIC SELECTION, AND RESTRICTION

When you begin your research project, your teacher may assign a topic or give you a list of topics to choose from. Or you may be free to select your own topic, one that has grown naturally from your personal experience or reading. Whatever the case, you may find that you know too little about the topic to begin your paper. You will have to do preliminary research that will help you settle on a subject and find a controversy.

The thinking skills you developed as you wrote exploratory and analytical essays should help you a great deal as you begin to read, analyze, and synthesize information. Think of your reading as an exploration; let your mind ramble, following what Sam Pickering calls your "willful curiosity." You're trying to make connections, trying to see things in a way in which no one else has seen them. You're doing what Tom Wolfe calls "locker-room digging," the work of the investigative reporter. As you begin digging, you will sift through the evidence, sort it, put an occasional marker in your book, take notes in your journal or on note cards, keep track of the things that occur to you. As you're sifting and sorting, you're also beginning to put your analytical skills to work: you're considering possibilities, asking questions, trying to focus your effort as soon as possible, making connections, forming tentative answers.

You can be sure that the topic you begin with will be too broad for your essay; you will have to restrict it. There is only so much you can do in a short paper. The idea is to restrict your topic so that you can learn a great deal about it. If the initial topic is Loren Eiseley, your essay cannot be about all of Eiseley's essays; there are too many of them. Neither can it be about Eiseley's development as a writer; he wrote too much over too many years. Such topics, restricted as they may seem, are still too broad. Focusing on one of Eiseley's essays or on the relationship between two of them might be more fruitful.

Intelligent restriction usually depends on active reading. If you are investigating a contemporary topic such as Eiseley, you ought to begin by looking through periodical indexes such as *The New York Times Index* and *Readers' Guide to Periodical Literature*. Scan those indexes for articles about your subject. If your topic is not contemporary and you know little about it, the best place to begin is usually a good encyclopedia. Often the articles you select from the indexes or read in encyclopedias will provide background and point to unresolved controversies.

You have to be on the lookout for controversy. The writer of the article does not have your research project in mind. That writer is trying to introduce readers to the subject in a general but authoritative way. You will have to read between the lines. At the end of many encyclopedia articles, you may find a short bibliography, a list of books and articles that you can consult to get more information about ideas that interest you. Some of those bibliographies and others that you consult will be annotated; they will give you a concise summary of each book or article. Use those valuable research aids wisely; they will save you time and energy. Pay attention to titles and subtitles. Often they will entice you or turn you away from a given article or book. Learn to trust your hunches.

RESTRICTED TOPIC QUESTION

Even the best researchers—and especially students who have limited time for exploration—need to focus their effort as soon as possible. Because the preliminary phase of research is generative, it can lead you in a number of different directions, any one of which might be fruitful. As you learn to become an efficient researcher, you will be better served if you investigate topics that interest you. Let personal interest set the restriction process in motion. If possible, find a topic that follows naturally from your studies. When you find that topic and discover through your initial reading how to restrict it, you will need to keep your research effort focused on that restricted topic. One way to do that is to form a *restricted topic question* (RTQ). The RTQ is nothing more than a question that will guide your research and keep you on track as you continue your investigation. A good RTQ has more than one answer.

Think back to the nursing home problem we considered at the beginning of this chapter. The RTQ for that research effort might be "To what extent is the nursing staff adequate in my grandmother's nursing home?" Such a question forces you to make a judgment based on adequacy; it also forces you to ask other questions to clarify the meaning of adequacy. Are there enough nurses to do essential tasks? What are the essential tasks? Are the tasks always routine? What about emergencies? What are the local guidelines for staffing nursing homes? Are there federal guidelines? What do those guidelines specify? All of these subordinate questions lead you back to the focusing question, the one that will require you to make a judgment.

As you investigate, you consider a number of possible answers to the RTQ; each of those answers is a tentative hypothesis, an educated guess based on the evidence you've collected up to a point. In the nursing home investigation, you discover two possible answers to your RTQ: (1) The nursing staff in my grandmother's nursing home meets the needs of the residents most of the time; few problems are ignored. (2) The nursing staff seems unable to respond to multiple emergencies during the night. Evidence gathered during additional research could rule out one of these hypotheses and confirm the other, or that research might shed light on both hypotheses, giving you a thesis such as this one that more nearly accounts for the evidence you've turned up: *Although the nursing staff is perfectly adequate during the day, it seems unable to handle multiple emergencies during late evening and early morning hours, when fewer nurses are on duty.* You are looking always for the best answer in light of all available evidence. That answer will govern the development of your paper. Your task, when you begin to write, will be to convince your readers that you have indeed turned up the best answer.

IDEA AND THESIS

Earlier in this book, we made a distinction between idea and thesis. We said a thesis can often be reduced to a simple declarative sentence ("Water pollution in Albany must be brought under control"); that declarative judgment seems to call for proof, seems to call for a hearing in court. It wants a reasonable, direct, and persuasive defense. An idea, on the other hand, begs an inquiry, an exploration. An idea is more supple than a thesis; it gains appeal and power in the hands of an essayist who is willing to take us round that idea, make us see it as he or she sees it.

Unlike a thesis that can be reduced to a simple declarative sentence ("Water pollution in Albany must be brought under control" or "Final examinations should be abolished" or "Abortion laws in New York State are unfair"), a good idea loses much of its appeal and power if we limit it ("Ira Solenberger lived his life in accordance with the seasons"). We suggested earlier that if a thesis calls for "proof" and demands something akin to a hearing in court, an idea calls for a different kind of hearing, a different way of expressing itself.

Now, I want to suggest that instead of considering *thesis* in that early, narrower sense, we might benefit from considering its direct kinship with *idea*. In our short research essays we are trying to resolve a controversy, so we need something akin to a thesis, something direct and in a sense provable. But we do not write essays about things that we can prove conclusively. There's something highly controversial about bringing water pollution in Albany under control. If you doubt it, try to persuade an industrial firm in Albany that it ought to improve its method for disposing of industrial waste—a firm that is already meeting the minimum standards imposed by federal regulations. A thesis, no matter how hard-edged or how convincing it may sound, never represents more than the best decision a writer can make, given the available evidence. A thesis does not represent incontrovertible truth. It represents a reasoned conclusion.

An *idea*, as we have considered it thus far in this book, calls for exploration; the idea itself is enlarged as the essayist examines it, passes it through the filter of his or her imagination, and then presents it to us so that we get the benefit of the writer's hard-earned understanding. We come to know what the writer knows. Recall the way Reed began his essay about Ira Solenberger—by mere suggestion, by pinning Ira to a particular spring day. As Reed developed his essay, the relationship between the two became more and more interesting. Reading that essay, we find out how a man's personality can be affected by the seasons, how a man's gardening philosophy matches his philosophy about life, how a man can still believe in magic at 86, how man and nature can live in harmony—and all of this accumulation and amplification is a part of the exploration that takes place in the essay; the idea becomes more complex, more interesting, more enticing as we see the essayist's mind play over and shape his material. An idea doesn't call for proof; it asks for a hearing in the front porch swing instead of in a courtroom; it wants a receptive mind, an unhurried reader who has time to watch the idea evolve by piecemeal and accumulation at a fairly leisurely pace.

The short research essay, as we've said, must be more direct than the exploratory essay. But that research piece ought to be informed by that same process of exploration that is the focal point in the exploratory essay. Directness in the research essay cannot lead to single-mindedness, to narrowness and the exclusion of evidence that might cast doubt on the thesis. So the informing spirit of exploration and the largeness of idea must somehow find expression in the directness of the research essay. Such complexity is not as difficult to achieve as you might suppose. It simply requires thorough research and a careful, analytical consideration of the evidence. It requires as well that you as a writer acknowledge the limitations of your thesis, that you make reasonable concessions to those who would disagree with your conclusions. There is strength in concession, and there can be a supple play of mind behind a good thesis. Analysis and exploration and argument are not such strange bedfellows at all.

REPORT OR ESSAY?

Consider again this answer to the nursing home RTQ: *Although the nursing staff is perfectly adequate during the day, it seems unable to handle multiple emergencies during late evening and early morning hours, when fewer nurses are on duty.* If you think of this answer to the RTQ as a rigid thesis requiring proof, it seems to call for little more than a restatement of the facts about the nursing home's operation. The answer might become nothing more than a report about your findings:

After observing the operation of the nursing home for more than two months, I found no instances when the daytime staff couldn't handle the problems for the eighty-six residents who live in the home. On the other hand, I discovered that during the same two-month period, there were no fewer than ten emergencies late in the

evening and five early in the morning, when the few staff members
on duty could not handle additional problems as they occurred.
On each of those occasions, other staff members had to be called
from home; thus treatment for stricken patients was often delayed.

As the writer of this report, you might go on to provide the details
about those fifteen occasions as a way of substantiating your claims
about inadequate staffing. But such a report would not be an essay. It
would provide important information; it would present the facts; but
it would not develop a theory about those facts. A report has no
argumentative edge to it; it simply documents your findings.

Those findings, nevertheless, raise important questions about
the nursing home and about the *adequacy* of staffing—questions that
can lead you to a good thesis that requires interpretation of the
evidence, a thesis that has the suppleness and appeal of a good idea. To
get to that interesting, supple thesis, you need to think again about the
evidence and about the RTQ; you need to think as well about others
whose view might be quite different from yours. The manager of the
nursing home—following to the letter the federal, state, or county
staffing guidelines—would more than likely claim that the home has
adequate staffing based on those guidelines. In light of your discoveries, you must counter that manager's claims about adequacy. You
have complaints filed by the relatives of nursing home residents who
were quite upset about the way those residents were neglected during
multiple emergencies. Staff members have also told you about their
own sense of inadequacy during those critical periods: the emotional
burden was too great; often they were not qualified to deal with the
patients' problems; on three occasions doctors were not available,
even though they were on call. Some of the problems required the
staff's undivided attention for several hours. Problems did not always
subside after additional staff members responded to calls for help;
often emergency staff members were not qualified to deal with the
emergencies.

You discover as you sort out the evidence and begin to develop your theory that your answer to the RTQ hinges on your own notion of *adequacy;* you know that your notion will challenge that contained in the guidelines and that of the manager of the nursing home. You know, finally, that your essay will attempt to persuade local health officials that adequacy is in the mind of the beholder and that in your mind—following a careful analysis of the evidence—you are certain that staffing at the nursing home in inadequate. This tentative thesis will guide you as you write your initial draft: *Although my grandmother's nursing home complies with the state's staffing guidelines, the actual day-to-day staff cannot meet the needs of patients except under the most routine conditions; under other than routine conditions, staffing and staffing guidelines are inadequate.*

D. *The Developmental Process: A Research Essay, Start to Finish*

To see how you might actually do your research and your writing, let's apply the general principles outlined in the preceding sections of this chapter to a research project that you might complete for your composition class. This project depends almost exclusively on your use of primary sources. We'll look now at the various stages of research and writing that can lead to a coherent essay.

RESEARCH IN COMPOSITION: INTERPRETATION AS CONTROVERSY

Let's begin in the composition class. You are asked to become very familiar with a modern essayist, one whose essays have appeared primarily in the twentieth century, one who might still be publishing. Your aim, as you move through the various stages of this research process, will be to find an idea associated with this writer's work that will require you to be interpretive and judgmental when you finally

◊

write your essay. *You're looking for some gap in the knowledge about the writer, something that would require you to interpret some aspect of the writer's work to an interested audience.* Because you have been reading modern essays throughout the course, you can choose from a fairly long list of writers that includes Joan Didion, Annie Dillard, Samuel Pickering, Tom Wolfe, E. B. White, Roy Reed, Loren Eiseley, and Gretel Ehrlich.

STAGE 1—READING, ANALYZING, DRAFTING

During the *first stage* of this research process, you turn to the task of learning as much about the writer as you can; you're trying to get to know the writer's work so well that you can make judgments about his or her ideas. Much of what you learned about active reading and analysis in the last chapter should help you, but now, instead of focusing on technique, you'll be studying several essays by the same writer in order to develop a sense of that writer's imagination. You want to become familiar with the play of the writer's imagination. You're looking for the writer's favorite topics, for the way he or she actually develops an essay, for the writer's sense of the world. You decide that the best way into that writer's imagination is through the essays themselves, the primary texts. Later, you may want to consult secondary texts, the ones others have written about the writer. But at first, you decide to rely on your own thinking; you want to approach the essays with an open mind, unbiased by someone else's interpretation.

You choose Roy Reed's essays because "Spring Comes to Hogeye" grabbed your interest. You're interested in finding out more about the man who could see so clearly the connection between Ira Solenberger and the seasons. You know from class discussions that Reed has only one collection of published pieces called *Looking for Hogeye,* and you must select five essays from that collection for your preliminary reading: "Heading Home," "The Country," "Fall," "Vernon McCall and the Government," and "A Letter to My Great-

Grandfather." You want to find out as much as you can about Reed's imagination before you begin to restrict your topic and formulate a thesis, so you select a broad, flexible RTQ: "To what extent does Roy Reed reveal a consistent set of concerns in his essays?" You know that in a later stage of this research effort, you may want to change that RTQ, but for now it will guide you through Reed's essays as you read under the influence of a willful curiosity, trying to identify Reed's main concerns.

Your writing task in this first stage will be to present a "character sketch" that will give your readers some sense of Reed based on what you as a researcher could glean from his essays. You will not be permitted to cite any evidence from biographical sources; all of your evidence for the initial assignment must come from the five selected essays. You will be aiming to give your readers a sense of Reed using his essays as your primary evidence.

As you read the five essays, you find that they tell you a great deal about Reed—his concerns, his family, his imagination. Your problem, you begin to see quite early, is not whether you will have enough material for a two- or three-page paper on Reed; the problem is *how to select the evidence* from the five essays that will give your readers a clear sense of this man you are beginning to like so much. You begin to think about what to include in your initial response about Reed.

During a conference with your instructor, you go over what you have learned from Reed's essays; he was a reporter for *The New York Times* for a number of years; he left the *Times* while in London and went to Hogeye, Arkansas, with his wife to settle into a farmer's life; his father had had such a life years before in Yell County and moved to Hot Springs; Reed's son married a Catholic, going pretty far astray from the family's Baptist background.

After talking with your instructor about those *facts* you've uncovered, you turn to *interpretive* issues: why Reed moved back to Arkansas, what Reed thought about his father's moving to Hot Springs, what Reed thought about his son's marriage. As you reflect on the essays you have read, you begin to formulate a sense of Reed's values, values that seem to provide the foundation for all of his essay. You turn away from the details of Reed's life to those values that seem to inform his writing. You get interested in finding the essence of Reed's work. You know that you will have to develop your own personal sense of what is common to all of those pieces you have read, no matter what their subject.

You go away from your conference with a clearer notion of the requirement, and you know that your first effort to make sense of Reed need not turn out to be a finished, coherent essay. You try only to reveal the man and his concerns; you have found your *evidence* in those five essays. Here is your initial sense of Reed:

Roy Reed: A Country Boy

My aunt and uncle live on a little farm in southeast Arkansas just outside Snyder where they raise hogs and corn in fairly large number, and they have a small garden where they raise all the food they need to survive. I like to visit them because their life is so different from the life I live in Hamburg. When we need food, we go to the grocery store to buy it; when they need food, they grow it. I like the way they work together, growing food, looking after the pigs and cows, tending the chickens and dogs. They work hard, but they are happy. When I visit them, I get the idea that I have gone through a time warp, that I have gone back to another era. The car ride back to town is always a sad one because I begin to feel a deep sense of loss, wishing I could be back around Aunt Kate's dining room table, listening to the family jokes, eating her good food, reminiscing with my mom and her family. I feel sad too because Aunt Kate and Uncle Earnest are getting old, and I sense not only the end of their lives but also the end of a way of life.

When I first read Roy Reed's essay about Ira Solenberger, I was reminded of Uncle Earnest. Solenberger is a wise old man who, according to Reed, lived his life in harmony with the seasons. He knew things no one else in the farming community seemed to know. He knew when to plant because he was more observant than most of his neighbors. Maybe he had a sixth sense. Reed seems to suggest that he did. Whatever the case, Solenberger "raised the biggest watermelons in Northwest Arkansas," according to his neighbors' testimony.

Because I liked the way Reed treated Solenberger, I decided that I would like to know more about Reed. He made me remember my days in Snyder, and I wanted to know how he could know so much about farmers. Reading five of his essays from *Looking for Hogeye*, I discovered a number of things about Reed's life. He apparently grew up in northwest Arkansas but somehow ended up in London as a foreign correspondent for *The New York Times.* After what must have been a distinguished career as a newspaperman, he left London and went to Hogeye, Arkansas, back to a farm in the Ozarks. He doesn't tell us directly why he went back, but we can figure it out between the lines of his essays.

In an essay called "Heading Home," Reed tells us about the luxurious life he and his wife gave up in London to return to one of the worst winters he could remember. Icy winters in north Arkansas are especially bad because the power lines break, the wind roars, and there is no salt for the roads to make them passable. But from this essay, we see that Reed is happy with his choice; he's happy to be "pestering his rural origins" heating his house with a wood stove, happy too at the sight of his two tomcats playing outside his window. Sitting there, he yearns "to entwine himself in nature."

In "The Country" and "A Letter to My Great-Grandfather," Reed gives us a pretty good sense of his family background and how he feels about it. He claims to be "trash"—"country trash" to be more exact. According to Reed, the trash are survivors. They have a developed sense of community because they are outsiders. They either take care of themselves, or they perish. No one else cares about them. Reed likes them because they are ornery and tough, but he likes them too because they have a sense of humor, know how to survive during the hard times. The trash do not care much for outsiders, and when Reed's son decides to marry an Ulster Catholic, Reed decides to write a letter to his own Great-Grandfather to give him a sense of how the family line has been faring since his death. It's a great and funny essay.

I know from reading these essays and a couple more that Reed has a consistent philosophy, that he went back home to recover something he lost along the way. His essays tell me what he lost and what he's trying to recover.

You're not completely satisfied with your initial piece on Reed, but you know that you're on to something that interests you. You realize that you didn't have time to revise, and you didn't have space enough to write about "Vernon McCall" and "Fall," other important essays. You got the paper back from your instructor with these comments:

I like the way you begin this piece with the paragraph about your family, but in a piece this short you probably need to compress that paragraph so that you will have more space for Reed. You understand Reed's values quite well. But I would like more, more about Reed, more evidence from the other essays. Do not feel obligated to tell me step-by-step how you came to like Reed better and better. Your essay need not follow the chronology of your own discoveries or the path of your reading. Could you reorganize on the basis of important ideas about Reed and his work? In your next-to-last paragraph you seem to be doing that. By discussing two essays together in the same paragraph, you show me that you are beginning to make connections. *That is, after all, the point of your research, that and the resolution of an interpretive controversy.* Keep these considerations in mind as we continue the research project. Do not forget to document your summaries and quotations from Reed's work; document within parentheses in the text of your essay. See the Appendix (p. 227).

STAGE 2—FOCUSED RESEARCH: READING, DELIBERATING, AND INTERPRETING

You know from class discussions that your most pressing task in the *second stage* of your research is to extend the range of your reading. You must consider at least ten essays by Reed so that as you broaden your base of knowledge, you can check your preliminary assumptions about Reed. During this second phase, you can also consult biographies and critical essays about Reed, if those sources exist.

You decide to examine *Hogeye* more closely, looking for clues that might guide the rest of your research. On the back of the title page in the acknowledgment section, you notice that Reed has published some of his pieces in *Arkansas Times, Time,* the New Orleans *Times-Picayune,* and *The New York Times.* You know, too, from reading the preface that Reed is well connected with that last paper's editorial council. You find on the dust jacket for the book that he was a reporter for eight years for the *Arkansas Gazette.* He was with the *Gazette* from 1957 to 1965 and with *The New York Times* from 1965 to 1978.

You begin to think about research in the library and recall *The New York Times Index* and *Readers' Guide to Periodical Literature* from earlier discussions about preliminary research.

Because your research project has taken its own shape now, you pose a new RTQ for this second stage of the project. You will probably not find much biographical or critical information on Reed, so your project will depend entirely on what you can find of Reed's that is in print in newspapers and magazines. You decide that you would like to proceed with this question in mind: "To what extent do Reed's other pieces change my view of the Reed I found in the five essays from *Hogeye?*" You realize that this is a tentative question, but it will keep your mind engaged as you begin to read; it will also focus your reading.

In the library—when you are working on a project like this one where you must look for primary source material—there are few shortcuts. You know that Reed's professional writing life covers more than twenty years, so you will have to go through the indexes and

◊

guides very carefully. In *The New York Times Index,* you begin to strike pay dirt. You discover, too, that Reed is still writing in the *Times* (with a byline) and in a number of magazines.

As you turn up more and more primary material, you begin to wonder if you should write or call either the New Orleans or the Arkansas newspaper. Eager to find whatever you can, you decide to call the *Arkansas Gazette.* You find that the newspaper does in fact have a library service and a computer retrieval service. But the bad news is that the retrieval service goes back no farther than 1984. Nevertheless, you learn from the *Gazette*'s librarian that Reed's coverage of the civil rights movement was very important. You also learn from him that *The New York Times* has a byline retrieval service, so you go to the interlibrary loan office and ask the librarian to help you get from the *Times* a byline bibliography for Roy Reed. You can also consult the *Personal Name Index to The New York Times Index.* In the meantime, you go on with your research, using the guides and the indexes, photocopying when necessary articles and essays from microfilm and bound periodicals.

After another week or two of researching, you find that Reed is fairly consistent in the pieces you read, whether he's writing about blueberry growing in Arkansas or about his redneck neighbors and relatives. Your reading of pieces not included in *Hogeye* confirms the representative nature of that collection. As you look at all the material you have assembled, you know that you must reach some conclusions about it; you must focus your effort.

After much deliberation, you decide that you want to restrict your attention primarily to *Hogeye;* you want to write your final paper about that collection of pieces, highlighting your findings with evidence from pieces outside the collection. You're still interested in why Reed left that London assignment and went back to Arkansas, and you think it has something to do with mystery and spirit of place, something to do with family and roots and continuity. Reed doesn't make such a case straight out in his essays, but you find the evidence in that collection and in the other pieces you have read. You can sense it as you read.

Members of the class can't see it at first, even though they have also read a couple of Reed's essays, but as you give your oral report to the class about what you are discovering, they begin to get interested in your *interpretation*. They begin to see that you are making sense of what you have been reading. Although they offer some opposition, questioning Reed's hard-nosed values on occasion, they seem to respect your point of view. You know you have found an engaging controversy that hinges on your interpretation of Reed's work. That's the key to your essay, the idea that will keep it focused and coherent.

As it turns out, the course you are taking in southern literature begins to play in your imagination as you think about Reed. In that course, you are studying the Agrarians, a group of southern writers who, after the First World War, expressed concern about the rising tide of industrialism in the South; they were concerned about an erosion of values and a disintegration of the agricultural community as they understood it. In a book called *I'll Take My Stand*, a number of them, including Allen Tate, Robert Penn Warren, Andrew Lytle, and John Crowe Ransom, contributed essays aimed at keeping the older order of the South intact; these writers wanted to preserve agrarian values. Reading their essays, you begin to see that Reed might be a latter-day descendant, an heir to their legacy. Reading them, you begin to understand Reed; you begin to make connections that excite you. In your composition course, you've also read Annie Dillard, who spends a lot of time writing about gods and mysteries, especially the mysteries of nature. You see that she and Reed are different even when they write about the same subject.

STAGE 3 — ORGANIZING AND WRITING

During the *third stage* of your research and writing, you know that you have to begin to impose order on all of that material you have been examining; you have to organize your discoveries, always keeping a reader in mind who knows very little if anything about the idea you're working on. You want to think of that reader's needs as you organize your thoughts, as you consider how to present your case.

You have, of course, been taking notes and making connections during the first two stages of research, and you have discovered that there are recurring themes in each of Reed's essays. Two of the essays—"Fall" and "Spring Comes to Hogeye"—seem to have a great deal to say about mystery; "The Country" and "A Letter to My Great-Grandfather" emphasize the importance of community. Those groupings lead to others, and you begin to impose order even as you make connections. Mystery and community seem to be at the heart of Reed's essays; they seem to account for Reed's fascination with the place he has gone back to and reclaimed, that little farm and the life that surrounds it. You change your RTQ one more time, trying to focus your effort: "Just how important is Reed's fascination with mystery and community; how does that fascination manifest itself in his essays?" You read through the essays again with this two-part question in mind.

Before you begin to write, you consider the Agrarians and know that you want to place Reed against that earlier southern background; you know, too, that that connection will be an informing one, yet you do not want to devote too much of your essay to it. You decide finally that your main goal is to explain to your readers why Reed is so attracted to life in and around Hogeye that he will give up a plush London assignment to go back to an Arkansas farm and "plow Ozark rocks." You want to uncover for your readers the attraction, the fascination that took Reed back and that informs a coherent reading of his essays. You want to convince your classmates that community is paramount in Reed's imagination and that there is something mysterious that binds people together in that little Arkansas outpost. The tentative thesis that shapes your essay is not at all complicated; it comes directly from your reading and analysis: *Reed's strong fascination with the mysteries of community drew him out of a posh London assignment and into the Arkansas hills, and those mysteries inform much of his best writing.*

Your conclusion is controversial because it is based on your own interpretation of Reed's work; you have drawn that conclusion following your exploration and your analysis; it accounts for your assessment of the central meaning in a number of Reed's essays. Other students in the class see Reed as nothing more than a retired reporter who writes interesting travel pieces and occasional essays about his family and folks around Hogeye. One student thinks of Reed as a redneck apologist; he thinks Reed couldn't possibly like the rednecks he writes about, even if some of them are family members. As you begin to understand your opponents' objections, you become more sure that your sense of Reed is correct. The evidence is in the essays. The more you read, the more you find to confirm your thesis.

Here is your final polished effort, your sustained attempt to write a coherent essay about Reed.

Back Home

1   Roy Reed left his choice London assignment with *The New York Times,* to go back to Hogeye, Arkansas. He went back, he tells us, "to try to discover where his heart is." Writing out of the Agrarian tradition, he takes his place alongside Tate, Ransom, Davidson, and Lytle. But Reed writes after the fall to industrialism, after the fall away from values, and his is a voice that differs from those earlier voices. In his essays, sketches, and travel pieces in *Looking for Hogeye,* he takes us back into what patches of garden remain in northwest Arkansas, tries to convince us that reentry is worth it even if we end up plowing rocks, scraping around, trying to dig ourselves back to life.

2   No sentimentalist, Reed has a keen awareness of what can't be, but what can't be seems no less possible for him. Back in his farmhouse, sitting hemmed in by his first winter's ice storm, he meditates: "I am stricken with regret. I yearn to entwine myself in

nature, but the simplest feat—one that my cat performs without effort—is beyond me. So for a few minutes I stand at the window and become a child. I walk in my mind to the base of the tree and look up. I select a spot fifteen or twenty feet high (that is reasonable, considering the greater size and strength of a man) and coil my muscles. I leap" (Reed 6). When Reed finishes such feats of imaginative derring-do—moving in and out of imagination, in and out of the seasons, in and out of nature—he is younger, more aware, more at home.

3   Dissolving the barriers between man and nature, Reed moves us as close to The Mysteries as Annie Dillard does trading glances with a weasel on Tinker Creek. In "Fall" we enter the woods with a "bunch" of hunters, some old, some young. We might just be in the Mississippi woods with Faulkner tracking bear, but this ritual develops on a smaller, more accessible scale. The hunters' primary business is squirrel hunting; Reed's is "the exhilarating mystery that puzzles every hunter: the discovery that he can detect the presence of game by some sense that is beyond hearing, seeing or even smelling" (44).

4   Mystery is again close in "Spring Comes to Hogeye." Eighty-six-year-old Ira Solenberger is late planting his crop because spring itself is late. Reed manages to get Solenberger to tell him why: "Well, sir, I believe the world twists a little bit. You know, everything that grows twists around to the right. Follows the sun. Even our storms that come out of the Gulf, they twist to the right. It's just nature" (28). Reed respects this old man's perception, loves him, and as he renders Ira, he not only gives us touches of Ozark wisdom, he also makes us see that Ira dies in harmony with the seasons. His existence has followed a mysterious rhythm of ebb and flow.

5   Ira's death signals the loss of that special breed of hill people. "The Country" is Reed's answer to Lytle—a confirmation of terrible loss. While relishing the country folk's laziness, their love of fishing, their carelessness, their contentiousness, their distrust of

education, their fire-and-brimstone religion, their "plain damned meanness," Reed also savors their sense of community (22): "Country people look after one another. . . . The trash take care of their own, not out of goodness but out of necessity" (20). Back in Hogeye, Reed is trying to reclaim and preserve values, but he's also there out of necessity. He's checking the vitality of his own "rootstock," trying to find out if he's got the "Mother of vinegar— the few drops that contain the life of the entire line and from which a new batch of vinegar can be started anytime" (12).

6   Reed's own rootstock comes clear in "A Letter to My Great-Grandfather." The wedding of Reed's son to an Ulster Catholic gives him occasion to write this spirited account of how the line has been faring for the last hundred or so years. Tongue in cheek, Reed writes about rednecks and survival, but what he says is only half in jest. Folks marrying outsiders and those "leaving the hills and hollers" under the influence of Sears and Roebuck catalogues do themselves and their kind no favors (127). The men die too young in town; they wear "themselves out on the pavement, running after the dream" (129). The women with their washing machines do no better. "And they are," Reed tells his great-grandpa, "the unhappiest people I know" (128).

7   In the sketches and travel reports in *Hogeye,* Reed takes a wider view of the South. He attends a camp meeting in Tennessee; watches a steamboat race in New Orleans; renders observations on wine tasting, country music, and other Ozark delights; and goes searching through Louisiana for Cajun delicacies. The same irresistible spirit of place that he finds in Hogeye, he senses elsewhere. At home in the hills and in the backwaters, he makes discoveries that only a country boy can make. People tell him things because they trust him. Reading these pieces, we understand why.

8   Reed is a great essayist, not only because he finds general truths embedded in the particularity of his own experience, but also because he knows what the good journalist knows, about immediacy, about dialogue, about economy. Reed, like Ira Solenberger,

understands magic. He's interested in the spirit of things. He's also interested in preservation and endurance, interested even in the longevity of his own life and ours. He puts us in Hogeye without wasting a word. And once we're there, we too are back home.

Works Cited

Reed, Roy. "The Country." *Looking for Hogeye*. Fayetteville: Arkansas UP, 1986. 10–14. [Additional essays, same collection:]
"Fall." 42–44.
"Heading Home." 1–6.
"A Letter to My Great-Grandfather." 117–132.
"Spring Comes to Hogeye." 25–29.

STAGE 4—REVISING

As a way of initiating the *fourth stage* of the process—the final revision—you distribute copies of your paper on Reed to other class members so they can prepare for an in-class workshop. They respond to your essay by writing notes in the margin, telling you where they would like to know more; they also identify those places in the essay that really please them. The exchange in the classroom leads finally to a thorough appraisal of your essay that is reflected in this summary from the workshop:

> We really like your essay. You've found an important idea that connects much of what is interesting and central to Reed's work. The writing is good too, but we'd like you to make the connection more explicit between mystery and community. What part does mystery play in that community? What kind of binding power do you think Reed associates with the various mysteries that he uncovers?
>
> Think about your essay's structure. Paragraphs 2–4 focus on mystery; paragraphs 5–7 touch on aspects of community—the family as well as the larger community in and around Hogeye. Can you find new ways to bring those two sections of your essay

together more effectively so that we know more about what you know, more about how mystery and community inform one another in Reed's imagination?

We like your quotations throughout the essay; they are well chosen to illustrate your points, but we'd like to know a little bit more about what you think about those quotations. Look, for example, at the quotation that ends paragraph 3. Could you reflect on that evidence from Reed's essay, tell us a little more about what it means to you. Does the hunter's ability to detect the presence of game have something to do with what brings these men together in the first place; does it draw them into community? What does Reed say in that same essay about what happens to the sense of community when the hunters just go on the hunt once a year? Why does he call the essay "Fall"? Could he be suggesting a "fall" out of community, like the fall out of paradise, out of unity? Try to give us a clearer sense of what Reed means by community. Look through your essay and see if there are not other places where you might *reflect* a bit more about your evidence. Remember, we really want to know what you think about Reed's ideas. You're behind this whole effort; you're the one selecting the evidence, arranging it in some order, making it make sense to us, your readers.

We know you've chosen to focus on *Hogeye,* but we'd like to see you make your case a bit more convincingly about Reed's values. Could you bring in two or three essays from outside the collection to give your essay a little more depth, to make it more convincing. Let those two or three essays comment on essays you've already cited. Strengthen your case; try not to discuss Reed's essays one at a time. Show us how similar ideas show up in a number of essays; bring those essays together in a single paragraph or in a section of your paper where you develop one of your subordinate ideas. We'd like to see you extend your reach while bringing your evidence together.

The beginning and ending are effective, but we all wanted to know just a little more about that last sentence in the introduction.

Could you elaborate? Are you saying that Reed wants to tell us that it's worth trying to reenter paradise, worth trying to go back in the garden, that going back to Arkansas was like going back to reclaim something that had been lost? How does that closing sentence of the introduction tie in with the closing sentences of your essay?

A reminder about documentation. You have done a good job of quoting from Reed's essays, but each one of those quotations must have parenthetical documentation to accompany it within the text of your essay. Be consistent. And you'll need a bibliography of works cited. Going back to check all of your quotations for accuracy will give you a chance to complete your documentation and make it consistent throughout your essay. Remember to follow the Modern Language Association guidelines [pp. 227–248].

After looking over this appraisal and thinking about it, you realize that you do not have a great deal of research left to do. You see how to connect two or three other essays; you've already done the reading. You know, too, about documentation and have kept careful track of the page numbers for your quotations, and you'll even be able to check them against the original sources instead of relying on your notes.

Your biggest effort must be directed toward the text of the essay itself. Revision, at this point, means clarifying and adding to what you have already written. It means working harder to make your various sources come together. You want to make better use of those sources, to let them comment on each other in your essay. And you want to reflect more on the evidence that you cite to ensure that your readers know why you have cited the evidence and what it means to you, what it has to do with your thesis.

You feel confident that you can make your readers see clearly the connection between mystery and community. You realize that when you clarify that connection, they will understand why Reed is so fascinated with life in the Ozarks; his fascination is implicit throughout the essays. It is especially implicit when he turns to that sense of community, that power of the land to draw people to it and together.

You realize from reading the class's appraisal that the class members have understood your interpretation. They like your discoveries, so you can finish your effort confident that you have their stamp of approval. This particular research project has led you to important discoveries about Reed. It has highlighted a research process and revealed to you some of the ways writers reveal themselves in the pieces they write. It has shown you, too, how your own interpretations lead to ideas and to essays—essays that can be graceful while being direct, essays that depend on research and on the play of your mind over a variety of texts. You have also discovered that interpretation, your interpretation, is controversial; it is your way of making sense of someone else's work; it is your way of seeing. Writing out that interpretation in the form of an essay is your way of asking others to see Reed as you do.

THE FINAL PAPER

Back Home

1   Roy Reed left his choice London assignment with *The New York Times,* to go back to Hogeye, Arkansas. He went back, he tells us, "to try to discover where his heart is." Writing out of the Agrarian Tradition, he takes his place alongside Tate, Ransom, Davidson, and Lytle. But Reed writes after the South's fall into industrialism, after the fall away from values, and his is a restorative voice, less strident, more appealing, more artful than those earlier agrarian voices. In his essays, sketches, and travel pieces in *Looking for Hogeye* and in other essays as well, he takes us back into what patches of garden remain in northwest Arkansas, tries to convince us that reentry is worth it even if we end up plowing rocks, scraping around, trying to dig ourselves back to life. What Reed finds there in

the Ozarks is solid; Hogeye lasts even when the world outside changes—bound together as it is by the mysteries of community.

2   No sentimentalist, Reed has a keen awareness of what can't be, but what can't be seems no less possible for him. Back in his own farmhouse, sitting hemmed in by his first winter's ice storm, he meditates: "I am stricken with regret. I yearn to entwine myself in nature, but the simplest feat—one that my cat performs without effort—is beyond me. So for a few minutes I stand at the window and become a child. I walk in my mind to the base of the tree and look up. I select a spot fifteen or twenty feet high (that is reasonable, considering the greater size and strength of a man) and coil my muscles. I leap" ("Home" 6). When Reed finishes such feats of imaginative derring-do—moving in and out of imagination, in and out of the seasons, in and out of nature—he is younger, more aware, more at home.

3   Even in London, reporting for the *The New York Times,* Reed had his mind on home. He never says that straight out, but two of his pieces from England suggest as much. He went to Laugharne, Wales, to Dylan Thomas's "adopted home," and discovered his own regret that the fishing industry—victim of industrial pollution, perhaps, or "overpicking by cockle collectors"—no longer bound the villagers to place, no longer spawned and sustained the tough breed of men whose brawling fascinated Reed as it had Thomas. The toughness and the brawling and the binding power of place, those were the qualities that spoke to Reed in that Welsh village so far away from home ("Boisterous" 2).

4   But "In an English Village, Bells Toll the Dying of Old Ways," we learn even more about why Reed, a temporary exile, was starting to itch for Arkansas. Visiting Radwinter, he was struck first by the bantam rooster and then by the church bells that woke the town each day. "Their message," Reed said, "is not merely the time but an affirmation of what they have been saying every 15 minutes for generations: No one in Radwinter is alone" (B1). Yet he tells us that "History is assaulting Radwinter," and he senses the

loss, the change, the disintegration of a way of life that troubles him and the older members of the village. Feudalism that had bound people to the land had been replaced by "a kind of do-it-yourself democracy" that was losing ground, finally, to a transient community of commuters (B10).

5   Reed reminds us that "Radwinter once provided everything its people needed. That was its purpose—meeting its people's needs, including employment" (B10). But the loss of the windmill was followed by a decline in churchgoing, and what counted was left in the hands of the old people. What interested Reed most in that village were the "sure throngs of community" that bound people together, year after year, century after century (B1): the Bowls Club, the cricket season, the planting, the barn dances—the events that "possess and perpetuate regularity" (B10). But Reed sensed loss. The record in the church tower, the signature of the ringer himself, showed that the bells last rang for the gleaning of harvest on August 29, 1917. Reed tells us that twenty-eight of the village's own had been claimed by the Great War (B10). The center was not holding in Radwinter, might not be holding anywhere else. Disintegration was on Reed's mind, and my guess is that he went back home, back to Arkansas, to see if he could find the "sure throngs of community"; he went back to see if he could find something close to the earth that would last.

6   Home in Hogeye, Reed wanted to leap 20 feet high into the air and become a squirrel; he wanted to be on the earth and defy it at the same time. Reed's Hogeye essays move us as close to The Mysteries as Annie Dillard does trading glances with a weasel on Tinker Creek. In "Fall," we enter the woods with a "bunch" of hunters, some old, some young. The hunter's primary business is squirrel hunting. Reed's is the "exhilarating mystery that puzzles every hunter: the discovery that he can detect the presence of game by some sense that is beyond hearing, seeing or even smelling" (44).

7   Throughout this essay, Reed intersperses another narrative that begins in 1943 against the backdrop of war. It is a story about the "expectations that every Southern boy has a right to see filled at a certain time"—a narrative of male ritual: the first hunt, the first drink, the first kill (42–43). That ritual "tied the boy not only to the uncle but, more importantly, to his father, and tied the two of them to the ancestral woods." But then, "the son lost his taste for it." Hunting became a "single ritual hunt each year," and the government flooded the land (43). The "bond was dissolved and the son set adrift from his own blood" (44). "Fall" is a story of cultural disintegration embedded in a story of perpetuation, of renewal and mystery. Reed's hunting neighbors in Hogeye live close enough to the land to live the myth. The stories they tell each other come from experience itself; they bind men together.

8   Mystery is again close in "Spring Comes to Hogeye." Eighty-six-year-old Ira Solenberger is late planting his crop because spring itself is late. Reed manages to get Solenberger to tell him why: "Well, sir, I believe the world twists a little bit. You know, everything that grows twists around to the right. Follows the sun. Even our storms that come out of the Gulf, they twist to the right. It's just nature" (28). Reed respects this old man's perception, loves him, and as he renders Ira, he not only gives us touches of Ozark wisdom, he also makes us see that Ira dies in harmony with the seasons. His existence has followed a mysterious rhythm of ebb and flow.

9   Ira's death signals the loss of that special breed of hill people that so fascinates Reed. "The Country" is Reed's answer to Lytle—a confirmation of terrible loss. While relishing the country folk's laziness, their love of fishing, their carelessness, their contentiousness, their distrust of education, their fire-and-brimstone religion, their "plain damned meanness," Reed also savors their sense of community (22): "Country people look after one another. . . . The trash take care of their own, not out of goodness but out of necessity" (20). Back in Hogeye, Reed is trying to reclaim and

preserve values, but he's also there out of necessity. He's checking the vitality of his own "rootstock," trying to find out if he's got the "Mother of vinegar—the few drops that contain the life of the entire line and from which a new batch of vinegar can be started anytime" (12).

10   Reed's own rootstock comes clear in "A Letter to My Great-Grandfather." The wedding of Reed's son to an Ulster Catholic gives him occasion to write this spirited account of how the family line has been faring for the last hundred or so years. Tongue in cheek, Reed writes about rednecks and survival, but what he says is only half in jest. Folks marrying outsiders and those "leaving the hills and hollers" under the influence of Sears and Roebuck catalogues do themselves and their kind no favors (127). The men die too young in town; they wear "themselves out on the pavement, running after the dream" (129). The women with their washing machines do no better. "And they are," Reed tells his great-grandpa, "the unhappiest people I know" (128).

11   In the sketches and travel reports in *Hogeye,* Reed takes a wider view of the South. He attends a camp meeting in Tennessee; watches a steamboat race in New Orleans; renders observations on wine tasting; country music, and other Ozark delights; and goes searching through Louisiana for Cajun delicacies. The same irresistible spirit of place that he finds in Hogeye, he senses elsewhere in the South. At home in the hills and in the backwaters, he makes discoveries that only a country boy can make. People tell him things because they trust him.

12   In a small Arkansas town, Crescent Dragonwagon, a writer and local innkeeper, tells Reed a secret that takes him finally to a place he had been looking for . . . perhaps for a long, long time. The town turned out to be Gilbert (pop. 45), but the place itself was a "gravel bar" on the Buffalo, a place where Reed could stand facing the river and the wind and know that he had found, for a moment, the "quietness" he had been looking for: "You cannot go any farther. Since you have run out of choices, you stop" ("Ozark" 105). Reed

had set out, he told us, to "explore some of the remaining re-
moteness" in the Ozarks (66). He wanted solitude, and he had
found it by lollygagging from place to place, talking to the people,
listening, taking note of the "new prosperity" and the tastes
brought in by the "outlanders," but revelling finally in what was
most remote and most isolated (95).

13   What he found there in Gilbert on the banks of the river was, I
suspect, akin to what he had written about years before as he left
New Orleans for the London assignment. He found magic and a
few possessions that belonged only to him and the place itself—
nothing more noteworthy than a "table at Al Pierce's restaurant in
the crawfish season," or a worrisome "contrary ole dog named
Wilhelminia." Those possessions of mind and others, he said as he
left Louisiana, were his—"mine merely because of where I have
stood for seven years to perceive them" ("Farewell" 12). By the
time Reed got to Gilbert, more than a decade later, his possessions
were accumulating . . . most likely to his liking. What he found at
the end of the road, up there in the Ozarks, seems to suit him. We
can sense it in his words. His tough nostalgia moves us around,
makes us take stock.

14   Like Ira Solenberger, Reed understands magic, something about
the spirit of place that yokes people. Like Lytle, Reed wants to stave
off disintegration. He wants to preserve and endure, interested as
he is in the longevity of his own life and ours as well. Reed serves up
his own brand of magic, embedding general truths in the particularity of his own experience—truths about the binding throngs of
community. He puts us in Hogeye, and once we're there, we too
are back home, bound to the mysteries of place—whatever they
may be.

Works Cited

*I'll Take My Stand: The South and the Agrarian Tradition by Twelve
    Southerners.* New York: Harper (Torchbook), 1962.

Reed, Roy. "In an English Village, Bells Toll the Dying of Old Ways." *New York Times* 17 Apr. 1978: B1+.

———. "The Country." *Looking for Hogeye.* Fayetteville: Arkansas UP, 1986. 10–24.

"Fall." 42–44.

"Heading Home." 1–6.

"A Letter to My Great-Grandfather." 117–132.

"Spring Comes to Hogeye." 25–29.

———. "Boisterous Days Are Over in 'Under Milk Wood' Town." *New York Times* 16 Apr. 1977: 2.

———. "A Nostalgic Farewell to New Orleans." *New York Times* 31 Jan. 1977: 12.

———. "Ozark Lollygagging." *New York Times* 13 Mar. 1988, sec. 4:66+.

EVALUATING *Compare this final version of "Back Home" with the earlier version (p. 190). Using as a guide the class's evaluation following that earlier version, consider the changes in this final essay. What specific changes seem to bring mystery and community closer together? How effective are those changes? What are the effects of the new material, those additional newspaper pieces about New Orleans, England, and the Ozarks? Look at two or three of the paragraphs that make use of the new material, and see if you can distinguish mere summary from analysis. What are the differences? What is gained by adding those new paragraphs? Identify places in the text of the final essay where you would like further clarification.*

WRITING—YOUR OWN RESEARCH ESSAY *With the essay about Reed in your mind, you turn now to your own process, your own developmental sequence:*

READING AND RESEARCHING *Select any modern essayist who is still alive and writing essays. Read five essays by that essayist, and write a short piece like "Country Boy" in which you try to identify a set of underlying concerns common to all the essays. After completing your initial piece, develop a flexible RTQ to guide further research and reading. Write a paragraph or two explaining why you have chosen that particular RTQ.*

READING, TAKING NOTES, AND CONNECTING *As you continue reading primary works by your selected essayist, and as you take notes about recurring ideas that carry over from essay to essay, stop for a while and think about other connections that come to mind. How do your essayist's ideas connect with ideas you have come across in other sources: books, articles, movies, poems? Keep track of connections that seem pertinent; make notes for future reference. Go to the periodical indexes and look for essays that have not been collected, essays that might broaden your sense of your essayist. Begin to formulate an answer to your RTQ; develop a tentative thesis for your short research essay. Remember that your thesis must have the appeal of an idea; it must be interpretive.*

ORGANIZING AND WRITING *Write the first draft of your research essay. Remember that your aim is to interpret your essayist's work, to reveal to your readers what you think is central to that writer's vision. As you write your draft, remember that your readers may know little about your essayist; they will not know enough about any of the essays you cite to fill in gaps that you leave in your explanation about that evidence. Remember, too, that you are writing an essay, not a report or a review that might consider a number of essays one at a time. In your essay, you want to show us how two or three essays make the same pertinent point and how two or three others make a related point. Your task is to make connections, to make sense of a large body of work. You want to let us see what you have discovered about your essayist's central concerns.*

POLISHING *Ask one or two people outside of class to read your initial draft and make comments in the margins. Ask them to mark places where they do not understand what you have written. Ask them, too, to mark places where you have interested them, where they want to know more. Ask them to be especially attentive to the evidence you cite from the essays and to your interpretation of that evidence. You want to make sure they know what you're doing. After reviewing their comments, write out your thesis on a separate sheet of paper; think about it; make sure that it governs everything you're doing in the essay. In light of all these considerations, revise your essay; prepare a polished draft for a group workshop in class.*

WRITING—THE FINAL COPY *Take your notes from the class workshop and plan your final revision. A short conference with your instructor might help you gain a final perspective on your work. Review documentation guidelines in Chapter 2, at the end of this chapter, and in the Appendix.*

E. *A Student's Sequence of Essays—Toward a Broader View of Process*

You have just considered a writing process that can lead you from start to finish as you write a short research essay such as "Back Home." That essay was based almost entirely on *primary* sources, the collected and occasional writings of Reed himself. This section considers a research essay that uses both primary and secondary sources—a paper by Jadran Lee about the essayist George Orwell. (Later we will turn to an entirely different type of research essay, one that uses no primary sources.) In looking at Jadran's essay, we will study more than the stages he went through to write that particular essay. We will focus on a larger process in order to gain insight into how Jadran's other writing in his composition course came into play as he wrote "An Appreciation of George Orwell." We want to examine Jadran's evolution as a writer—to see how one essay led to another, to watch a recursive writing process move to and fro through the entire composition course.

JADRAN LEE'S EVOLVING SENSE OF PERSONA AND STYLE—HIS OWN AND ORWELL'S

We want to consider briefly Jadran Lee's development as a thinker and as a writer, highlighting his writing from the first essay in his composition course to the last. Looking at his earlier work should give you a sense of the developmental process that led eventually to his research essay, "An Appreciation of George Orwell." That process includes much more than the stages necessary to produce a single essay, and it is equally important to his development.

You may recall Jadran's *exploratory* essay about snowboarding that we examined in the Coda to Chapter 3 (p. 161). Two versions of that essay, "Lucky Icarus," are included in the Essays for Additional Reading section (pp. 358 and 361). In the initial writing sequence that led Jadran to write "Icarus," he learned to use and shape his own lived experience, to tell his story in such a way that it would help him develop his *idea* about fear and death and close encounters. Jadran learned—we speculated in the Coda to Chapter 3—by writing an *analytical* essay (the second in the course) about George Orwell's "Shooting an Elephant." We noted that between Version 1 and Version 2 of "Icarus," Jadran learned to create a more reflective persona, one capable of presenting experiences and then commenting on them with hindsight. By so doing, he broadened our perspective on events.

One of the requirements in the writing sequence that led to the final version of "Orwell's 'Shooting an Elephant' " gives us insight into Jadran's development. The requirement asked Jadran to assume that Orwell was alive and to write him a letter about some interesting aspect of "Shooting an Elephant." Here is the first of three paragraphs from that letter; they point back to Jadran's revisions of "Icarus," and they anticipate both the *analytical* essay on "Elephant" and the *research* essay on Orwell that came later in the course. This paragraph from Jadran's letter reflects his evolving interest in Orwell's work, in the notion of persona, and in his own writing:

"Shooting an Elephant" is not a piece I enjoyed; but I do not think you meant us to enjoy it. When I read it I felt myself drawn into the uncomfortable role of the white man with the gun, almost without noticing it. I shared the sense of bewildered nausea you felt about your task as enforcer of an immoral social order. Perhaps the chief reason for my being able to empathize so fully with the young Orwell is your discrete way of detaching yourself from this literary persona in a way that lets us know that what he thought is not enough to convey the full nature of his experience. You are unafraid to break a recollected sequence of thoughts with an idea formulated later. When you first realize that the Burmese are willing to shoot, you insert hindsight by digressing: "Here was I, the white man with his gun, standing in front of an unarmed native crowd. . . ." This technique is effective because thoughts that are not formed but felt constitute an essential aspect of immediate experience.

In this passage from his letter to Orwell, Jadran is beginning to examine Orwell's persona; he's beginning to see how an older Orwell comments on and distances himself from the experiences of a younger, more naive Orwell. He's also beginning to see how Orwell actually detaches himself from his younger self. In his letter, Jadran also comments on Orwell's racial frankness as well as on a recurring stylistic problem of his own:

Your frankness in the matter of your own racial attitudes also strengthens ["Elephant"]. You clearly state your leftist sympathy for "prostrate peoples" at the outset, yet make no attempt to cover the hostile gut reaction you feel against the Burmese. You admit that the diminutive Burmans are to you an alien "sea of yellow faces," "evil-spirited little beasts" who cannot even give clear instructions as to the whereabouts of the elephant. It is this detached, honest exposition of the tension between your political liberality and your xenophobic instincts which provides the real interest of the essay, elevating it far above the obvious allegory in some of your fiction. . . .

Finally, I praise your offhand, dry prose, which is ideally suited to an episode that is so troubling. I know from experience that it is easy to fly into the most unmoving, heady rhetoric when one is moved by one's topic, as you obviously are. . . .

We'll return to Jadran's comments about "heady rhetoric" in a later exercise. For now, let's see how he incorporates these preliminary thoughts from his letter to Orwell in his analytical essay about "Elephant." Here are his first two paragraphs from that essay and an excerpt from the third:

In "Shooting an Elephant," George Orwell draws us into one of his experiences as a British police officer in Burma to give us a compelling view of "the real nature of imperialism—the real motives for which despotic governments act" (188). He shoots an apparently harmless elephant because a Burmese crown wills him to. The sahib cannot but make a show of force because the natives expect it of him. We are led irresistibly to Orwell's conclusion that colonial dominion is futile: "when the white man becomes a tyrant it is his own freedom that he destroys . . . he has got to do what the 'natives' expect of him" (190).

Orwell made me appreciate his unusual point about imperialism largely through techniques that pulled me into near-complete empathy with the younger Orwell of the story. I felt his bewildered nausea and internal struggles as he tried to reconcile himself to the dirty work of empire: the clash of wills between him and the two thousand Burmese; the tension between his political hatred of imperialism and his dislike of the Burmese. When one has shared Orwell's feelings and thoughts throughout the essay, his conclusions follow almost as naturally as one's own.

Perhaps the chief reason for my being able to empathize with the young Orwell is the mature writer's discrete way of detaching himself from his youthful self. Orwell is thus unafraid to break a recollected sequence of thoughts with ideas he must have felt only vaguely at the time; the mind of the mature writer will superimpose itself on that of the young man. This happens most noticeably in Orwell's recounting of the moment when he has to decide whether or not to shoot the elephant. He narrates all of the physical events and tells us how he suddenly realizes that the Burmese crowd's expectations are forcing him to shoot. Then he digresses from that realization to a meditation on the nature of imperialism . . . (190). The calculated insertion of his mature reflections serves two purposes: it provides the essay with a unifying interpretation of a bewildering experience, and at the same time draws us into further empathy with the younger Orwell. It is in a sense paradoxical that when Orwell distances himself from the protagonist, layers his recent thinking on top of that of the perplexed colonial officer, he draws us closer to his younger persona. Yet this technique is highly effective because it allows us to enter Orwell's mind. We watch his memory very naturally blur remembered attitudes and subsequent thinking; so that the past Orwell describes becomes real to us in the same way that our own experience is, for we see both slightly altered by the memory's instinct for simplification and rationalization. We come to share the writer's perspective on his past, a privileged vantage point that allows us to look back on his experience as our own.

Jadran goes on in this analytical essay to praise Orwell for revealing his racial attitudes and for his "pithy prose"; both of those qualities appeal to Jadran and make him more prone to accept Orwell's idea about the misguiding power of imperialism. Jadran's analysis of "Elephant" ends this way:

All the literary techniques discussed here cohere to produce a hypnotic, persuasive essay. Perhaps Orwell never even thought he was using disparate tools; his style, use of imagery, and psychological intentions are so closely intertwined. His goal of drawing us into empathy with him by merging the thoughts of the mature writer with those of the young man—so that we feel ourselves to be remembering the scene rather than reading about it—depends on his perfect frankness. The self-deprecating style also comes as a natural support to this aim, for these are recollections that the writer is not proud of. And the recurrent pictures of the coolie and of laughing Burmans are woven into the fabric of the essay in the same way that a few meaningful, striking images pervade our memories of our own experience.

This effective ending pulls together the various strands of Jadran's essay, reminding us, too, of his interest in Orwell's persona, which is the focal point of the essay. But the ending also points to a minor problem in the essay. Because Jadran discusses a number of what he calls "literary techniques," we often seem to be moving methodically through a list of those techniques as Jadran devotes a paragraph to each. He understands quite well the techniques he discusses, but he doesn't always show us how they work together to create the "drawing" effect that so pleases him about Orwell's essay. Aware of that lingering problem, Jadran sets out to find an idea that would permit him to write a fully integrated research essay about a dozen of Orwell's essays. He would not take up those essays one at a time but would consider them in a more comprehensive way in a polished essay of his own: that was his aim.

ANALYZING   *Go back to the excerpts from Jadran's letter to Orwell. How do those passages change when they appear revised in Jadran's analytical essay? How do you account for those changes? Are they related to audience or to purpose or both? Explain.*

WRITING   *Jadran mentions that "it is easy to fly into the most unmoving, heady rhetoric when one is moved by one's topic." Find two or three instances in the excerpts from Jadran's work that seem to be "heady" and "unmoving" or just difficult to understand. Study them, and then rewrite them so that they are clear, reasonable, and persuasive.*

IMAGINING AND EDITING   *In the third paragraph of Jadran's analytical essay, how might he be more persuasive? How might he make it easier for you to understand his point about the difference between the two Orwells? Could you shorten that paragraph, or might you break it into two? Edit the paragraph in response to these questions.*

JADRAN'S RESEARCH ESSAY — SOME HIGHLIGHTS

Jadran turned quite easily from Orwell's techniques in the analytical essay to Orwell's ideas in the short research essay. For the final course project, Jadran was asked to write an essay similar to the one on Reed (Section D) with the added proviso that he consider secondary sources as well as the primary ones. Orwell has attracted a host of critics.

Jadran's first writing requirement in the sequence was to prepare a short piece based on a close reading of only five of Orwell's essays; the aim of the piece was to identify a central facet of Orwell's imagination, some interesting concern of his that an attentive reader could detect in all the essays. Jadran discovered two aspects of Orwell's imagination that interested him: the political and the moral. In response to the second requirement in the writing sequence, Jadran read several more of Orwell's essays and a few important secondary sources. His reading confirmed his initial hunch that some of Orwell's radical tendencies (deriving largely from his morals) rested uneasily with his conservative political temperament. That uneasiness became the focal point for Jadran's research essay.

Let's consider Jadran's beginning, keeping in mind that he is still interested in Orwell's duality; he's still interested in Orwell's complexity, even though he has wisely dropped the term "persona." He's focusing now on Orwell's mind and his ideas:

In the thirties and forties George Orwell wrote roughly thirty essays, most of which had leftist political content. Some were literary criticism or commentaries on contemporary British culture; others were autobiographical pieces about injustices he had witnessed in coal mines, industrial cities, and overseas colonies. He had "the power of facing unpleasant facts," like hangings and poverty, and a contagious indignation at injustice which made him "the conscience of his generation" (*Essays* 419; qtd. in *Prose Pieces* 171). In an essay entitled "Why I Write," Orwell gave four reasons for which people wrote: sheer egoism, aesthetic enthusiasm, historical impulse, and political purpose; and stated that the last was the most important to him. Yet it would be a grave misreading to see Orwell simply as a political pamphleteer; much of his writing has only tangential bearing on politics. In this paper I shall argue that what he called *political* purpose might better be called moral purpose, and that his aesthetic enthuasiasm and conservative temperament were uneasy with the radicalism that his morals imposed on him.

Jadran goes on from this terse, effective beginning to examine many of Orwell's essays as he lays out the inherent clash between that conservative temperament and the morality that overshadowed his politics. On two occasions in his essay, he plays off his own ideas against the criticism from the secondary sources, but for the most part his effort is focused on his own analysis and his own attempt to bring together Orwell's work in a comprehensive way. These two paragraphs from the middle of his essay give you a sense of his method:

> Orwell's conscience pervades his writing. His best essays derive their strength from the sense of moral urgency with which his conscience imbues recollected experience. "Shooting an Elephant" describes how Orwell, a sahib Burma Police sergeant, feels compelled to kill an apparently harmless beast to make a show of force to the natives. The essay exposes the "futility of the white man's dominion in the East," a dominion which requires foolish and immoral violence to gain grudging acceptance (*Prose Pieces* 190). "How the Poor Die" describes his experience of the atrocious conditions in a Paris hospital. Both essays are highly representative of Orwell because they criticize the status quo on moral grounds; Orwell's hypnotic prose makes us resent British imperialism and Paris poverty, just as a generation earlier *Oliver Twist*

made people hate the poorhouse. There is nothing in most of Orwell's essays which might be called reasoned, prescriptive political argument. Orwell was not a political writer, but a moralist who focused on what bothered his sense of justice in order to make sure it bothers ours too. The vagueness of his political thinking is nowhere better illustrated than in "A Hanging," where we are given a surrealistic account of an execution in Burma and made to feel the nauseating immorality of capital punishment without even an attempt by the author to argue against hangings on anything but impressionistic moral grounds.

Orwell generally did not write as a smug, judgmental prig. He was of the upper class in a nation with what he saw as an unjust colonial empire. He seems as a result to have felt himself to be partially responsible for the misery of the poor and oppressed in England and abroad. This guilt can be inferred from the tense unease of some of his essays, which have the sound of a man unburdening his soul. His essays on imperialism, "Shooting an Elephant," "A Hanging," and "Marrakech" illustrate this best. "Marrakech" differs from the other two in its setting and development; it is a series of reflections and poignant vignettes arising from a stroll through a French North African city. Each essay is a moral attack on imperialism which contains discrete, but unmerciful, self-recrimination. The whole premise of "Shooting an Elephant," that of "the futility of the white man's dominion in the East," rests on his confessed weakness in the face of an expectant Burmese crowd (*Prose Pieces* 190). The essay's analysis of "the real motives for which despotic governments act" demands that Orwell expose his culpable mindset as an officer in the Raj. Hence, he confesses to being glad the elephant had trampled to death a coolie, since this offered a pretext for destroying the elephant. This admission must have tormented Orwell, because the sight and memory of that poor, tortured man is haunting, especially as Orwell recounts it. Similar confessions appear in "Marrakech" and "A Hanging,": *he, the unfeeling European, fails to notice the plight of the Moroccan* women who struggle past his house carrying huge bundles of wood; *he* joins in the ghastly gaiety that follows the hanging in Burma. Orwell felt guilty, and needed to express himself to expiate his guilt: "the wretched prisoners huddling in the stinking cages of the lock-ups, the gray, cowed faces of the long-term convicts, the scarred buttocks of the men who had been flogged with bamboos—all of these oppressed me with an intolerable sense of guilt . . . [furthermore] I had had to think out my problems in the utter silence that is imposed on every Englishman in the East" (*Prose Pieces* 188). Come home to England, he could not remain silent. His writing thus possesses a moral urgency even greater than Dickens's, for Orwell's voice has less of the preacher and more of the intensity of a man crying *mea culpa*.

Orwell wrote with a hair shirt on. . . .

We see from these paragraphs how Jadran uses yet again material from his earlier exercises and essays and how he modifies them for a new purpose. We see, too, how he is learning to look across a number of essays and to find in two or three of them similar ideas. We see Jadran evolving as a writer, a writer at home with ideas and with large bodies of evidence.

ANALYZING, DOCUMENTING *Turn to "An Appreciation of George Orwell" (Essays for Additional Reading section, p. 363). Jadran did not make extensive use of secondary sources, but he did cite works by Jeffrey Meyers and Averil Gardner; both works appear in his bibliography. Go through the essay and see where Jadran cites Meyers and where he cites Gardner. Why does Jadran put Meyers's discussion about the word "smelly" in a note instead of putting it in the text of his essay? Would you prefer it in the text? Why? Jadran uses Gardner in two different ways: (Gardner 132) and (qtd. in Gardner 132). What do those two different citations mean? At the library, check them or any of Jadran's other citations against the original sources. Are you satisfied with the way Jadran cites and uses his sources, or can you improve his method?*

◊

Explain. Jadran also includes this information about two of his sources: (Essays 218; Meyers 63). Look at the sentence in Jadran's essay (p. 369) that goes with this parenthetical documentation *and at his Works Cited list in the bibliography. What does the information in parentheses tell us? Go to the library and check Jadran's accuracy against the Orwell and Meyers texts.*

IMAGINING AND WRITING *Select an established essayist such as Orwell, E. M. Forster, Virginia Woolf, or Annie Dillard; read five or six essays by that essayist, and identify an underlying, unifying concern in the selected essays. Then go to the library and find secondary criticism about the writer—either in a critical book or in reviews or occasional pieces about the writer. Make sure that you select secondary sources that focus on essays rather than on novels or other forms of writing. Imagine, finally, a conversation between you and one or two of the critics. Outline the conversation, showing how you agree and disagree with what they have said about your selected writer. To what extent do those other voices help you come to terms with your evaluation of the writer? Explain. Read five or six more essays. How does your evaluation change in the face of additional primary evidence?*

F. *Another Student Essay—Cross-Disciplinary Applications*

IAN WATSON'S CROSS-DISCIPLINARY APPLICATIONS: AREA CODES AND OTHER CONNECTIONS

As a way of extending our research principles to other projects—as a way of extending the range of this book beyond its fascination with the essay—let's turn to telephone area codes, a topic that seems quite far from the essayist's world. We want to see how, in his composition class, Ian Watson created an essay on a subject as commonplace as area codes and still made use of exploration, enrichment, and analysis—

how he took a workaday subject, researched it, studied it, and gave it new meaning.

Ian had worked up to this subject by writing three other essays. The first was an exploratory one about his visit to the Faeroe Islands, where, in flight from his own values, he rediscovered a need for something distinctly American as he sat around a bare wooden table eating puffins with an island family. The second and third essays were analytical, one about the ironic complexity of the cozy comfort *Yankee* magazine affords its readers and another about the restrictive nature of the MLA system of documentation. As it turned out, these were warm-up pieces for his essay on area codes. But in writing them, he learned that the essay itself—its changing, malleable shape—could accommodate his way of thinking and that within the essay's structure, he could create his own. He found a playground for his lively imagination.

Ian had been thinking about area codes for some time, interested as he is in systems: computer systems, value systems, numbering systems, lettering systems, linguistic systems—any system that tries to impose order, and therefore meaning, on the world we live in. As kids he and his friends had played area-code games with each other. Ian admitted that he was prone to imagine a regional personality, one tied to an area code. "Oh, you're from 501, probably a country boy who doesn't mind dragging his feet in the mud, or an Ozark mountain woman used to defining herself against a bunch of rednecks." Ian's is a quirky scientific mind colored by the imagination of a poet. He likes making odd sense out of the commonplace.

The research for this project began in the library with a conversation between him and someone on the library staff. That conversation led him to a couple of technical pieces on area codes; those pieces led to others, as they often do. Research is generative. He spent some time in a large public library looking at old telephone books so that he could trace firsthand the evolution of area codes. But as you can see from his Works Cited list, his sources were limited. The sources gave him the facts about how area codes were set up and how they had to be modified as needs changed, but he developed an idea of his own; his thinking created the essay. The sources gave him the foundation he needed to understand area codes. They set his mind to work.

We want to look now at parts of Ian's product, parts of the essay itself, instead of at the research process that led to it; his process is implicit in the product. Reading "Equilibrium and Exhaustion" (Essays for Additional Reading section, p. 372), we can guess about the other things Ian had to do, the additional research and reading he had to do to prepare himself to write the essay. We can always guess that about any essay, if we take the time; the work and the life and the values are always there behind the words, no matter what the subject.

Here's Ian's introduction:

There are children starving in Northern Botswana. The continental shelf is wearing away and New Jersey is going to slip into the ocean. The icebergs are melting and soon Hawaii will become a chain of underwater seamounts. The Russians are planting anti-American triple megaphasers in the Arctic icecap. And America is running out of area codes.

Yes, it's true. There are only five area codes left on the North American Numbering Plan. They will be exhausted by 1995 or 1996. One day, every idealist in America, dutifully working their lives away fighting homelessness, nuclear proliferation, discriminatory college admissions policies, the slaughter of baby harp seals, and all those horribly imminent natural catastrophes, will wake up and find out that they can't call each other. The phone system will be completely paralyzed from sheer overload, and just picking up the handset will throw your phone into jerking, twitching spasms and seizures. People will rush out into the streets to console each other as they watch the coherence, the structure, the security of America melt and slither away into vast existential nothingness.

Well, maybe it won't work quite like that. Enough people have been thinking about area codes to have formulated a plan to deal with area code exhaustion. These are the prescient few who have realized that area codes are as much of a pressing social problem as computer viruses or saturated fat, and certainly much less trendy. And perhaps America's well-meaning social activists should pay a little more attention to area codes, because they use them every day whenever they dial long distance, which is certainly more often than they get face-to-face with a drum of disposable nuclear waste. Maybe the basic structural systems that we take for granted every day, like area codes, are no less important than the latest horrifying social concern on the cover of *Time* or *Newsweek.*

As a matter of fact, the problem of area code exhaustion leads us into a whole way of thinking about systems of organization and identification. You see, when we run out of area codes, something is going to have to change in the telephone system, some rule that used to restrict the phone system in some way that made sense. In the case of area codes, the rule that now says that their second digit has to be a zero or a one will be eliminated. If and when we run out of area codes again, some other restriction will have to be changed. What we see here is that to keep any system working, we must always strike a balance between the idea of exhaustion—an inexorable process in the case of telephones, since there will always be more and more customers—and the rules and conventions that give sense and order to the system. Even in something seemingly trivial like area codes, we see the importance of compromise and balance. And that's not trivial at all.

Let's see if we can go back to a notion we considered near the beginning of this chapter, the notion that thesis and idea are not strange bedfellows. The *thesis* of Ian's piece is sitting right there where it ought to be, near the end of the last paragraph of the essay's *beginning*: "What we see here is that to keep any system working, we must always strike a balance between the idea of exhaustion—an inexorable process in the case of telephones, since there will always be more and more customers—and the rules and conventions that give sense and order to the system." We know from looking at that thesis that it's fraught with danger. Ian could spend the rest of his life writing about the way "we must always strike a balance between the idea of exhaustion . . . and the rules and conventions that give sense and order to the system," and he could never prove his point conclusively: there would always be another system to analyze, another possibility that might disprove his thesis. But it is precisely this danger, precisely this logician's nightmare, precisely this uncertainty, that makes Ian's proposition so interesting, so worthy of an essay—a try, if you will. And that's not all.

Ian takes on more because he sees this problem of exhaustion in a much larger cultural context; he has an *idea* about the importance of this matter, and he reminds us of it in the final sentences of his beginning: "Even in something seemingly trivial like area codes, we see the importance of compromise and balance. And that's not trivial at all." With those two sentences, Ian enlarges his contract. It will not be enough just to show us how the area-code system works, how its own rules become inadequate over time, how they lead to exhaustion, how those rules must be changed, modified, to keep the phones working; Ian must also show us how other systems exhaust them-selves, and finally (because of those last two sentences of the begin-ning), he must show us why the "compromise and balance" so necessary to a system's operation are "not trivial at all."

Let's see how Ian manages to present his case, as we occasionally listen in on his *conversations* when he tries to talk us through all of these complexities. The first section of the middle of his essay focuses on the history of the area-code system. What he does in this section is tell us the story of how area codes came into being in the first place. But he does more: he tells us how they had to change over time to serve the needs of more and more people; how they had to change to accommo-date an overseas audience; how even now, after all of those changes, the current system faces exhaustion. His story follows a natural, chronological progression, but it's not just a story told for its own sake, not just a straightforward historical account of what happened.

Ian has his mind on *why* it happened and why it will continue to happen, and he keeps reminding us about exhaustion and equilibrium as he lays out quite lucidly the complex intricacies of the area-code system. Wrapping up that story, summing it up, Ian moves us into the second of the two major sections of his essay:

> The conclusion from this mathematical sort of give-and-take is, then, that anything that makes the telephone numbering plan sensible also limits its development, and that this is an example of an equilibrium forced by the necessity to make hard choices so that our telephone networks will be able to function understandably.
>
> Now comes the fun part, because with knowledge of the compromises in the phone system we can go on to apply what we've learned to a whole lot of other systems in the world. But first we need to go through several different types of sense-making to get an idea of the terms we're dealing with. The best way to do this is with a purely theoretical example:
>
> Let's say we are making a city and we want to number every street in it. The freest way would be to pick an arbitrary number for each street. There would be no restrictions on length or relation to any other street number. So one street could be called 4 and the next one over called 356812 and a cross-street 67. We would never run out of numbers and we would never see an end to our system.
>
> Unfortunately, that sort of numbering plan doesn't satisfy people's need for order. It is easier for people to work within a system—in this case, to find their way around the streets of the city—if they have some secure base of reference. For instance, we could number our streets from one on, starting with the very first street and working on up. The basis of our system would then be *chronology.* Or we could number our streets according to what sector of the city they are in. So we could have Sector 4, Street 17, and we might write it as 4/17 Street. Washington's street system works like this. A simpler form of this *geographical relevance* system is something like New York's numbered streets and ave-

nues. Geographical relevance is a specific case of *general relevance,* in which *discrete levels of significance* such as the two levels of the hierarchy Sector Number–Street Number stand for the relevant concrete entities (the sector and the street). We might also find that for reference purposes, or perhaps for purposes of simpler computer storage, it's easier to have all our street numbers be of a uniform, predictable length—like two numbers. This would be a *closed-length* system. Each of these italicized features is one of many ways to make a system sensible.

The problem that we will see is that anything that makes a system make sense also limits it, because the real world tends not to always fit in the nice square boxes that we create for it. If we number a system chronologically, what happens when one street is demolished to create a shopping mall, or when we find that we've forgotten to number a street because it was so small and insignificant? When we have sequentially numbered, geographically related (e.g., parallel) streets, what happens when we stick another street in between them? We get something weird and unstable like Forty-Three-and-a-Half Street. And what happens when we have a closed-length system that consists of three digits from 0 to 9 and suddenly we find out that we have more than 1,000 things to number—that our system has been *exhausted?* This problem of exhaustion is the most critical one in an age when world population and its technological reverberations such as telephone networks, postal systems, and automobile registration have been multiplying at an exponential rate. What we are always forced to do is change the systems that once made sense to us to accommodate the increased use that will always come through population and technological growth. Yet at the same time we must make sure that we don't destroy the sensibility that makes these systems usable. We return, in the abstract this time, to the notion of a settled equilibrium between competing forces in a system.

We can almost hear Ian's concern for us as readers; he's talking us through a complex process, writing like a good teacher who wants to make sure we're following the play of his mind. His aim here is to win us over to his notion about other systems: the street numbering system, the zip-code system, the automobile registration system, the national interstate highway numbering plan. Ian doesn't write exhaustively about each of these systems, but as he develops his argument, he points always to exhaustion and equilibrium; he writes enough about these selected systems to make us know that he understands how they were set up, how they operate, how they must be changed as the world changes. What he makes us begin to see is how much our lives are affected by these systems—and we are reminded, without his having to tell us, how little consideration we give to them. As an essayist, Ian seems to know that he must keep our attention focused on his thesis, so he never strays very far afield; we're always looking directly at a system and its far-reaching implications. Here's the way he focuses our attention at the end of the second major section of the essay; here, too, is his *ending*:

I expect that every other identification system you will come across will work similarly. Vehicle identification numbers, Social Security numbers, two-letter airline and three-letter airport codes, bank account numbers, license plates, library cataloguing systems—they're all subject to the same problems.[15] We build these things up and try to make them make sense to ourselves—even a five-year-old can learn to use the telephone—and then slowly their limits become apparent and we see how they will break down, and then they do break down, and we have to find something else.

We could take the concept of systems equilibrium further into the snowy mountains of philosophical thought, discuss its relationship to dialectical materialism and change through Darwinian gradualism, derive and construct an ideal model of social change based originally on change in theoretical systems of identification, and then reapply that into the social concerns that were satirized at the beginning of this discussion. We're not going to do that. It would be too alarmingly Marxist and philosophically pompous. We could also try to say that whether it is telephone systems, zip codes, fossil fuel reserves, alternative education, baby harp seals, or Amazonian rain forests, we're all dealing with fairly similar problems: always there is inevitable change, and we must react to it, and somebody trying to solve the problems of the environment or of society should look to the clear-cut mathematical simplicity of area codes and their kin for ideas on how to fix things out in the real world. We're not going to do that either. In the real world many problems are complicated metasystems, the simple models that we have seen in identification systems are overlaid with all sorts of messy stuff that obscures their real usefulness, and even those few masters who understand the interacting, competing forces haven't got the power to set them right. What I really want to say is that thinking critically about technological trivia is not dry, not trivial, not uninteresting, and not a rejection of our supposed moral and ethical duty to do whatever is currently moral and ethical. *Right now America simply would not function without well-managed area codes.* Planning them, and watching them settle and work properly, is no less valuable than helping the homeless, saving the whales, or considering the great moral questions of Life. And it's perhaps more satisfying, because we can sit back at the end and say, "It works; it's an endless battle to keep the system happy, but at least we know we can do it."

ANALYZING *Consider within your class discussion group whether Ian's ending is effective and whether he manages in his essay to fulfill all of those contract elements that we considered earlier. To answer the question about the essay's overall effectiveness, you might want to study the entire essay. What part do you think his Notes play in his presentation?*

WRITING *Write Ian a short note, 200 to 300 words, telling him what you liked most about his essay. Identify any points in his essay where you would like to have more information, and at the end of your note, tell him, in your own words, what you think his idea is in this essay.*

WRITING   *In another short note, classify Ian's essay. Is it exploratory, analytical, argumentative? Is it something else? Explain.*

WRITING   *Write an essay that will replace Ian's essay in the second edition of this book. Write about something commonplace, something taken from the workaday world, something interesting. Ian said one of his teachers told him that for a subject to be interesting, it had to be susceptible to further analysis. . . like an idea, perhaps. See if you can find something going on in the world you live in that will be susceptible to further analysis even when you have finished your essay. Write that essay to get the analysis started.*

G.   *Guidelines for Future Research*

The general principles outlined in earlier sections of this chapter underscore the process that led to each essay. Critical, exploratory reading lies at the back of the research process. You read to discover, but you also read to test tentative hypotheses, hunches. The sooner you can narrow your topic, the sooner you can begin to do directed reading. Find your controversy as quickly as possible, and begin to restrict your topic.

Be open to authorities; consult them freely. You will not normally need to call editors and researchers away from your college or university, but on occasion there may be a compelling need to do so. Teachers, other professors, and members of the library staff will generally be glad to answer your calls for assistance. Consult the experts on your subject after you have done enough research to be thoroughly conversant with your topic. Remember, too, that these are busy people; if you decide to consult one, make an appointment and be prepared to do your work with that person expeditiously.

Keep your restricted topic question (RTQ) in your mind's eye at all times. Focus your effort, but work open-mindedly. Continue to pose questions for yourself that anticipate your audience's questions. Do not skirt the difficult questions. Continue reading. Follow clues and trust your intuition. Develop an efficient system for taking notes. If you use an informal system, discuss it with your teacher, who may want to review your notes on occasion.

When you develop your writing strategy, do so with your audience in mind. Make good assumptions about what the audience will know about your topic and what you have to tell them so that they can understand your findings. Try not to leave gaps in your explanations. Always assume that your readers are skeptical but interested. The burden of proof and of explanation lies with you, not with your readers. After you have written a good draft, give it to several other people to read. Ask them to put question marks in the manuscript where they are confused. What you want from them is a clear indication about sections of the paper that need further development. Write your draft far enough ahead of time so that you can put it aside for a few days. Go back to it with a fresh mind. Try to read it as an editor would—from a distance, with interest but unwillingness to fill in the gaps.

Remember that revision is not simply a matter of going back through your paper to correct grammatical errors or to answer questions your readers have asked. You might very well write several versions of your paper before you decide how to develop your final version. Those early efforts may help you clarify certain difficulties. In working on your final version, you may have to discover ways to combine those preliminary efforts.

Always be willing to consider rearranging your paper after you have gotten feedback from other readers. You may have misjudged the way your audience would react. Often you can solve problems by reorganizing, by presenting the evidence in a way that seems more logical to your readers. Always keep in mind your major writing tasks: what to put in, what to leave out, how to shape the material. Work on these tasks with your audience in mind. Remember that you will not be able to prove your thesis; you are dealing with controversy. You are trying to develop the best answer to the question under consideration, on the basis of your assessment of the available evidence.

Revision may mean shortening your draft. Try to shorten your paper even when you are adding material to fill gaps readers have noticed. Although shortening while adding sounds like a contradiction, it really isn't. When you go back to read your writing, shorten or eliminate sentences. Often you can cut entire paragraphs that were written while you were exploring, searching for an answer by writing down preliminary ideas and supporting them with evidence gathered during research. Or you can make those paragraphs more direct during revision. Cutting whole paragraphs can lead to a clearer, more direct presentation of an idea.

Check thoroughly all of your quotations. Make sure they are accurate. Consult the style manual. Your teacher will normally specify the style manual. The essays in this book (except those written by the professional essayists) should conform to *The MLA Style Manual*, 1985. Other manuals in common use are *Publication Manual of the American Psychological Association, The Chicago Manual of Style*, and *A Manual for Writers of Term Papers, Theses, and Dissertations*.

THINKING AND PLANNING *Turn to Bernd Heinrich's essay "The Thesis Hunt" (Essays for Additional Reading section, p. 387). As you read the essay, make a list of the various steps in the process that led Heinrich to his thesis. Compare that list with our "Guidelines." How do the two processes differ, and how are they the same? To what extent are those differences a function of the scientific basis of Heinrich's research? What do you think Heinrich means at the very end of his essay by "the long struggle of ideas"?*

◊

H. *A Coda—Thoughts on Development*

The Reed essay and those essays by Jadran and Ian reflect this book's major lesson: writing and reading and thinking are always exploratory, just as they are always analytical. We see from those essays that the distinctions between the various *forms* of the essay become less and less critical as your argumentative essays draw their sustenance from exploratory research and from rigorous, analytical thinking. Neither disciplined directness nor the call for objectivity need mask a lively, inquisitive mind. The essay need never be flat and unimaginative.

As you become more adept at exploration, analysis, and argument, your most important imaginative task may very well be to decide how to combine characteristics of the three forms to serve a particular need. You have a sense of your options now, and you know what it means to ramble under the influence of a willful curiosity, what it means to let your mind reach out and make those connections that both surprise and convince your readers, just as you know what it means to be more direct and forceful in your analysis. You know, too, how to meet your listener on the front porch swing or in the chambers of the municipal courthouse. Your task, the most pleasing writer's task of all, will be to design and tailor each of your essays, searching always for another way to give your readers the pleasure of a fine idea.

Appendix

MLA
DOCUMENTATION
—
A
SHORT
GUIDE

A. *Documentation Guidelines—*
What They Mean, How to Apply Them

A CROSS-REFERENTIAL SYSTEM

Your *documentation* within an essay lets your readers know what you have borrowed from primary and secondary sources and incorporated into your own written work. You must document your sources—whether the borrowed material is quoted, paraphrased, or summarized—for two very important reasons: you want to give credit always for someone else's words, ideas, programs, conclusions, or rationale; *and* your readers want to know your sources so that they can do additional research, extending the range and depth of their own inquiries as well as yours. In short, you document your sources to give credit where credit is due and to provide helpful information for other researchers and writers.

There are a number of manuals that provide guidance for documentation: *The MLA Style Manual, Publication Manual of the American Psychological Association, The Chicago Manual of Style,* and *A Manual for Writers of Term Papers, Theses, and Dissertations.* In this textbook, we rely on the documentation guidelines formulated by the Modern Language Association and published in *The MLA Style Manual.*

The MLA guidelines suggest that you use *parenthetical documentation* within the text of your essay as the primary means for citing your sources. This parenthetical method replaces traditional footnotes and endnotes, and it eliminates much of the duplication of information that was inherent in the older method. With parenthetical documentation, sources are identified within parentheses in the text of your essay, as they are in this excerpt from a paragraph in progress:

```
In "Anonymity: An Enquiry," E. M. Forster tells us
that "each human mind has two personalities, one on
the surface, one deeper down. The upper personality
has a name" (Two Cheers 83). The lower does not.
Forster goes on to argue that there is something
special about the deeper personality and that if
writers do not tap into it occasionally, they will
never produce "first-class work" (83).
```

The information within the parentheses—(*Two Cheers* 83) and (83)—identifies the book and page number where Forster's words and ideas actually appear. Yet what you see within the parentheses is not a complete citation; it is a shorthand notation, based on *conventions* established by the MLA.

What you see within parentheses makes little sense unless you understand those conventions. The information within parentheses points your reader to the *bibliography* of your paper; the bibliography and the parenthetical information refer to and supplement one another. In the paragraph about Forster, the information within parentheses tells your reader that you have cited material from Forster's book *Two Cheers for Democracy;* the quoted and summarized material comes from page 83 of that collection of essays. The bibliography at the end of your essay would contain a section called "Works Cited"; that section would include the following entry:

```
                  Works Cited
Forster, E. M. Two Cheers for Democracy. New York:
     Harvest-Harcourt, 1951.
```

Subsequent citations in the same paragraph need not include *Two Cheers* within parentheses when it is clear from your essay that you are still referring to the same book. But if there can be any doubt in your reader's mind, repeat the information. You—and you alone—are responsible for making clear the source of your cited material.

Information that you provide in the text of your essay need not be repeated within parentheses. Notice, for example, that in the excerpted paragraph, the writer told you that Forster's words came from an essay entitled "Anonymity: An Enquiry." (Titles of essays always appear in quotation marks; titles of books are always underlined or in italics.) Because the writer named the essay within the paragraph, the essay's title need not be repeated within parentheses. Had the title of the essay been omitted in the paragraph, the documentation might have appeared this way:

```
E. M. Forster tells us that "each human mind has two
personalities, one on the surface, one deeper down.
The upper personality has a name" ("Anonymity,"
Two Cheers 83). The lower does not. Forster goes on
to argue that there is something special about the
deeper personality and that if writers do not tap
```

```
into it occasionally, they will never produce
"first-class work" (83).
```

If the title of the essay were not within the text or within the parentheses, the reader would have to refer to the Works Cited list and then to the book itself to find that title. As a writer, you have to decide how much you want to give your reader. Too many parenthetical references that are too long clutter up the text of your essay, so you have to strike a balance between what is essential and what your readers might like to know as they read your essay. Within parentheses, always use short titles for both the essay and the book; select a word or two from each complete title that will make it easy for your reader to locate the source in the Works Cited section of your bibliography.

Occasionally, you will find that what you need to know about the format for citing a source does not appear in *The MLA Style Manual* or in an Appendix such as this one. In that case you have to use your best judgment, following as closely as possible the conventions that do apply. Your watchword should always be *consistency*. Make a decision that is in keeping with the guidelines and stick with it.

Let's consider an actual problem that I had to solve in the text of this book, a problem related to those essays in Chapter 4 that included citations from a number of different essays by the same author; many of those essays were from a single collection of that author's essays. The problem I faced was twofold: how to minimize the parenthetical clutter within the text of the essay and at the same time provide important source information for the reader. If I had followed the MLA guidelines to the letter, every entry in the text for an essay from *Looking for Hogeye* would have appeared this way: (Reed 26), or this: (Reed, *Hogeye* 26), or this: (*Hogeye* 26), or this ("Spring," *Hogeye* 26), depending on what other information I provided outside the parentheses in my essay on Reed. I could not use (Reed   ) every time because there were other Reed items in the bibliography; just citing his name with a page number would not lead the reader to the correct text. I also wanted to avoid repeating *Hogeye* over and over, and yet I wanted my reader to know the particular essay of Reed's that I was citing. I was trying to meet competing demands: one for brevity, another for source information that would be helpful to my reader.

I decided to name within my text each of the Reed essays that I cited, just as I have done here in this Appendix with the paragraph on Forster. But in the Works Cited section of the bibliography for my essay on Reed, I treated *Hogeye,* a *collection* of essays, as if it were an *anthology*. Anthologies, of course, usually contain various kinds of material—poems, essays, stories, articles. The convention for an anthology entry in the Works Cited list is to give the name of the individual essay, poem, story, or article as part of the documentation; you must also include the editor's name, if there is one. Here is an example:

```
                    Works Cited
Garrett, George. "My Two One-Eyed Coaches." The
     Best American Essays 1988. Ed. Annie Dillard
     and Robert Atwan. New York: Ticknor, 1988.
     141-161.
```

This entry tells you that Garrett's essay "Coaches" appears on pages 141–161 in an anthology entitled *The Best American Essays 1988.* The anthology was edited by Annie Dillard and Robert Atwan and published by Ticknor & Fields.

Treating *Looking for Hogeye* as an anthology allowed me to provide important source information at a quick glance (both in my essay and in the bibliography), and at the same time, this approach allowed me to keep the text of the essay itself uncluttered. Let's consider a sample paragraph from an early draft of my text and the appropriate entries from the Works Cited list:

```
     In two of Reed's essays, he gives us a pretty
good sense of his family background and how he feels
```

about it. He claims to be "trash"--"country
trash" to be more exact. According to Reed, the
trash are survivors. They have a developed sense of
community because they are outsiders. They either
take care of themselves, or they perish. No one else
cares about them ("Country" 20). Reed likes them
because they are ornery and tough, but he likes them
too because they have a sense of humor, know how to
survive during the hard times (22). The trash do not
care much for outsiders, and when Reed's son decides
to marry an Ulster Catholic, Reed decides to write a
letter to his own Great-Grandfather to give him a
sense of how the family line has been faring since
his death ("Letter" 131).

Works Cited

Reed, Roy. "The Country." <u>Looking for Hogeye.</u>
    Fayetteville: Arkansas UP, 1986. 10-24.
    [Additional essays from this collection are
    also cited within the text:]
    "A Letter to My Great-Grandfather." 117-132.

There is no authority in *The MLA Style Manual* for my decision to treat
a collection of essays as an anthology; nor is there an example of a
Works Cited section exactly like this one, where I list additional essays
from the collection in an abbreviated form. But *The MLA Style
Manual* does associate collections with anthologies. So in the interest
of solving a documentation problem peculiar to a particular kind of
research essay, I made a decision that minimizes clutter in the text,
provides within-the-text source information at a glance, makes it easy
to locate the essay *and* the title of the collection in the Works Cited list,
and eliminates unnecessary duplication of the Works Cited entries.
Your editor or your teacher will be the final arbiter about a matter of

this kind. The example, nevertheless, raises a pertinent question: What do you do when the MLA guidelines seem inadequate for the particular problem that you have to solve? Answer: Consider the guidelines, make a decision, and be consistent.

TYPICAL EXAMPLES—PARENTHETICAL ENTRIES AND WORKS CITED

A Book

When you refer to a book by an author who appears only once in your bibliography, you need to include only the writer's last name and the page number in parentheses within the text of your essay:

```
(Forster 165)
```

The entry in the Works Cited list should include three elements: author, title, and publishing information:

```
Forster, E. M. Aspects of the Novel. New York: Har-
     vest-Harcourt, 1951.
```

If you cite two sources by Forster within your essay, you must in some way distinguish one from the other. If in the text of your essay you say, "In *Two Cheers for Democracy,* Forster argues that 'each human mind has two personalities,'" your parenthetical documentation should be "(83)." But if you say in one place, "E. M. Forster argues that 'each human mind has two personalities,'" and you say in another, "Forster contends that even when a book seems to have no 'external shape,' we can see that it 'hangs together because it is stitched internally, because it contains rhythms,'" you need to distinguish Forster's two sources one from the other: "(*Two Cheers* 83)" and "(*Aspects* 165)." Within the text of your essay, the documentation should appear this way:

E. M. Forster argues that "each human mind has two personalities" (<u>Two Cheers</u> 83). Forster goes on to suggest that there is something special about a writer's deeper personality. He believes that if writers do not tap into the deeper personality occasionally while they're writing, they will never produce "first-class work" (83).

In a subsequent paragraph in the same essay:

Forster contends that even when a book seems to have no "external shape," we can see that it "hangs together because it is stitched internally, because it contains rhythms" (<u>Aspects</u> 165). When he talks about rhythms, he has Proust and Beethoven on his mind, and he's trying to ascribe musical qualities to certain novels.

The Works Cited list should include these two entries:

Forster, E. M. <u>Aspects of the Novel</u>. New York: Harvest-Harcourt, 1955.

---. <u>Two Cheers for Democracy</u>. New York: Harvest-Harcourt, 1951.

In a Works Cited list, works are arranged alphabetically by the author's last name or by the first significant word of the title when the author is unknown. If there are two or more works by the same author, they are arranged alphabetically by the first significant word of each title. You should not repeat the author's name for each entry following the first one. Instead, use "---." for subsequent entries.

A Work in an Anthology with an Editor

When citing a work from an anthology, give the author of the work, the title of the work, the title of the anthology, the editor of the anthology, and publishing information. The last element of the entry gives the inclusive page numbers for the work cited, not just the pages from which you borrowed information:

```
White, E. B. "The Ring of Time." Literature: Read-
     ing Fiction, Poetry, Drama, and the Essay. Ed.
     Robert DiYanni. New York: Random, 1986. 1414-
     1418.
```

Within the text, your parenthetical reference could read this way, if this is the only work by White that you are citing:

```
(White 1415)
```

If there are other works by White taken from other sources, the parenthetical information could look this way if, within your own text, you identify White as the writer of the cited material:

```
("Ring" 1415)
```

An Article in a Periodical

When citing an article in a periodical, give the author, the title of the article, the title of the periodical, the series number or name, if there is a series, the volume number, the date of publication, and the inclusive page numbers. The second citation in this entry shows how to document an essay that has been reprinted in a second source:

```
Sanders, Scott. "The Singular First Person." The
     Sewanee Review 96 (1988): 658-672. Rpt. in
     Essays on the Essay: Redefining the Genre. Ed.
```

```
Alexander J. Butrym. Athens: Georgia UP,
    1989. 31-42.
```

Within the text:

```
(Sanders 659)
```

A Newspaper Article

When citing an article in a newspaper, give the author, the title of the article, the name of the newspaper, the date, and the page number; the plus sign after the page number indicates that the article continues on scattered pages:

```
Reed, Roy. "In an English Village, Bells Toll the
    Dying of Old Ways." New York Times 17 Apr.
    1978: B1+.
```

Within the text:

```
(Reed B10)
```

A Work in More than One Volume

The volume comes after the title:

```
Parker, William R. Milton: A Biography. 2 vols. Ox-
    ford: Clarendon, 1968.
```

Within the text:

```
(Parker 1:63)
```

A Recording

In the Works Cited list:

Beethoven, Ludwig van. Symphony no. 7 in A, op. 92.
    Cond. Herbert von Karajan. Vienna Philhar-
    monic Orch. London, STS 15107, 1966.

Within the text:

(Beethoven)

A Movie
In the Works Cited list:

Citizen Kane. Dir. Orson Welles. RKO. 1941.

Within the text:

(Citizen Kane)

A Poem
In the Works Cited list:

Lawrence, D. H. "Whales Weep Not!" D. H. Lawrence:
    Selected Poems. Ed. Kenneth Rexroth. New
    York: Penguin, 1957. 133–135.

Within the text:

(Lawrence 134)

An Interview
In the Works Cited list:

Sommers, Nancy. Telephone Interview. 7 Sept. 1990.

Within the text:

(Sommers Interview)

A Play
In the Works Cited list:

Shakespeare, William. <u>King Lear. Shakespeare: The
    Complete Works</u>. Ed. G. B. Harrison. New York:
    Harcourt, 1968.

Within the text:

(<u>Lear</u> IV.vi.162)

Be as specific as possible in the parenthetical text reference: act, scene, page.

A Lecture
In the Works Cited list:

Wolfe, Tom. "The Meaning of Freedom." The 14th Sol
    Feinstone Lecture. West Point, New York,
    8 Oct. 1986.

Within the text:

(Wolfe)

You can find documentation examples for other sources in *The MLA Style Manual* or in handbooks.

B. *Citing Sources—Quoting or Summarizing*

No matter what form of the essay you're writing—exploratory, analytical, or argumentative—you must decide whether to quote or summarize material from your sources. There is no hard-and-fast rule, but a general guideline is to use few block quotations—quotations of more than four typed lines that must be set off from your own text (that is, indented an additional five spaces and blocked). Block quotations are double-spaced like the rest of the essay, and *they do not require quotation marks.* Here is a passage that lets you see how to combine a block quotation, a straight summary, and a summary with quoted phrases. Note that with the blocked material, the parentheses and page number go outside the final period (this is only the case with block quotations):

In "Anonymity: An Enquiry," E. M. Forster tells us
that "each human mind has two personalities, one on
the surface, one deeper down. The upper personality
has a name" (<u>Two Cheers</u> 83). The lower does not:

> It has something in common with all other
> deeper personalities, and the mystic will
> assert that the common quality is God. . . .
> It is in any case the force that makes for an-
> onymity. . . . The poet wrote the poem, . . .
> but he forgot himself while he wrote it, and
> we forget him while we read. (84)

Forster sounds a bit like T. S. Eliot in an early essay about impersonality. Eliot compares the poet's
mind to a "shred of platinum" and calls to our attention a creative force that is somehow apart from
the poet himself. The poet's mind, like the "shred
of platinum," is a "transforming catalyst" that
converts feelings and emotions into a work of art

```
(Eliot 41). That mind, according to Eliot, acts
almost independently of the man himself.
```

Instead of quoting extensively, as this writer did with Forster, always consider quoting only the most telling phrases, as this writer did with Eliot. Try to select phrases that convey the essence of the source you are citing. Whether you are quoting or summarizing (reducing material from the source to the essence, in your own words), you must document what you have cited. Your reader will want to know the source and the page number for everything that you have included in your essay from that source. Your Works Cited list would include these two entries:

```
Eliot, T. S. "Tradition and the Individual Tal-
     ent." Selected Prose of T. S. Eliot. Ed. Frank
     Kermode. New York: Harcourt, 1975. 37-49.

Forster, E. M. Two Cheers for Democracy. New York:
     Harvest-Harcourt, 1951.
```

C. *Documenting the Exploratory Essay—A Slight Variation*

THE TECHNIQUE OF INCORPORATION

The rigorous scholarly work associated with both the analytical and the argumentative essay calls for the kind of precise documentation that we are considering in this Appendix. The exploratory essay generally calls for something different. Rarely do such essays have page numbers within the text or a Works Cited list at the end. Nevertheless, the writer of an exploratory essay must also give credit where credit is due. The obligation to acknowledge sources applies there as well as in the other forms of the essay. The most effective way to give that credit is to write it into the text of the essay in a way that is consistent with the style of the passage where it appears:

> Years later, after Vietnam, after my father's death, when I finally turned my mind south again, I began to understand what Allen Tate meant in "A Southern Mode of the Imagination" about the change that took place after World War I, the change that turned the southern mind inward, causing it to "shift from rhetoric to dialectic," creating what he later characterized as a "literature of introspection" rather than a "literature of romantic illusion." I was not the "old Southern <u>rhetor</u>, the speaker who was eloquent before the audience but silent in himself." Rummaging around inside my head, I was discovering my heritage, recovering lost remnants of masculinity, developing a sense of irony.

A reader wanting to locate Tate's essay in a larger collection of essays could not do so from the citation within this paragraph, but the writer of an essay of this type has no inherent obligation to provide such information; the writer's obligation is to give credit where credit is due. This writer does just that.

On occasion you can find an exploratory essay in an anthology or collection of essays that includes a Works Cited list at the end, but such a list is an exception rather than the rule. It is nevertheless a good idea for students to include a Works Cited list at the end of an exploratory essay that includes material from sources. Again, your teacher or your editor will be the arbiter in these cases.

FURTHER RHETORICAL CONSIDERATIONS

The technique we have just considered for writing your source information into your essay can be used to good advantage in analytical and argumentative essays. For one thing, as we have already seen, you often reduce what needs to be put within parentheses when you include the name of the author and the title of the book or article or essay within the text of your essay. For another, you gain a certain rhetorical advantage by being as specific as possible within your essay. Finally, by naming the book's title or the essay's, you might even add clarity to your own paragraph. Let's consider again the passage about the southern imagination. But this time, let's look at the passage without the title of Tate's essay:

> Years later, after Vietnam, after my father's death, when I finally turned my mind south again, I began to understand what Allen Tate meant about the change that took place after World War I, the change that turned the southern mind inward, causing it to "shift from rhetoric to dialectic," creating what he later characterized as a "literature of intro-spection" rather than a "literature of romantic illusion." I was not the "old Southern <u>rhetor</u>, the speaker who was eloquent before the audience but si-lent in himself." Rummaging around inside my head, I was discovering my heritage, recovering lost remnants of masculinity, developing a sense of irony.

Taking out the title of the essay strips this passage of some of its authority; that's especially true if you as a reader do not know that Allen Tate is an important southern writer whose critical essays and critical theories about literature are held in high esteem by many scholars. But whether you know Tate or not, the title and the author's name in combination convey a certain authority. In the case of this essay of Tate's, the title—"A Southern Mode of the Imagination"—prepares you for the rest of the paragraph about the southern imagination and a southern way of thinking. Tate's words, the quoted passages themselves, clarify aspects of that southern frame of mind, giving you the essence of Tate's argument. They also establish a context for this writer's claim: he is telling you that he is not silent within himself; he is not the "old Southern *rhetor.*" So the name, the title, and the selected passages suggest authority and help clarify the writer's claim. If readers know of Tate's critical reputation, this writer may gain even more of a persuasive advantage with his readers. But the point is this: leaving nothing more than Tate's name and the title of his essay out of this passage diminishes its effectiveness.

There is a second point worth repeating. This technique of writing the sources into the text of your essay will stand you in good stead for analytical and argumentative essays too. Write in that authority (the writer's name and the title of the specific essay or book), and all you have left to include within parentheses for those essays is a page number. To make the Tate passage suitable for a scholarly essay, you need only add appropriate page numbers within parentheses and include this entry in a Works Cited list:

Tate, Allen. <u>Essays for Four Decades</u>. Chicago:
    Swallow, 1968.

The differences—as far as documentation is concerned—between the various forms of the essays are few: page numbers within parentheses and Works Cited list. Rhetorical considerations vary from essay to essay depending on purpose and style. Fundamental principles remain the same.

D. *Incidentals—Mechanical Niceties*

NOTES

You can use two kinds of notes with parenthetical documentation: content notes, where you offer comments, explanations, or information that the text cannot accommodate, *and* bibliographic notes, where you give either several sources or evaluative comments on sources. Refer your reader to such notes by placing superscript arabic numerals at the appropriate places in your essay; make the numbers consecutive. Number each note in a section at the end of the essay titled "Notes." See the "Notes" at the end of Jadran Lee's and Ian Watson's essays in the Essays for Additional Reading section (pp. 371 and 385) for a range of possibilities.

ELLIPSIS

When you wish to omit a word, phrase, sentence, or paragraph from the text that you are quoting, use some form of ellipsis: three periods with a space between each (. . .) to indicate that you have omitted a word or phrase within a sentence, or four periods (. . . .) to indicate the end of a sentence or the omission of a whole sentence or more.

Let's reconsider the block quotation from the Forster-Eliot passage:

```
In "Anonymity: An Enquiry," E. M. Forster tells us
that "each human mind has two personalities, one on
the surface, one deeper down. The upper personality
has a name" (Two Cheers 83). The lower does not:

        It has something in common with all other
        deeper personalities, and the mystic will
        assert that the common quality is God. . . .
        It is in any case the force that makes for an-
        onymity. . . . The poet wrote the poem, . . .
```

but he forgot himself while he wrote it, and
we forget him while we read. (84)

Forster sounds a bit like T. S. Eliot in an early essay about impersonality. Eliot compares the poet's
mind to a "shred of platinum" and calls to our attention a creative force that is somehow apart from
the poet himself. The poet's mind, like the "shred
of platinum," is a "transforming catalyst" that
converts feelings and emotions into a work of art
(Eliot 41). That mind, according to Eliot, acts
almost independently of the man himself.

Here is the way that blocked passage appears, without the omissions,
in Forster's essay. I have underlined the omitted passages for purposes
of illustration:

It has something in common with all other deeper
personalities, and the mystic will assert that the
common quality is God, <u>and that here, in the obscure
recesses of our being, we near the gates of the Di-
vine</u>. It is in any case the force that makes for anonymity. <u>As it came from the depths, so it soars to
the heights, out of local questionings; as it is
general to all men, so the works it inspires have
something general about them, namely beauty</u>. The
poet wrote the poem, <u>no doubt</u>, but he forgot himself
while he wrote it, and we forget him while we read.
(84)

The three ellipses in the initial passage reflect, in order, three types of
omissions: the final clause of a sentence, material between quoted
sentences, and material within a sentence. Final sentence punctuation
in the case of the first and second omissions accounts for the fourth

period. In a block quotation, which is indented in order to be set off, the documentation comes after the final period in the quotation. Both the spacing of periods and their placement are important in all of these cases. Note in the first example where there is spacing and where there is not.

Had the quoted passage been only the first sentence, it would not have been blocked and set off; the parenthetical documentation would have come between the third and fourth periods: "It has something in common with all other deeper personalities, and the mystic will assert that the common quality is God . . ." (Forster 84).

When you omit something from a quoted passage, you must ensure that you do not change the meaning of the passage. Fairness to the source is paramount.

QUOTED IN

Occasionally you will decide to requote a quotation that you find in a secondary source. Let's say you are reading Joyce Carol Oates's essay "Against Nature," and you find a brief quotation from Thoreau's journal at the beginning of Oates's essay. In writing your own essay, you decide to cite a part of that same quotation. You have not read Thoreau's journal; you have taken the words from Oates's essay. Your citation within the text of your essay would appear this way:

```
Nature seems quite fickle to me. I never quite know
whether I can depend on her. Occasionally, I will
feel at home in the woods, comfortable and secure.
At other times, I encounter the most insurmountable
obstacles: rivers to cross, swarming bees to avoid,
poison ivy. At those times I side with Thoreau, who
found that Nature "excites an expectation which she
cannot satisfy" (qtd. in Oates 236).
```

The Works Cited list would include this entry:

```
Oates, Joyce Carol. "Against Nature." Antaeus 57
    (1986): 236-243.
```

EDITORIAL INTERPOLATIONS

When you want to add something within a quoted passage, you must put the added material within square brackets. You usually make such changes so that the quoted material will blend into your own sentence:

> George Core, in "Lives Fugitive and Unwritten,"
> argues that until very recently most southern writ-
> ers have chosen not to write autobiography and mem-
> oir. Core predicts, nevertheless, that because the
> "politics of our culture are far more confused"
> than in the past and because we "live in a society
> that has no underlying common myth," we're entering
> a time when "each writer [will] probably . . . be
> more inclined to set sails on the seas of the self."

In the original text, that last clause read: "each writer is probably going to be more inclined to set sails on the seas of the self." I chose to change the tense of the verb so that it would fit more naturally into my own sentence; to do so, I also had to omit two words, hence the ellipsis as well as the brackets.

PREPARING YOUR MANUSCRIPT—SOME GUIDELINES

Use 16-to-20-pound, 8½- by 11-inch white bond paper. Do not use erasable paper. Use 1-inch margins on all sides—a 1¼-inch left margin if you intend to put your essay in a binder. Indent the first word of each paragraph five spaces.

Use a fresh black ribbon on your typewriter or printer.

Double-space the entire manuscript.

Number pages consecutively in the upper right-hand corner, $\frac{1}{2}$ inch from the top. Your name can precede the page number on each page: Smit, D.   1

Prepare a title page. Center the title a third of the way down; center your name a double space below the title. Leave the rest of the page blank so that your teacher can write comments.

Underline the titles of books, plays, periodicals, films, record albums, and paintings; put the title of poems, essays, articles, short stories, television programs, and chapters in quotation marks.

If a comma or a period appears after a title that is in quotation marks (or at the end of a quoted passage), put the comma or period inside the closing quotation mark. Put a colon or semicolon outside the closing quotation mark.

Dashes are always made with two hyphens; there is no space before the two hyphens and no space following them: Loved people-- no matter what they claim--are among the happiest people alive.

ESSAYS
FOR
ADDITIONAL
READING
—
STUDENT
AND
PROFESSIONAL

A CONFUSED IDEALIST
by Jay Varma

1   With the dispassionate power of a camera, Annie Dillard's "The Deer at Providencia" presents the death and consumption of a deer as a poignant commentary on suffering—how one woman and, on a larger level, all humans confront violence. To that end, her images, and the pain they convey, penetrate our consciousness with stunning skill. Described with the vivid clarity of immediate narratives, these potent visions expose the randomness and pain of suffering—a brutal continuum permitted by God and ignored by humanity. She argues that the agony of a deer's exhausted, wracked limbs and of a man's charred flesh, are part of our daily baggage; we feed off their misery, never acknowledging its exis-

tence or our own moral cannibalism. Charging all humans with insensitivity, Dillard draws portraits of brutality, savagery, and despair for us to explore and understand—to bring into our hearts—and then admonishes our empathy with moral indignance.

2 It is this philosophical exposition, however, that eventually undermines Dillard's effectiveness as a social commentator. Retreating to moral higher ground, Dillard grows sententious and self-righteous at the end of "The Deer at Providencia"—"This is the Big Time here, every minute of it," she warns, reproving both the reader and the "gentlemen of the city" for allegedly ignoring the inevitability of suffering (559). But, as a result, the reader is dragged from self-reflection, ostensibly Dillard's goal, into defensive posturing: Dillard becomes a hypocritical whiner, feeding off the pain of the burnt man and decrying, not accepting, the immutability of misery—the same failings she condemns so forthrightly. In "The Deer at Providencia," Dillard guides us into suffering with compelling images but, eventually, leaves us disoriented, mired in her own idealistic confusion.

3 In her essay, Dillard brings us close to pain with her most powerful vision—the death of the deer and the circle of onlookers. Her description is plain and selective, vivid and real; it is straightforward, matter-of-fact storytelling that, while ostensibly objective, imparts a compelling immediacy and passion to her writing. To depict the deer's final gyrations, Dillard eschews sympathetic euphemisms and complex syntax: the deer becomes "it," the sentences noun/verb/noun (557). We see the deer desperately twisting and pawing to free its head and feet, but merely tearing at its own flesh; we see the "raw underside of its neck . . . bruises bleeding inside the muscles," the only outcome of its painful and fruitless struggle (557). But Dillard does not stop; she must consummate the horror. "Its hip jerked; its spine shook. Its eyes rolled; its tongue, thick with spittle, pushed in and out," Dillard writes (557). And, as the tension rises, she strikes the final blow: "Then it would

rest again. We watched this for fifteen minutes" (557). The delivery of these lines is straight and powerful; Dillard stresses the deer's torture in visual and temporal terms, portraying a violent, repetitious struggle. And the meaning is clear: the tragedy of death, of suffering continues. We see the deer's demise in anatomical detail; and its agony unavoidably becomes ours.

4 But to create this narrative power, Dillard emphasizes the outside forces surrounding the deer's death, placing that event between two closely related scenes: humans watching suffering; and humans savoring its consequences.

5 Dillard begins the essay like a camera, panning the surroundings, bringing the reader closer to the horror. The "village headman," "several village boys," "four businessmen from Quito," and Dillard stand around the deer as it initially struggles to loosen its neck and feet from a rope (557). "We watched the deer, and no one said much" (557). On one level, this image of the onlookers captivated by the deer exemplifies the casual sympathy Dillard condemns so forcefully. As if this is their first experience with pain, the people watch in silence, each stunned by the deer's hopeless struggle and the cruelty it endures—that is their only "common language" (557).

6 But Dillard also seems to draw a deeper, more symbolic parallel. She suggests that, while appearing sympathetic, these men, rather, glean a bizarre sense of power from the cruelty they observe. Though they may stare intensely at the pitiful deer and contemplate the moral justification of its death, the onlookers, Dillard argues, are actually enjoying this scene, relishing their power: the humans stand, while the deer writhes on the ground; they are strong and safe, the deer tortured and helpless. The onlookers emotionally feed off the deer's misery—their sympathy is a facade, Dillard suggests.

7 Dillard also relays that philosophical message in the scene following the deer's death, translating a venison lunch into a metaphor for her meaning: in eating animal flesh, the humans quite

literally feed off another's misery. Her lunch with the villagers and the "gentlemen of the city" is more than another midday meal; it is a kind of animal ritual carried through in vivid detail: she tears at the "delicate fish-flesh" and savors the "sweet and full of flavor" fried bananas (557–8). But, most important, she enjoys her venison stew, devouring it "in shreds," savage onlooker that she is (557).

8   "It was good," Dillard writes, "I was surprised at its tenderness" (557). And why was the deer meat so tender, so good? "It is a fact that high levels of lactic acid, which builds up in muscle tissues during exertion, tenderizes," she intones (558). Her plain, scientific answer brings home the emotional message, her delicate subtlety masterfully accentuating its power: the more violent the kill—and the more painful the suffering—the tastier the reward. It is an unwritten law, the violent code of humanity, the underlying force driving us, Dillard argues. And that is Dillard's brutal revelation, her passionate thesis. Why should the "metropolitan men" cringe at a deer's misery (556)? Why should they be so shocked at cruelty? They live it, thrive off it, and encourage it, Dillard tells us. Humans are carnivores—whether at the dinner table or in a circle of "very different people" or in the work office—a fact Dillard would probably see evidenced in the violence and immorality currently plaguing our culture. "These things are not issues; they are mysteries," Dillard states (558). A subtle, urgent narrative, this passage reflects human savagery: we are all cruel and insensitive in Dillard's eyes.

9   Dillard's experience in the woods, her powerful descriptions of the deer and even the savage meal itself, reveal a sensitive heart. She is clearly troubled by the death scene and the symbolic import of the humans' carnivorousness—why else would she describe those events so carefully, so vividly? But she tries to hide that reality. Stoicism is worn like a badge—"Gentlemen of the city, what surprises you? That there is suffering here, or that I know it?" she rails, obviously proud of her presumed awareness (558). But it is this arrogant confusion that eventually undermines the essence

◊

of Dillard's essay: she forces us to confront suffering, to analyze our morality with sensitivity; but her tone and actions at the end of the essay painfully offend the reader and destroy that self-reflection. With an inner conflict obviously boiling within her, flamed by her insecurity over the implications of worldwide suffering, she tries to hide those central emotions behind a guise of cynicism. It does not work.

10   She concludes her first two presentations of brutality on a note of despair: a burnt man's and Annie Dillard's. Bringing the essay out of the Ecuadorian jungle, Dillard describes her obsession with a photograph of Alan McDonald, a man "burned for second time" (558). Her description is a flash of reality: narrative interspersed with quotes from a newspaper. Dillard incorporates that method to focus her meaning and amplify its impact. "Every morning for the past two years I have seen in that mirror, beside my sleep-softened face, the blackened face of a burnt man," Dillard writes (558). And she focuses on his desperate history to bring the pain home—"a burnt boy . . . he had already been stunned by what could happen, by how life could veer" (559). By placing him on her mirror to stare at daily and by describing his fate in such detail, Dillard attaches symbolic importance to McDonald: he exemplifies suffering. And her observance of him every morning is a kind of religious ritual. McDonald is a martyr, a visual, vibrant countenance of suffering, and she confronts it daily, on literal and symbolic terms, adding to her own moral and theological unrest. "Why does God hate me?" McDonald implores in the newspaper (559). But, Dillard wonders, why does God hate all animals? She highlights the man's pain— "that the world included such suffering"—and questions the meaning of its existence: "What is going on?" she cries out in desperation (559).

11   Her tone in this passage, though, seems hypocritical: earlier she condemned the "gentlemen of the city" ("What surprises you?") for their empathy; but now she appears equally guilty of that crime, commiserating with "Alan McDonald in his dignity . . . [and] the

deer at Providencia in his dignity" (559). And, more important, while she waxes sympathetic, she maintains an air of self-importance: "And mail me the carbon," she writes, commanding someone to answer her pleas (559). She plays the cold cynic in her scathing criticism of humanity, attacking those who acknowledge the world's pain only when confronted by it, while still feeding off its consequences. But is Dillard so different from those she denounces? She feasts on Alan McDonald's suffering, just as she did the deer's; his countenance of despair gives her life daily meaning, cause for moral urgency. And, more important, she rejects her own proposition—that suffering has consumed the world. The pervasive spread of suffering is still "a mystery" to her, she states, seeking spiritual guidance, a moral justification. But if she "knows . . . that there is suffering," why does she continue to question it so intensely (558)? It is perfectly appropriate to acknowledge a problem—in this instance, suffering—and then question its roots; but Dillard seems more confused about than critical of her beliefs. She cannot accept the world's pain, yet she condemns us for that same failing.

12   Though its first half resounds with force and emotional passion, "The Deer at Providencia" disintegrates towards the end into Dillard's idealistic confusion. Dillard succeeds admirably in transmitting her two main images; the reader feels the pain of the deer and senses the savagery of the venison lunch. But when Dillard tries to relate those scenes to everyday existence, to elicit further moral self-reflection, she descends into an idealism belied by her harsh denunciations of humanity. We don't know whether to become cynical, but potentially enlightened citizens by vigorously espousing her thesis (that suffering is omnipresent), or to return to "ignorance," a kind of healthy, perpetual confusion over the meaning of suffering and our relationship with it. It is a tall order—a dilemma Dillard herself fails to resolve.

◊

Work Cited

Dillard, Annie. "The Deer at Providencia." *Prose Pieces: Essays and Stories.* Ed. Pat C. Hoy II and Robert DiYanni. New York: Random, 1988. 556–559.

ONAMAEWA
(WHAT IS YOUR NAME?)
by Leon Yen

1   A person's name is a person's identity. I lost mine when I immigrated to this foreign land; I have been searching for it ever since. Throughout the years I have adopted other names to use as my own, only to find myself enmeshed with their reality and going around in a circle, gradually returning to the starting point, a point where I should always have been. I never thought I would be able to find myself again.

2   When I first entered elementary school in the States, I went by many names. One day I might call myself John, another day Steve, Devin, so on, and so on. My teacher didn't care, really. She just thought I was kind of queer and liked to play this identity game that kids like to play sometimes. To her I was number eleven in her roll book, and so I called myself Eleven. My classmates never got used to that. One day this bully cornered me during recess and demanded to know my name.

3   "Eleven," I answered him.

4   "No, stupid! You can't have a number for a name," he yelled at me. "What is your REAL name?"

5   I told him I didn't have one. He badgered me and twisted my arm. Finally, I relented and said that I had had a name before, but that it was dead, and so it didn't matter anymore.

6   "What is your old name then," he insisted.

7   "Shih-Wei," I said flatly, unconvinced that the name belonged to me.

8   Hearing my gibberish, he burst out, "What kind of a name is that? That's not a name; I've never heard of it. Why can't you have a normal name like the rest of us. Get a real name! Will ya?"

9   I did.

10   When I was in high school I was eager to distinguish myself, to establish my name, so to say. I was awed by the seniors who played water polo and absorbed by the spectacle when they came back from their conquest bathed in all their glory. For these same grandiose dreams I also played water polo.

11   I was number sixteen on the team. But even though I tried very hard to be a good water polo player, I always remained a normal Sixteen compared to the other studs on the team. Every day, practice before dawn, practice after school. No weekends, no spring break, no summer vacation. For two years, Sixteen hoped that he could start someday. Still, Sixteen would be on second string. It wasn't really Sixteen's fault or anybody's fault; it's just that he had played for all the wrong reasons. Sixteen thought that water polo was an easy means to a glorious end. He didn't count on the competition, much less defeat. Out of pride, he stuck with the team, thinking that he was sure to have his day. He waited and waited and waited.

12   One day Sixteen couldn't wait any longer. He broke down in the middle of a game and felt his whole world crumbling in on him. The funny thing was that Sixteen didn't get played in the game; Sixteen had been sitting on the icy bench for the past three quarters or, for all that matter, the past two years. What happened was that Sixteen suddenly felt bone-chilling, got up, ran into the locker room, and took a long hot shower that never quite eased the numbness or the emptiness within him. As though the dream that had shaped and sustained him for these past two years had been consumed and spent, he felt like a dry husk, burnt out, his reality crumbling in. And like an old man, he was shaking. It was Sixteen's debut into the world.

13　　Mid-July summer in the subterranean city of Tokyo was unbearable. The heat and humidity outside were magnified tenfold underground, but I didn't mind that really. It was the facelessness of the crowd that killed me; they reminded me of my own anonymity. As I tip-toed on the deck of the Ginza Station with the mob of rush-hour people enveloping me, I grew nervous; wiping my face and my neck with a towel became a preoccupation. I sweat too much. A heightened uneasiness emanated from the mob like a breathing heat wave. It was intimidation, but then none of us had any choice but to suffer each other. It seemed as though the train and the mob had a mind of their own, and yet they never seemed to understand each other. Nor did they understand me.

14　　A gush of cool air. A sigh of relief. Then the rail and the whole underground structure hummed, echoed, and rattled. Three-two-one. The train roared into the station with unfailing punctuality.

15　　"Three rows! Three rows," the conductor yelled as the mob, ant-like, split neatly into three columns and filed into the tin can while the hired hands tackled and shoved the last few unfortunate ones through the threshold of the boxcar so that the door would engage and close.

16　　The boxcar thundered through the subterranean world amidst the illuminating lights shooting by like a meteor shower. Out of boredom I decided to check out the crowd around me. Stacked against my right hip stood a student in his hideous, black uniform. I couldn't understand the name sewn on his shirt, only the I.D. number 724. Somehow, this 724 managed to grab on to a seat and read and sweat at the same time in this cramped, overheated world. Cramming for college exams, I presumed. He reminded me of Sixteen. Sixteen thought that the way to distinguish himself in this world was to conquer himself, the competition, and the system. Perhaps 724 had been told that getting into Tokyo University would be his ticket to success with the promise of a solid, steady job upon graduation. However, neither Sixteen nor 724 had intended on being reduced to a statistic.

17   In front of me stood a thin, gaunt businessman in his thirties. Sweat had formed a crescent under his armpit, but the man stared mindlessly out of the window at the shooting stars, oblivious to his surroundings and sealed in his own private world. He seemed like someone who had conquered the odds and carved out his turf in the world. And yet he was forlorn, perhaps troubled by some remote possibility that he might have found happiness if he had been a carpenter instead of a manager, or perhaps upon reflection he might have asked himself, "Is this all worth it?" Sixteen asked himself the same questions when he was taking that long hot shower in the locker room. Could it be a case of mid-life crisis? I didn't know. I was only a kid with no name. Somehow I had this urge to get 724 and this sweaty man together; perhaps the sparks from the dry husks of this man could cause an inflammation in the mind of 724. But alas, I didn't speak Japanese.

18   I was so busy trying to steady myself and looking in front of me that I almost stumbled on someone behind me. I turned around and there was this short, old woman dressed in her kimono with a baby strapped at her back. Her face looked wrinkled like raisin's skin, old and haggard except for those two tiny beads that shone with kindness and equanimity. Even with the weight of the baby she withstood the push and shove of the mob; even in this unbearable heat she was serene and unruffled in her thick kimono. As my fascination with the old woman grew, I realized that if I stretched my ears I could hear her humming an ancient lullaby, her lone voice crisp and clear against the thundering metallic roar. Mo-mo-ta-ro . . .

19   I had heard of that voice somewhere in my past when I still had my name. That melancholic tune lingered round and round in my head like a voice leading me out of this subterranean darkness until suddenly I realized that of all these people, she was the only person who had told me her name. To me her stamina in the midst of this faceless, sweaty crowd could only come from the strength of her character; her lone voice wrote a signature in my heart. Her lullaby

defined her identity, her immortality in that cramped space and time.

20   I realized at that moment that I had a name all along, except that I had abandoned it in search of something more grandiose. At eleven I was unsure of who I was. At sixteen I was too eager to live someone else's reality, adopting for myself a clay cast to mold into even if it didn't fit me. I wasn't meant to be Eleven or John or Steve, much less Sixteen, 724, the sweaty man, or the old woman. I was meant to be only myself, like the old woman was herself. But I found myself in her nevertheless. She showed me what I could not see by myself.

21   Some people told me that if I traveled far enough I would meet myself eventually. That was why I went to Japan in the first place. And I did see what I had set out to see, what I wanted to see, and what I needed to see. I saw myself in the reflection of that old woman, and it came as a shock because I had always thought I would see myself in the crowd. I didn't believe in miracles, but she had awakened me. Her lullaby still rings in my ear, louder even than the metallic roar of the subway.

SPRING COMES TO HOGEYE
by Roy Reed

1   Spring was late in the Ozark Mountains. The first week of April had passed, and the oaks and maples were only then risking a few pale green shoots, tentative little leaves that would not constitute much of a loss if another frost stole in at night on the villainous northwest air.

2   Ira Solenberger was also late. Practically everybody else in Hogeye had braved the hazard of frost and had planted corn, onions, English peas and Irish potatoes. A few, emulating the bold dogwood and redbud trees, which for more than a week had been blooming bright white and purple against the dark hills, had gone so far as to put out beans, squash and even tender tomato plants.

3   But Mr. Solenberger, who was regarded as the best gardener in Washington County, had not plowed a furrow or planted a seed. Like the craggy maple in front of his house (itself one of the oldest things in Hogeye, a relic of the Butterfield Stage era), he found that his sap was slow to rise that spring. It had not occurred to him to blame it on his eighty-six years.

4   "It's that old flu," he said. "Got it back in the winter and can't get rid of it. First time I've had it since 19 and 18."

5   He opened the door of his heating stove and threw another chunk of wood on the fire. He closed it a little sharply and glanced out the window toward his empty garden.

6   Every April, the main thing going on in the rural South is vegetable gardening. A farmer might take an hour to talk politics or help a cow give birth, but the really urgent business for him, his wife and all of the children who are old enough to keep their feet off the onion sets is getting seeds and plants in the ground to take advantage of the warming days. With a little luck, the sweet corn planted in early April will have roasting ears ("roashnears," they are called) by the middle of June.

7   This is a pursuit that seeks every year to outwit the awful force that pushes the shoots from the oak's branches, and that turns Seth Timmons's meadow from brown to green, and impels swallows to build nests in weathered barns.

8   It was the same force, that spring, that pushed Ira Solenberger out the door in a hat and coat, hunched against the biting bright air blowing up from the Illinois River, to kick the dirt and study the sky, and then retreat to the house to throw another chunk of wood on the fire.

9   There is still a poet up the road at Fayetteville who, in those days, drove into the hills every April to study the hills and watch for Robert Frost's signs—the gold that is nature's first evidence, "her hardest hue to hold"—and for private signs of his own that stirred his spirit.

10 Ira Solenberger's mind ran less to poetry than to science. He was an amateur magician, and he performed magic with plants as well as cards.

11 "Summer before last, I grafted some tomatoes on some poke stalks."

12 Why?

13 "Just to see if they would grow."

14 But when he talked of nature and growth, he used words that Frost might have used, or Thoreau.

15 "Plow deep. There's one acre right under another acre. I plow both of them."

16 "Phosphorous makes things grow roots. If you get roots, you're going to get something else."

17 "I farm with a tractor. But when it gets rowed up and a-growing, I use a roan horse."

18 He was now in the April sun, away from the stove. His eye scanned the three and a half acres where, just a year earlier—unencumbered by the flu—he had planted rhubarb, corn, tomatoes, squash, sweet potatoes, Irish potatoes, okra, green beans, cantaloupes, radishes, onions, cucumbers and strawberries. He had harvested a bumper crop of everything. He had eaten what he wanted and sold the rest at the farmers' market on the square at Fayetteville.

19 He pointed to a fallow patch and said, "That's where I had my watermelons last year." He spoke in a loud, professorial voice, as if addressing the cows at the top of the hill.

20 "They told me I raised the biggest watermelons in Northwest Arkansas. One of them weighed eighty-three pounds.

21 "I've had people ask me, 'What's your secret for raising watermelons?' I tell them, 'I ain't got no secret.' "

22 Then, still addressing the cows, he proceeded to tell the secret. Plow the ground deep. Watermelons need more air than water, and deep plowing lets in air.

23 "I plow turrible deep. Eight or ten inches." He grinned with private satisfaction and moved on to a strawberry patch.

24 Mr. Solenberger believed in humus. He produced it by placing mulch between the rows. I once knew a Mississippi liberal who enjoyed a minor reputation as a gardener by mulching old copies of *The New York Times.* Mr. Solenberger did not take the *Times.* He used dead crab grass.

25 "Make sure it's rotten," he said, jabbing the air with an open pocket knife. "If you plow under something that ain't rotten, it's a detriment to you for the first season."

26 Many of his neighbors planted by the moon, and still do. Mr. Solenberger did not.

27 "I don't pay any attention to the moon, and I'll tell you why. I've got a neighbor that plants by the moon, and I asked him a question one day that he couldn't answer. I said, 'You plant a seed in dry ground, when the moon is right, and it won't come up. Then ten days later it comes a rain and that seed sprouts and comes up. But by then the sign of the moon is wrong. How do you account for that?' He couldn't answer that. I don't plant by the moon. I plant by the ground."

28 He was troubled, though, by another phenomenon, and he was a little reluctant to talk about it. He said the frosts seemed to come later each spring, just as the force that drove him to the plow seemed to have arrived late that year.

29 "The timber's awful slow a-leafing out." He cast a blue eye toward the hill across the road. "When I was a boy, we weren't bothered with frost. When spring come, it come. Our spring's almost a month later than it used to be."

30 I asked him what he thought the reason was. He glanced at my face to see whether I was ready to accept what he had to say. He decided to risk it.

31 "Well, sir, I believe the world twists a little bit. You know, everything that grows twists around to the right. Follows the sun.

Even our storms that come out of the Gulf, they twist to the right. It's just nature."

32   Why was a man of eighty-six still involved every April with the earth's greening, as if it were his own? He passed the question off quickly. He indicated that it was merely the same motive that led him to do card tricks and tell jokes and graft tomatoes to poke weed.

33   "I just like to be doing things."

34   He returned to the question later, however, sidling up to it so as not to sound too serious. He began by confessing that spring was his favorite season. I asked him why, and he said, "Life is at a high ebb in the spring."

35   He leaned his chair back against the porch wall and hooked his shoe heels over the lower rung. He studied the trees on the hill across the road, and then he said, "People who are getting up in years, more of them die in the winter when the days are short, and in the hours after midnight. Life is at a low ebb after midnight and in the short days. Did you know that? And the shorter the days, the lower the ebb."

36   Thus it was the lengthening days that sent Ira Solenberger to the garden, and he could no more resist than the hapless oak bud could resist becoming a leaf.

37   He was also right about the other. He thrived for one more season of the high ebb. He made one more garden. Then he died in the winter, during the short days.

THE MEN WE CARRY IN OUR MINDS
by Scott Russell Sanders

1   "This must be a hard time for women," I say to my friend Anneke. "They have so many paths to choose from, and so many voices calling them."

2   "I think it's a lot harder for men," she replies.

3   "How do you figure that?"

4   "The women I know feel excited, innocent, like crusaders in a just cause. The men I know are eaten up with guilt."

5   We are sitting at the kitchen table drinking sassafras tea, our hands wrapped around the mugs because this April morning is cool and drizzly. "Like a Dutch morning," Anneke told me earlier. She is Dutch herself, a writer and midwife and peacemaker, with the round face and sad eyes of a woman in a Vermeer painting who might be waiting for the rain to stop, for a door to open. She leans over to sniff a sprig of lilac, pale lavender, that rises from a vase of cobalt blue.

6   "Women feel such pressure to be everything, do everything," I say. "Career, kids, art, politics. Have their babies and get back to the office a week later. It's as if they're trying to overcome a million years' worth of evolution in one lifetime."

7   "But we help one another. We don't try to lumber on alone, like so many wounded grizzly bears, the way men do." Anneke sips her tea. I gave her the mug with owls on it, for wisdom. "And we have this deep-down sense that we're in the *right*—we've been held back, passed over, used—while men feel they're in the wrong. Men are the ones who've been discredited, who have to search their souls."

8   I search my soul. I discover guilty feelings aplenty—toward the poor, the Vietnamese, Native Americans, the whales, an endless list of debts—a guilt in each case that is as bright and unambiguous as a neon sign. But toward women I feel something more confused, a snarl of shame, envy, wary tenderness, and amazement. This muddle troubles me. To hide my unease I say, "You're right, it's tough being a man these days."

9   "Don't laugh." Anneke frowns at me, mournful-eyed, through the sassafras steam. "I wouldn't be a man for anything. It's much easier being the victim. All the victim has to do is break free. The persecutor has to live with his past."

10   How deep is that past? I find myself wondering after Anneke has left. How much of an inheritance do I have to throw off? Is it just the

beliefs I breathed in as a child? Do I have to scour memory back through father and grandfather? Through St. Paul? Beyond Stonehenge and into the twilit caves? I'm convinced the past we must contend with is deeper even than speech. When I think back on my childhood, on how I learned to see men and women, I have a sense of ancient, dizzying depths. The back roads of Tennessee and Ohio where I grew up were probably closer, in their sexual patterns, to the campsites of Stone Age hunters than to the genderless cities of the future into which we are rushing.

11   The first men, besides my father, I remember seeing were black convicts and white guards, in the cottonfield across the road from our farm on the outskirts of Memphis. I must have been three or four. The prisoners wore dingy gray-and-black zebra suits, heavy as canvas, sodden with sweat. Hatless, stooped, they chopped weeds in the fierce heat, row after row, breathing the acrid dust of boll-weevil poison. The overseers wore dazzling white shirts and broad shadowy hats. The oiled barrels of their shotguns flashed in the sunlight. Their faces in memory are utterly blank. Of course those men, white and black, have become for me an emblem of racial hatred. But they have also come to stand for the twin poles of my early vision of manhood—the brute toiling animal and the boss.

12   When I was a boy, the men I knew labored with their bodies. They were marginal farmers, just scraping by, or welders, steelworkers, carpenters; they swept floors, dug ditches, mined coal, or drove trucks, their forearms ropy with muscle; they trained horses, stoked furnaces, built tires, stood on assembly lines wrestling parts onto cars and refrigerators. They got up before light, worked all day long whatever the weather, and when they came home at night they looked as though somebody had been whipping them. In the evenings and on weekends they worked on their own places, tilling gardens that were lumpy with clay, fixing broken-down cars, hammering on houses that were always too drafty, too leaky, too small.

13   The bodies of the men I knew were twisted and maimed in ways visible and invisible. The nails of their hands were black and split, the hands tattooed with scars. Some had lost fingers. Heavy lifting had given many of them finicky backs and guts weak from hernias. Racing against conveyor belts had given them ulcers. Their ankles and knees ached from years of standing on concrete. Anyone who had worked for long around machines was hard of hearing. They squinted, and the skin of their faces was creased like the leather of old work gloves. There were times, studying them, when I dreaded growing up. Most of them coughed, from dust or cigarettes, and most of them drank cheap wine or whiskey, so their eyes looked bloodshot and bruised. The fathers of my friends always seemed older than the mothers. Men wore out sooner. Only women lived into old age.

14   As a boy I also knew another sort of men, who did not sweat and break down like mules. They were soldiers, and so far as I could tell they scarcely worked at all. During my early school years we lived on a military base, an arsenal in Ohio, and every day I saw GIs in the guardshacks, on the stoops of barracks, at the wheels of olive drab Chevrolets. The chief fact of their lives was boredom. Long after I left the Arsenal I came to recognize the sour smell the soldiers gave off as that of souls in limbo. They were all waiting—for wars, for transfers, for leaves, for promotions, for the end of their hitch— like so many braves waiting for the hunt to begin. Unlike the warriors of older tribes, however, they would have no say about when the battle would start or how it would be waged. Their waiting was broken only when they practiced for war. They fired guns at targets, drove tanks across the churned-up fields of the military reservation, set off bombs in the wrecks of old fighter planes. I knew this was all play. But I also felt certain that when the hour for killing arrived, they would kill. When the real shooting started, many of them would die. This was what soldiers were *for,* just as a hammer was for driving nails.

15   Warriors and toilers: those seemed, in my boyhood vision, to be the chief destinies for men. They weren't the only destinies, as I learned from having a few male teachers, from reading books, and from watching television. But the men on television—the politicians, the astronauts, the generals, the savvy lawyers, the philosophical doctors, the bosses who gave orders to both soldiers and laborers—seemed as remote and unreal to me as the figures in tapestries. I could no more imagine growing up to become one of these cool, potent creatures than I could imagine becoming a prince.

16   A nearer and more hopeful example was that of my father, who had escaped from a red-dirt farm to a tire factory, and from the assembly line to the front office. Eventually he dressed in a white shirt and tie. He carried himself as if he had been born to work with his mind. But his body, remembering the earlier years of slogging work, began to give out on him in his fifties, and it quit on him entirely before he turned sixty-five. Even such a partial escape from man's fate as he had accomplished did not seem possible for most of the boys I knew. They joined the Army, stood in line for jobs in the smoky plants, helped build highways. They were bound to work as their fathers had worked, killing themselves or preparing to kill others.

17   A scholarship enables me not only to attend college, a rare enough feat in my circle, but even to study in a university meant for the children of the rich. Here I met for the first time young men who had assumed from birth that they would lead lives of comfort and power. And for the first time I met women who told me that men were guilty of having kept all the joys and privileges of the earth for themselves. I was baffled. What privileges? What joys? I thought about the maimed, dismal lives of most of the men back home. What had they stolen from their wives and daughters? The right to go five days a week, twelve months a year, for thirty or forty years to a steel mill or a coal mine? The right to drop bombs and die in war? The right to feel every leak in the roof, every gap in the fence, every

cough in the engine, as a wound they must mend? The right to feel, when the lay-off comes or the plant shuts down, not only afraid but ashamed?

18   I was slow to understand the deep grievances of women. This was because, as a boy, I had envied them. Before college, the only people I had ever known who were interested in art or music or literature, the only ones who read books, the only ones who ever seemed to enjoy a sense of ease and grace were the mothers and daughters. Like the menfolk, they fretted about money, they scrimped and made-do. But, when the pay stopped coming in, they were not the ones who had failed. Nor did they have to go to war, and that seemed to me a blessed fact. By comparison with the narrow, ironclad days of fathers, there was an expansiveness, I thought, in the days of mothers. They went to see neighbors, to shop in town, to run errands at school, at the library, at church. No doubt, had I looked harder at their lives, I would have envied them less. It was not my fate to become a woman, so it was easier for me to see the graces. Few of them held jobs outside the home, and those who did filled thankless roles as clerks and waitresses. I didn't see, then, what a prison a house could be, since houses seemed to me brighter, handsomer places than any factory. I did not realize— because such things were never spoken of—how often women suffered from men's bullying. I did learn about the wretchedness of abandoned wives, single mothers, widows; but I also learned about the wretchedness of lone men. Even then I could see how ex- hausting it was for a mother to cater all day to the needs of young children. But if I had been asked, as a boy, to choose between tending a baby and tending a machine, I think I would have chosen the baby. (Having now tended both, I know I would choose the baby.)

19   So I was baffled when the women at college accused me and my sex of having cornered the world's pleasures. I think something like my bafflement has been felt by other boys (and by girls as well) who grew up in dirt-poor farm country, in mining country, in black

ghettos, in Hispanic barrios, in the shadows of factories, in Third World nations—any place where the fate of men is as grim and bleak as the fate of women. Toilers and warriors. I realize now how ancient these identities are, how deep the tug they exert on men, the undertow of a thousand generations. The miseries I saw, as a boy, in the lives of nearly all men I continue to see in the lives of many—the body-breaking toil, the tedium, the call to be tough, the humiliating powerlessness, the battle for a living and for territory.

20   When the women I met at college thought about the joys and privileges of men, they did not carry in their minds the sort of men I had known in my childhood. They thought of their fathers, who were bankers, physicians, architects, stockbrokers, the big wheels of the big cities. These fathers rode the train to work or drove cars that cost more than any of my childhood houses. They were attended from morning to night by female helpers, wives and nurses and secretaries. They were never laid off, never short of cash at month's end, never lined up for welfare. These fathers made decisions that mattered. They ran the world.

21   The daughters of such men wanted to share in this power, this glory. So did I. They yearned for a say over their future, for jobs worthy of their abilities, for the right to live at peace, unmolested, whole. Yes, I thought, yes yes. The difference between me and these daughters was that they saw me, because of my sex, as destined from birth to become like their fathers, and therefore as an enemy to their desires. But I knew better. I wasn't an enemy, in fact or in feeling. I was an ally. If I had known, then, how to tell them so, would they have believed me? Would they now?

BEING FAMILIAR
by Samuel F. Pickering, Jr.

1   Last spring I published a familiar essay in the *Kenyon Review.* The essay contained some untoward parts, and for a while I thought about suppressing it. Eventually, though, I decided that no one in

my family was liable to read the *Kenyon Review.* I was mistaken. Like sin, words will out, particularly if they involve, as mine did, youthful indiscretions. A week after the essay appeared, Mother telephoned. A friend, she informed me, sent her the *Review.* The essay had not gone down well in Tennessee. "We are," Mother said, "people of some reputation in this town, and this kind of thing."

2   Before she could sink her teeth into the piece and shake it back and forth, I interrupted. "Mamma," I said, straining to change the grounds of conversation, "Mamma, don't think of the essay as truth; think of it as literature."

3   "Literature," Mother exclaimed after a slight pause, "it's not literature. It's bullshit!"

4   Mother's reaction was not surprising. In my essays being familiar means being personal and approachable. My life furnishes matter for writing, and although my essays don't always describe what really happened, they often strike readers as true. Unlike members of my family, who, understandably enough, are often embarrassed by my writing, readers are generally attracted. Being personal makes me approachable, and they write me almost as a friend, in the process brightening my days and giving me material for more essays. "Mr. Pickering," a woman wrote this September, "You don't know us, but we are a black preacher and wife from Tennessee—Waverley, Tennessee. So I thought if you had the time you might want to come to our Fiftieth Wedding Anniversary. We would be glad to see someone from Tennessee." Accompanying the letter was a gold-and-claret invitation from the couple's children and grandchildren and the members of the minister's congregation, inviting me to the "joyful Fiftieth Wedding Celebration." Although the day of the celebration was cold and rainy, the mood inside the church was warm and sunny. Carrying a ring, a little boy dressed in white nervously picked his way down the aisle. Behind him skipped a small girl, plucking petals from daisies, all the while saying "He loves me" and "She loves me."

5 Although I often spend days wandering about in old graveyards, picnicking and reading tombstones, I had not been in a church for a long time. I no longer believe, and although I long for faith, I avoid churches. I am afraid of entering that world redolent with sweet memories—birthday parties for the baby Jesus, mite boxes, and soothing calls to Abide with Him. Once within the fold I might not have will enough to kick loose. Instead of living the sad joy of this dark earth, I might spend my time dreaming of life to come. The pull of church, though, is strong, and at the end of the celebration when a big woman stood up and sang the Lord's Prayer, I almost cried. For a moment, years and hard-edged knowledge fell away. I saw myself in Sunday school, an awkward little boy in a gray coat and gray short pants, wonderfully happy as he looked at a silver star beside his name on an attendance chart.

6 I don't attend all the celebrations to which I am invited, but I try to go to most. Sometimes being approachable leads to physical rather than mental pain. Occasionally I run road races. I don't run for prizes. I am remarkably slow afoot; what is a sprint to me is a crawl to the young and the fleet. In truth, if I were fast, I would probably stop running. Competition makes me uncomfortable, and I labor to avoid it. Road races are simply my excuse for traveling around New England, breathing the salt air along the Maine coast and wandering through the green-and-white villages of Vermont. In my essays on running, losers appear wise; at the back of the pack, I argue, a person has time to look around, to talk, and to appreciate. Probably because they, too, have not won a race, many people like the essays. As a result a race director will sometimes ask me to run in his race. In October I was invited to a half-marathon in New Hampshire. "A road race entry from the Lone Ranger of Running," the director wrote, "would boost morale and increase the respectability of the race, especially if you happen to be old." The letter was light and seductive. "Your personal safety," the director continued, "will be guaranteed. Several hours before the race, police will arrest all those citizens with a previous

history of gunplay involving joggers, and the Dog Officer will cudgel all loose dogs on the route itself."

7   Although I had not run thirteen miles in eight years, I began training. "There is no telling what this will lead to," I told my wife, Vicki, when she said I was too old and fat for such a race; "maybe a running magazine will make me a correspondent."

8   "The only thing this is going to lead to," she answered, "is the bed." Alas, she was right. One afternoon a week before the race as I ran up a tall hill, my heel began to ache. The next morning my Achilles tendon was as hard and as thick as a two-by-four. Six weeks have passed, and the Lone Ranger of Running still has trouble mounting the stairs in his house, much less hills in New England.

9   Beginning an essay is difficult. Unlike academic writing, for which one can imagine a specific audience and which generates its own urgency, pushing a person to put his thoughts down before someone else gets the same idea, the writer of familiar essays feels little compulsion to write. Often about the inconsequential, the familiar essay adds nothing to knowledge. No experts wait, minds sharpened, ready to cut and slice and then weigh the learning and find it wanting. Unable to imagine particular readers and under no pressure to publish, the essayist is tempted to live ordinary life rather than to write about it. I planned to spend last Saturday writing, but when Vicki said she wanted to visit local church bazaars to search for Christmas presents and asked me to mind the children, I gladly put my pencils aside and turned to other things. Two years ago I bought three cords of firewood. Although the woodsman assured me that it was split, much of the wood consisted of logs fit more for factory heating plants than living-room stoves. This year I purchased a maul, and while the children spun up and down the driveway on Big Wheels, I split wood.

10   Splitting wood is remarkably satisfying. There is something heartily primitive about wresting logs out from the bottom of an old woodpile and then smashing them into splinters. I like my maul,

but while splitting wood I dreamed about a chainsaw. Most of my friends own them, but Vicki won't let me have one. Whenever my friends use their saws, they wear caps—tough caps that belie their ages and sit boldly on their heads, proclaiming in black letters Echo or Stihl. I would like such a cap. By comparison my only hat seems weak and intellectual. It is a tweedy, checkered English cap. On top is a big brown spot. One day after the cap got soaked in a storm, I hung it on a lamp to dry. Unfortunately, heat from the light bulb burned it, not badly enough for me to throw it away but badly enough to leave a mark everybody notices.

11   By the time Vicki came home, I had split most of the wood, at least all I was going to split. I did not, however, settle down to writing. That morning Tom, the UPS man, delivered a box of peonies from Spring Hill Nurseries in Tipp City, Ohio. Since the weather was good and rain was forecast for Sunday, after lunch I dug holes for the peonies along the edge of the driveway. Then when Vicki went to Ledgecrest to buy bone meal, the children and I went into the woods behind the house, and I dug up several cartloads of rich, black humus for the holes. Digging, carting, and planting took most of the afternoon, and I put off writing until after dinner. I didn't expect to get much done; something always comes up after dinner, and, sure enough, while I was looking through my notebooks, Vicki called from the kitchen. Edward, our two-and-a-half-year-old, had stuck a raisin up his nose. Instead of blowing as Vicki instructed, Edward snorted, and snorted like a bull let out to cows in the spring. And the raisin which had once hung loosely in mid-passage took off and, flying upward like a rocket, was now firmly lodged beyond the reach of tweezers, ready and indeed eager, I was sure, to dive into Edward's sinuses. I did not know what to do, but since Edward was screaming, Vicki said we had to try something. I carried Edward into the living room and stretched him out on a sofa. Vicki got a toothpick and then went harpooning. I held Edward down with one hand; with the other I pried open his nose. In my mouth was a flashlight; by humping over I was able to

shine it in the general vicinity of Edward's face. Although Vicki proved herself a master harpooner and quickly speared the raisin, the excitement wore me out, making me fit only for television.

12   Since Sunday was supposed to be rainy, I had every intention of writing. Unpredictably, though, Sunday dawned warm and bright and was much too pretty to spend at a desk. After breakfast Vicki, the boys, and Eliza and I set out on a walk. Since she was only six months old, Eliza rode in a baby carrier strapped to my back. We crossed Horsebarn Hill on the university farm and, cutting through fields of newly harvested corn, drifted toward the Fenton River. *Drifted* is the right word. Direction, like my determination to write, came and went. The boys explored the fields and found several half-eaten ears of hard, yellow corn. For the boys the corn was golden treasure, and soon I looked like a scarecrow with shucks sticking out of my pockets. In the trees along one side of the field grew bittersweet; we noted it and said we would return later and pick some. At the edge of another field grew pokeberries. I crushed a handful, and after telling the boys that Cherokee Indians used them to make ink, I painted my face. Much to Vicki's dismay, the boys did the same. Earlier in the fall, a hurricane tore through Connecticut, and throughout the woods lay the broken tops of oak trees, bushy with dried leaves and heavy with acorns. These, too, were judged treasure, and I crammed handfuls into my pockets along with the corn.

13   The woods were quiet, and except for the sound of our walking, we heard little. I have never seen or heard an owl in the wild, and I hoped I might see one sitting wide-eyed, deep in the hollow of a rotten tree. I didn't, and nothing appeared to mark place or time until Edward suddenly plopped heavily down on the ground. He was worn out. To get him going again, I promised to buy him a treat at the university's ice cream bar. For a while he stumbled along, but then he collapsed for good. I picked him up and, turning back through the woods, took what I hoped was a short cut home. My sense of direction is pretty good, and soon we were back at the

cornfields. Near the edge of the fields grew cattails, ready to go to seed. Ducking down, I crawled through a hole in the fence and picked one. When I rubbed it, the seeds with their long silky tails burst out and, catching the breeze, blew around us like snow. Next I saw some cockleburs; I picked a handful and, sticking them on Francis's shirt, made a smiling face. Just then, Vicki looked at Eliza; blood ran down Eliza's forehead. A wire had scraped the top of her head when I crawled under the fence. All plans for the dairy bar were off, and we hurried home. Before we got there, Francis began to scream. Prickles on the cockleburs worked through his sweater and shirt and irritated his chest, making his skin break out in red bumps. As soon as we were home, I bathed Francis with calamine lotion, and Vicki cleaned Eliza's cut with hydrogen peroxide. This bothered me because I thought Vicki ought to use an ointment crammed with antibiotics. "You will have only yourself to blame if she gets lockjaw and dies," I said and went to read Dr. Spock on tetanus. And so the day passed. Again I did not write, although I eventually went to the dairy bar. The boys and I ate fudge-cake sundaes, hot fudge poured over chocolate ice cream and a piece of fudge. For her part Vicki had an apple sundae, apple ice cream buried under a thick applesauce topping.

14   The weekend's having gone by with my writing nothing did not bother me. Rarely does the familiar essay set out hiking boots afoot and compass in hand; instead it meanders, picking cockleburs and cattails, hoping to see an owl and eating ice cream. Over the years I have grown accustomed to its ways and satisfied with an easy, meandering life. I don't know whether the essay has influenced me, or whether writing it has just coincided with the growth of family and the slowing of my own pace. Whatever the case, faraway places with their sounding cataracts and stony castles no longer attract me. Living at home is good enough. In the fall I look forward to Vicki's tying an orange ribbon around Indian corn and hanging the corn on the front door. On the stoop she puts pots of yellow chrysanthemums; in late spring she puts out red and, if she

can get them, white geraniums; in summer, first pansies, then marigolds. In ordinary life I now find the stuff of poetry and research. Almost everything, even a day's dull walk, can be matter for a familiar essay.

15   This fall when the weather turned cold, scores of insects rushed to my house for shelter. Since they were little, Vicki and I generally ignored them. The only time we were really aware of them was at night. The ceiling of our bedroom seemed to be a gathering place. Before turning out the light, Vicki and I stretched out and watched them rush busily about. Occasionally, one tumbled off the ceiling and landed scurrying on the covers. Often the insects that fell were click beetles or, as they have also been known, spring bugs, blacksmiths, and skipjacks. For years I caught them in the house and tossed them outside without a thought. Now under the influence of the familiar essay I looked at them closely and wondered how such small creatures could jump so fast and so high. One morning shortly afterwards I went to the bug section of the university library. I soon realized how little I knew about my everyday world. Among the ordinary inhabitants of my bedroom, the little click beetle was extraordinary. Compared to him the world's best high jumper is a stumbling amateur. When the beetle jumps, his speed is eight feet per second; not only that but while in the air he does up to six end-over-end somersaults. To get off the ground, he snaps the top half of his body forward. The motion resembles that of the old-fashioned wooden mousetrap. When a mouse takes the cheese and releases the catch, the trap's arm flies up and over, pulling the trap into the air. In less than two thousandths of a second, the upper half of the beetle's body moves in a similar fashion, accelerating to several hundred times the force of gravity, pulling him off the ground. When he is dozing or just visiting with acquaintances, a small peg on the upper part of the beetle keeps his body straight. A catch holds the peg in place until the beetle decides to jump. When the catch is released, the peg

slams forward into a pocket on the lower part of the beetle's body. It slams into the pocket so hard that it makes a snapping sound.

16   There are over five hundred varieties of click beetles in the United States. The small suburban family with its two children, a marble cat, and a dachshund is not for the click beetle. Since it spends three to five years underground, feeding on roots and tubers, few people, aside from farmers and gardeners, know just how prolific the beetle is. Called wire worms, the young of some varieties flourish in wild numbers. If the wire worms on an acre of land are fewer than three hundred thousand, an agricultural journal stated, almost any crop can be planted. Cereals, but not potatoes, can be grown on land that contains more than three but less than six hundred thousand wire worms per acre. When the worms number more than six hundred thousand, it is difficult to grow any crop on light soil. On heavy soil, barley is likely to succeed. Beyond a million worms per acre, no matter what the texture of the soil, no crop can be grown.

17   The information that I found in the library fascinated me, and that night as Vicki and I lay in bed, watching our visitors traipse about, I told her what I had learned. For a time she was interested, or at least she pretended to be interested, until I started talking about the number of wire worms on an acre of land. "That's enough about beetles," she said, turning off the light; "three children is enough for man or bug. That's all we have, and that's all we are going to have. You had better study something less prolific. Good night."

18   Although familiar essays have changed the way I live, even creeping into the bedroom on six legs, they have not increased the size of my family. Some things are beyond the power of the pen. What the essays have influenced, though, is my academic career. Scholarly writing and the familiar essay are very different. Instead of driving hard to prove a point, the essay saunters, letting the writer follow the vagaries of his own willful curiosity. Instead of reaching conclusions, the essay ruminates and wonders. Rather than being

right or informative, it is thoughtful. Instead of being serious, it is often lighthearted, pondering subjects like the breeding habits of beetles, and alas, of people. Of course as a person ages it becomes increasingly difficult to be scholarly or definitive. Truth seems beside the point, or at least amid the many doings of a day it seems to have progressively less to do with living. Years have passed since I have read a study advertised as definitive. Being definitive, and perhaps even clever, is an activity for youth. Certainly it was in my case. Not long ago a university press that just reprinted an academic book I wrote in fresher days rejected a new manuscript. "You don't reach enough conclusions," the editor explained; "writing essays seems to have affected your scholarship." The editor was right; I now have trouble reaching conclusions. Instead of cudgeling stray dogs along the route I travel, as the director of that half-marathon in New Hampshire promised, I stop and pet them. If they could talk, I'd probably sit down, start chatting, and forget about the race.

19   Miss Dotty Brice lived in the small town in which my father grew up. The daughter of Shubael Brice, who owned the hardware store, Miss Dotty never married. An only child, she lived at home and nursed her parents to the grave. Shubael Brice was not a good businessman, and at his death when the store was sold and the debts paid off, Miss Dotty was left with little. Over the years her little shrank to nothing; yet she never went without. Relatives mended her roof, and neighbors brought her firewood and coal, chickens and eggs. Several nights a week at dinnertime, Miss Dotty put on her best clothes and started uptown. The townspeople watched for her, and before she walked far, someone always invited her in for dinner. "Don't you look nice, Miss Dotty," a neighbor would say; "we are just sitting down to eat. We are not having anything fancy, but we'd be pleased if you would join us." Like Miss Dotty, the familiar essay isn't a rich literary form. It doesn't have much of its own, yet it never goes wanting. Whenever writing time rolls around, it starts ambling along and before it has

gotten far from the front stoop it has met someone or something and is sitting down at the table, head bowed, ready for life's blessings.

THE ILLUSION OF THE TWO CULTURES
by Loren Eiseley

1   Not long ago an English scientist, Sir Eric Ashby, remarked that "to train young people in the dialectic between orthodoxy and dissent is the unique contribution which universities make to society." I am sure that Sir Eric meant by this remark that nowhere but in universities are the young given the opportunity to absorb past tradition and at the same time to experience the impact of new ideas—in the sense of a constant dialogue between past and present—lived in every hour of the student's existence. This dialogue, ideally, should lead to a great winnowing and sifting of experience and to a heightened consciousness of self which, in turn, should lead on to greater sensitivity and perception on the part of the individual.

2   Our lives are the creation of memory and the accompanying power to extend ourselves outward into ideas and relive them. The finest intellect is that which employs an invisible web of gossamer running into the past as well as across the minds of living men and which constantly responds to the vibrations transmitted through these tenuous lines of sympathy. It would be contrary to fact, however, to assume that our universities always perform this unique function of which Sir Eric speaks, with either grace or perfection; in fact our investment in man, it has been justly remarked, is deteriorating even as the financial investment in science grows.

3   More than thirty years ago, George Santayana had already sensed this trend. He commented, in a now-forgotten essay, that one of the strangest consequences of modern science was that as the visible wealth of nature was more and more transferred and abstracted, the mind seemed to lose courage and to become

ashamed of its own fertility. "The hard-pressed natural man will not indulge his imagination," continued Santayana, "unless it poses for truth; and being half-aware of this imposition, he is more troubled at the thought of being deceived than at the fact of being mechanized or being bored; and he would wish to escape imagination altogether."

4   "Man would wish to escape imagination altogether." I repeat that last phrase, for it defines a peculiar aberration of the human mind found on both sides of that bipolar division between the humanities and the sciences, which C. P. Snow has popularized under the title of *The Two Cultures.* The idea is not solely a product of this age. It was already emerging with the science of the seventeenth century; one finds it in Bacon. One finds the fear of it faintly foreshadowed in Thoreau. Thomas Huxley lent it weight when he referred contemptuously to the "caterwauling of poets."

5   Ironically, professional scientists berated the early evolutionists such as Lamarck and Chambers for overindulgence in the imagination. Almost eighty years ago John Burroughs observed that some of the animus once directed by science toward dogmatic theology seemed in his day increasingly to be vented upon the literary naturalist. In the early 1900s a quarrel over "nature faking" raised a confused din in America and aroused W. H. Hudson to some dry and pungent comment upon the failure to distinguish the purposes of science from those of literature. I know of at least one scholar who, venturing to develop some personal ideas in an essay for the layman, was characterized by a reviewer in a leading professional journal as a worthless writer, although, as it chanced, the work under discussion had received several awards in literature, one of them international in scope. More recently, some scholars not indifferent to humanistic values have exhorted poets to leave their personal songs in order to portray the beauty and symmetry of molecular structures.

6   Now some very fine verse has been written on scientific subjects, but, I fear, very little under the dictate of scientists as such.

Rather there is evident here precisely that restriction of imagination against which Santayana inveighed; namely, an attempt to constrain literature itself to the delineation of objective or empiric truth, and to dismiss the whole domain of value, which after all constitutes the very nature of man, as without significance and beneath contempt.

7 Unconsciously, the human realm is denied in favor of the world of pure technics. Man, the tool user, grows convinced that he is himself only useful as a tool, purpose, even, in some indefinable way, sinful. I was reading J. R. R. Tolkien's great symbolic trilogy, *The Fellowship of the Ring,* a few months ago, when a young scientist of my acquaintance paused and looked over my shoulder. After a little causal interchange the man departed leaving an accusing remark hovering in the air between us. "I wouldn't waste my time with a man who writes fairy stories." He might as well have added, "or with a man who reads them."

8 As I went back to my book I wondered vaguely in what leafless landscape one grew up without Hans Christian Anderson, or Dunsany, or even Jules Verne. There lingered about the young man's words a puritanism which seemed the more remarkable because, as nearly as I could discover, it was unmotivated by any sectarian religiosity unless a total dedication to science brings to some minds a similar authoritarian desire to shackle the human imagination. After all, it is this impossible, fertile world of our imagination which gave birth to liberty in the midst of oppression, and which persists in seeking until what is sought is seen. Against such invisible and fearful powers, there can be found in all ages and in all institutions—even the institutions of professional learning—the humorless man with the sneer, or if the sneer does not suffice, then the torch, for the bright unperishing letters of the human dream.

9 One can contrast this recalcitrant attitude with an 1890 reminiscence from that great Egyptologist Sir Flinders Petrie, which steals

over into the realm of pure literature. It was written, in unconscious symbolism, from a tomb:

10   "I here live, and do not scramble to fit myself to the requirements of others. In a narrow tomb, with the figure of Néfermaat standing on each side of me—as he has stood through all that we know as human history—I have just room for my bed, and a row of good reading in which I can take pleasure after dinner. Behind me is that Great Peace, the Desert. It is an entity—a power—just as much as the sea is. No wonder men fled to it from the turmoil of the ancient world."

11   It may now reasonably be asked why one who has similarly, if less dramatically, spent his life among the stones and broken shards of the remote past should be writing here about matters involving literature and science. While I was considering this with humility and trepidation, my eye fell upon a stone in my office. I am sure that professional journalists must recall times when an approaching deadline has keyed all their senses and led them to glance wildly around in the hope that something might leap out at them from the most prosaic surroundings. At all events my eyes fell upon this stone.

12   Now the stone antedated anything that the historians would call art; it had been shaped many hundreds of thousands of years ago by men whose faces would frighten us if they sat among us today. Out of old habit, since I like the feel of worked flint, I picked it up and hefted it as I groped for words over this difficult matter of the growing rift between science and art. Certainly the stone was of no help to me; it was a utilitarian thing which had cracked marrow bones, if not heads, in the remote dim morning of the human species. It was nothing if not practical. It was, in fact, an extremely early example of the empirical tradition which has led on to modern science.

13   The mind which had shaped this artifact knew its precise purpose. It had found out by experimental observation that the stone was tougher, sharper, more enduring than the hand which

wielded it. The creature's mind had solved the question of the best form of the implement and how it could be manipulated most effectively. In its day and time this hand ax was as grand an intellectual achievement as a rocket.

14   As a scientist my admiration went out to that unidentified workman. How he must have labored to understand the forces involved in the fracturing of flint, and all that involved practical survival in his world. My uncalloused twentieth-century hand caressed the yellow stone lovingly. It was then that I made a remarkable discovery.

15   In the mind of this gross-featured early exponent of the practical approach to nature—the technician, the no-nonsense practitioner of survival—two forces had met and merged. There had not been room in his short and desperate life for the delicate and supercilious separation of the arts from the sciences. There did not exist then the refined distinctions set up between the scholarly percipience of reality and what has sometimes been called the vaporings of the artistic imagination.

16   As I clasped and unclasped the stone, running my fingers down its edges, I began to perceive the ghostly emanations from a long-vanished mind, the kind of mind which, once having shaped an object of any sort, leaves an individual trace behind it which speaks to others across the barriers of time and language. It was not the practical experimental aspect of this mind that startled me, but rather that the fellow had wasted time.

17   In an incalculably brutish and dangerous world he had both shaped an instrument of practical application and then, with a virtuoso's elegance, proceeded to embellish his product. He had not been content to produce a plain, utilitarian implement. In some wistful, inarticulate way, in the grip of the dim aesthetic feelings which are one of the marks of man—or perhaps I should say, some men—this archaic creature had lingered over his handiwork.

18   One could still feel him crouching among the stones on a long-vanished river bar, turning the thing over in his hands, feeling its

polished surface, striking, here and there, just one more blow that no longer had usefulness as its criterion. He had, like myself, enjoyed the texture of the stone. With skills lost to me, he had gone on flaking the implement with an eye to beauty until it had become a kind of rough jewel, equivalent in its day to the carved and gold-inlaid pommel of the iron dagger placed in Tutankhamen's tomb.

19   All the later history of man contains these impractical exertions expended upon a great diversity of objects, and, with literacy, breaking even into printed dreams. Today's secular disruption between the creative aspect of art and that of science is a barbarism that would have brought lifted eyebrows in a Cro-Magnon cave. It is a product of high technical specialization, the deliberate blunting of wonder, and the equally deliberate suppression of a phase of our humanity in the name of an authoritarian institution, science, which has taken on, in our time, curious puritanical overtones. Many scientists seem unaware of the historical reasons for this development or the fact that the creative aspect of art is not so remote from that of science as may seem, at first glance, to be the case.

20   I am not so foolish as to categorize individual scholars or scientists. I am, however, about to remark on the nature of science as an institution. Like all such structures it is apt to reveal certain behavioral rigidities and conformities which increase with age. It is no longer the domain of the amateur, though some of its greatest discoverers could be so defined. It is now a professional body, and with professionalism there tends to emerge a greater emphasis upon a coherent system of regulations. The deviant is more sharply treated, and the young tend to imitate their successful elders. In short, an "Establishment"—a trade union—has appeared.

21   Similar tendencies can be observed among those of the humanities concerned with the professional analysis and interpretation of the works of the creative artist. Here too, a similar rigidity and exclusiveness make their appearance. It is not that in the case of both the sciences and the humanities standards are out of place.

What I am briefly cautioning against is that too frequently they afford an excuse for stifling original thought or constricting much latent creativity within traditional molds.

22 Such molds are always useful to the mediocre conformist who instinctively castigates and rejects what he cannot imitate. Tradition, the continuity of learning, are, it is true, enormously important to the learned disciplines. What we must realize as scientists is that the particular institution we inhabit has its own irrational accretions and authoritarian dogmas which can be as unpleasant as some of those encountered in sectarian circles—particularly so since they are frequently unconsciously held and surrounded by an impenetrable wall of self-righteousness brought about because science is regarded as totally empiric and open-minded by tradition.

23 This type of professionalism, as I shall label it in order to distinguish it from what is best in both the sciences and humanities, is characterized by two assumptions: that the accretions of fact are cumulative and lead to progress, whereas the insights of art are, at best, singular, and lead nowhere, or, when introduced into the realm of science, produce obscurity and confusion. The convenient label "mystic" is, in our day, readily applied to men who pause for simple wonder, or who encounter along the borders of the known that "awful power" which Wordsworth characterized as the human imagination. It can, he says, rise suddenly from the mind's abyss and enwrap the solitary traveler like a mist.

24 We do not like mists in this era, and the word imagination is less and less used. We like, instead, a clear road, and we abhor solitary traveling. Indeed one of our great scientific historians remarked not long ago that the literary naturalist was obsolescent if not completely outmoded. I suppose he meant that with our penetration into the biophysical realm, life, like matter, would become increasingly represented by abstract symbols. To many it must appear that the more we can dissect life into its elements, the closer we are getting to its ultimate resolution. While I have some reservations on

this scope, they are not important. Rather, I should like to look at the symbols which in the one case denote science and in the other constitute those vaporings and cloud wraiths that are the abomination, so it is said, of the true scientist but are the delight of the poet and literary artist.

25   Creation in science demands a high level of imaginative insight and intuitive perception. I believe no one would deny this, even though it exists in varying degrees, just as it does, similarly, among writers, musicians, or artists. The scientist's achievement, however, is quantitatively transmissible. From a single point his discovery is verifiable by other men who may then, on the basis of corresponding data, accept the innovation and elaborate upon it in the cumulative fashion which is one of the great triumphs of science.

26   Artistic creation, on the other hand, is unique. It cannot be twice discovered, as, say, natural selection was discovered. It may be imitated stylistically, in a genre, a school, but, save for a few items of technique, it is not cumulative. A successful work of art may set up reverberations and is, in this, just as transmissible as science, but there is a qualitative character about it. Each reverberation in another mind is unique. As the French novelist François Mauriac has remarked, each great novel is a separate and distinct world operating under its own laws with a flora and fauna totally its own. There is communication, or the work is a failure, but the communication releases our own visions, touches some highly personal chord in our own experience.

27   The symbols used by the great artist are a key releasing our humanity from the solitary tower of the self. "Man," says Lewis Mumford, "is first and foremost the self-fabricating animal." I shall merely add that the artist plays an enormous role in this act of self-creation. It is he who touches the hidden strings of pity, who searches our hearts, who makes us sensitive to beauty, who asks questions about fate and destiny. Such questions, though they lurk always around the corners of the external universe which is the

peculiar province of science, the rigors of the scientific method do not enable us to pursue directly.

28   And yet I wonder.

29   It is surely possible to observe that it is the successful analogy or symbol which frequently allows the scientist to leap from a generalization in one field of thought to a triumphant achievement in another. For example, Progressionism in a spiritual sense later became the model contributing to the discovery of organic evolution. Such analogies genuinely resemble the figures and enchantments of great literature, whose meanings similarly can never be totally grasped because of their endless power to ramify in the individual mind.

30   John Donne gave powerful expression to a feeling applicable as much to science as to literature when he said devoutly of certain Biblical passages: "The literall sense is always to be preserved; but the literall sense is not always to be discerned; for the literall sense is not always that which the very letter and grammar of the place presents." A figurative sense, he argues cogently, can sometimes be the most "literall intention of the Holy Ghost."

31   It is here that the scientist and artist sometimes meet in uneasy opposition, or at least along lines of tension. The scientist's attitude is sometimes, I suspect, that embodied in Samuel Johnson's remark that, wherever there is mystery, roguery is not far off.

32   Yet surely it was not roguery when Sir Charles Lyell glimpsed in a few fossil prints of raindrops the persistence of the world's natural forces through the incredible, mysterious aeons of geologic time. The fossils were a symbol of a vast hitherto unglimpsed order. They are, in Donne's sense, both literal and symbolic. As fossils they merely denote evidence of rain in a past era. Figuratively they are more. To the perceptive intelligence they afford the hint of lengthened natural order, just as the eyes of ancient trilobites tell us similarly of the unchanging laws of light. Equally, the educated mind may discern in a scratched pebble the retreating shadow of vast ages of ice and gloom. In Donne's archaic phraseology these

objects would bespeak the principal intention of the Divine Being—that is, of order beyond our power to grasp.

33 Such images drawn from the world of science are every bit as powerful as great literary symbolism and equally demanding upon the individual imagination of the scientist who would fully grasp the extension of meaning which is involved. It is, in fact, one and the same creative act in both domains.

34 Indeed evolution itself has become such a figurative symbol, as has also the hypothesis of the expanding universe. The laboratory worker may think of these concepts in a totally empirical fashion as subject to proof or disproof by the experimental method. Like Freud's doctrine of the subconscious, however, such ideas frequently escape from the professional scientist into the public domain. There they may undergo further individual transformation and embellishment. Whether the scholar approves or not, such hypotheses are now as free to evolve in the mind of the individual as are the creations of art. All the resulting enrichment and confusion will bear about it something suggestive of the world of artistic endeavor.

35 As figurative insights into the nature of things, such embracing conceptions may become grotesquely distorted or glow with added philosophical wisdom. As in the case of the trilobite eye or the fossil raindrop, there lurks behind the visible evidence vast shadows no longer quite of that world which we term natural. Like the words in Donne's Bible, enormous implications have transcended the literal expression of the thought. Reality itself has been superseded by a greater reality. As Donne himself asserted, "The substance of the truth is in the great images which lie behind."

36 It is because these two types of creation—the artistic and the scientific—have sprung from the same being and have their points of contact even in division that I have the temerity to assert that, in a sense, the "two cultures" are an illusion, that they are a product of unreasoning fear, professionalism, and misunderstanding. Be-

cause of the emphasis upon science in our society, much has been said about the necessity of educating the layman and even the professional student of the humanities upon the ways and the achievements of science. I admit that a barrier exists, but I am also concerned to express the view that there persists in the domain of science itself an occasional marked intolerance of those of its own membership who venture to pursue the way of letters. As I have remarked, this intolerance can the more successfully clothe itself in seeming objectivity because of the supposed open nature of the scientific society. It is not remarkable that this trait is sometimes more manifest in the younger and less secure disciplines.

37   There was a time, not too many centuries ago, when to be active in scientific investigation was to invite suspicion. Thus it may be that there now lingers among us, even in the triumph of the experimental method, a kind of vague fear of that other artistic world of deep emotion, of strange symbols, lest it seize upon us or distort the hard-won objectivity of our thinking—lest it corrupt, in other words, that crystalline and icy objectivity which, in our scientific guise, we erect as a model of conduct. This model, incidentally, if pursued to its absurd conclusion, would lead to a world in which the computer would determine all aspects of our existence; one in which the bomb would be as welcome as the discoveries of the physician.

38   Happily, the very great in science, or even those unique scientist-artists such as Leonardo, who foreran the emergence of science as an institution, have been singularly free from this folly. Darwin decried it even as he recognized that he had paid a certain price in concentrated specialization for his achievement. Einstein, it is well known, retained a simple sense of wonder; Newton felt like a child playing with pretty shells on a beach. All show a deep humility and an emotional hunger which is the prerogative of the artist. It is with the lesser men, with the institutionalization of method, with the appearance of dogma and mapped-out territories, that an unpleas-

ant suggestion of fenced preserves begins to dominate the university atmosphere.

39   As a scientist, I can say that I have observed it in my own and others' specialties. I have had occasion, also, to obseve its effects in the humanities. It is not science *per se;* it is, instead, in both regions of thought, the narrow professionalism which is also plainly evident in the trade union. There can be small men in science just as there are small men in government or business. In fact it is one of the disadvantages of big science, just as it is of big government, that the availability of huge sums attracts a swarm of elbowing and contentious men to whom great dreams are less than protected hunting preserves.

40   The sociology of science deserves at least equal consideration with the biographies of the great scientists, for powerful and changing forces are at work upon science, the institution, as contrasted with science as a dream and an ideal of the individual. Like other aspects of society, it is a construct of men and is subject, like other social structures, to human pressures and inescapable distortions.

41   Let me give an illustration. Even in learned journals, clashes occasionally occur between those who would regard biology as a separate and distinct domain of inquiry and the reductionists who, by contrast, perceive in the living organism only a vaster and more random chemistry. Understandably, the concern of the reductionists is with the immediate. Thomas Hobbes was expressing a similar point of view when he castigated poets as "working on mean minds with words and distinctions that of themselves signifie nothing, but betray (by their obscurity) that there walketh . . . another kingdome, as it were a kingdome of fayries in the dark." I myself have been similarly criticized for speaking of a nature "beyond the nature that we know."

42   Yet consider for a moment this dark, impossible realm of "fayrie." Man is not totally compounded of the nature we profess to understand. He contains, instead, a lurking unknown future, just

as the man-apes of the Pliocene contained in embryo the future that surrounds us now. The world of human culture itself was an unpredictable fairy world until, in some pre-ice-age meadow, the first meaningful sounds in all the world broke through the jungle babble of the past, the nature, until that moment, "known."

43   It is fascinating to observe that, in the very dawn of science, Francis Bacon, the spokesman for the empirical approach to nature, shared with Shakespeare, the poet, a recognition of the creativeness which adds to nature, and which emerges from nature as "an art which nature makes." Neither the great scholar nor the great poet had renounced this "kingdome of fayries." Both had realized what Henri Bergson was later to express so effectively, that life inserts a vast "indetermination into matter." It is, in a sense, an intrusion from a realm which can never be completely subject to prophetic analysis by science. The novelties of evolution emerge; they cannot be predicted. They haunt, until their arrival, a world of unimaginable possibilities behind the living screen of events, as these last exist to the observer confined to a single point on the time scale.

44   Oddly enough, much of the confusion that surrounded my phrase, "a nature beyond the nature that we know," resolves itself into pure semantics. I might have pointed out what must be obvious even to the most dedicated scientific mind—that the nature which we know has been many times reinterpreted in human thinking, and that the hard, substantial matter of the nineteenth century has already vanished into a dark, bodiless void, a web of "events" in space-time. This is a realm, I venture to assert, as weird as any we have tried, in the past, to exorcise by the brave use of seeming solid words. Yet some minds exhibit an almost instinctive hostility toward the mere attempt to wonder or to ask what lies below that microcosmic world out of which emerge the particles which compose our bodies and which now take on this wraithlike quality.

45   Is there something here we fear to face, except when clothed in safely sterilized professional speech? Have we grown reluctant in this age of power to admit mystery and beauty into our thoughts, or to learn where power ceases? I referred earlier to one of our own forebears on a gravel bar, thumbing a pebble. If, after the ages of building and destroying, if after the measuring of light-years and the powers probed at the atom's heart, if after the last iron is rust-eaten and the last glass lies shattered in the streets, a man, some savage, some remnant of what once we were, pauses on his way to the tribal drinking place and feels rising from within his soul the inexplicable mist of terror and beauty that is evoked from old ruins—even the ruins of the greatest city in the world—then, I say, all will still be well with man.

46   And if that savage can pluck a stone from the gravel because it shone like crystal when the water rushed over it, and hold it against the sunset, he will be as we were in the beginning, whole—as we were when we were children, before we began to split the knowledge from the dream. All talk of the two cultures is an illusion; it is the pebble which tells man's story. Upon it is written man's two faces, the artistic and the practical. They are expressed upon one stone over which a hand once closed, no less firm because the mind behind it was submerged in light and shadow and deep wonder.

47   Today we hold a stone, the heavy stone of power. We must perceive beyond it, however, by the aid of the artistic imagination, those humane insights and understandings which alone can lighten our burden and enable us to shape ourselves, rather than the stone, into the forms which great art has anticipated.

LIVING LIKE WEASELS
by Annie Dillard

1   A weasel is wild. Who knows what he thinks? He sleeps in his underground den, his tail draped over his nose. Sometimes he lives

in his den for two days without leaving. Outside, he stalks rabbits, mice, muskrats, and birds, killing more bodies than he can eat warm, and often dragging the carcasses home. Obedient to instinct, he bites his prey at the neck, either splitting the jugular vein at the throat or crunching the brain at the base of the skull, and he does not let go. One naturalist refused to kill a weasel who was socketed into his hand deeply as a rattlesnake. The man could in no way pry the tiny weasel off, and he had to walk half a mile to water, the weasel dangling from his palm, and soak him off like a stubborn label.

2   And once, says Ernest Thompson Seton—once, a man shot an eagle out of the sky. He examined the eagle and found the dry skull of a weasel fixed by the jaws to his throat. The supposition is that the eagle had pounced on the weasel and the weasel swiveled and bit as instinct taught him, tooth to neck, and nearly won. I would like to have seen that eagle from the air a few weeks or months before he was shot: was the whole weasel still attached to his feathered throat, a fur pendant? Or did the eagle eat what he could reach, gutting the living weasel with his talons before his breast, bending his beak, cleaning the beautiful airborne bones?

3   I have been reading about weasels because I saw one last week. I startled a weasel who startled me, and we exchanged a long glance.

4   Twenty minutes from my house, through the woods by the quarry and across the highway, is Hollins Pond, a remarkable piece of shallowness, where I like to go at sunset and sit on a tree trunk. Hollins Pond is also called Murray's Pond; it covers two acres of bottomland near Tinker Creek with six inches of water and six thousand lily pads. In winter, brown-and-white steers stand in the middle of it, merely dampening their hooves; from the distant shore they look like miracle itself, complete with miracle's nonchalance. Now, in summer, the steers are gone. The water lilies have blossomed and spread to a green horizontal plane that is terra firma to

plodding blackbirds, and tremulous ceiling to black leeches, crayfish, and carp.

5   This is, mind you, suburbia. It is a five-minute walk in three directions to rows of houses, though none is visible here. There's a 55 mph highway at one end of the pond, and a nesting pair of wood ducks at the other. Under every bush is a muskrat hole or a beer can. The far end is an alternating series of fields and woods, fields and woods, threaded everywhere with motorcycle tracks—in whose bare clay wild turtles lay eggs.

6   So. I had crossed the highway, stepped over two low barbed-wire fences, and traced the motorcycle path in all gratitude through the wild rose and poison ivy of the pond's shoreline up into high grassy fields. Then I cut down through the woods to the mossy fallen tree where I sit. This tree is excellent. It makes a dry, upholstered bench at the upper, marshy end of the pond, a plush jetty raised from the thorny shore between a shallow blue body of water and a deep blue body of sky.

7   The sun had just set. I was relaxed on the tree trunk, ensconced in the lap of lichen, watching the lily pads at my feet tremble and part dreamily over the thrusting path of a carp. A yellow bird appeared to my right and flew behind me. It caught my eye; I swiveled around—and the next instant, inexplicably, I was looking down at a weasel, who was looking up at me.

8   Weasel! I'd never seen one wild before. He was ten inches long, thin as a curve, a muscled ribbon, brown as fruitwood, soft-furred, alert. His face was fierce, small and pointed as a lizard's; he would have made a good arrowhead. There was just a dot of chin, maybe two brown hairs' worth, and then the pure white fur began that spread down his underside. He had two black eyes I didn't see, any more than you see a window.

9   The weasel was stunned into stiffness as he was emerging from beneath an enormous shaggy wild rose bush four feet away. I was

stunned into stillness twisted backward on the tree trunk. Our eyes locked, and someone threw away the key.

10   Our look was as if two lovers, or deadly enemies, met unexpectedly on an overgrown path when each had been thinking of something else: a clearing blow to the gut. It was also a bright blow to the brain, or a sudden beating of brains, with all the charge and intimate grate of rubbed balloons. It emptied our lungs. It felled the forest, moved the fields, and drained the pond; the world dismantled and tumbled into that black hole of eyes. If you and I looked at each other that way, our skulls would split and drop to our shoulders. But we don't. We keep our skulls. So.

11   He disappeared. This was only last week, and already I don't remember what shattered the enchantment. I think I blinked, I think I retrieved my brain from the weasel's brain, and tried to memorize what I was seeing, and the weasel felt the yank of separation, the careening splashdown into real life and the urgent current of instinct. He vanished under the wild rose. I waited motionless, my mind suddenly full of data and my spirit with pleadings, but he didn't return.

12   Please do not tell me about "approach-avoidance conflicts." I tell you I've been in that weasel's brain for sixty seconds, and he was in mine. Brains are private places, muttering through unique and secret tapes—but the weasel and I both plugged into another tape simultaneously, for a sweet and shocking time. Can I help it if it was a blank?

13   What goes on in his brain the rest of the time? What does a weasel think about? He won't say. His journal is tracks in clay, a spray of feathers, mouse blood and bone: uncollected, unconnected, loose-leaf, and blown.

14   I would like to learn, or remember, how to live. I come to Hollins Pond not so much to learn how to live as, frankly, to forget about it. That is, I don't think I can learn from a wild animal how to live in particular—shall I suck warm blood, hold my tail high, walk with my footprints precisely over the prints of my hands?—but I might

learn something of mindlessness, something of the purity of living in the physical senses and the dignity of living without bias or motive. The weasel lives in necessity and we live in choice, hating necessity and dying at the last ignobly in its talons. I would like to live as I should, as the weasel lives as he should. And I suspect that for me the way is like the weasel's: open to time and death painlessly, noticing everything, remembering nothing, choosing the given with a fierce and pointed will.

15   I missed my chance. I should have gone for the throat. I should have lunged for that streak of white under the weasel's chin and held on, held on through mud and into the wild rose, held on for a dearer life. We could live under the wild rose wild as weasels, mute and uncomprehending. I could very calmly go wild. I could live two days in the den, curled, leaning on mouse fur, sniffing bird bones, blinking, licking, breathing musk, my hair tangled in the roots of grasses. Down is a good place to go, where the mind is single. Down is out, out of your ever-loving mind and back to your careless senses. I remember muteness as a prolonged and giddy fast, where every moment is a feast of utterance received. Time and events are merely poured, unremarked, and ingested directly, like blood pulsed into my gut through a jugular vein. Could two live that way? Could two live under the wild rose, and explore by the pond, so that the smooth mind of each is as everywhere present to the other, and as received and as unchallenged, as falling snow?

We could, you know. We can live any way we want. People take vows of poverty, chastity, and obedience—even of silence—by choice. The thing is to stalk your calling in a certain skilled and supple way, to locate the most tender and live spot and plug into that pulse. This is yielding, not fighting. A weasel doesn't "attack" anything; a weasel lives as he's meant to, yielding at every moment to the perfect freedom of single necessity.

16   I think it would be well, and proper, and obedient, and pure, to grasp your one necessity and not let it go, to dangle from it limp wherever it takes you. Then even death, where you're going no matter how you live, cannot you part. Seize it and let it seize you up aloft even, till your eyes burn out and drop; let your musky flesh fall off in shreds, and let your very bones unhinge and scatter, loosened over fields, over fields and woods, lightly, thoughtless, from any height at all, from as high as eagles.

MANY RIVERS TO CROSS
DECEMBER, 1981
by June Jordan

1   When my mother killed herself I was looking for a job. That was fifteen years ago. I had no money and no food. On the pleasure side I was down to my last pack of Pall Malls plus half a bottle of J & B. I needed to find work because I needed to be able fully to support myself and my eight-year-old son, very fast. My plan was to raise enough big bucks so that I could take an okay apartment inside an acceptable public school district, by September. That deadline left me less than three months to turn my fortunes right side up.

2   It seemed that I had everything to do at once. Somehow, I must move all of our things, mostly books and toys, out of the housing project before the rent fell due, again. I must do this without letting my neighbors know because destitution and divorce added up to personal shame, and failure. Those same neighbors had looked upon my husband and me as an ideal young couple, in many ways: inseparable, doting, ambitious. They had kept me busy and laughing in the hard weeks following my husband's departure for graduate school in Chicago; they had been the ones to remember him warmly through teasing remarks and questions all that long year that I remained alone, waiting for his return while I became the "temporary," sole breadwinner of our peculiar long-distance family by telephone. They had been the ones who kindly stopped the

teasing and the queries when the year ended and my husband, the father of my child, did not come back. They never asked me and I never told them what that meant, altogether. I don't think I really knew.

3   I could see how my husband would proceed more or less naturally from graduate school to a professional occupation of his choice, just as he had shifted rather easily from me, his wife, to another man's wife—another woman. What I could not see was how I should go forward, now, in any natural, coherent way. As a mother without a husband, as a poet without a publisher, a freelance journalist without assignment, a city planner without a contract, it seemed to me that several incontestable and conflicting necessities had suddenly eliminated the whole realm of choice from my life.

4   My husband and I agreed that he would have the divorce that he wanted, and I would have the child. This ordinary settlement is, as millions of women will testify, as absurd as saying, "I'll give you a call, you handle everything else." At any rate, as my lawyer explained, the law then was the same as the law today; the courts would surely award me a reasonable amount of the father's income as child support, but the courts would also insist that they could not enforce their own decree. In other words, according to the law, what a father owes to his child is not serious compared to what a man owes to the bank for a car, or a vacation. Hence, as they say, it is extremely regrettable but nonetheless true that the courts cannot garnish a father's salary, nor freeze his account, nor seize his property on behalf of his children, in our society. Apparently this is because a child is not a car or a couch or a boat. (I would suppose this is the very best available definition of the difference between an American child and a car.)

5   Anyway, I wanted to get out of the projects as quickly as possible. But I was going to need help because I couldn't bend down and I couldn't carry anything heavy and I couldn't let my parents know about these problems because I didn't want to fight

with them about the reasons behind the problems—which was the same reason I couldn't walk around or sit up straight to read or write without vomiting and acute abdominal pain. My parents would have evaluated that reason as a terrible secret compounded by a terrible crime; once again an unmarried woman, I had, nevertheless, become pregnant. What's more I had tried to interrupt this pregnancy even though this particular effort required not only one but a total of three abortions—each of them illegal and amazingly expensive, as well as, evidently, somewhat poorly executed.

6   My mother, against my father's furious rejections of me and what he viewed as my failure, offered what she could; she had no money herself but there was space in the old brownstone of my childhood. I would live with them during the summer while I pursued my crash schedule for cash, and she would spend as much time with Christopher, her only and beloved grandchild, as her worsening but partially undiagnosed illness allowed.

7   After she suffered a stroke, her serenely imposing figure had shrunk into an unevenly balanced, starved shell of chronic disorder. In the last two years, her physical condition had forced her retirement from nursing, and she spent most of her days on a makeshift cot pushed against the wall of the dining room next to the kitchen. She could do very few things for herself, besides snack on crackers, or pour ready-made juice into a cup and then drink it.

8   In June, 1966, I moved from the projects into my parents' house with the help of a woman named Mrs. Hazel Griffin. Since my teens, she had been my hairdresser. Every day, all day, she stood on her feet, washing and straightening hair in her crowded shop, the Arch of Beauty. Mrs. Griffin had never been married, had never finished high school, and she ran the Arch of Beauty with an imperturbable and contagious sense of success. She had a daughter as old as I who worked alongside her mother, coddling customer fantasy into confidence. Gradually, Mrs. Griffin and I became close; as my own mother became more and more bedridden and demoralized, Mrs. Griffin extended herself—dropping by my par-

ents' house to make dinner for them, or calling me to wish me good luck on a special freelance venture, and so forth. It was Mrs. Griffin who closed her shop for a whole day and drove all the way from Brooklyn to my housing project apartment in Queens. It was Mrs. Griffin who packed me up, so to speak, and carried me and the boxes back to Brooklyn, back to the house of my parents. It was Mrs. Griffin who ignored my father standing hateful at the top of the stone steps of the house and not saying a word of thanks and not once relieving her of a single load she wrestled up the stairs and past him. My father hated Mrs. Griffin because he was proud and because she was a stranger of mercy. My father hated Mrs. Griffin because he was like that sometimes: hateful and crazy.

9   My father alternated between weeping bouts of self-pity and storm explosions of wrath against the gods apparently determined to ruin him. These were his alternating reactions to my mother's increasing enfeeblement, her stoic depression. I think he was scared; who would take care of him? Would she get well again and make everything all right again?

10   This is how we organized the brownstone; I fixed a room for my son on the top floor of the house. I slept on the parlor floor in the front room. My father slept on the same floor, in the back. My mother stayed downstairs.

11   About a week after moving in, my mother asked me about the progress of my plans. I told her things were not terrific but that there were two different planning jobs I hoped to secure within a few days. One of them involved a study of new towns in Sweden and the other one involved an analysis of the social consequences of a huge hydro-electric dam under construction in Ghana. My mother stared at me uncomprehendingly and then urged me to look for work in the local post office. We bitterly argued about what she dismissed as my "high-falutin" ideas and, I believe, that was the last substantial conversation between us.

12 From my first memory of him, my father had always worked at the post office. His favorite was the night shift, which brought him home usually between three and four o'clock in the morning.

13 It was hot. I finally fell asleep that night, a few nights after the argument between my mother and myself. She seemed to be rallying; that afternoon, she and my son had spent a long time in the backyard, oblivious to the heat and the mosquitoes. They were both tired but peaceful when they noisily re-entered the house, holding hands awkwardly.

14 But someone was knocking at the door to my room. Why should I wake up? It would be impossible to fall asleep again. It was so hot. The knocking continued. I switched on the light by the bed: 3:30 a.m. It must be my father. Furious, I pulled on a pair of shorts and a t-shirt. "What do you want' What's the matter?" I asked him, through the door. Had he gone berserk? What could he have to talk about at that ridiculous hour?

15 "OK, all right," I said, rubbing my eyes awake as I stepped to the door and opened it. "What?"

16 To my surprise, my father stood there looking very uncertain.

17 "It's your mother," he told me, in a burly, formal voice. "I think she's dead, but I'm not sure." He was avoiding my eyes.

18 "What do you mean," I answered.

19 "I want you to go downstairs and figure it out."

20 I could not believe what he was saying to me. "You want me to figure out if my mother is dead or alive?"

21 "I can't tell! I don't know!!" he shouted angrily.

22 "Jesus Christ," I muttered, angry and beside myself.

23 I turned and glanced about my room, wondering if I could find anything to carry with me on this mission; what do you use to determine a life or a death? I couldn't see anything obvious that might be useful.

24 "I'll wait up here," my father said. "You call up and let me know."

25   I could not believe it; a man married to a woman more than forty
years and he can't tell if she's alive or dead and he wakes up his kid
and tells her, "You figure it out."

26   I was at the bottom of the stairs. I halted just outside the dining
room where my mother slept. Suppose she really was dead?
Suppose my father was not just being crazy and hateful? "Naw," I
shook my head and confidently entered the room.

27   "Momma?!" I called, aloud. At the edge of the cot, my mother
was leaning forward, one arm braced to hoist her body up. She was
trying to stand up! I rushed over. "Wait. Here, I'll help you!" I said.

28   And I reached out my hands to give her a lift. The body of my
mother was stiff. She was not yet cold, but she was stiff. Maybe I had
come downstairs just in time! I tried to loosen her arms, to change
her position, to ease her into lying down.

29   "Momma!" I kept saying. "Momma, listen to me! It's OK! I'm
here and everything. Just relax. Relax! Give me a hand, now. I'm
trying to help you lie down!"

30   Her body did not relax. She did not answer me. But she was not
cold. Her eyes were not shut.

31   From upstairs my father was yelling, "Is she dead? Is she dead?"

32   "No!" I screamed at him. "No! She's not dead!"

33   At this, my father tore down the stairs and into the room. Then he
braked.

34   "Milly?" he called out, tentative. Then he shouted at me and
banged around the walls. "You damn fool. Don't you see now
she's gone. Now she's gone!" We began to argue.

35   "She's alive! Call the doctor!"

36   "No!"

37   "Yes!"

38   At last my father left the room to call the doctor.

39   I straightened up. I felt completely exhausted from trying to gain
a response from my mother. There she was, stiff on the edge of her
bed, just about to stand up. Her lips were set, determined. She

would manage it, but by herself. I could not help. Her eyes fixed on some point below the floor.

40   "Momma!" I shook her hard as I could to rouse her into focus. Now she fell back on the cot, but frozen and in the wrong position. It hit me that she might be dead. She might be dead.

41   My father reappeared at the door. He would not come any closer. "Dr. Davis says he will come. And he call the police."

42   The police? Would they know if my mother was dead or alive? Who would know?

43   I went to the phone and called my aunt. "Come quick," I said. "My father thinks Momma has died but she's here but she's stiff."

44   Soon the house was weird and ugly and crowded and I thought I was losing my mind.

45   Three white policemen stood around telling me my mother was dead. "How do you know?" I asked, and they shrugged and then they repeated themselves. And the doctor never came. But my aunt came and my uncle and they said she was dead.

46   After a conference with the cops, my aunt disappeared and when she came back she held a bottle in one of her hands. She and the police whispered together some more. Then one of the cops said, "Don't worry about it. We won't say anything." My aunt signalled me to follow her into the hallway where she let me understand that, in fact, my mother had committed suicide.

47   I could not assimilate this information: suicide.

48   I broke away from my aunt and ran to the telephone. I called a friend of mine, a woman who talked back loud to me so that I could realize my growing hysteria, and check it. Then I called my cousin Valerie who lived in Harlem; she woke up instantly and urged me to come right away.

49   I hurried to the top floor and stood my sleeping son on his feet. I wanted to get him out of this house of death more than I ever wanted anything. He could not stand by himself so I carried him down the two flights to the street and laid him on the backseat and then took off.

50   At Valerie's, my son continued to sleep, so we put him to bed, closed the door, and talked. My cousin made me eat eggs, drink whiskey, and shower. She would take care of Christopher, she said. I should go back and deal with the situation in Brooklyn.

51   When I arrived, the house was absolutely full of women from the church dressed as though they were going to Sunday communion. It seemed to me they were, every one of them, wearing hats and gloves and drinking coffee and solemnly addressing invitations to a funeral and I could not find my mother anywhere and I could not find an empty spot in the house where I could sit down and smoke a cigarette.

52   My mother was dead.

53   Feeling completely out of place, I headed for the front door, ready to leave. My father grabbed my shoulder from behind and forcibly spun me around.

54   "You see this?" he smiled, waving a large document in the air. "This am insurance paper for you!" He waved it into my face. "Your mother, she left you insurance, see?"

55   I watched him.

56   "But I gwine burn it in the furnace before I give it you to t'row away on trash!"

57   "Is that money?" I demanded. "Did my mother leave me money?"

58   "Eh-heh!" he laughed. "And you don't get it from me. Not today, not tomorrow. Not until I dead and buried!"

59   My father grabbed for my arm and I swung away from him. He hit me on my head and I hit back. We were fighting.

60   Suddenly, the ladies from the church bustled about and pushed, horrified, between us. This was a sin, they said, for a father and a child to fight in the house of the dead and the mother not yet in the ground! Such a good woman she was, they said. She was a good woman, a good women, they all agreed. Out of respect for the memory of this good woman, in deference to my mother who had

committed suicide, the ladies shook their hats and insisted we should not fight; I should not fight with my father.

61   Utterly disgusted and disoriented, I went back to Harlem. By the time I reached my cousin's place I had begun to bleed, heavily. Valerie said I was hemorrhaging so she called up her boyfriend and the two of them hobbled me into Harlem Hospital.

62   I don't know how long I remained unconscious, but when I opened my eyes I found myself on the women's ward, with an intravenous setup feeding into my arm. After a while, Valerie showed up. Christopher was fine, she told me; my friends were taking turns with him. Whatever I did, I should not admit I'd had an abortion or I'd get her into trouble, and myself in trouble. Just play dumb and rest. I'd have to stay on the ward for several days. My mother's funeral was tomorrow afternoon. What did I want her to tell people to explain why I wouldn't be there? She meant, what lie?

63   I thought about it and I decided I had nothing to say; if I couldn't tell the truth then the hell with it.

64   I lay in that bed at Harlem Hospital, thinking and sleeping. I wanted to get well.

65   I wanted to be strong. I never wanted to be weak again as long as I lived. I thought about my mother and her suicide and I thought about how my father could not tell whether she was dead or alive.

66   I wanted to get well and what I wanted to do as soon as I was strong again, actually, what I wanted to do was I wanted to live my life so that people would know unmistakably that I am alive, so that when I finally die people will know the difference for sure between my living and my death.

67   And I thought about the idea of my mother as a good woman and I rejected that, because I don't see why it's a good thing when you give up, or when you cooperate with those who hate you or when you polish and iron and mend and endlessly mollify for the sake of the people who love the way that you kill yourself day by day silently.

68 And I think all of this is really about women and work. Certainly this is all about me as a woman and my life work. I mean I am not sure my mother's suicide was something extraordinary. Perhaps most women must deal with a similar inheritance, the legacy of a woman whose death you cannot possibly pinpoint because she died so many, many times and because, even before she became your mother, the life of that woman was taken; I say it was taken away.

69 And really it was to honor my mother that I did fight with my father, that man who could not tell the living from the dead.

70 And really it is to honor Mrs. Hazel Griffin and my cousin Valerie and all the women I love, including myself, that I am working for the courage to admit the truth that Bertolt Brecht has written, he says, "It takes courage to say that the good were defeated not because they were good, but because they were weak."

71 I cherish the mercy and the grace of women's work. But I know there is new work that we must undertake as well: that new work will make defeat detestable to us. That new women's work will mean we will not die trying to stand up: we will live that way: standing up.

72 I came too late to help my mother to her feet.

73 By way of everlasting thanks to all of the women who have helped me to stay alive I am working never to be late again.

REPORT FROM THE BAHAMAS
1982
by June Jordan

1 I am staying in a hotel that calls itself The Sheraton British Colonial. One of the photographs advertising the place displays a middle-aged Black man in a waiter's tuxedo, smiling. What intrigues me most about the picture is just this: while the Black man bears a tray full of "colorful" drinks above his left shoulder, both of

his feet, shoes and trouserlegs, up to ten inches above his ankles, stand in the also "colorful" Caribbean salt water. He is so delighted to serve you he will wade into the water to bring you Banana Daquiris while you float! More precisely, he will wade into the water, fully clothed, oblivious to the ruin of his shoes, his trousers, his health, and he will do it with a smile.

2   I am in the Bahamas. On the phone in my room, a spinning complement of plastic pages offers handy index clues such as CAR RENTAL and CASINOS. A message from the Ministry of Tourism appears among these travellers tips. Opening with a paragraph of "WELCOME," the message then proceeds to "A PAGE OF HIS-TORY," which reads as follows:

> New World History begins on the same day that modern Bahamian history begins—October 12, 1492. That's when Columbus stepped ashore—British influence came first with the Eleutherian Adventurers of 1647—After the Revolutions, American Loyalists fled from the newly independent states and settled in the Bahamas. Confederate blockade-runners used the island as a haven during the War between the States, and after the War, a number of Southerners moved to the Bahamas . . .

There it is again. Something proclaims itself a legitimate history and all it does is track white Mr. Columbus to the British Eleutherians through the Confederate Southerners as they barge into New World surf, land on New World turf, and nobody saying one word about the Bahamian people, the Black peoples, to whom the only thing new in their island world was this weird succession of crude intruders and its colonial consequences.

3   This is my consciousness of race as I unpack my bathing suit in the Sheraton British Colonial. Neither this hotel nor the British nor the long ago Italians nor the white Delta airline pilots belong here, of course. And every time I look at the photograph of that fool standing in the water with his shoes on I'm about to have a West

307

Indian fit, even though I know he's no fool; he's a middle-aged Black man who needs a job and this is his job—pretending himself a servile ancillary to the pleasures of the rich. (Compared to his options in life, I am a rich woman. Compared to most of the Black Americans arriving for this Easter weekend on a three nights four days' deal of bargain rates, the middle-aged waiter is a poor Black man.)

4   We will jostle along with the other (white) visitors and join them in the tee shirt shops or, laughing together, learn ruthless rules of negotiation as we, Black Americans as well as white, argue down the price of handwoven goods at the nearby straw market while the merchants, frequently toothless Black women seated on the concrete in their only presentable dress, humble themselves to our careless games:

5   "Yes? You like it? Eight dollar."

6   "Five."

7   "I give it to you. Seven."

8   And so it continues, this weird succession of crude intruders that, now, includes me and my brothers and my sisters from the North.

9   This is my consciousness of class as I try to decide how much money I can spend on Bahamian gifts for my family back in Brooklyn. No matter that these other Black women incessantly weave words and flowers into the straw hats and bags piled beside them on the burning dusty street. No matter that these other Black women must work their sense of beauty into these things that we will take away as cheaply as we dare, or they will do without food.

10   We are not white, after all. The budget is limited. And we are harmlessly killing time between the poolside rum punch and "The Native Show on the Patio" that will play tonight outside the hotel restaurant.

11   This is my consciousness of race and class and gender identity as I notice the fixed relations between these other Black women and

myself. They sell and I buy or I don't. They risk not eating. I risk going broke on my first vacation afternoon.

12   We are not particularly women anymore; we are parties to a transaction designed to set us against each other.

13   "Olive" is the name of the Black woman who cleans my hotel room. On my way to the beach I am wondering what "Olive" would say if I told her why I chose The Sheraton British Colonial; if I told her I wanted to swim. I wanted to sleep. I did not want to be harassed by the middle-aged waiter, or his nephew. I did not want to be raped by anybody (white or Black) at all and I calculated that my safety as a Black woman alone would best be assured by a multinational hotel corporation. In my experience, the big guys take customer complaints more seriously than the little ones. I would suppose that's one reason why they're big; they don't like to lose money anymore than I like to be bothered when I'm trying to read a goddamned book underneath a palm tree I paid $264 to get next to. A Black woman seeking refuge in a multinational corporation may seem like a contradiction to some, but there you are. In this case it's a coincidence of entirely different self-interests: Sheraton/cash = June Jordan's short run safety.

14   Anyway, I'm pretty sure "Olive" would look at me as though I came from someplace as far away as Brooklyn. Then she'd probably allow herself one indignant query before righteously removing her vacuum cleaner from my room; "and why in the first place you come down you without your husband?"

15   I cannot imagine how I would begin to answer her.

16   My "rights" and my "freedom" and my "desire" and a slew of other New World values; what would they sound like to this Black woman described on the card atop my hotel bureau as "Olive the Maid"? "Olive" is older than I am and I may smoke a cigarette while she changes the sheets on my bed. Whose rights? Whose freedom? Whose desire?

17   And why should she give a shit about mine unless I do something, for real, about hers?

18   It happens that the book that I finished reading under a palm tree earlier today was the novel, *The Bread Givers,* by Anzia Yezierska. Definitely autobiographical, Yezierska lays out the difficulties of being both female and "a person" inside a traditional Jewish family at the start of the 20th century. That any Jewish woman became anything more than the abused servant of her father or her husband is really an improbable piece of news. Yet Yezierska managed such an unlikely outcome for her own life. In *The Bread Givers,* the heroine also manages an important, although partial, escape from traditional Jewish female destiny. And in the unpardonable, despotic father, the Talmudic scholar of that Jewish family, did I not see my own and hate him twice, again? When the heroine, the young Jewish child, wanders the streets with a filthy pail she borrows to sell herring in order to raise the ghetto rent and when she cries, "Nothing was before me but the hunger in our house, and no bread for the next meal if I didn't sell the herring. No longer like a fire engine, but like a houseful of hungry mouths my heart cried, 'herring—herring! Two cents apiece!' " who would doubt the ease, the sisterhood of conversation possible between that white girl and the Black women selling straw bags on the streets of paradise because they do not want to die? And is it not obvious that the wife of that Talmudic scholar and "Olive," who cleans my room here at the hotel, have more in common than I can claim with either one of them?

19   This is my consciousness of race and class and gender identity as I collect wet towels, sunglasses, wristwatch, and head towards a shower.

20   I am thinking about the boy who loaned this novel to me. He's white and he's Jewish and he's pursuing an independent study project with me, at the State University where I teach whether or not I feel like it, where I teach without stint because, like the waiter, I am no fool. It's my job and either I work or I do without everything you need money to buy. The boy loaned me the novel because he thought I'd be interested to know how a Jewish-American writer

used English so that the syntax, and therefore the cultural habits of mind expressed by the Yiddish language, could survive translation. He did this because he wanted to create another connection between us on the basis of language, between his knowledge/his love of Yiddish and my knowledge/my love of Black English.

21   He has been right about the forceful survival of the Yiddish. And I had become excited by this further evidence of the written voice of spoken language protected from the monodrone of "standard" English, and so we had grown closer on this account. But then our talk shifted to student affairs more generally, and I had learned that this student does not care one way or the other about currently jeopardized Federal Student Loan Programs because, as he explained it to me, they do not affect him. He does not need financial help outside his family. My own son, however, is Black. And I am the only family help available to him and that means, if Reagan succeeds in eliminating Federal programs to aid minority students, he will have to forget about furthering his studies, or he or I or both of us will have to hit the numbers pretty big. For these reasons of difference, the student and I had moved away from each other, even while we continued to talk.

22   My consciousness turned to race, again, and class.

23   Sitting in the same chair as the boy, several weeks ago, a graduate student came to discuss her grade. I praised the excellence of her final paper; indeed it had seemed to me an extraordinary pulling together of recent left brain/right brain research with the themes of transcendental poetry.

24   She told me that, for her part, she'd completed her reading of my political essays. "You are so lucky!" she exclaimed.

25   "What do you mean by that?"

26   "You have a cause. You have a purpose to your life."

27   I looked carefully at this white woman; what was she really saying to me?

28   "What do you mean?" I repeated.

29   "Poverty. Police violence. Discrimination in general."

30   (Jesus Christ, I thought: Is that her idea of lucky?)

31   "And how about you?" I asked.

32   "Me?"

33   "Yeah, you. Don't you have a cause?"

34   "Me? I'm just a middle-aged woman: a housewife and a mother. I'm a nobody."

35   For a while, I made no response.

36   First of all, speaking of race and class and gender in one breath, what she said meant that those lucky preoccupations of mine, from police violence to nuclear wipe-out, were not shared. They were mine and not hers. But here she sat, friendly as an old stuffed animal, beaming good will or more "luck" in my direction.

37   In the second place, what this white woman said to me meant that she did not believe she was "a person" precisely because she had fulfilled the traditional female functions revered by the father of that Jewish immigrant, Anzia Yezierska. And the woman in front of me was not a Jew. That was not the connection. The link was strictly female. Nevertheless, how should that woman and I, another female, connect beyond this bizarre exchange?

38   If she believed me lucky to have regular hurdles of discrimination then why shouldn't I insist that she's lucky to be a middle class white Wasp female who lives in such well-sanctioned and normative comfort that she even has the luxury to deny the power of the privileges that paralyze her life?

39   If she deserts me and "my cause" where we differ, if, for example, she abandons me to "my" problems of race, then why should I support her in "her" problems of housewifely oblivion?

40   Recollection of this peculiar moment brings me to the shower in the bathroom cleaned by "Olive." She reminds me of the usual Women's Studies curriculum because it has nothing to do with her or her job: you won't find "Olive" listed anywhere on the reading list. You will likewise seldom hear of Anzia Yezierska. But yes, you will find, from Florence Nightingale to Adrienne Rich, a white procession of independently well-to-do women writers. (Gertrude

312

Stein/Virginia Woolf/Hilda Doolittle are standard names among the "essential" women writers.)

41　　In other words, most of the women of the world—Black and First World and white who work because we must—most of the women of the world persist far from the heart of the usual Women's Studies syllabus.

42　　Similarly, the typical Black History course will slide by the majority experience it pretends to represent. For example, Mary McLeod Bethune will scarcely receive as much attention as Nat Turner, even though Black women who bravely and efficiently provided for the education of Black people hugely outnumber those few Black men who led successful or doomed rebellions against slavery. In fact, Mary McLeod Bethune may not receive even honorable mention because Black History too often apes those ridiculous white history courses which produce such dangerous gibberish as The Sheraton British Colonial "history" of the Bahamas. Both Black and white history courses exclude from their central consideration those people who neither killed nor conquered anyone as the means to new identity, those people who took care of every one of the people who wanted to become "a person," those people who still take care of the life at issue: the ones who wash and who feed and who teach and who diligently decorate straw hats and bags with all of their historically unrequited gentle love: the women.

> *Oh the old rugged cross*
> *on a hill far away*
> *Well I cherish the old rugged cross*

It's Good Friday in the Bahamas. Seventy-eight degrees in the shade. Except for Sheraton territory, everything's closed.

43　　It so happens that for truly secular reasons I've been fasting for three days. My hunger has now reached nearly violent proportions. In the hotel sandwich shop, the Black woman handling the counter complains about the tourists; why isn't the shop closed and why don't the tourists stop eating for once in their lives. I'm famished and I order chicken salad and cottage cheese and lettuce and tomato and a hard boiled egg and a hot cross bun and apple juice.

44   She eyes me with disgust.

45   To be sure, the timing of my stomach offends her serious religious practices. Neither one of us apologizes to the other. She seasons the chicken salad to the peppery max while I listen to the loud radio gospel she plays to console herself. It's a country Black version of "The Old Rugged Cross."

46   As I heave much chicken into my mouth tears start. It's not the pepper. I am, after all, a West Indian daughter. It's the Good Friday music that dominates the humid atmosphere.

Well I cherish the old rugged cross

And I am back, faster than a 747, in Brooklyn, in the home of my parents where we are wondering, as we do every year, if the sky will darken until Christ has been buried in the tomb. The sky should darken if God is in His heavens. And then, around 3 p.m., at the conclusion of our mournful church service at the neighborhood St. Phillips, and even while we dumbly stare at the black cloth covering the gold altar and the slender unlit candles, the sun should return through the high gothic windows and vindicate our waiting faith that the Lord will rise again, on Easter.

47   How I used to bow my head at the very name of Jesus: ecstatic to abase myself in deference to His majesty.

48   My mouth is full of salad. I can't seem to eat quickly enough. I can't think how I should lessen the offense of my appetite. The other Black woman on the premises, the one who disapprovingly prepared this very tasty break from my fast, makes no remark. She is no fool. This is a job that she needs. I suppose she notices that at least I included a hot cross bun among my edibles. That's something in my favor. I decide that's enough.

49   I am suddenly eager to walk off the food. Up a fairly steep hill I walk without hurrying. Through the pastel desolation of the little

town, the road brings me to a confectionary pink and white plantation house. At the gates, an unnecessarily large statue of Christopher Columbus faces me down, or tries to. His hand is fisted to one hip. I look back at him, laugh without deference, and turn left.

50   It's time to pack it up. Catch my plane. I scan the hotel room for things not to forget. There's that white report card on the bureau.

51   "Dear Guests:" it says, under the name "Olive." I am your maid for the day. Please rate me: Excellent. Good. Average. Poor. Thank you."

52   I tuck this momento from the Sheraton British Colonial into my notebook. How would "Olive" rate *me*? What would it mean for us to seem "good" to each other? What would that rating require?

53   But I am hastening to leave. Neither turtle soup nor kidney pie nor any conch shell delight shall delay my departure. I have rested, here, in the Bahamas, and I'm ready to return to my usual job, my usual work. But the skin on my body has changed and so has my mind. On the Delta flight home I realize I am burning up, indeed.

54   So far as I can see, the usual race and class concepts of connection, or gender assumptions of unity, do not apply very well. I doubt that they ever did. Otherwise why would Black folks forever bemoan our lack of solidarity when the deal turns real. And if unity on the basis of sexual oppression is something natural, then why do we women, the majority people on the planet, still have a problem?

55   The plane's ready for takeoff. I fasten my seatbelt and let the tumult inside my head run free. Yes: race and class and gender remain as real as the weather. But what they must mean about the contact between two individuals is less obvious and, like the weather, not predictable.

56   And when these factors of race and class and gender absolutely collapse is whenever you try to use them as automatic concepts of connection. They may serve well as indicators of commonly felt conflict, but as elements of connection they seem about as reliable

315

as precipitation probability for the day after the night before the day.

57   It occurs to me that much organizational grief could be avoided if people understood that partnership in misery does not necessarily provide for partnership for change: *When we get the monsters off our backs all of us may want to run in very different directions.*

58   And not only that: even though both "Olive" and "I" live inside a conflict neither one of us created, and even though both of us therefore hurt inside that conflict, I may be one of the monsters she needs to eliminate from her universe and, in a sense, she may be one of the monsters in mine.

59   I am reaching for the words to describe the difference between a common identity that has been imposed and the individual identity any one of us will choose, once she gains that chance.

60   That difference is the one that keeps us stupid in the face of new, specific information about somebody else with whom we are supposed to have a connection because a third party, hostile to both of us, has worked it so that the two of us, like it or not, share a common enemy. *What happens beyond the idea of that enemy and beyond the consequences of that enemy?*

61   I am saying that the ultimate connection cannot be the enemy. The ultimate connection must be the need that we find between us. It is not only who you are, in other words, but what we can do for each other that will determine the connection.

62   I am flying back to my job. I have been teaching contemporary women's poetry this semester. One quandary I have set myself to explore with my students is the one of taking responsibility without power. We had been wrestling ideas to the floor for several sessions when a young Black woman, a South African, asked me for help, after class.

63   Sokutu told me she was "in a trance" and that she'd been unable to eat for two weeks.

64   "What's going on?" I asked her, even as my eyes startled at her trembling and emaciated appearance.

65 "My husband. He drinks all the time. He beats me up. I go to the hospital. I can't eat. I don't know what/anything."

66 In my office, she described her situation. I did not dare to let her sense my fear and horror. She was dragging about, hour by hour, in dread. Her husband, a young Black South African, was drinking himself into more and more deadly violence against her.

67 Sokutu told me how she could keep nothing down. She weighed 90 lbs. at the outside, as she spoke to me. She'd already been hospitalized as a result of her husband's battering rage.

68 I knew both of them because I had organized a campus group to aid the liberation struggles of Southern Africa.

69 Nausea rose in my throat. What about this presumable connection: this husband and this wife fled from that homeland of hatred against them, and now what? He was destroying himself. If not stopped, he would certainly murder his wife.

70 She needed a doctor, right away. It was a medical emergency. She needed protection. It was a security crisis. She needed refuge for battered wives and personal therapy and legal counsel. She needed a friend.

71 I got on the phone and called every number in the campus directory that I could imagine might prove helpful. Nothing worked. There were no institutional resources designed to meet her enormous, multifaceted, and ordinary woman's need.

72 I called various students. I asked the Chairperson of the English Department for advice. I asked everyone for help.

73 Finally, another one of my students, Cathy, a young Irish woman active in campus IRA activities, responded. She asked for further details. I gave them to her.

74 "Her husband," Cathy told me, "is an alcoholic. You have to understand about alcoholics. It's not the same as anything else. And it's a disease you can't treat any old way.

75 I listened, fearfully. Did this mean there was nothing we could do?

76   "That's not what I'm saying," she said. "But you have to keep the alcoholic part of the thing central in everybody's mind, otherwise her husband will kill her. Or he'll kill himself."

77   She spoke calmly, I felt there was nothing to do but to assume she knew what she was talking about.

78   "Will you come with me?" I asked her, after a silence. "Will you come with me and help us figure out what to do next?"

79   Cathy said she would but that she felt shy: Sokutu comes from South Africa. What would she think about Cathy?

80   "I don't know," I said. "But let's go."

81   We left to find a dormitory room for the young battered wife.

82   It was late, now, and dark outside.

83   On Cathy's VW that I followed behind with my own car, was the sticker that reads BOBBY SANDS FREE AT LAST. My eyes blurred as I read and reread the words. This was another connection: Bobby Sands and Martin Luther King Jr. and who would believe it? I would not have believed it; I grew up terrorized by Irish kids who introduced me to the word "nigga."

84   And here I was following an Irish woman to the room of a Black South African. We were going to that room to try to save a life together.

85   When we reached the little room, we found ourselves awkward and large. Sokutu attempted to treat us with utmost courtesy, as though we were honored guests. She seemed surprised by Cathy, but mostly Sokutu was flushed with relief and joy because we were there, with her.

86   I did not know how we should ever terminate her heartfelt courtesies and address, directly, the reason for our visit: her starvation and her extreme physical danger.

87   Finally, Cathy sat on the floor and reached out her hands to Sokutu.

88   "I'm here," she said quietly, "Because June has told me what has happened to you. And I know what it is. Your husband is an alcoholic. He has a disease. I know what it is. My father was an

alcoholic. He killed himself. He almost killed my mother. I want to be your friend.''

89   ''Oh,'' was the only small sound that escaped from Sokutu's mouth. And then she embraced the other student. And then everything changed and I watched all of this happen so I know that this happened: this connection.

90   And after we called the police and exchanged phone numbers and plans were made for the night and for the next morning, the young South African woman walked down the dormitory hallway, saying goodbye and saying thank you to us.

91   I walked behind them, the young Irish woman and the young South African, and I saw them walking as sisters walk, hugging each other, and whispering and sure of each other and I felt how it was not who they were but what they both know and what they were both preparing to do about what they know that was going to make them both free at last.

92   And I look out the windows of the plane and I see clouds that will not kill me and I know that someday soon other clouds may erupt to kill us all.

93   And I tell the stewardess No thanks to the cocktails she offers me. But I look about the cabin at the hundred strangers drinking as they fly and I think even here and even now I must make the connection real between me and these strangers everywhere before those other clouds unify this ragged bunch of us, too late.

LOS ANGELES NOTEBOOK
by Joan Didion

1   There is something uneasy in the Los Angeles air this afternoon, some unnatural stillness, some tension. What it means is that tonight a Santa Ana will begin to blow, a hot wind from the northeast whining down through the Cajon and San Gorgonio Passes, blowing up sandstorms out along Route 66, drying the hills and the nerves to the flash point. For a few days now we will see

smoke back in the canyons, and hear sirens in the night. I have neither heard nor read that a Santa Ana is due, but I know it, and almost everyone I have seen today knows it too. We know it because we feel it. The baby frets. The maid sulks. I rekindle a waning argument with the telephone company, then cut my losses and lie down, given over to whatever it is in the air. To live with the Santa Ana is to accept, consciously or unconsciously, a deeply mechanistic view of human behavior.

2   I recall being told, when I first moved to Los Angeles and was living on an isolated beach, that the Indians would throw themselves into the sea when the bad wind blew. I could see why. The Pacific turned ominously glossy during a Santa Ana period, and one woke in the night troubled not only by the peacocks screaming in the olive trees but by the eerie absence of surf. The heat was surreal. The sky had a yellow cast, the kind of light sometimes called "earthquake weather." My only neighbor would not come out of her house for days, and there were no lights at night, and her husband roamed the place with a machete. One day he would tell me that he had heard a trespasser, the next a rattlesnake.

3   "On nights like that," Raymond Chandler once wrote about the Santa Ana, "every booze party ends in a fight. Meek little wives feel the edge of the carving knife and study their husbands' necks. Anything can happen." That was the kind of wind it was. I did not know then that there was any basis for the effect it had on all of us, but it turns out to be another of those cases in which science bears out folk wisdom. The Santa Ana, which is named for one of the canyons it rushes through, is a *foehn* wind, like the *foehn* of Austria and Switzerland and the *hamsin* of Israel. There are a number of persistent malevolent winds, perhaps the best known of which are the mistral of France and the Mediterranean sirocco, but a *foehn* wind has distinct characteristics: it occurs on the leeward slope of a mountain range and, although the air begins as a cold mass, it is warmed as it comes down the mountain and appears finally as a hot dry wind. Whenever and wherever a *foehn* blows, doctors hear

about headaches, and nausea and allergies, about "nervousness," about "depression." In Los Angeles some teachers do not attempt to conduct formal classes during a Santa Ana, because the children become unmanageable. In Switzerland the suicide rate goes up during the *foehn,* and in the courts of some Swiss cantons the wind is considered a mitigating circumstance for crime. Surgeons are said to watch the wind, because blood does not clot normally during a *foehn.* A few years ago an Israeli physicist discovered that not only during such winds, but for the ten or twelve hours which precede them, the air carries an unusually high ratio of positive to negative ions. No one seems to know exactly why that should be; some talk about friction and others suggest solar disturbances. In any case the positive ions are there, and what an excess of positive ions does, in the simplest terms, is make people unhappy. One cannot get much more mechanistic than that.

4   Easterners commonly complain that there is no "weather" at all in Southern California, that the days and the seasons slip by relentlessly, numbingly bland. That is quite misleading. In fact the climate is characterized by infrequent but violent extremes: two periods of torrential subtropical rains which continue for weeks and wash out the hills and send subdivisions sliding toward the sea; about twenty scattered days a year of the Santa Ana, which, with its incendiary dryness, invariably means fire. At the first prediction of a Santa Ana, the Forest Service flies men and equipment from northern California into the southern forests, and the Los Angeles Fire Department cancels its ordinary non-firefighting routines. The Santa Ana caused Malibu to burn the way it did in 1956, and Bel Air in 1961, and Santa Barbara in 1964. In the winter of 1966–67 eleven men were killed fighting a Santa Ana fire that spread through the San Gabriel Mountains.

5   Just to watch the front-page news out of Los Angeles during a Santa Ana is to get very close to what it is about the place. The longest Santa Ana period in recent years was in 1957, and it lasted not the usual three or four days but fourteen days, from November

21 until December 4. On the first day 25,000 acres of the San Gabriel Mountains were burning, with gusts reaching 100 miles an hour. In town, the wind reached Force 12, or hurricane force, on the Beaufort Scale; oil derricks were toppled and people ordered off the downtown streets to avoid injury from flying objects. On November 22 the fire in the San Gabriels was out of control. On November 24 six people were killed in automobile accidents, and by the end of the week the Los Angles *Times* was keeping a box score of traffic deaths. On November 26 a prominent Pasadena attorney, depressed about money, shot and killed his wife, their two sons, and himself. On November 27 a South Gate divorcee, twenty-two, was murdered and thrown from a moving car. On November 30 the San Gabriel fire was still out of control, and the wind in town was blowing eighty miles an hour. On the first day of December four people died violently, and on the third the wind began to break.

6   It is hard for people who have not lived in Los Angeles to realize how radically the Santa Ana figures in the local imagination. The city burning is Los Angeles's deepest image of itself: Nathanael West perceived that, in *The Day of the Locust;* and at the time of the 1965 Watts riots what struck the imagination most indelibly were the fires. For days one could drive the Harbor Freeway and see the city on fire, just as we had always known it would be in the end. Los Angeles weather is the weather of catastrophe, of apocalypse, and, just as the reliably long and bitter winters of New England determine the way life is lived there, so the violence and the unpredictability of the Santa Ana affect the entire quality of life in Los Angeles, accentuate its impermanence, its unreliability. The wind shows us how close to the edge we are.

2

7   "Here's why I'm on the beeper, Ron," said the telephone voice on the all-night radio show. "I just want to say that this *Sex for the Secretary* creature—whatever her name is—certainly isn't con-

tributing anything to the morals in this country. It's pathetic. Statistics *show*."

8   "It's *Sex and the Office,* honey," the disc jockey said. "That's the title. By Helen Gurley Brown. Statistics show what?"

9   "I haven't got them right here at my fingertips, naturally. But they *show*."

10 "I'd be interested in hearing them. Be constructive, you Night Owls."

11 "All right, let's take *one* statistic," the voice said, truculent now. "Maybe I haven't read the book, but what's this business she recommends about *going out with married men for lunch?*'

12 So it went, from midnight until 5 a.m., interrupted by records and by occasional calls debating whether or not a rattlesnake can swim. Misinformation about rattlesnakes is a leitmotiv of the insomniac imagination in Los Angeles. Toward 2 a.m. a man from "out Tarzana way" called to protest. "The Night Owls who called earlier must have been thinking about, uh, *The Man in the Gray Flannel Suit* or some other book," he said, "because Helen's one of the few authors trying to tell us what's really going *on.* Hefner's another, and he's also controversial, working in, uh, another area."

13 An old man, after testifying that he "personally" had seen a swimming rattlesnake, in the Delta-Mendota Canal, urged "moderation" on the Helen Gurley Brown question. "We shouldn't get on the beeper to call things pornographic before we've read them," he complained, pronouncing it porn-ee-oh-graphic. "I say, get the book. Give it a chance." The original *provocateur* called back to agree that she would get the book. "And then I'll burn it," she added.

14 "Book burner, eh?" laughed the disc jockey good-naturedly.

15 "I wish they still burned witches," she hissed.

3

16 It is three o'clock on a Sunday afternoon and 105° and the air so thick with smog that the dusty palm trees loom up with a sudden

and rather attractive mystery. I have been playing in the sprinklers with the baby and I get in the car and go to Ralph's Market on the corner of Sunset and Fuller wearing an old bikini bathing suit. That is not a very good thing to wear to the market but neither is it, at Ralph's on the corner of Sunset and Fuller, an unusual costume. Nonetheless a large woman in a cotton muumuu jams her cart into mine at the butcher counter. *"What a thing to wear to the market,"* she says in a loud but strangled voice. Everyone looks the other way and I study a plastic package of rib lamb chops and she repeats it. She follows me all over the store, to the Junior Food, to the Dairy Products, to the Mexican Delicacies, jamming my cart whenever she can. Her husband plucks at her sleeve. As I leave the check-out counter she raises her voice one last time: *What a thing to wear to Ralphs,"* she says.

4

17   A party at someone's house in Beverly Hills: a pink tent, two orchestras, a couple of French Communist directors in Cardin evening jackets, chili and hamburgers from Chasen's. The wife of an English actor sits at a table alone, she visits California rarely although her husband works here a good deal. An American who knows her slightly comes over to the table.

18   "Marvelous to see you here," he says.

19   "Is it," she says.

20   "How long have you been here?"

21   "Too long."

22   She takes a fresh drink from a passing waiter and smiles at her husband, who is dancing.

23   The American tries again. He mentions her husband.

24   "I hear he's marvelous in this picture."

25   She looks at the American for the first time. When she finally speaks she enunciates every word very clearly. "He . . . is . . . also . . . a . . . fag," she says pleasantly.

5

26   The oral history of Los Angeles is written in piano bars. "Moon River," the piano player always plays, and "Mountain Greenery." "There's a Small Hotel" and "This Is Not the First Time." People talk to each other, tell each other about their first wives and last husbands. "Stay funny," they tell each other, and "This is to die over." A construction man talks to an unemployed screenwriter who is celebrating, alone, his tenth wedding anniversary. The construction man is on a job in Montecito: "Up in Montecito," he says, "they got one square mile with 135 millionaires."

27   "Putrescence," the writer says.

28   "That's all you got to say about it?"

29   "Don't read me wrong, I think Santa Barbara's one of the most— Christ, *the* most—beautiful places in the world, but it's a beautiful place that contains a . . . *putrescence.* They just live on their putrescent millions."

30   "So give me putrescent."

31   "No, no," the writer says. "I just happen to think millionaires have some sort of lacking in their . . . in their elasticity."

32   A drunk requests "The Sweetheart of Sigma Chi." The piano player says he doesn't know it. "Where'd you learn to play the piano?" the drunk asks. "I got two degrees," the piano player says. "One in musical education." I go to a coin telephone and call a friend in New York. "Where are you?" he says. "In a piano bar in Encino," I say. "Why?" he says. "Why not," I say.

COCKSURE WOMEN AND HENSURE MEN
by D. H. Lawrence

1   It seems to me there are two aspects to women. There is the demure and the dauntless. Men have loved to dwell, in fiction at least, on the demure maiden whose inevitable reply is: Oh, yes, if you please, kind sir! The demure maiden, the demure spouse, the demure mother—this is still the ideal. A few maidens, mistresses

and mothers *are* demure. A few pretend to be. But the vast majority are not. And they don't pretend to be. We don't expect a girl skilfully driving her car to be demure, we expect her to be dauntless. What good would demure and maidenly Members of Parliament be, inevitably responding: Oh, yes, if you please, kind sir!—Though of course there are masculine members of that kidney.—And a demure telephone girl? Or even a demure stenographer? Demureness, to be sure, is outwardly becoming, it is an outward mark of femininity, like bobbed hair. But it goes with inward dauntlessness. The girl who has got to make her way in life has got to be dauntless, and if she has a pretty, demure manner with it, then lucky girl. She kills two birds with two stones.

2   With the two kinds of femininity go two kinds of confidence: There are the women who are cocksure, and the women who are hensure. A really up-to-date woman is a cocksure woman. She doesn't have a doubt nor a qualm. She is the modern type. Whereas the old-fashioned demure woman was sure as a hen is sure, that is, without knowing anything about it. She went quietly and busily clucking around, laying the eggs and mothering the chickens in a kind of anxious dream that still was full of sureness. But not mental sureness. Her sureness was a physical condition, very soothing, but a condition out of which she could easily be startled or frightened.

3   It is quite amusing to see the two kinds of sureness in chickens. The cockerel is, naturally, cocksure. He crows because he is *certain* it is day. Then the hen peeps out from under her wing. He marches to the door of the hen-house and pokes out his head assertively: *Ah ha! daylight, of course, just as I said!*—and he majestically steps down the chicken ladder towards *terra firma,* knowing that the hens will step cautiously after him, drawn by his confidence. So after him, cautiously, step the hens. He crows again: *Ha-ha! here we are!*—It is indisputable, and the hens accept it entirely. He marches toward the house. From the house a person ought to appear, scattering corn. Why does the person not appear? The cock will see to it. He is cocksure. He gives a loud crow in the

doorway, and the person appears. The hens are suitably impressed but immediately devote all their henny consciousness to the scattered corn, pecking absorbedly, while the cock runs and fusses, cocksure that he is responsible for it all.

4   So the day goes on. The cock finds a tit-bit, and loudly calls the hens. They scuffle up in henny surety, and gobble the tit-bit. But when they find a juicy morsel for themselves, they devour it in silence, hensure. Unless, of course, there are little chicks, when they most anxiously call the brood. But in her own dim surety, the hen is really much surer than the cock, in a different way. She marches off to lay her egg, she secures obstinately the nest she wants, she lays her egg at last, then steps forth again with prancing confidence, and gives that most assured of all sounds, the hensure cackle of a bird who has laid her egg. The cock, who is never so sure about anything as the hen is about the egg she has laid, immediately starts to cackle like the female of his species. He is pining to be hensure, for hensure is so much surer than cocksure.

5   Nevertheless, cocksure is boss. When the chicken-hawk appears in the sky, loud are the cockerel's calls of alarm: Then the hens scuffle under the verandah, the cock ruffles his feathers on guard. The hens are numb with fear, they say: Alas, there is no health in us! How wonderful to be a cock so bold!—And they huddle, numbed. But their very numbness is hensurety.

6   Just as the cock can cackle, however, as if he had laid the egg, so can the hen bird crow. She can more or less assume his cocksureness. And yet she is never so easy, cocksure, as she used to be when she was hensure. Cocksure, she is cocksure, but uneasy. Hensure, she trembles, but is easy.

7   It seems to me just the same in the vast human farmyard. Only nowadays all the cocks are cackling and pretending to lay eggs, and all the hens are crowing and pretending to call the sun out of bed. If women today are cocksure, men are hensure. Men are timid, tremulous, rather soft and submissive, easy in their very henlike

tremulousness. They only want to be spoken to gently. So the women step forth with a good loud *cock-a-doodle-do!*

8   The tragedy about cocksure women is that they are more cocky, in their assurance, than the cock himself. They never realize that when the cock gives his loud crow in the morning, he listens acutely afterwards, to hear if some other wretch of a cock dare crow defiance, challenge. To the cock, there is always defiance, challenge, danger and death on the clear air; or the possibility thereof.

9   But alas, when the hen crows, she listens for no defiance or challenge. When she says *cock-a-doodle-do!* then it is unanswerable. The cock listens for an answer, alert. But the hen knows she is unanswerable. *Cock-a-doodle-do!* and there it is, take it or leave it!

10   And it is this that makes the cocksureness of women so dangerous, so devastating. It is really out of scheme, it is not in relation to the rest of things. So we have the tragedy of cocksure women. They find, so often, that instead of having laid an egg, they have laid a vote, or an empty ink-bottle, or some other absolutely unhatchable object, which means nothing to them.

11   It is the tragedy of the modern woman. She becomes cocksure, she puts all her passion and energy and years of her life into some effort or assertion, without ever listening for the denial which she ought to take into count. She is cocksure, but she is a hen all the time. Frightened of her own henny self, she rushes to mad lengths about votes, or welfare, or sports, or business: she is marvellous, out-manning the man. But alas, it is all fundamentally disconnected. It is all an attitude, and one day the attitude will become a weird cramp, a pain, and then it will collapse. And when it has collapsed, and she looks at the eggs she has laid, votes, or miles of typewriting, years of business efficiency—suddenly, because she is a hen and not a cock, all she has done will turn into pure nothingness to her. Suddenly it all falls out of relation to her basic henny self, and she realizes she has lost her life. The lovely henny surety, the hensureness which is the real bliss of every

female, has been denied her: she had never had it. Having lived her life with such utmost strenuousness and cocksureness, she has missed her life altogether. Nothingness!

BEAUTY: WHEN THE OTHER DANCER IS THE SELF
by Alice Walker

1   It is a bright summer day in 1947. My father, a fat, funny man with beautiful eyes and a subversive wit, is trying to decide which of his eight children he will take with him to the county fair. My mother, of course, will not go. She is knocked out from getting most of us ready: I hold my neck stiff against the pressure of her knuckles as she hastily completes the braiding and then beribboning of my hair.

2   My father is the driver for the rich old white lady up the road. Her name is Miss Mey. She owns all the land for miles around, as well as the house in which we live. All I remember about her is that she once offered to pay my mother thirty-five cents for cleaning her house, raking up piles of her magnolia leaves, and washing her family's clothes, and that my mother—she of no money, eight children, and a chronic earache—refused it. But I do not think of this in 1947. I am two and a half years old. I want to go everywhere my daddy goes. I am excited at the prospect of riding in a car. Someone has told me fairs are fun. That there is room in the car for only three of us doesn't faze me at all. Whirling happily in my starchy frock, showing off my biscuit-polished patent-leather shoes and lavender socks, tossing my head in a way that makes my ribbons bounce, I stand, hands on hips, before my father. "Take me, Daddy," I say with assurance; "I'm the prettiest!"

3   Later, it does not surprise me to find myself in Miss Mey's shiny black car, sharing the back seat with the other lucky ones. Does not surprise me that I thoroughly enjoy the fair. At home that night I tell the unlucky ones all I can remember about the merry-go-round, the

man who eats live chickens, and the teddy bears, until they say: that's enough, baby Alice. Shut up now, and go to sleep.

4   It is Easter Sunday, 1950. I am dressed in a green, flocked, scalloped-hem dress (handmade by my adoring sister, Ruth) that has its own smooth satin petticoat and tiny hot-pink roses tucked into each scallop. My shoes, new T-strap patent leather, again highly biscuit-polished. I am six years old and have learned one of the longest Easter speeches to be heard that day, totally unlike the speech I said when I was two: "Easter lilies/pure and white/blossom in/the morning light." When I rise to give my speech I do so on a great wave of love and pride and expectation. People in the church stop rustling their new crinolines. They seem to hold their breath. I can tell they admire my dress, but it is my spirit, bordering on sassiness (womanishness), they secretly applaud.

5   "That girl's a little *mess*," they whisper to each other, pleased.

6   Naturally I say my speech without stammer or pause, unlike those who stutter, stammer, or, worst of all, forget. This is before the word "beautiful" exists in people's vocabulary, but "Oh, isn't she the *cutest* thing!" frequently floats my way. "And got so much sense!" they gratefully add . . . for which thoughtful addition I thank them to this day.

7   *It was great fun being cute. But then, one day, it ended.*

8   I am eight years old and a tomboy. I have a cowboy hat, cowboy boots, checkered shirt and pants, all red. My playmates are my brothers, two and four years older than I. Their colors are black and green, the only difference in the way we are dressed. On Saturday nights we all go to the picture show, even my mother; Westerns are her favorite kind of movie. Back home, "on the ranch," we pretend we are Tom Mix, Hopalong Cassidy, Lash LaRue (we've even named one of our dogs Lash LaRue); we chase each other for hours rustling cattle, being outlaws, delivering damsels from distress.

Then my parents decide to buy my brothers guns. These are not "real" guns. They shoot "BBs," copper pellets my brothers say will kill birds. Because I am a girl, I do not get a gun. Instantly I am relegated to the position of Indian. Now there appears a great distance between us. They shoot and shoot at everything with their new guns. I try to keep up with my bow and arrows.

9   One day while I am standing on top of our makeshift "garage"—pieces of tin nailed across some poles—holding my bow and arrow and looking out toward the fields, I feel an incredible blow in my right eye. I look down just in time to see my brother lower his gun.

10   Both brothers rush to my side. My eye stings, and I cover it with my hand. "If you tell," they say, "we will get a whipping. You don't want that to happen, do you?" I do not. "Here is a piece of wire," says the older brother, picking it up from the roof; "say you stepped on one end of it and the other flew up and hit you." The pain is beginning to start. "Yes," I say. "Yes, I will say that is what happened." If I do not say this is what happened, I know my brothers will find ways to make me wish I had. But now I will say anything that gets me to my mother.

11   Confronted by our parents we stick to the lie agreed upon. They place me on a bench on the porch and I close my left eye while they examine the right. There is a tree growing from underneath the porch that climbs past the railing to the roof. It is the last thing my right eye sees. I watch as its trunk, its branches, and then its leaves are blotted out by the rising blood.

12   I am in shock. First there is intense fever, which my father tries to break using lily leaves bound around my head. Then there are chills: my mother tries to get me to eat soup. Eventually, I do not know how, my parents learn what has happened. A week after the "accident" they take me to see a doctor. "Why did you wait so long to come?" he asks, looking into my eye and shaking his head. "Eyes are sympathetic," he says. "If one is blind, the other will likely become blind too."

13   This comment of the doctor's terrifies me. But it is really how I look that bothers me most. Where the BB pellet struck there is a glob of whitish scar tissue, a hideous cataract, on my eye. Now when I stare at people—a favorite pastime, up to now—they will stare back. Not at the "cute" little girl, but at her scar. For six years I do not stare at anyone, because I do not raise my head.

14   Years later, in the throes of a mid-life crisis, I ask my mother and sister whether I changed after the "accident." "No," they say, puzzled. "What do you mean?"

15   *What do I mean?*

16   I am eight, and, for the first time, doing poorly in school, where I have been something of a whiz since I was four. We have just moved to the place where the "accident" occurred. We do not know any of the people around us because this is a different county. The only time I see the friends I knew is when we go back to our old church. The new school is the former state penitentiary. It is a large stone building, cold and drafty, crammed to overflowing with boisterous, ill-disciplined children. On the third floor there is a huge circular imprint of some partition that has been torn out.

17   "What used to be here?" I ask a sullen girl next to me on our way past it to lunch.

18   "The electric chair," says she.

19   At night I have nightmares about the electric chair, and about all the people reputedly "fried" in it. I am afraid of the school, where all the students seem to be budding criminals.

20   "What's the matter with your eye?" they ask, critically.

21   When I don't answer (I cannot decide whether it was an "accident" or not), they shove me, insist on a fight.

22   My brother, the one who created the story about the wire, comes to my rescue. But then brags so much about "protecting" me, I become sick.

23   After months of torture at the school, my parents decide to send me back to our old community, to my old school. I live with my

grandparents and the teacher they board. But there is no room for Phoebe, my cat. By the time my grandparents decide there *is* room, and I ask for my cat, she cannot be found. Miss Yarborough, the boarding teacher, takes me under her wing, and begins to teach me to play the piano. But soon she marries an African—a "prince," she says—and is whisked away to his continent.

24   At my old school there is at least one teacher who loves me. She is the teacher who "knew me before I was born" and bought my first baby clothes. It is she who makes life bearable. It is her presence that finally helps me turn on the one child at the school who continually calls me "one-eyed bitch." One day I simply grab him by his coat and beat him until I am satisfied. It is my teacher who tells me my mother is ill.

25   My mother is lying in bed in the middle of the day, something I have never seen. She is in too much pain to speak. She has an abscess in her ear. I stand looking down on her, knowing that if she dies, I cannot live. She is being treated with warm oils and hot bricks held against her cheek. Finally a doctor comes. But I must go back to my grandparents' house. The weeks pass but I am hardly aware of it. All I know is that my mother might die, my father is not so jolly, my brothers still have their guns, and I am the one sent away from home.

26   "You did not change," they say.

27   *Did I imagine the anguish of never looking up?*

28   I am twelve. When relatives come to visit I hide in my room. My cousin Brenda, just my age, whose father works in the post office and whose mother is a nurse, comes to find me. "Hello," she says. And then she asks, looking at my recent school picture, which I did not want taken, and on which the "glob," as I think of it, is clearly visible, "You still can't see out of that eye?"

29   "No," I say, and flop back on the bed over my book.

30   That night, as I do almost every night, I abuse my eye. I rant and rave at it, in front of the mirror. I plead with it to clear up before morning. I tell it I hate and despise it. I do not pray for sight. I pray for beauty.

31   "You did not change," they say.

32   I am fourteen and baby-sitting for my brother Bill, who lives in Boston. He is my favorite brother and there is a strong bond between us. Understanding my feelings of shame and ugliness he and his wife take me to a local hospital, where the "glob" is removed by a doctor named O. Henry. There is still a small bluish crater where the scar tissue was, but the ugly white stuff is gone. Almost immediately I become a different person from the girl who does not raise her head. Or so I think. Now that I've raised my head I won the boyfriend of my dreams. Now that I've raised my head I have plenty of friends. Now that I've raised my head classwork comes from my lips as faultlessly as Easter speeches did, and I leave high school as valedictorian, most popular student, and *queen,* hardly believing my luck. Ironically, the girl who was voted most beautiful in our class (and was) was later shot twice through the chest by a male companion, using a "real" gun, while she was pregnant. But that's another story in itself. Or is it?

33   "You did not change," they say.

34   It is now thirty years since the "accident." A beautiful journalist comes to visit and to interview me. She is going to write a cover story for her magazine that focuses on my latest book. "Decide how you want to look on the cover," she says. "Glamorous, or whatever."

35   Never mind "glamorous," it is the "whatever" that I hear. Suddenly all I can think of is whether I will get enough sleep the night before the photography session: if I don't, my eye will be tired and wander, as blind eyes will.

36   At night in bed with my lover I think up reasons why I should not appear on the cover of a magazine. "My meanest critics will say I've sold out," I say. "My family will now realize I write scandalous books."

37   "But what's the real reason you don't want to do this?" he asks.

38   "Because in all probability," I say in a rush, "my eye won't be straight."

39   "It will be straight enough," he says. Then, "Besides, I thought you'd made your peace with that."

40   And I suddenly remember that I have.

41   *I remember:*

42   I am talking to my brother Jimmy, asking if he remembers anything unusual about the day I was shot. He does not know I consider that day the last time my father, with his sweet home remedy of cool lily leaves, chose me, and that I suffered and raged inside because of this. "Well," he says, "all I remember is standing by the side of the highway with Daddy, trying to flag down a car. A white man stopped, but when Daddy said he needed somebody to take his little girl to the doctor, he drove off."

43   *I remember:*

44   I am in the desert for the first time. I fall totally in love with it. I am so overwhelmed by its beauty, I confront for the first time, consciously, the meaning of the doctor's words years ago: "Eyes are sympathetic. If one is blind, the other will likely become blind too." I realize I have dashed about the world madly, looking at this, looking at that, storing up images against the fading of the light. *But I might have missed seeing the desert!* The shock of that possibility—and gratitude for over twenty-five years of sight—sends me literally to my knees. Poem after poem comes—which is perhaps how poets pray.

ON SIGHT

I am so thankful I have seen
The Desert
And the creatures in the desert
And the desert Itself.

The desert has its own moon
Which I have seen
With my own eye.

There is no flag on it.

Trees of the desert have arms
All of which are always up
That is because the moon is up
The sun is up
Also the sky
The stars
Clouds
None with flags.

If there were flags, I doubt
the trees would point.
Would you?

45   *But mostly, I remember this:*

46   I am twenty-seven, and my baby daughter is almost three. Since her birth I have worried about her discovery that her mother's eyes are different from other people's. Will she be embarrassed? I think. What will she say? Every day she watches a television program called "Big Blue Marble." It begins with a picture of the earth as it appears from the moon. It is bluish, a little battered-looking, but full of light, with whitish clouds swirling around it. Every time I see it I weep with love, as if it is a picture of Grandma's house. One day when I am putting Rebecca down for her nap, she suddenly focuses on my eye. Something inside me cringes, gets ready to try to protect

myself. All children are cruel about physical differences, I know from experience, and that they don't always mean to be is another matter. I assume Rebecca will be the same.

47   But no-o-o-o. She studies my face intently as we stand, her inside and me outside her crib. She even holds my face maternally between her dimpled little hands. Then, looking every bit as serious and lawyerlike as her father, she says, as if it may just possibly have slipped my attention: "Mommy, there's a *world* in your eye." (As in, "Don't be alarmed, or do anything crazy.") And then, gently, but with great interest: "Mommy, where did you *get* that world in your eye?"

48   For the most part, the pain left then. (So what, if my brothers grew up to buy even more powerful pellet guns for their sons and to carry real guns themselves. So what, if a young "Morehouse man" once nearly fell off the steps of Trevor Arnett Library because he thought my eyes were blue.) Crying and laughing I ran to the bathroom, while Rebecca mumbled and sang herself off to sleep. Yes indeed, I realized, looking into the mirror. There *was* a world in my eye. And I saw that it was possible to love it: that in fact, for all it had taught me of shame and anger and inner vision, I *did* love it. Even to see it drifting out of orbit in boredom, or rolling up out of fatigue, not to mention floating back at attention in excitement (bearing witness, a friend has called it), deeply suitable to my personality, and even characteristic of me.

49   That night I dream I am dancing to Stevie Wonder's song "Always" (the name of the song is really "As," but I hear it as "Always"). As I dance, whirling and joyous, happier than I've ever been in my life, another bright-faced dancer joins me. We dance and kiss each other and hold each other through the night. The other dancer has obviously come through all right, as I have done. She is beautiful, whole and free. And she is also me.

THE DEER AT PROVIDENCIA
by Annie Dillard

1 There were four of us North Americans in the jungle, in the Ecuadorian jungle on the banks of the Napo River in the Amazon watershed. The other three North Americans were metropolitan men. We stayed in tents in one riverside village, and visited others. At the village called Providencia we saw a sight which moved us, and which shocked the men.

2 The first thing we saw when we climbed the riverbank to the village of Providencia was the deer. It was roped to a tree on the grass clearing near the thatch shelter where we would eat lunch.

3 The deer was small, about the size of a whitetail fawn, but apparently full-grown. It had a rope around its neck and three feet caught in the rope. Someone said that the dogs had caught it that morning and the villagers were going to cook and eat it that night.

4 This clearing lay at the edge of the little thatched-hut village. We could see the villagers going about their business, scattering feed corn for hens about their houses, and wandering down paths to the river to bathe. The village headman was our host; he stood beside us as we watched the deer struggle. Several village boys were interested in the deer; they formed part of the circle we made around it in the clearing. So also did four businessmen from Quito who were attempting to guide us around the jungle. Few of the very different people standing in this circle had a common language. We watched the deer, and no one said much.

5 The deer lay on its side at the rope's very end, so the rope lacked slack to let it rest its head in the dust. It was "pretty," delicate of bone like all deer, and thin-skinned for the tropics. Its skin looked virtually hairless, in fact, and almost translucent, like a membrane. Its neck was no thicker than my wrist; it was rubbed open on the rope, and gashed. Trying to paw itself free of the rope, the deer had scratched its own neck with its hooves. The raw underside of its

neck showed red stripes and some bruises bleeding inside the muscles. Now three of its feet were hooked in the rope under its jaw. It could not stand, of course, on one leg, so it could not move to slacken the rope and ease the pull on its throat and enable it to rest its head.

6   Repeatedly the deer paused, motionless, its eyes veiled, with only its rib cage in motion, and its breaths the only sound. Then, after I would think, "It has given up; now it will die," it would heave. The rope twanged; the tree leaves clattered; the deer's free foot beat the ground. We stepped back and held our breaths. It thrashed, kicking, but only one leg moved; the other three legs tightened inside the rope's loop. Its hip jerked; its spine shook. Its eyes rolled; its tongue, thick with spittle, pushed in and out. Then it would rest again. We watched this for fifteen minutes.

7   Once three young native boys charged in, released its trapped legs, and jumped back to the circle of people. But instantly the deer scratched up its neck with its hooves and snared its forelegs in the rope again. It was easy to imagine a third and then a fourth leg soon stuck, like Brer Rabbit and the Tar Baby.

8   We watched the deer from the circle, and then we drifted on to lunch. Our palm-roofed shelter stood on a grassy promontory from which we could see the deer tied to the tree, pigs and hens walking under village houses, and black-and-white cattle standing in the river. There was even a breeze.

9   Lunch, which was the second and better lunch we had that day, was hot and fried. There was a big fish called *doncella,* a kind of catfish, dipped whole in corn flour and beaten egg, then deep fried. With our fingers we pulled soft fragments of it from its sides to our plates, and ate; it was delicate fish-flesh, fresh and mild. Someone found the roe, and I ate of that too—it was fat and stronger, like egg yolk, naturally enough, and warm.

10   There was also a stew of meat in shreds with rice and pale brown gravy. I had asked what kind of deer it was tied to the tree; Pepe had answered in Spanish, "*Gama*." Now they told us this was *gama* too, stewed. I suspect the word means merely game or venison. At any rate, I heard that the village dogs had cornered another deer just yesterday, and it was this deer which we were now eating in full sight of the whole article. It was good. I was surprised at its tenderness. But it is a fact that high levels of lactic acid, which builds up in muscle tissues during exertion, tenderizes.

11   After the fish and meat we ate bananas fried in chunks and served on a tray; they were sweet and full of flavor. I felt terrific. My shirt was wet and cool from swimming; I had had a night's sleep, two decent walks, three meals, and a swim—everything tasted good. From time to time each one of us, separately, would look beyond our shaded roof to the sunny spot where the deer was still convulsing in the dust. Our meal completed, we walked around the deer and back to the boats.

12   That night I learned that while we were watching the deer, the others were watching me.

13   We four North Americans grew close in the jungle in a way that was not the usual artificial intimacy of travelers. We liked each other. We stayed up all that night talking, murmuring, as though we rocked on hammocks slung above time. The others were from big cities: New York, Washington, Boston. They all said that I had no expression on my face when I was watching the deer—or at any rate, not the expression they expected.

14   They had looked to see how I, the only woman, and the youngest, was taking the sight of the deer's struggles. I looked detached, apparently, or hard, or calm, or focused, still. I don't know. I was thinking. I remember feeling very old and energetic. I could say like Thoreau that I have traveled widely in Roanoke, Virginia. I have thought a great deal about carnivorousness; I eat meat. These things are not issues; they are mysteries.

15 Gentlemen of the city, what surprises you? That there is suffering here, or that I know it?

16 We lay in the tent and talked. "If it had been my wife," one man said with special vigor, amazed, "she wouldn't have cared *what* was going on; she would have dropped *everything* right at that moment and gone in the village from here to there to there, she would not have *stopped* until that animal was out of its suffering one way or another. She couldn't *bear* to see a creature in agony like that."

17 I nodded.

18 Now I am home. When I wake I comb my hair before the mirror above my dresser. Every morning for the past two years I have seen in that mirror, beside my sleep-softened face, the blackened face of a burnt man. It is a wire-service photograph clipped from a newspaper and taped to my mirror. The caption reads: "Alan McDonald in Miami hospital bed." All you can see in the photograph is a smudged triangle of face from his eyelids to his lower lip; the rest is bandages. You cannot see the expression in his eyes; the bandages shade them.

19 The story, headed MAN BURNED FOR SECOND TIME, begins:

"Why does God hate me?" Alan McDonald asked from his hospital bed.

"When the gunpowder went off, I couldn't believe it," he said. "I just couldn't believe it. I said, 'No, God couldn't do this to me again.' "

He was in a burn ward in Miami, in serious condition. I do not even know if he lived. I wrote him a letter at the time, cringing.

20 He had been burned before, thirteen years previously, by flaming gasoline. For years he had been having his body restored and his face remade in dozens of operations. He had been a boy,

and then a burnt boy. He had already been stunned by what could happen, by how life could veer.

21   Once I read that people who survive bad burns tend to go crazy; they have a very high suicide rate. Medicine cannot ease their pain; drugs just leak away, soaking the sheets, because there is no skin to hold them in. The people just lie there and weep. Later they kill themselves. They had not known, before they were burned, that the world included such suffering, that life could permit them personally such pain.

22   This time a bowl of gunpowder had exploded on McDonald.

"I didn't realize what had happened at first," he recounted. "And then I heard that sound from 13 years ago. I was burning. I rolled to put the fire out and I thought, 'Oh God, not again.'

"If my friend hadn't been there, I would have jumped into a canal with a rock around my neck."

His wife concludes the piece, "Man, it just isn't fair."

23   I read the whole clipping again every morning. This is the Big Time here, every minute of it. Will someone please explain to Alan McDonald in his dignity, to the deer at Providencia in his dignity, what is going on? And mail me the carbon.

24   When we walked by the deer at Providencia for the last time, I said to Pepe with a pitying glance at the deer, *"Pobrecito"*—"poor little thing." But I was trying out Spanish. I knew at the time it was a ridiculous thing to say.

◊

THE DANCE OF THE FROGS
by Loren Eiseley

I

1   He was a member of the Explorers Club, and he had never been outside the state of Pennsylvania. Some of us who were world travelers used to smile a little about that, even though we knew his scientific reputation had been, at one time, great. It is always the way of youth to smile. I used to think of myself as something of an adventurer, but the time came when I realized that old Albert Dreyer, huddling with his drink in the shadows close to the fire, had journeyed farther into the Country of Terror than any of us would ever go, God willing, and emerge alive.

2   He was a morose and aging man, without family and without intimates. His membership in the club dated back into the decades when he was a zoologist famous for his remarkable experiments upon amphibians—he had recovered and actually produced the adult stage of the Mexican axolotl, as well as achieving remarkable tissue transplants in salamanders. The club had been flattered to have him then, travel or no travel, but the end was not fortunate. The brilliant scientist had become the misanthrope; the achievement lay all in the past, and Albert Dreyer kept to his solitary room, his solitary drink, and his accustomed spot by the fire.

3   The reason I came to hear his story was an odd one. I had been north that year, and the club had asked me to give a little talk on the religious beliefs of the Indians of the northern forest, the Naskapi of Labrador. I had long been a student of the strange mélange of superstition and woodland wisdom that makes up the religious life of the nature peoples. Moreover, I had come to know something of the strange similarities of the "shaking tent rite" to the phenomena of the modern medium's cabinet.

4   "The special tent with its entranced occupant is no different from the cabinet," I contended. "The only difference is the type of

343

voices that emerge. Many of the physical phenomena are identical—the movement of powerful forces shaking the conical hut, objects thrown, all this is familiar to Western psychical science. What is different are the voices projected. Here they are the cries of animals, the voices from the swamp and the mountain—the solitary elementals before whom the primitive man stands in awe, and from whom he begs sustenance. Here the game lords reign supreme; man himself is voiceless."

5 A low, halting query reached me from the back of the room. I was startled, even in the midst of my discussion, to note that it was Dreyer.

6 "And the game lords, what are they?"

7 "Each species of animal is supposed to have gigantic leaders of more than normal size," I explained. "These beings are the immaterial controllers of that particular type of animal. Legend about them is confused. Sometimes they partake of human qualities, will and intelligence, but they are of animal shape. They control the movements of game, and thus their favor may mean life or death to man."

8 "Are they visible?" Again Dreyer's low, troubled voice came from the back of the room.

9 "Native belief has it that they can be seen on rare occasions," I answered. "In a sense they remind one of the concept of the archetypes, the originals behind the petty show of our small, transitory existence. They are the immortal renewers of substance—the force behind and above animate nature."

10 "Do they dance?" persisted Dreyer.

11 At this I grew nettled. Old Dreyer in a heckling mood was something new. "I cannot answer that question," I said acidly. "My informants failed to elaborate upon it. But they believe implicitly in these monstrous beings, talk to and propitiate them. It is their voices that emerge from the shaking tent."

12 "The Indians believe it," pursued old Dreyer relentlessly, "but do *you* believe it?"

13   "My dear fellow"—I shrugged and glanced at the smiling audience—"I have seen many strange things, many puzzling things, but I am a scientist." Dreyer made a contemptuous sound in his throat and went back to the shadow out of which he had crept in his interest. The talk was over. I headed for the bar.

II

14   The evening passed. Men drifted homeward or went to their rooms. I had been a year in the woods and hungered for voices and companionship. Finally, however, I sat alone with my glass, a little mellow, perhaps, enjoying the warmth of the fire and remembering the blue snowfields of the North as they should be remembered—in the comfort of warm rooms.

15   I think an hour must have passed. The club was silent except for the ticking of an antiquated clock on the mantel and small night noises from the street. I must have drowsed. At all events it was some time before I grew aware that a chair had been drawn up opposite me. I started.

16   "A damp night," I said.

17   "Foggy," said the man in the shadow musingly. "But not too foggy. They like it that way."

18   "Eh?" I said. I knew immediately it was Dreyer speaking. Maybe I had missed something; on second thought, maybe not.

19   "And spring," he said. "Spring. That's part of it. God knows why, of course, but we feel it, why shouldn't they? And more intensely."

20   "Look—" I said. "I guess—" The old man was more human than I thought. He reached out and touched my knee with the hand that he always kept a glove over—burn, we used to speculate—and smiled softly.

21   "You don't know what I'm talking about," he finished for me. "And, besides, I ruffled your feelings earlier in the evening. You must forgive me. You touched on an interest of mine, and I was

perhaps overeager. I did not intend to give the appearance of heckling. It was only that . . ."

22 "Of course," I said. "Of course." Such a confession from Dreyer was astounding. The man might be ill. I rang for a drink and decided to shift the conversation to a safer topic, more appropriate to a scholar.

23 "Frogs," I said desperately, like any young ass in a china shop. "Always admired your experiments. Frogs. Yes."

24 I give the old man credit. He took the drink and held it up and looked at me across the rim. There was a faint stir of sardonic humor in his eyes.

25 "Frogs, no," he said, "or maybe yes. I've never been quite sure. Maybe yes. But there was no time to decide properly." The humor faded out of his eyes. "Maybe I should have let go," he said. "It was what they wanted. There's no doubting that at all, but it came too quick for me. What would you have done?"

26 "I don't know," I said honestly enough and pinched myself.

27 "You had better know," said Albert Dreyer severely, "if you're planning to become an investigator of primitive religions. Or even not. I wasn't, you know, and the things came to me just when I least suspected—But I forget, you don't believe in them."

28 He shrugged and half rose, and for the first time, really, I saw the black-gloved hand and the haunted face of Albert Dreyer and knew in my heart the things he had stood for in science. I got up then, as a young man in the presence of his betters should get up, and I said, and I meant it, every word: "Please, Dr. Dreyer, sit down and tell me. I'm too young to be saying what I believe or don't believe in at all. I'd be obliged if you'd tell me."

29 Just at that moment a strange, wonderful dignity shone out of the countenance of Albert Dreyer, and I knew the man he was. He bowed and sat down, and there were no longer the barriers of age and youthful ego between us. There were just two men under a lamp, and around them a great waiting silence. Out to the ends of the universe, I thought fleetingly, that's the way with man and his

lamps. One has to huddle in, there's so little light and so much space. One——

III

30   "It could happen to anyone," said Albert Dreyer. "And especially in the spring. Remember that. And all I did was to skip. Just a few feet, mark you, but I skipped. Remember that, too.

31   "You wouldn't remember that place at all. At least not as it was then." He paused and shook the ice in his glass and spoke more easily.

32   "It was a road that came out finally in a marsh along the Schuylkill River. Probably all industrial now. But I had a little house out there with a laboratory thrown in. It was convenient to the marsh, and that helped me with my studies of amphibia. Moreover, it was a wild, lonely road, and I wanted solitude. It is always the demand of the naturalist. You understand that?"

33   "Of course," I said. I knew he had gone there, after the death of his young wife, in grief and loneliness and despair. He was not a man to mention such things. "It is best for the naturalist," I agreed.

34   "Exactly. My best work was done there." He held up his black-gloved hand and glanced at it meditatively. "The work on the axolotl, newt neoteny. I worked hard. I had—" he hesitated— "things to forget. There were times when I worked all night. Or diverted myself, while waiting the result of an experiment, by midnight walks. It was a strange road. Wild all right, but paved and close enough to the city that there were occasional street lamps. All uphill and downhill, with bits of forest leaning in over it, till you walked in a tunnel of trees. Then suddenly you were in the marsh, and the road ended at an old, unused wharf.

35   "A place to be alone. A place to walk and think. A place for shadows to stretch ahead of you from one dim lamp to another and spring back as you reached the next. I have seen them get tall, tall, but never like that night. It was like a road into space."

36   "Cold?" I asked.

37   "No. I shouldn't have said 'space.' It gives the wrong effect. Not cold. Spring. Frog time. The first warmth, and the leaves coming. A little fog in the hollows. The way they like it then in the wet leaves and bogs. No moon, though; secretive and dark, with just those street lamps wandered out from the town. I often wondered what graft had brought them there. They shone on nothing—except my walks at midnight and the journeys of toads, but still . . ."

38   "Yes?" I prompted, as he paused.

39   "I was just thinking. The web of things. A politician in town gets a rake-off for selling useless lights on a useless road. If it hadn't been for that, I might not have seen them. I might not even have skipped. Or, if I had, the effect—How can you tell about such things afterwards? Was the effect heightened? Did it magnify their power? Who is to say?"

40   "The skip?" I said, trying to keep things casual. "I don't understand. You mean, just skipping? Jumping?"

41   Something like a twinkle came into his eyes for a moment. "Just that," he said. "No more. You are a young man. Impulsive? You should understand."

42   "I'm afraid—" I began to counter.

43   "But of course," he cried pleasantly. "I forget. You were not there. So how could I expect you to feel or know about this skipping. Look, look at me now. A sober man, eh?"

44   I nodded. "Dignified," I said cautiously.

45   "Very well. But, young man, there is a time to skip. On country roads in the spring. It is not necessary that there be girls. You will skip without them. You will skip because something within you knows the time—frog time. Then you will skip."

46   "Then I will skip," I repeated, hypnotized. Mad or not, there was a force in Albert Dreyer. Even there under the club lights, the night damp of an unused road began to gather.

47   "It was a late spring," he said. "Fog and mist in those hollows in
a way I had never seen before. And frogs, of course. Thousands of
them, and twenty species, trilling, gurgling, and grunting in as
many keys. The beautiful keen silver piping of spring peepers
arousing as the last ice leaves the ponds—if you have heard that
after a long winter alone, you will never forget it." He paused and
leaned forward, listening with such an intent inner ear that one
could almost hear that far-off silver piping from the wet meadows of
the man's forgotten years.

48   I rattled my glass uneasily, and his eyes came back to me.

49   "They come out then," he said more calmly. "All amphibia
have to return to the water for mating and egg laying. Even toads
will hop miles across country to streams and waterways. You don't
see them unless you go out at night in the right places as I did, but
that night—

50   "Well, it was unusual, put it that way, as an understatement. It
was late, and the creatures seemed to know it. You could feel the
forces of mighty and archaic life welling up from the very ground.
The water was pulling them—not water as we know it, but the
mother, the ancient life force, the thing that made us in the days of
creation, and that lurks around us still, unnoticed in our sterile
cities.

51   "I was no different from any other young fool coming home on a
spring night, except that as a student of life, and of amphibia in
particular, I was, shall we say, more aware of the creatures. I had
performed experiments"—the black glove gestured before my
eyes. "I was, as it proved, susceptible.

52   "It began on that lost stretch of roadway leading to the river, and
it began simply enough. All around, under the street lamps, I saw
little frogs and big frogs hopping steadily toward the river. They
were going in my direction.

53   "At that time I had my whimsies, and I was spry enough to feel the tug of that great movement. I joined them. There was no mystery about it. I simply began to skip, to skip gaily, and enjoy the great bobbing shadow I created as I passed onward with that leaping host all headed for the river.

54   "Now skipping along a wet pavement in spring is infectious, particularly going downhill, as we were. The impulse to take mightier leaps, to soar farther, increases progressively. The madness worked into me. I bounded till my lungs labored, and my shadow, at first my own shadow, bounded and labored with me.

55   "It was only midway in my flight that I began to grow conscious that I was not alone. The feeling was not strong at first. Normally a sober pedestrian, I was ecstatically preoccupied with the discovery of latent stores of energy and agility which I had not suspected in my subdued existence.

56   "It was only as we passed under a street lamp that I noticed, beside my own bobbing shadow, another great, leaping grotesquerie that had an uncanny suggestion of the frog world about it. The shocking aspect of the thing lay in its size, and the fact that, judging from the shadow, it was soaring higher and more gaily than myself.

57   " 'Very well,' you will say"—and here Dreyer paused and looked at me tolerantly—" 'Why didn't you turn around? That would be the scientific thing to do.'

58   "It would be the scientific thing to do, young man, but let me tell you it is not done—not on an empty road at midnight—not when the shadow is already beside your shadow and is joined by another, and then another.

59   "No, you do not pause. You look neither to left nor right, for fear of what you might see there. Instead, you dance on madly, hopelessly. Plunging higher, higher, in the hope the shadows will be left behind, or prove to be only leaves dancing, when you reach the next street light. Or that whatever had joined you in this midnight bacchanal will take some other pathway and depart.

60   "You do not look—you cannot look—because to do so is to destroy the universe in which we move and exist and have our transient being. You dare not look, because, beside the shadows, there now comes to your ears the loose-limbed slap of giant batrachian feet, not loud, not loud at all, but there, definitely there, behind you at your shoulder, plunging with the utter madness of spring, their rhythm entering your bones until you too are hurtling upward in some gigantic ecstasy that it is not given to mere flesh and blood to long endure.

61   "I was part of it, part of some mad dance of the elementals behind the show of things. Perhaps in that night of archaic and elemental passion, that festival of the wetlands, my careless hopping passage under the street lights had called them, attracted their attention, brought them leaping down some fourth-dimensional roadway into the world of time.

62   "Do not suppose for a single moment I thought so coherently then. My lungs were bursting, my physical self exhausted, but I sprang, I hurtled, I flung myself onward in a company I could not see, that never outpaced me, but that swept me with the mighty ecstasies of a thousand springs, and that bore me onward exultantly past my own doorstep, toward the river, toward some pathway long forgotten, toward some unforgettable destination in the wetlands and the spring.

63   "Even as I leaped, I was changing. It was this, I think, that stirred the last remnants of human fear and human caution that I still possessed. My will was in abeyance; I could not stop. Furthermore, certain sensations, hypnotic or otherwise, suggested to me that my own physical shape was modifying, or about to change. I was leaping with a growing ease. I was—

64   "It was just then that the wharf lights began to show. We were approaching the end of the road, and the road, as I have said, ended in the river. It was this, I suppose, that startled me back into some semblance of human terror. Man is a land animal. He does not

willingly plunge off wharfs at midnight in the monstrous company of amphibious shadows.

65   "Nevertheless their power held me. We pounded madly toward the wharf, and under the light that hung above it, and the beam that made a cross. Part of me struggled to stop, and part of me hurtled on. But in that final frenzy of terror before the water below engulfed me I shrieked, *'Help! In the name of God, help me! In the name of Jesus, stop!'*"

66   Dreyer paused and drew in his chair a little closer under the light. Then he went on steadily.

67   "I was not, I suppose, a particularly religious man, and the cries merely revealed the extremity of my terror. Nevertheless this is a strange thing, and whether it involves the crossed beam, or the appeal to a Christian deity, I will not attempt to answer.

68   "In one electric instant, however, I was free. It was like the release from demoniac possession. One moment I was leaping in an inhuman company of elder things, and the next moment I was a badly shaken human being on a wharf. Strangest of all, perhaps, was the sudden silence of that midnight hour. I looked down in the circle of the arc light, and there by my feet hopped feebly some tiny froglets of the great migration. There was nothing impressive about them, but you will understand that I drew back in revulsion. I have never been able to handle them for research since. My work is in the past."

69   He paused and drank, and then, seeing perhaps some lingering doubt and confusion in my eyes, held up his black-gloved hand and deliberately pinched off the glove.

70   A man should not do that to another man without warning, but I suppose he felt I demanded some proof. I turned my eyes away. One does not like a webbed batrachian hand on a human being.

71   As I rose embarrassedly, his voice came up to me from the depths of the chair.

72   "It is not the hand," Dreyer said. "It is the question of choice. Perhaps I was a coward, and ill prepared. Perhaps"—his voice

searched uneasily among his memories—"perhaps I should have taken them and that springtime without question. Perhaps I should have trusted them and hopped onward. Who knows? They were gay enough, at least."

73   He sighed and set down his glass and stared so intently into empty space that, seeing I was forgotten, I tiptoed quietly away.

OLD MRS. GREY
by Virginia Woolf

1   There are moments even in England, now, when even the busiest, most contented suddenly let fall what they hold—it may be the week's washing. Sheets and pyjamas crumble and dissolve in their hands, because, though they do not state this in so many words, it seems silly to take the washing round to Mrs. Peel when out there over the fields over the hills, there is no washing; no pinning of clotheslines; mangling and ironing; no work at all, but boundless rest. Stainless and boundless rest; space unlimited; untrodden grass; wild birds flying; hills whose smooth uprise continues that wild flight.

2   Of all this however only seven foot by four could be seen from Mrs. Grey's corner. That was the size of her front door which stood wide open, though there was a fire burning on the grate. The fire looked like a small spot of dusty light feebly trying to escape from the embarrassing pressure of the pouring sunshine.

3   Mrs. Grey sat on a hard chair in the corner looking—but at what? Apparently at nothing. She did not change the focus of her eyes when visitors came in. Her eyes had ceased to focus themselves; it may be that they had lost the power. They were aged eyes, blue, unspectacled. They could see, but without looking. She had never used her eyes on anything minute and difficult; merely upon faces, and dishes and fields. And now at the age of ninety-two they saw nothing but a zigzag of pain wriggling across the door, pain that twisted her legs as it wriggled; jerked her body to and fro like a

marionette. Her body was wrapped round the pain as a damp sheet is folded over a wire. The wire was spasmodically jerked by a cruel invisible hand. She flung out a foot, a hand. Then it stopped. She sat still for a moment.

4   In that pause she saw herself in the past at ten, at twenty, at twenty-five. She was running in and out of a cottage with eleven brothers and sisters. The line jerked. She was thrown forward in her chair.

5   'All dead. All dead,' she mumbled. 'My brothers and sisters. And my husband gone. My daughter too. But I go on. Every morning I pray God to let me pass.'

6   The morning spread seven foot by four green and sunny. Like a fling of grain the birds settled on the land. She was jerked again by another tweak of the tormenting hand.

7   'I'm an ignorant old woman. I can't read or write, and every morning when I crawls downstairs, I say I wish it were night; and every night, when I crawls up to bed, I say I wish it were day. I'm only an ignorant old woman. But I prays to God: O let me pass. I'm an ignorant old woman—I can't read or write.'

8   So when the colour went out of the doorway, she could not see the other page which is then lit up; or hear the voices that have argued, sung, talked for hundreds of years.

9   The jerked limbs were still again.

10   'The doctor comes every week. The parish doctor now. Since my daughter went, we can't afford Dr. Nicholls. But he's a good man. He says he wonders I don't go. He says my heart's nothing but wind and water. Yet I don't seem able to die.'

11   So we—humanity—insist that the body shall still cling to the wire. We put out the eyes and the ears; but we pinion it there, with a bottle of medicine, a cup of tea, a dying fire, like a rook on a barn door; but a rook that still lives, even with a nail through it.

LOOKING FOR A LOST DOG
by Gretel Ehrlich

The most valuable thoughts which I entertain are anything but what I thought. Nature abhors a vacuum, and if I can only walk with sufficient carelessness I am sure to be filled.

—HENRY DAVID THOREAU

1   I started off this morning looking for my lost dog. He's a red heeler, blotched brown and white, and I tell people he looks like a big saddle shoe. Born at Christmas on a thirty-below-zero night, he's tough, though his right front leg is crooked where it froze to the ground.

2   It's the old needle-in-the-haystack routine: small dog, huge landscape, and rugged terrain. While moving cows once, he fell in a hole and disappeared. We heard him whining but couldn't see him. When we put our ears to the ground, we could hear the hole that had swallowed him.

3   It's no wonder human beings are so narcissistic. The way our ears are constructed, we can only hear what's right next to us or else the internal monologue inside. I've taken to cupping my hands behind my ears—mule-like—and pricking them all the way forward or back to hear what's happened or what's ahead.

4   "Life is polyphonic," a Hungarian friend in her eighties said. She was a child prodigy from Budapest who had soloed on the violin in Paris and Berlin by the time she was twelve. "Childishly, I once thought hearing had mostly to do with music," she said. "Now that I'm too old to play the fiddle, I know it has to do with the great suspiration of life everywhere."

5   But back to the dog. I'm walking and looking and listening for him, though there is no trail, no clue, no direction to the search. Whimsically, I head north toward the falls. They're set in a deep gorge where Precambrian rock piles up to ten thousand feet on either side. A raven creaks overhead, flies into the cleft, glides

toward a panel of white water splashing over a ledge, and comes out cawing.

6   To find what is lost is an art in some cultures. The Navajos employ "hand tremblers," usually women, who go into a trance and "see" where the lost article or person is located. When I asked one such diviner what it was like when she was in trance, she said, "Lots of noise, but noise that's hard to hear."

7   Near the falls the ground flattens into a high-altitude valley before the mountains rise vertically. The falls roar, but they're overgrown with spruce, pine, willow, and wild rose, and the closer I get, the harder it is to see the water. Perhaps that is how it will be in my search for the dog.

8   We're worried about Frenchy because last summer he was bitten three times by rattlesnakes. After the first bite he walked toward me, reeled dramatically, and collapsed. I could see the two holes in his nose where the fangs went in, and I felt sure he was dying. I drove him twenty miles to the vet; by the time we arrived, Frenchy resembled a monster. His nose and neck had swollen as though a football had been sewn under the skin.

9   I walk and walk. Past the falls, through a pass, toward a larger, rowdier creek. The sky goes black. In the distance snow on the Owl Creek Mountains glares. A blue ocean seems to stretch between, and the black sky hangs over like a frown. A string of cottonwoods whose new, tender leaves are the color of limes pulls me downstream. I come into the meadow with the abandoned apple orchard. The trees have leaves but have lost most of their blossoms. I feel as if I had caught strangers undressed.

10   The sun comes back, and the wind. It brings no dog, but ducks slide overhead. An Eskimo from Barrow, Alaska, told me the reason spring has such fierce winds is so birds coming north will have something to fly on.

11   To find what's lost; to lose what's found. Several times I've thought I might be "losing my mind." Of course, minds aren't literally misplaced—on the contrary, we live too much under

them. As with viewing the falls, we can lose sight of what is too close. It is between the distant and close-up views that the struggle between impulse and reason, logic and passion takes place.

12 The feet move; the mind wanders. In his journals Thoreau wrote: "The saunterer, in the good sense, is no more vagrant than the meandering river, which is all the while sedulously seeking the shortest course to the sea."

13 Today I'm filled with longings—for what I'm not, for what is impossible, for people I love who can't be in my life. Passions of all sorts struggle soundlessly, or else, like the falls, they are all noise but can't be seen. My hybrid anguish spends itself as recklessly and purposefully as water.

14 Now I'm following a game trail up a sidehill. It's a mosaic of tracks—elk, deer, rabbit, and bird. If city dwellers could leave imprints in cement, it would look this way; tracks would overlap, go backward and forward like the peregrine saunterings of the mind.

15 I see a dog's track, or is it a coyote's? I get down on my hands and knees to sniff out a scent. What am I doing? I entertain expectations of myself as preposterous as when I landed in Tokyo—I felt so at home there that I thought I would break into fluent Japanese. Now I sniff the ground and smell only dirt. If I spent ten years sniffing, would I learn scents?

16 The tracks veer off the trail and disappear. Descending into a dry wash whose elegant, tortured junipers and tumbled boulders resemble a Japanese garden, I trip on a sagebrush root. I look. Deep in the center of the plant there is a bird's nest, but instead of eggs, a locust stares up at me.

17 Some days I think this one place isn't enough. That's when nothing is enough, when I want to live multiple lives and be allowed to love without limits. Those days, like today, I walk with a purpose but no destination. Only then do I see, at least momentarily, that everything is here. To my left a towering cottonwood is lunatic with birdsong. Under it I'm a listening post while its great

gray trunk—like a baton or the source of something—heaves its green symphony into the air.

18   I walk and walk: from the falls, over Grouse Hill, to the dry wash. Today it is enough to make a shadow.

LUCKY ICARUS
(VERSION 1)
by Jadran Lee

1   The snow had been growing wet and heavy in the warm weather of the past week. The lower reaches of the mountain had bare patches of damp earth and strawlike grass. Higher up the Swiss had posted emphatic warnings against skiing outside of marked slopes, for wet snow is prone to avalanches. I felt that the prospect of not skiing or snowsurfing again until Christmas called for some memorable bravado. Although not an exceptionally good snowsurfer, I was hopelessly addicted to the sensate rush one experiences when tearing down a powder field upon this modern relative of the ski.

2   I took the cable car up to the highest point I could reach far above the treeline. All of that week I had taken no risks, never skiing or surfing without a friend. The view from the top station of the cable car was one of the most imposing I had ever seen. The sky was of a strong blue unknown at lower altitudes; the snow was obviously dying yet it retained a brilliance that almost hurt the eyes. This was a landscape that wanted a story. I was a deity atop Mount Olympus; the dingy, settled valleys were in a different plane of existence, separated from me by white clouds that mingled with the snow.

3   I followed the slope until the first bend. There I had the option of branching off onto forbidden ground which looked fairly easy from the cable car but which now was covered in cloud. Temptation carried the day, and I found myself pushing into the little-known. I was surfing full tilt when I hit a cloud. It was exceptionally beautiful to be utterly engulfed in white. I could barely see a meter in front of

358

me, as the snow I raised on my snowboard mingled with the crisp white mist.

4   I was a lucky Icarus. A clear pocket in the cloud enabled me to see the three-meter dropoff just as I came upon it. I stopped and sat down on the forty-degree slope at the brink of the cliff to take stock of my situation. Should I jump? I had never tried so large a dropoff, and was unsure of getting help if I should hurt myself. Besides, there was a crevasse at the foot of the drop which seemed wide enough to accommodate my body. Until then, death had been a terrifying proposition which fortunately had no bearing on my life. Never had I seen danger that was not fleeting or been forced to think about survival. Yet I was strangely calm. Why? Sitting on a precipice and peering into a crevasse, I felt that I wanted to go on living, but that whether I did or not was unimportant. I consciously thought about not existing, and found the prospect no more fearsome than that of never having been born. What had been so frightening about death was not the idea of ceasing to be, but the awesome mystery that shrouded the manner and time of its coming. We are unnerved by the Grim Reaper because of his intractable and mysterious presence: he stalks forever at the periphery of our consciousness. A silent, implacable partner, he unmans by the arbitrary nature of his decision to strike. I was unafraid because the scythe was no longer a shadow, but the tangible reality of an icy crevasse which would only swallow me if I was unskillful.

5   Exhilarated with my victory over fear, I began to cast about for a practical way of leaving the mountain alive. A better snowboarder might have jumped, hoping to make it over the crevasse, but I knew my limitations. I would have to backtrack. It was clearly hopeless to try to carry my snowboard up with me, for the sagging snow looked as if it might avalanche even if I were unencumbered with that heavy object. I unfastened the board from my feet and stepped in the snow. My legs sank straight down as if I had been trying to stand on water, and I heard a substantial amount of snow slip away. Another step created a similar result. It was impossible to climb

uphill in this slush, so I decided to move away from the danger sideways, edging along with at least three of my limbs sunk in the snow at any one time. In this I must have resembled Spiderman moving sideways on the face of the skyscraper. The maneuver proved successful. I had only to get my surfboard that had fallen into the crevasse. I was able to approach the crack from below, where the snow was firmer and the slope was less steep; there I found that my board had gotten stuck in the fissure high enough for me to reach it.

6   Surfing to the nearest shelter was easy enough after that. Rather more difficult was the task of coming to grips with what I had thought and done. I ordered a beer at a cafe on the slopes, and found myself to be shivering convulsively as I thought of what I had confronted. Would I never be afraid of death again, by virtue of once having asked: "Death, where is thy sting?" Clearly not, for we are created with a deep-rooted emotional aversion to death. One can no more rationalize away this dread than one can be blind to that redness which affrights in the blood. Yet I knew my attitude towards dying to have evolved irrevocably. The change was not purely intellectual; it involved a distinct diminishing of fear which could not have come from reading a well-argued book. For there is a quintessential difference between ideas and attitudes springing from what Virginia Woolf termed "moments of being," such as my time on the rock, and those drawn from vicarious experience and the thoughts of others. The distinction for me was not heightened confidence, in my judgment by virtue of its being my own; but a deep-rooted sense that this was what I truly believed, that these were thoughts drawn from the very core rather than feeble casuistry to sweeten the prospect of passing.

7   It was dusk by the time I was able to stop thinking and surf down the last part of the mountain, into the hotel.

LUCKY ICARUS
(VERSION 2)
by Jadran Lee

1   The snow had been growing wet and heavy in the warm sunshine of the past week. From the ascending cable car I saw that at lower altitudes the melt had exposed patches of damp earth and strawlike grass. Spring was climbing out of the valley. All week I had taken no risks, always skiing or surfing with at least one friend, but today I was alone. I felt that winter's end called for memorable bravado. Although I could not ride a snowboard exceptionally well, I was helplessly addicted to the sensate rush one feels when tearing down a powdery slope on this modern relative of the ski.

2   I rode the cable car to its highest station, far above the treeline. At the exit from the cable car the Swiss had posted emphatic warnings against skiing outside of marked slopes, for wet snow is prone to avalanches. The warnings did not hold my attention nearly as long as did the view of the Alps. I took a long time to strap on my snowboard, savouring the beauty of a landscape that I would soon be rushing through. Wet snow reflected the April sun with unmerciful brilliance. The sky was of a strong blue seldom seen from below the clouds; a blue without hazy paleness; vigorous and beautiful, like a woman with character. It offset frozen peaks: regal, jagged, perhaps impregnable; relics of geological violence in epochs so ancient as to make men seem transient as the snow. Brown valleys far below were obscured by clouds merging into the snow of the slopes. Up there I felt god-like, with the Mont Fort my Olympus. I stood up, lingered for an instant like a projectile at the apex of its flight, then pushed downhill.

3   I followed the slope until its first bend. There I had the option of branching off onto forbidden ground, which had looked fairly easy from the cable car but was now partly covered in cloud. Temptation won. I was surfing full tilt when I hit the cloud and was utterly engulfed in white. The snow and mist seemed to form a

single medium through which I floated, so that I felt briefly an exhilarating sense of being free from the ground. I could hardly see a meter ahead of me, and did not especially care to.

4   I was a lucky Icarus. A clear pocket in the cloud enabled me to see the three-meter dropoff just as I came upon it. I stopped and sat down at the brink of the little cliff to take stock of my situation. Should I jump? I had never tried so large a fall, and was unsure of getting help if I should hurt myself. Besides, I could just see a crevasse at the foot of the drop which seemed wide enough to accommodate my body.

5   Suddenly it struck me that I might die here. Until then, death had been an unsettling abstraction. Never before had I faced danger that was not fleeting, nor been forced to think to survive. Yet I felt unexpectedly calm, almost unafraid. Peering into the crevasse, I wanted to go on living, but felt that it was of no real importance whether I died now or later. Death would mean not existing, which seemed a prospect no worse than that of never having been born. What is normally so unnerving about death is our impotence in the face of it; the ghastly mystery of when the Grim Reaper will strike. I felt almost secure on the edge of the cliff for I knew I had some say in my destiny: I could die if I chose to let myself slip, or was unskillful; but if I were calm and resolute, I might be safe.

6   Gladdened by my small victory over fear, I began to cast about for a way to leave the mountain alive. A better snowboarder might have jumped, hoping to make it over the crevasse, but I knew my limitations. I would have to backtrack. It would clearly be hopeless to try to carry my snowboard with me, for the sagging snow looked as if it might avalanche even if I were not carrying the board. I unstrapped it from my feet and stepped into the snow. My legs sank deep into the slush, and I heard a substantial amount of snow slip away. Another step produced an even larger slippage which carried my board over the edge. It would be impossible to climb uphill, so I moved sideways, like a crab, until I reached a point where the dropoff shrank into a lump in the slope. If my snowboard

were lost I would face many difficulties, not the least of which would be a long walk into the valley. I circled around the base of the drop, hoping to reach my snowboard without stepping into snow that could collapse and let me fall to a rocky depth. Happily, the board had fallen obliquely into the crevasse, and wedged within reach.

7   Surfing into the valley was easy enough after that. Rather more difficult was the task of coming to grips with my experience. I ordered a beer at a cafe and sat down to think. Would my little tryst with fear mean that I would never again be afraid of dying? Clearly not, for I was shivering. I could no more rationalize away the innate dread of death than I could become blind to the redness which affrights in the blood. Perhaps people who face danger daily, like soldiers, completely lose their fear of death, as paramedics learn to master their inborn aversion to gore; but I had not seen nearly enough to count myself so brave. Yet I was less afraid of death now than I had ever been. Some of the awful mystery of dying was gone: I now had an inkling of what it must be like to face imminent death; I now had some reason to hope that I might greet my passing with dignity. I was frightened, but my fear was the quieter and more reasoned fear of one who has come to know himself better.

AN APPRECIATION OF GEORGE ORWELL
by Jadran Lee

1   In the thirties and forties George Orwell wrote roughly thirty essays, most of which had leftist political content. Some were literary criticism or commentaries on contemporary British culture; others were autobiographical pieces about injustices he had witnessed in coal mines, industrial cities, and overseas colonies. He had "the power of facing unpleasant facts," like hangings and poverty, and a contagious indignation at injustice which made him "the conscience of his generation" (*Essays* 419; qtd. in *Prose Pieces* 171). In an essay entitled "Why I Write," Orwell gave four

reasons for which people wrote: sheer egoism, aesthetic enthusiasm, historical impulse, and political purpose; and stated that the last was the most important to him. Yet it would be a grave misreading to see Orwell simply as a political pamphleteer; much of his writing has only tangential bearing on politics. In this paper I shall argue that what he called *political* purpose might better be called moral purpose, and that his aesthetic enthusiasm and conservative temperament were uneasy with the radicalism that his morals imposed on him.

2   We may better understand Orwell's motives for writing by observing in his work the moralistic tendencies he ascribed to Dickens. In the critical essay "Charles Dickens," Orwell examines the work of that author and concludes that Dickens was not the revolutionary political writer he was understood to be. Dickens described poorhouses and class cruelty, Orwell says, but expressed moral outrage rather than any prescriptive, political agenda. Orwell is disappointed at what he perceives as Dickens's political naivete, yet defends the author's moral purpose. He pictures Dickens as "a man who is *generously angry* . . . a nineteenth century liberal, a type hated with equal intensity by all the smelly[1] little orthodoxies that are now contending for our souls" (*Essays* 87). Orwell was of an age more politicized than Dickens's, yet he too seems motivated more by conscience than by political affiliation.

3   For Orwell was far too honest and independently-minded to enter factional politics wholeheartedly. He detested political orthodoxy because it required one to lie, which was unacceptable to a writer whose concern for politics was, he claimed, not intrinsic, but forced upon him by events and a fine conscience. Although he was broadly leftist, and once wrote: "Every line of serious work I have written since 1936 has been written, directly or indirectly, against totalitarianism and for democratic socialism," he constantly criticized aspects of the Left his conscience would not let him espouse. In the quotation above from "Charles Dickens," he

dismisses modern factions as "smelly little orthodoxies" (*Essays*
87). In "Looking Back on the Spanish War," there is a long tirade
against ideologues' rejection of objective truth where political
struggle was concerned. Wild stories of war atrocities were
concocted by both Republicans and Fascists, and true stories were
given credence only where they showed the enemy to be barba-
rous. He clarifies his revolt against political factionalism in the
essay "Writers and Leviathan," where he argues that in such a
turbulent age as his, it is one's duty to engage in politics, although
"in politics one can never do more than decide which of two evils
is less" (*Essays* 434). Politics, he declares, is a "dirty, degrading
business," so that the "acceptance of any political discipline seems
incompatible with literary integrity" (*Essays* 432, 434). These are
not the words of a man who had any natural relish for politics. He
says, in "Why I Write," that in a peaceful age he might have
concentrated on aesthetic writing, but that he was "forced" by the
twentieth century "into becoming a sort of pamphleteer" (*Essays*
423). Orwell, then, advocated Socialism *faute de mieux*, his social
awareness arising essentially from a Dickensian ethical concern.

4   Orwell's conscience pervades his writing. His best essays derive
their strength from the sense of moral urgency with which his
conscience imbues recollected experience. "Shooting an Elephant" describes how Orwell, a sahib Burma Police sergeant, feels
compelled to kill an apparently harmless beast to make a show of
force to the natives. The essay exposes the "futility of the white
man's dominion in the East," a dominion which requires foolish
and immoral violence to gain grudging acceptance (*Prose Pieces*
190). "How the Poor Die" describes his experience of the atro-
cious conditions in a Paris hospital. Both essays are highly representative of Orwell because they criticize the status quo on moral
grounds; Orwell's hypnotic prose makes us resent British imperialism and Paris poverty, just as a generation earlier *Oliver Twist*
made people hate the poorhouse. There is nothing in most of
Orwell's essays which might be called reasoned, prescriptive

political argument. Orwell was not a political writer, but a moralist who focused on what bothered his sense of justice in order to make sure it bothers ours too. The vagueness of his political thinking is nowhere better illustrated than in "A Hanging," where we are given a surrealistic account of an execution in Burma and made to feel the nauseating immorality of capital punishment without even an attempt by the author to argue against hangings on anything but impressionistic moral grounds.

5   Orwell generally did not write as a smug, judgmental prig. He was of the upper class in a nation with what he saw as an unjust colonial empire. He seems as a result to have felt himself to be partially responsible for the misery of the poor and oppressed in England and abroad. This guilt can be inferred from the tense unease of some of his essays, which have the sound of a man unburdening his soul. His essays on imperialism, "Shooting an Elephant," "A Hanging," and "Marrakech" illustrate this best. "Marrakech" differs from the other two in its setting and development; it is a series of reflections and poignant vignettes arising from a stroll through a French North African city. Each essay is a moral attack on imperialism which contains discrete, but unmerciful, self-recrimination. The whole premise of "Shooting an Elephant," that of "the futility of the white man's dominion in the East," rests on his confessed weakness in the face of an expectant Burmese crowd (*Prose Pieces* 190). The essay's analysis of "the real motives for which despotic governments act" demands that Orwell expose his culpable mindset as an officer in the Raj. Hence, he confesses to being glad the elephant had trampled to death a coolie, since this offered a pretext for destroying the elephant. This admission must have tormented Orwell, because the sight and memory of that poor, tortured man is haunting, especially as Orwell recounts it. Similar confessions appear in "Marrakech" and "A Hanging": *he,* the unfeeling European, fails to notice the plight of the Moroccan women who struggle past his house carrying huge bundles of wood; *he* joins in the ghastly gaiety that follows the hanging in

Burma. Orwell felt guilty, and needed to express himself to expiate his guilt: "the wretched prisoners huddling in the stinking cages of the lock-ups, the gray, cowed faces of the long-term convicts, the scarred buttocks of the men who had been flogged with bamboos—all of these oppressed me with an intolerable sense of guilt . . . [furthermore] I had had to think out my problems in the utter silence that is imposed on every Englishman in the East" (*Prose Pieces* 188). Come home to England, he could not remain silent. His writing thus possesses a moral urgency even greater than Dickens's, for Orwell's voice has less of the preacher and more of the intensity of a man crying *mea culpa*.

6   Orwell wrote with a hair shirt on. He felt forced by his conscience to advocate socialism, albeit with the deep reservations discussed earlier in this paper, as a cure to the wretched iniquities of the world. Yet his character was uneasy with this moral chore: for him "writing a book [was] a horrible, exhausting struggle" (*Essays* 426). He sometimes strove to paper over this unease, perhaps because he felt it a weakness, saying things like "all art is propaganda," or "what I have most wanted to do in the past ten years is to make political writing into an art," or "it is invariably where I lacked *political* purpose that I wrote lifeless books . . . and humbug generally"; all of which can be taken to mean that Orwell felt no unsatisfying tradeoff between writing as a radical and writing as an artist, a conclusion that is flatly untrue (*Essays* 73, 424, 426). Orwell himself admits, in "Why I Write," that the politically calculated inclusion of a long historical passage in "Homage to Catalonia" was a painful violation of the artistic unity of the book. The few bad parts of his essays are where he loses sight of moral or aesthetic inspiration and lapses into political rambling. The perceptiveness of Orwell the observer is obscured in leftist jargon; as in his long-winded attempt in "Looking Back on the Spanish War" to explain the war as a class struggle; and in his convincing attempt to see Dali's "decadent" Surrealism in terms of the "decay of capitalist civilization" (*Essays* 215). Fortunately, Orwell rarely

makes such slips, for he usually steered clear of fanatical party lines; it being, as he says in "Politics and the English Language," "Orthodoxy, of whatever color, [that] seems to demand a lifeless, imitative style."

7   The radical politics Orwell felt bound to uphold sat ill, not only with his aesthetic sensibilities, but with a naturally conservative disposition that left traces everywhere in his writing. Orwell was "a revolutionary in love with 1910"; in love with almost anything old and English that did not clash with his ideology (qtd. in Gardner 132).

8   This conservatism is expressed in his attitude to prose style. In the essay "Politics and the English Language," he argues brilliantly for saving the language from obscure waffle, all the while revealing deep-seated nostalgia in his outlook (qtd. in Gardner 132). His strong preference of Anglo-Saxon words over Latin and foreign ones makes him look a little like a grumbly old xenophobe. Furthermore, his choice of the old-fashioned language of the King James Bible as a model of stylistic clarity is a questionable result of an austere respect for tradition.

9   Orwell's regard for tradition also manifests itself in his literary technique. His essays mostly have the structure of straightforward dissertations (Gardner 132). There is very little Woolfian experimentation with form, except in "Marrakech," which is a compilation of images structured like a rock-music video. His attachment to linear development is seen in his frequent use of lists. In "Why I Write" he enumerates four reasons for writing professionally, in "Boys' Weeklies" he lists national stereotypes appearing in those periodicals, in "Anti-Semitism in Britain" he provides a catalogue of anti-semitic remarks, and in "Politics and the English Language" he gives numbered lists of what a writer should and shouldn't do. Orwell has essentially one literary technique of his own: he makes us live one of his experiences vicariously so as to draw us into strong empathy with him, in the hope that an intimate appreciation of the causes that led him to an opinion will lead us there also. This

technique can be supremely effective, as in "How the Poor Die," a chronicle of inhumanity at a hospital for the poor in Paris. It can also be quite limited in impact when the recollected experience is unmoving. This happens in "Looking Back on the Spanish War," where we are told that a "wild-looking boy" in Orwell's militia was kind to him; the benevolence may have been moving at the time, but when retold has the boring character of Dickensian sentimentality.

10   Orwell's radicalism was indeed limited to politics, and subject to an essentially Victorian set of values. Nowhere does his essential conservatism show so clearly as in his attack on Salvador Dali in "Benefit of Clergy." Dali, in the tradition of artists like Byron and Baudelaire, led a notoriously wicked, dissipated life; perhaps believing that this might heighten his creativity (Meyers 63). Orwell is indignant in his review of Dali's autobiography that the man should flaunt his necrophilia, exhibitionism, and sadism. This annoyance at perversion is understandable, but unfortunately Orwell manages to sound prudish. He calls Dali a "disgusting human being" and a "diseased intellect," and "does not grasp the fact that Dali's book is basically Surrealistic fiction and deliberately designed to attack bourgeois values. Orwell naively rises to Dali's obvious bait, and unleashes his rather puritanical indignation at the artist . . ." (*Essays* 218; Meyers 63). The problem was that Orwell had the habit of seeing "all art [as] propaganda," and of interpreting all of life in earnest, moral terms. This analytical penchant falls short when confronted with anything so unconventional as Dali; it is simplistic to dismiss Dali as a propagandist for moral perversity.

11   Orwell's nationalism reinforces one's perception of him as a Dickensian moralist who espoused Socialism because that seemed the decent thing, rather than because he was temperamentally suited for it. In "Note on Nationalism" he criticizes the anglophobic sentiments of the British Left. In other essays he shows himself to be very much in love with things English. He wrote an

essay "In Defence of English Cooking," when all but the most die-hard anglophiles will tell you it is rather unappetizing. Another essay, "The Decline of the English Murder," laments the supplanting of prewar murders that were committed after "long and terrible struggles with . . . conscience" with an unthinking, presumably foreign type of butchery (qtd. in Gardner 88). It seems slightly jingoistic to associate a fine conscience with one nation, even if it was the home of Cardinal Newman.

12   This native love of his own people assumed a charmless dimension in his attitude to nonwhites. As a Socialist, he resented racism and imperialism; yet seems to have entertained a visceral dislike of colored peoples. He perceived the Burmese as an alien "sea of yellow faces," "evil-spirited little beasts" incapable of giving clear directions (*Prose Pieces* 188, 190). In "Shooting an Elephant," he describes the contradiction thus: "With one part of my mind I thought of the British Raj as an unbreakable tyranny . . . clamped down . . . upon the will of prostrate peoples; with another part I thought the greatest joy in the world would be to drive a bayonet into a Buddhist priest's guts" (*Prose Pieces* 188). Everywhere in his writing, natives are presented as specimens of a type rather than as individuals: hence his description of the convict in "A Hanging" as having "the bobbing gait of the Indian who never straightens his knees," and of the black soldier in "Marrakech" as having "the shy, wide-eyed Negro look" (*Prose Pieces* 172, 198). He even explains that pigmented people are harder to empathize with because they look different: "The people have brown faces— besides, there are so many of them! Are they really the same flesh as yourself? Do they even have names? Or are they merely a kind of undifferentiated brown stuff, about as individual as bees or coral insects" (*Prose Pieces* 194)? Orwell, of course, *did* care and *did* recognize the immorality that arose from such perceptions; I merely point to another instance of his instinctive disposition being more old-fashioned than radical.

13   What, then, are we to make of Orwell? He has been claimed as a spokesman by Socialists who point to his essays about the oppressed, and by Conservatives who point to *1984*. Like Dickens, he is "one of those writers who is felt to be worth stealing" (*Essays* 73). To understand his writing it is not useful to push him into a political mold. Instead, we must recognize him as an artist with a strong conscience; a man who would have been glad "to write enormous naturalistic novels . . . full of detailed passages and arresting similes . . . in which words were used partly for the sake of their sound" (*Essays* 421). He was a literary Cincinnatus with old-fashioned ideals of virtue, a man who entered the madding crowd of partisan politics because the time and his honor demanded it of him.

Note

[1]His intention in using the word "smelly" can better be understood thanks to this passage by Jeffrey Meyers: "Orwell . . . uses odour as a kind of ethical touchstone. . . . [He] concludes his essay on Gandhi by remarking, 'how clean a smell he has managed to leave behind!'; and he writes that the autobiography of Dali, the personal and moral antithesis of Gandhi, 'is a book that stinks' " (Meyers 62).

Works Cited

Gardner, Averil. *George Orwell*. Boston: Twayne, 1987.

Meyers, Jeffrey. *A Reader's Guide to George Orwell*. London: Thames, 1975.

Orwell, George. *Collected Essays*. London: Secker, 1961.

———. "A Hanging." *Prose Pieces: Essays and Stories*. Ed. Pat C. Hoy II and Robert DiYanni. New York, Random House, 1985. 171–74. [Additional essays from the same source:] "Marrakech." 194–98.

"Shooting an Elephant." 187–92.

Works Consulted

Hunter, Lynette. *George Orwell: The Search for Voice*. Milton Keynes: Open UP, 1984.

Lewis, Peter. *George Orwell: The Road to 1984*. New York: Harcourt, 1981.

EQUILIBRIUM AND EXHAUSTION
CAN AMERICA SURVIVE WHEN WE RUN
OUT OF AREA CODES?
by Ian Watson

1   There are children starving in Northern Botswana. The continental shelf is wearing away and New Jersey is going to slip into the ocean. The icebergs are melting and soon Hawaii will become a chain of underwater seamounts. The Russians are planting anti-American triple megaphasers in the Arctic icecap. And America is running out of area codes.

2   Yes, it's true. There are only five area codes left on the North American Numbering Plan. They will be exhausted by 1995 or 1996. One day, every idealist in America, dutifully working their lives away fighting homelessness, nuclear proliferation, discriminatory college admissions policies, the slaughter of baby harp seals, and all those horribly imminent natural catastrophes, will wake up and find out that they can't call each other. The phone system will be completely paralyzed from sheer overload, and just picking up the handset will throw your phone into jerking, twitching spasms and seizures. People will rush out into the streets to console each other as they watch the coherence, the structure, the security of America melt and slither away into vast existential nothingness.

3   Well, maybe it won't work quite like that. Enough people have been thinking about area codes to have formulated a plan to deal with area code exhaustion. These are the prescient few who have realized that area codes are as much of a pressing social problem as computer viruses or saturated fat, and certainly much less trendy. And perhaps America's well-meaning social activists should pay a little more attention to area codes, because they use them every day

whenever they dial long distance, which is certainly more often than they get face-to-face with a drum of disposable nuclear waste. Maybe the basic structural systems that we take for granted every day, like area codes, are no less important than the latest horrifying social concern on the cover of *Time* or *Newsweek*.

4   As a matter of fact, the problem of area code exhaustion leads us into a whole way of thinking about systems of organization and identification. You see, when we run out of area codes, something is going to have to change in the telephone system, some rules that used to restrict the phone system in some way that made sense. In the case of area codes, the rule that now says that their second digit has to be a zero or a one will be eliminated. If and when we run out of area codes again, some other restriction will have to be changed. What we see here is that to keep any system working, we must always strike a balance between the idea of exhaustion—an inexorable process in the case of telephones, since there will always be more and more customers—and the rules and conventions that give sense and order to the system. Even in something seemingly trivial like area codes, we see the importance of compromise and balance. And that's not trivial at all.

5   Perhaps the best way to understand area codes and telephone numbering plans is to take a look at the history of the current system. Area codes trace back to a 1952 article in the Bell System Technical Journal by W. H. Nunn describing a new "nationwide numbering plan covering the United States and Canada" (Nunn 854). The creation of this North American Numbering Plan (NANP), as it's now known,[1] was an attempt to make it easier and cheaper for operators and customers to make long distance or "toll" calls by creating a standard system of reference for each telephone number in America. The problem had been that each local telephone system had expanded to whatever extent and in whatever ways it saw fit, so that Nunn describes ten different ways of local numbering, which he temperately calls "a source of some difficulty and confusion to the operators." In addition, long dis-

tance calls had to be operator-assisted, and required complicated and error-prone routing codes instead of the simplicity of the new area code system.

6   The way to do this was to prescribe a national standard for the numbering system. There has also been a need for terminology to describe this standard. The essential part of the terminology is fairly simple: "X" stands for any number from 0 to 9, "N" for any number from 2 to 9, and "0/1" for either zero or one (Rey 115).[2] Now the system that the terminology describes, in its original 1952 conception, consisted of three parts:

1. A three-digit area code consisting of the form N0/1X, in other words 1) a number between 2 and 9; 2) either 0 or 1; and 3) a number between 0 and 9; with the following additional rules:

a. There were three types of area codes, covering 1) several states or provinces 2) one state or province or 3) a part of one and only one state or province.

b. Area codes of types 1 and 2 would have zero as the middle digit; area codes of type 3 would have 1 as the middle digit.[3]

c. Area codes of the form N00 and N11 would be unassigned and reserved for special applications such as 800 numbers and 911 service; traditionally, N10 area codes have not been used either, but N01 codes are fully functional (Rhode Island's area code is 401).

2. A three-digit exchange code, designating a particular telephone office within an area code, of the form NNX, with the NN originally transcribed as letters for directory purposes; the letter code was generally related to the geographical name of the area it served, so that, for instance, TR6 (876) derived from TRafalgar 6.[4]

3. A four-digit line number of the unrestricted form XXXX.

4. A final aspect of the system was that the telephone switching technology then in general use was of a step-by-step type: in other words, it could not consider an entire sequence of dialed numbers as a whole and then decide where to route the call, but instead made individual switching decisions after each number.

Therefore we had an original system which had two types of home telephone numbers:

N0X-NNX-XXXX, for states with just one area code, and N1X-NNX-XXXX, for states with more than one area code, with the -NN- of the exchange as geographically relevant letters for directory purposes.

7   We need to go through the technical rigor of this description in order to understand the importance of how the system has changed, because most of these rules limited telephone system expansion at the same time as they helped the numbering plan make sense for its users. So one by one, as Americans got themselves more and more telephones, the rules were done away with.

8   The first one to go was the rule that area codes that covered entire states had to have a medial zero and that area codes that covered parts of states had to have a one. Not only was its original purpose (operator convenience) outmoded with the availability of direct long-distance dialing, but it was also impractical. Single-area-code states such as North Carolina (704) and Washington (206) became too populous for one area code, and had to be split. And regardless of whether the new area code had a medial zero (like Washington's 509) or a one (like North Carolina's 919), the logical chain which predicted how many area codes a state had from any given one of its codes no longer worked. If the one-zero distinction had been preserved by changing the original area code of single-code states that had to be split, it would have also proved impractical because the stock of medial-one area codes would

have been exhausted long ago.[5] So from the start, the one-zero distinction was doomed by the inevitable process of American population growth.

9   This change created a system with numbers described by a new system:

> N0/1X-NNX-XXXX with the -NN- of the exchange as geographically relevant letters for directory purposes.

10   The next thing that went was the letter system. First of all, the geographical significance of the first two letters of the exchange could not always be maintained because, as more and more exchanges were created, the two numbers that corresponded to the first two letters of the exchange name were sometimes already used; it no longer became always possible to have the letters have any relevance to the location of the exchange. Second, it was in the interests of international standardization to have an all-number code (Rey 118).[6] So what happened was that one exhaustible system (geographical relevance) was exchanged for one that was not exhaustible but made just as much sense (international numbering plan coherence). So the new North American system was simply:

> N0/1X-NNX-XXXX

11   The next problem came when exchanges started to use up all 10,000 possible line numbers, new exchanges were created, and then area codes started to run out of their 640 possible exchanges. The solution to this was to remove the rule that said that the second digit of exchange codes could run only from two through nine. This sort of system is said to have "interchangeable codes." So, for example, the exchange that serves the University of Chicago is numbered 702, and University of Chicago numbers assume the form 312-702-XXXX. The problem with this is that traditionally there have been three levels of calling distance for American customers:

a. (exchange)+(line number): within a designated local calling area

b. 1+(exchange)+(line number): outside (a) but within one's area code

c. 1+(area code)+(exchange)+(line number): to other area codes

12 Now it had always been true that calls of type (b) could be easily distinguished from type (c), since they had different initial sequences: 1+NNX versus 1+N0/1X. But with elimination of the medial exchange number restriction, we get an overlapping situation: 1+NXX versus 1+N0/1X, where zero and one can be used by both types as the third digit dialed. Now, when someone on the outer edges of area code 312 dials 1-702-, it is no longer apparent whether they are dialing according to level (b) (exchange 702, the University of Chicago exchange within area code 312) or (c) (area code 702, or Nevada). Only knowing the rest of the number will give us the answer. This is a big problem for step-by-step destination processing, which must deal with the "702" before it considers the rest of the number. There are two ways to deal with this. One is by creating another restriction that would be consistent with step-by-step processing: eliminate level (b), so that in area codes with interchangeable codes, a prefixed 1- always means that the next three digits will designate an area code, and use level (a) for all numbers in the same area code as the caller. The other method is to process telephone calls with new computerized equipment that considers how many digits have been dialed before it thinks about what those digits are, and to then decide whether the -702- is an area code or an exchange based on whether seven or four numbers follow it. This approach demands some way of determining when a caller has stopped dialing—either a manual termination code (such as dialing #) or a computer-monitored time limit between dialed digits (known as a "critical time").[7]

13   The introduction of these interchangeable exchange codes in selected areas in 1974 left us with the following system.[8]

N0/1X-NXX-XXXX

This is where we are now. Unfortunately, interchangeable exchange codes only expand an area code's capacity by 25 percent, not enough to stave off exhaustion for very long. And our store of area codes is low. There are now five left, and they are going fast: since 1984 New York City has been given 718, Colorado 719, Florida 407, and Massachusetts 508. More are on the way: 708, for example, is coming soon to Chicago.[9] Officials at Bellcore (Bell Communications Research) in New Jersey, which administers the NANP, estimate that complete exhaustion will occur in 1995 or 1996.[10] There are some small measures that we could take to prevent this, such as using unassigned and practically usable (but systemically prohibited) N1X and N00 codes. But that would only be a stopgap measure.

14   Instead, what will happen is that the idea of interchangeable exchange codes will be applied to area codes. Exchange codes formerly prohibited medial zeroes and ones; area codes currently prohibit *anything but* zeros and ones medially. Exchange codes now allow any medial digit (providing that the associated problems have been solved); so, eventually, will area codes, and with similar switching needs. And by doing this the theoretical area code reserve will jump by 640 ($8 \times 8 \times 10$) codes, and we will be safe from the inexorable process of exhaustion for a long time to come.[11] Our system will then be:

NXX-NXX-XXXX

for longer than we can predict right now. Now, what will happen if exhaustion catches up with us again? Well, perhaps we'll change to an XXX-XXX-XXXX format; more likely, we'll have to add an extra digit to all our phone numbers. But somehow, we'll manage it. We'll have to.

15   We had to go through the complexity of the system to understand the sort of logical reasoning that it demands. Now we're in a
position to draw some conclusions. The most important of these is
that there is a basic similarity in all the North American Numbering
Plan changes. For each change, there was a cause, and there was
an effect. The projected exhaustion of appropriate area codes
caused the demise of the medial zero/medial one distinction in
area codes. The desire for standardization caused the elimination
of the letter system. In each case we witness two competing needs
which come head to head. To keep the system alive though, they
have to find an equilibrium (which usually eliminates one of the
two forces), and this balancing process seems to be the one
common link to all systemic changes. The two forces that are most
important in maintaining equilibrium are (1) the desire that systems
make sense, so that their users can understand them, and (2) the
desire that systems be able to expand, so that they will not be
exhausted. The fact is that there is little way to stop the process of
telephone exhaustion, but it's easy to fudge on sense-making, so
the forces of expansion usually win out. It's just like balancing an
algebraic equation:

Need for SENSE	System Equilibrium	Size CONSTRAINT
−SENSE Loss of relevant N01/N1X distinction	balances	−CONSTRAINT Additional area codes available
−SENSE No geographical relevance of letters	balances	+CONSTRAINT All-numeric, standardized numbers
−SENSE Exchanges go from NNX to NXX[12]	balances	−CONSTRAINT Additional exchanges available

A minus on both sides, or a plus and a minus on the same side, cancel each other out, and everything works again. The only deviation we had was when we ran into problems with dialing processing: the changes we had to make in the numbering plan affected a whole other system, which is itself an analogous equilibrium between (1) the simplicity and sensibility of dialing methods and (2) the constraints of switching technology to handle dialing method changes. We had a sort of metasystem, a meta-equilibrium where two linked systems had to settle themselves before our telephone could work right.

16   The conclusion from this mathematical sort of give-and-take is, then, that anything that makes the telephone numbering plan sensible also limits its development, and that this is an example of an equilibrium forced by the necessity to make hard choices so that our telephone networks will be able to function understandably.

17   Now comes the fun part, because with knowledge of the compromises in the phone system we can go on to apply what we've learned to a whole lot of other systems in the world. But first we need to go through several different types of sense-making to get an idea of the terms we're dealing with. The best way to do this is with a purely theoretical example:

18   Let's say we are making a city and we want to number every street in it. The freest way would be to pick an arbitrary number for each street. There would be no restrictions on length or relation to any other street number. So one street could be called 4 and the next one over called 356812 and a cross-street 67. We would never run out of numbers and we would never see an end to our system.

19   Unfortunately, that sort of numbering plan doesn't satisfy people's need for order. It is easier for people to work within a system—in this case, to find their way around the streets of the city—if they have some secure base of reference. For instance, we could number our streets from one on, starting with the very first street and working on up. The basis of our system would then be

chronology. Or we could number our streets according to what sector of the city they are in. So we could have Sector 4, Street 17, and we might write it as 4/17 Street. Washington's street system works like this. A simpler form of this *geographical relevance* system is something like New York's numbered streets and avenues. Geographical relevance is a specific case of *general relevance,* in which *discrete levels of significance* such as the two levels of the hierarchy Sector Number–Street Number stand for the relevant concrete entities (the sector and the street). We might also find that for reference purposes, or perhaps for purposes of simpler computer storage, it's easier to have all our street numbers be of a uniform, predictable length—like two numbers. This would be a *closed-length* system. Each of these italicized features is one of many ways to make a system sensible.

20   The problem that we will see is that anything that makes a system make sense also limits it, because the real world tends not to always fit in the nice square boxes that we create for it. If we number a system chronologically, what happens when one street is demolished to create a shopping mall, or when we find that we've forgotten to number a street because it was so small and insignificant? When we have sequentially numbered, geographically related (e.g., parallel) streets, what happens when we stick another street in between them? We get something weird and unstable like Forty-Three-and-a-Half Street. And what happens when we have a closed-length system that consists of three digits from 0 to 9 and suddenly we find out that we have more than 1,000 things to number—that our system has been *exhausted?* This problem of exhaustion is the most critical one in an age when world population and its technological reverberations such as telephone networks, postal systems, and automobile registration have been multiplying at an exponential rate. What we are always forced to do is change the systems that once made sense to us to accommodate the increased use that will always come through population and technological growth. Yet at the same time we must make sure that

we don't destroy the sensibility that makes these systems usable. We return, in the abstract this time, to the notion of a settled equilibrium between competing forces in a system.

21   When we look at other numbering plans, we find them dealing with these very same problems in the very same ways. The national interstate highway numbering plan, for instance, specifies that long-distance interstates be two digits, odd-numbered for north–south routes starting with I-5 in the west and even-numbered for east–west routes starting with I-4 in the south, and specifies a complicated three-number system for short-distance bypass-type interstates depending on whether they go through, into, or around a city. There are two problems that balance out this sort of sense-making. The real-life interstates do not always correspond to their theoretical conception: long-distance interstates are not always parallel but sometimes cross, and it's sometimes hard to tell whether a short interstate goes through, into, or around a city, and even more complicated when it connects two different cities. Also, this severely limits the supply of interstate numbers, which has forced things like the fact that there are I-190s in Massachusetts, New York, and South Dakota: the everpresent effects of exhaustion.[13]

22   Exhaustion—opposed to a system of relevance—is a sort of shadowy worry in the system of two-letter state and province abbreviations used by the U.S. Postal Service. Notice I said "abbreviations" instead of "codes." This is because the abbreviations are specifically designed to approximate—in other words, be relevant to—the states they refer to. Otherwise no one would know what they meant. It wouldn't work quite so well, it wouldn't feel so correct, if Utah were 47 and Georgia were 09. So our sense-making system consists of two components: one, that the abbreviation must resemble the state name (which generally means that the first letters of the abbreviation and the state must be the same, and that the second letter of the abbreviation ought to be somewhere in the state name, preferably in a stressed position), and,

two, that the abbreviation must be limited to two letters. Strangely enough, this system is very limiting. But its limitation is in turn compensated for by the fact that the rate of change for the system is rather slow (we haven't had a new state or territory in quite a while now) and we don't anticipate exhaustion right now. But still, look at the problem that the post office must have had in finding a two-letter code for Manitoba. We start it with "M," of course, but find in trying to use any of the next five letters of "Manitoba" that they have been exhausted by Massachusetts, Minnesota, Michigan, Montana, and Missouri respectively. The only choice left is "MB," which works fairly nicely, but we start to wonder what would have happened to our nice, sensible system if that "B" weren't there.

23   We feel fairly sure of our zip code system. It covers the country geographically, not according to shifty, unstable population distribution; it makes sense on five discrete levels; and we don't expect new land to suddenly surface off the coast of Oregon, exhausting our supply of zip codes.[14] But there is just no permanence in these kinds of systems either. A new offshore island, like the volcanic one that surfaced off Iceland during the fifties, would demand modification, and California falling into the ocean would really do the trick. Give things about a hundred million years and the United States will probably look so different that today's zip codes won't work at all.

24   I expect that every other identification system you will come across will work similarly. Vehicle identification numbers, Social Security numbers, two-letter airline and three-letter airport codes, bank account numbers, license plates, library cataloguing systems—they're all subject to the same problems.[15] We build these things up and try to make them make sense to ourselves—even a five-year-old can learn to use the telephone—and then slowly their limits become apparent and we see how they will break down, and then they do break down, and we have to find something else.

25   We could take the concept of systems equilibrium further into the snowy mountains of philosophical thought, discuss its relationship to dialectical materialism and change through Darwinian gradualism, derive and construct an ideal model of social change based originally on change in theoretical systems of identification, and then reapply that into the social concerns that were satirized at the beginning of this discussion. We're not going to do that. It would be too alarmingly Marxist and philosophically pompous. We could also try to say that whether it is telephone systems, zip codes, fossil fuel reserves, alternative education, baby harp seals, or Amazonian rain forests, we're all dealing with fairly similar problems: always there is inevitable change, and we must react to it, and somebody trying to solve the problems of the environment or of society should look to the clear-cut mathematical simplicity of area codes and their kin for ideas on how to fix things out in the real world. We're not going to do that either. In the real world many problems are complicated metasystems, the simple models that we have seen in identification systems are overlaid with all sorts of messy stuff that obscures their real usefulness, and even those few masters who understand the interacting, competing forces haven't got the power to set them right. What I really want to say is that thinking critically about technological trivia is not dry, not trivial, not uninteresting, and not a rejection of our supposed moral and ethical duty to do whatever is currently moral and ethical. *Right now America simply would not function without well-managed area codes.* Planning them, and watching them settle and work properly, is no less valuable than helping the homeless, saving the whales, or considering the great moral questions of Life. And it's perhaps more satisfying, because we can sit back at the end and say, "It works; it's an endless battle to keep the system happy, but at least we know we can do it."

◊

Notes

[1] I should briefly discuss telephone terminology here because this article set the standard for official numbering system jargon. What is commonly known as an "area code" is technically the numeric designation of a geographical "numbering plan area" or NPA; what we call an "exchange" (i.e., the first three numbers of a local telephone number) is really the entity served by a "central office" and designated by a "central office code"; the NANP refers to the planning of the entire system of NPA, central office code, and line number (Young; McAleese; Rey 115–116). Since the terms "exchange" and "area code" have become part of standard American English, I'll use them instead of their technical synonyms.

[2] My discussion of these changes is essentially an expansion of the diagram in Rey 118.

[3] This system was put in for the convenience of operators when long-distance calls were still operator-assisted; see (Nunn 856).

[4] Schwartz. The system for translating numbers to letters can still be found on your telephone dial.

[5] Of the sixty-four medial-one NANP area codes that exist exclusive of N10 and N11, fifty were included in the 1952 plan, and the fourteen remaining ones would have been exhausted very easily. Compare Nunn, Fig. 1, 858–859 and any current telephone directory.

[6] The unfortunate demise of the "personal appeal of names . . . which often had local geographical significance" is also mentioned in Rey. For more on the "personal appeal," see Schwartz.

[7] For the idea of critical time see (Rey 117). The # button is already recognized as a termination code by international switching technology, which must use critical time of "#" because international numbering length is not standardized; some telephone books, such as mine at home in Rochester, N.Y., are now advising the use of "#" at the end of all international calls to speed things up so that the computer won't have to waste time waiting for the critical time period to go by.

[8] See (Rey 118–119).

[9] 1986–87 Boston White Pages; McAleese. The five that are left are 708, 903, 908, 909, and 917. 903 was formerly used as a routing code to the Mexican telephone system but is not any longer (McAleese). The reason that the highest-numbered area codes are the ones still left is that they are most difficult to dial on rotary phones (Deford).

[10] McAleese, Bellcore was given NANP administrative responsibility after the AT&T breakup.

[11]N*(X-0/1)*X=(2 to 9)*(2 to 9)*(0 to 9=8*8*10=640, minus whatever restrictions are placed on NX0 and NX1 codes.

[12]The loss of sense here is in that it is no longer possible to tell on the basis of the middle number whether a given three-number sequence is an area code or an exchange.

[13]See the 1988 Rand McNally Road Atlas, particularly p. 3, for an explanation of the system.

[14]The standard references for zip codes are the ZIP and ZIP+4 guides published by the Postal Service and available at many post offices and reference libraries. The five discrete levels of a zip code are illustrated by my zip code, 14619-1816, where 1- covers New York, New Jersey, and Pennsylvania; 1-46- Rochester, New York, and selected suburbs; 1-46-19- a specific chunk of the southwestern section of the city of Rochester served by a branch post office, the Thurston Road Station; 1-46-19-18- a "sector" within 14619; and 1-46-19-18-16 a particular "segment" within sector 18, which often works out to just a few housing units. For instance, Thayer Hall, a Harvard dormitory, has three segments all to itself.

[15]Any of these systems would be interesting and fun to study. They are all documented in various types of literature, although the airline systems (which are administered by the International Air Transport Association) seem tough to find information on. One very soon gets into questions of international standardization and international conventions. The system of international country codes used in telephone dialing is one of the most interesting of these, but space prevents me from going into the detailed analysis it deserves. The country code system has two discrete levels of significance (the one-digit World Zone and the zero-to-two-digit affix that designates a particular country within that world zone), geographical relevance, and some limits on length (country codes can be from one to three digits long). The forces that undermine its sense-making have mostly to do with its questionable coverage (some countries have no code) and the resulting problems of expansion and possible exhaustion, plus the difficulties in case of boundary changes due to war, etc., not to mention the technological problems that must be involved. The system is overseen by the Comité Consultatif International Télégraphique et Téléphonique in Geneva, Switzerland. For more information, see (Rey 120–121), as well as your local phone book, which should have a section on international dialing.

◊

Works Cited

"718? 212!," *The New Yorker,* 2 May 1983, 29–31.

"Busy," *The New Yorker,* 27 August 1984, 28–29.

Deford, Frank. "Cracking the Area Code," *New York,* 29 July 1985, 23.

McAleese, Bob (Bellcore). Telephone conversation, 6 December 1988.

Nunn, W. H. "Nationwide Numbering Plan," *Bell System Technical Journal,* XXXI(1952): 851–859.

Rey, R. F., ed. *Engineering and Operations in the Bell System,* 2nd ed. Murray Hill, N.J.: AT&T Bell Laboratories, 1983.

Schwartz, Jonathan. "TRafalgar 6," *New York,* 21–28 December 1987, 89.

Young, Jackie (New England Telephone). Telephone conversation, 5 December 1988.

Please note: much of the basic reference material on zip codes, area codes, state codes, and so on, is general information that can be found in standard reference material such as the *World Almanac,* the USPS guides to zip codes and ZIP+4 materials, and your local phone book. In addition, much of the discussion is drawn from my own personal experience and observation, and any errors are, needless to say, my own.

THE THESIS HUNT
by Bernd Heinrich

1   The protozoa called Euglena are difficult to define as plant or animal. They have features of both. Under the microscope the organisms move rapidly, propelled by whiplike tails, or flagellae. When in the dark they can absorb nutrients and metabolize them by some of the same intricate metabolic pathways found in animal cells. On the other hand, when these organisms are put into water without organic food molecules, but in the light, they miraculously turn green as they become packed full of chloroplasts like those from any respectable plant. With the chloroplasts they can synthesize their own food energy out of the carbon dioxide they take in from the atmosphere.

2   Professor James Cook's laboratory in the basement of Coburn Hall, the ancient zoology building at the University of Maine, was filled with Euglena housed in Erlenmeyer flasks. The flasks in the

light contained a green broth, as millions of Euglena crowded into every milliliter. The Euglena cell suspensions from the dark, in temperature cabinets, were a pale transparent white. Other Euglena were held in temperature-controlled chemostats, where accurate pumps delivered nutrients at rates precisely adjusted to maintain specific population densities. There were centrifuges, an autoclave, a Beckman spectrophotometer with a recorder, a larger electronic box with a fluorescent screen, called a Coulter counter (for counting population densities of the protozoa), plus the usual shelves of chemicals and glassware.

3   I was majoring in zoology now and helping out in Cook's lab. By the end of the summer I had graduated from washing dishes to mixing nutrient media, pipetting cultures, making cell counts, and doing enzyme assays. I was even starting to wonder about many of the differences I was seeing between cells grown on sugar and cells grown on the salt of acetic acid, and so I decided to stay on for a master's degree. Despite my inclination to be outdoors, I felt I had to work in the laboratory to start learning the roots of biology. My thesis problem was on deciphering the metabolic pathways whereby these two entirely different food molecules might be used by Euglena, and how or why the different food molecules so drastically affected the cell's respiratory rates, culture acidity, and maximum population density.

4   Before I could get involved in this research, I did much reading on the biology of Euglena. I saw these organisms through the minds of others, in their brilliant experiments and insights. The beauty of Euglena was inside of them, and much of that beauty could only be seen with the aid of a laboratory and a sharp mind's eye. The seeing is in the head, which is where the excitement is. I rarely looked at them through the microscope; I was more like a blind man when it came to seeing the biochemical machinery in Euglena. But after a while some parts of that internal beauty lay tangible and exposed, as if in the palm of my hand. Perhaps beauty and the structure and functioning of nature, in each of its many dimensions, are one and

the same thing. Beauty is not only an inherent feature, like the molecules of Euglena, the feathers of a bird, or the trees of a forest.

5   Within two years I had published or helped publish four papers in leading scientific journals. My initial success encouraged me to continue on for a Ph.D., and within another year, in 1966, I was at UCLA, focusing more and more narrowly on cell physiology, working this time with Tetrahymena, another kind of protozoa.

6   I broke the Tetrahymena cells open to spill their contents by swirling them in a detergent that ruptured the cell walls. Now I had a soup of cell fragments, sugars, fats, amino acids, proteins, and many other chemicals. To isolate the DNA out of this soup of cell constituents and detergent, I added phenol and shook the broth until it was white and creamy. The DNA separated out, and I gently twirled the coils out of the beaker onto a glass rod.

7   I was not equipped to handle examination of the sequence of bases that made up the DNA code. For the time being, I only wanted to know if the "tape" lengths, or the overall composition of bases, varied between possibly diverse populations of DNA molecules within the same cells. One of the ways of separating different DNA molecules was by their density-dependent rates of sedimentation under a strong centrifugal force.

8   I took a small sample of DNA downstairs to spin it for a day in a cesium chloride gradient on the Beckman ultracentrifuge. I waited. Would I get a satellite peak or not? My densitometer reading said I didn't have one. Perhaps the machine didn't work properly. Perhaps I didn't spin long enough. Perhaps my sample wasn't pure. Perhaps I shook it too long and broke the DNA strands. Or did I do everything right and was there really no satellite DNA? The only way to find out was to do it again, and again. Same results. Surely there is supposed to be a satellite if the mitochondria have their own DNA. Like any art, biology takes skill. It is not always easy to do all of the mechanical details just right in the effort to bring any one intellectual idea to life. It is disquieting when you don't know whether a certain result is real or just the result of fumbling.

9   The ultracentrifuge was a rare and expensive machine. Many professors and graduate students at UCLA had to use it. A week passed before it was free for my sample. In the meantime I noticed, beyond the phenol fumes surrounding my workbench, the red-tailed hawk soaring up against the sky, over toward the canyon. I wondered where it was making its nest, but I didn't have time to look. I was studying physical chemistry and calculus, and that was taking most of my time and all of my patience. I realized then I was not in the right field. Certain keys to an understanding of "life" would indeed be found in physics and chemistry. But maybe there was more. Some of the great revolutions in biological thought were made by a naturalist who was a beetle and rock collector and by a monk who liked growing varieties of garden peas.

10   One of the beauties of the UCLA zoology department was its diversity. If you couldn't find a home to suit your individual needs or wants in one lab, then you might find it down the hall. There were people working on molecular biology, cellular biology, whole-organism biology, and ecology. There were also world-renowned people working on insects, fishes, birds, mammals, and vertebrate fossils. Still others studied not specific organisms as such, but the adaptations of organisms to common problems encountered in the environment, such as those relating to moisture, temperature, and pressure.

11   One of these was the eminent physiological ecologist George A. Bartholomew. Bart was only slightly wary when I told him I wanted to switch areas of study. He cut short our first meeting by telling me to come back in a week with six different potential Ph.D. thesis test problems. "Then we'll talk," he said.

12   During this time a paper by Phillip A. Adams and James R. Heath in the *Journal of Experimental Biology* caught my eye. The authors claimed that the white-lined sphinx moth stabilized its body temperature near 37.8°C (100°F) over a wide range of air temperatures. This seemed incredible. I had learned that the primitive birds and mammals maintain lower body temperatures than the more

advanced ones and that the still more primitive reptiles and amphibians are cold-blooded. Moths and other insects are considered to be very primitive indeed compared with vertebrate animals. Thermoregulation by internally generated heat was only known for the highly advanced birds and mammals, and it was unknown even in the lower vertebrates, the amphibians and reptiles. Insects, of course, are not lower on the phylogenetic scale than humans. They are merely an entirely different line that has advanced along its own trajectory.

13   Sphinx moths, sometimes called hummingbird moths, are large narrow-winged insects that superficially resemble hummingbirds when they are in flight. They and hummingbirds are a remarkable example of what biologists call convergent evolution. They have both become adapted to do the same things: to suck nectar while hovering in front of flowers. They could also have converged in some aspects of their physiology, such as thermoregulation, but such a prediction does not mean that it is true. Some of the methods used in the experiments on moths were less than clear. I felt that the claim that they regulated their body temperature should be reexamined.

14   It was in 1964 that Adams, an entomologist from Fullerton College in California, first approached Heath, from the University of Illinois at Urbana, to study some sphinx moths he thought might be keeping themselves warm by shivering, using their flight muscles in the thorax. Heath was a well-known authority on thermoregulation in vertebrate animals, and he agreed to help investigate the problem. The species of sphinx moth that Adams showed Heath was *Hyles* (then called *Celerio*) *lineata,* the white-lined sphinx moth. The moth has a tapered streamlined body with delicate white, light brown, green, and pink markings. It has huge bulging eyes and a long tongue that, when not in use, is tucked neatly under the chin in a tight coil. The tufts of long scales at the end of the abdomen resemble a short tail. It flies fast, and willingly.

15   Adams and Heath enclosed thermocouples (fine wires for measuring temperature electronically) in the moths' thorax (the body part where legs and wings are attached). Then they used the long, thin wire leads from the thermocouples, which were attached to a temperature readout meter, as a leash. They could take their moths out for a short morning flight down the halls of the zoology building and observe on an instrument dial if the thorax heated up. Flight is extremely rigorous exercise, which, as any runner knows, produces heat. As expected, the moths heated up in flight and, indeed, could not fly until the temperature in their thorax was close to that found at the end of their pre-flight shivering. This was because the hotter they were, the faster they could beat their wings, and they couldn't fly until their wings beat at a certain speed. The moths' thoracic temperature during flight was remarkably close to the normal body temperature of warm-blooded birds and mammals. But what was more surprising was not that thoracic temperature was higher than air temperature, but that it remained at approximately the *same* high temperature regardless of what air temperature they were flown at. The thoracic temperature of the sphinx moths during flight was regulated.

16   Regulation of body temperature is determined by Newton's law of cooling, which says that the greater the difference in temperature between a body and its surroundings, the faster heat will transfer between them. At around 68°F we feel comfortable, since the heat generated by our resting metabolism is just enough to keep our bodies stabilized at 98.6°. If it gets much colder than 68°, we must shiver to produce extra heat, much as a furnace kicks on when room temperature drops below some fixed point. Conversely, if it is very hot, we sweat and the blood vessels close to the skin dilate (we get red) in order to give off heat. Similarly, an air conditioner turns on when room temperatures rise above some fixed point.

17   If sphinx moths do maintain a steady thoracic temperature during flight, they could do so in one of two ways. If the heat produced from the flight activity was not enough, they would have

to produce an increasing amount of extra heat when flying at decreasingly lower air temperatures. However, if the heat produced as a by-product of flight was always more than they needed to maintain a fixed body temperature, even at low air temperature, then they would have to actively lose more and more heat when flying at increasingly high air temperatures. Birds and mammals use the first mechanism to keep their body temperatures stable over broad ranges of air temperature, but since no insect had ever before been shown to regulate, it was not obvious which method they would use to keep thoracic temperature stable during flight: extra heat production or active heat loss. Adams and Heath concluded, "Large moths increase metabolism during active periods to offset heat loss and thereby maintain a relatively constant internal temperature. In this regard they may be considered endothermic, like birds and mammals." Thus they were concluding that the moths regulate by the heat-production mechanism.

18   But what actually did these researchers mean by "active periods" in a sphinx moth? A sphinx moth feeds by hovering. When it is not hovering or flying from one place to another, it is totally at rest. For someone who knew sphinx moths, "active" seemed to mean *flight,* especially since the measurements of metabolism or heat production were made "during periods of uniform activity following warm-up." Moths warm up for one thing only, to fly. I could not visualize *how* the moths might increase their metabolism at low air temperatures in order to stabilize thoracic temperature, as Adams and Heath seemed to imply for flying moths. The upstroke and downstroke muscles of the wings in the thorax could be contracted simultaneously against each other for shivering, as in pre-flight warm-up. Or the muscles could contract alternately to move the wings up and down during flight. But they could not be used for warm-up and flight simultaneously. Did the moths beat their wings faster (to produce more heat) with decreasing air temperatures? The researchers made no mention that wingbeat frequency varied at all, implying instead that the muscle efficiency

varied. But heat production of an exercising muscle cannot be simply turned on or off. If the moths could do it, it would be a new biological phenomenon.

19   I had to think up other possible explanations. Heath and Adams had measured metabolism in small jars. I knew that if a moth is prevented from flight, it stops its wingbeat and cools immediately. After cooling it may again shiver to try to fly again. The lower the air temperature, the faster it would cool, and the more it would have to shiver to get ready for flight; the total metabolism averaged over a series of warm-up bouts would be higher. Were they really measuring warm-up rather than flight? On the other hand, maybe their conclusion was faulty and the moths were not regulating thoracic temperature at all—maybe they were not flown long enough following warm-up for thoracic temperature stabilization to have occurred. Or maybe if the moths did thermoregulate, they did it by getting rid of excess heat at the high air temperatures, rather than increasing heat production at the low air temperatures. Perhaps they did it by a combination of both heat production and heat loss.

20   I gave a seminar on my thoughts about the Heath and Adams paper to Bart's laboratory group. Bart accepted me as his student, and it was decided that "the moth problem" held more potentially interesting prospects than the other five thesis projects I had come up with. So I set out to investigate, first of all, whether or not sphinx moths can thermoregulate while they are in continuous flight.

21   It was a major problem simply to get sphinx moths. *Hyles,* the moths that Heath and Adams worked with, occur in outbreaks for a few weeks or so, at some times in some places. Then they are often gone for years. It might not be a good animal to work with for a thesis problem, since I would need a steady supply of many. If a moth is punctured to take its temperature, it will be dead or damaged and cannot be used a second time. Insects are very delicate and usually short-lived.

22   And then I discovered *Manduca sexta,* the common garden-variety tomato "worm." These caterpillars could also be found all

over the jimson weed out in the Mojave Desert. They also eat tobacco. The worms hatch out into beautiful moths with delicate gray and black markings and a brilliant patchwork of black and yellow on the abdomen. They were not only as beautiful as *Hyles,* but also bigger. I wanted large moths so that I could more easily insert thermocouples and other probes into them with a minimum of damage. The only problem was that the big moths mean big caterpillars. Each caterpillar ate about one fifteen-inch-tall green-house-grown tobacco plant per day, and I was rearing 50–100 moths at a time. It seemed for a while that I was becoming a tobacco farmer, although toward the end of my studies I discovered a synthetic diet of wheat germ, agar, sugar, and vitamins that the caterpillars thrived on quite readily.

23   Measurements of the thoracic temperature of moths that were either attached and flopping at the end of a short thermocouple lead or enclosed in small containers did not relate to the normal behavior of these animals. I wondered what the temperatures were like during *continuous* flight where the moths could fly as long and as fast as they chose. I considered implanting radio telemeters to monitor temperature, but that wouldn't work because the moths were too small to accommodate any known telemeter. Perhaps an infra-red spotting scope? No, that would only give me surface temperature of the moths' scales, and it wouldn't be accurate enough.

24   I had another idea. I would fly them suspended on a mill where they could fly in circles at any speed they chose, as I continually monitored thoracic temperature. The leads from the thermocouples would be strung through the hollow arm of the flight mill to a temperature recorder, where thoracic temperature could be continuously printed out on a chart. I designed the mill, rushed to the shop, and the thing was built. At the unveiling it sat on a little table in Bart's lab. A moth was put on. Graduate students gathered round. The temperature recorder started printing out the moth's temperature every three seconds. The chart paper started to roll,

and the moth took off. The moth flew slowly at first, when its thoracic temperature was low. Gradually, from the flight exercise, it got hotter and hotter and flew faster and faster. The hotter it got, the faster it flew (and the more heat it produced and lost). After three to four minutes the rates of heat production and loss were equal, and thoracic temperature stabilized. My new toy worked. I would fly the moths at different air temperatures to see whether or not sphinx moths really did regulate their thoracic temperatures during flight.

25   Moth after moth went through its paces, and moth after moth stabilized its thoracic temperature, generating an excess body temperature of about 10°C above whatever air temperature I tried. That is, not one of these moths regulated its thoracic temperature. If air temperature was 15°C (58°F) they flew with a thoracic temperature near 25°C (77°F), and if air temperature was 25°C they flew with a thoracic temperature near 35°C. I was disappointed. These humdrum results suggested that there was no mysterious new physiological mechanism for me to decipher after all. Perhaps worse, it meant that I still had no thesis problem.

26   I had examined thoracic temperature by more sophisticated methods than Adams and Heath had, and my results contradicted theirs. Should I publish a paper and then move on to a more promising subject? Adams had written to me saying that they had a workable hypothesis for the mechanism of regulation in flight, as well as four graduate students working on the problem. They would very likely scoop me with the same results, so I would have nothing to show for my second year at UCLA. Maybe I should at least try to get into print before they did. Fortunately I didn't publish just then. More sophisticated methods do not necessarily make for better results, if there is a flaw in the ideas behind them. In this case, however, it wasn't so much a flaw as it was an important detail I had overlooked. And that detail would ultimately stand everyone's ideas on their head.

27   It was December, a time when it could be cool in the Mojave at night. I and a fellow graduate student, Gary Stiles, had camped in a wash among barrel cacti, boulders, ocatillo, and bushes of tuperow with blazing red flowers. The wash also contained the mauve green bushes of a mint with delicate blue flowers that were abuzz with honeybees throughout the day. The patches of tuperow attracted hummingbirds in the daytime. As the sun set and the coyotes howled on the distant ridges, we sat down to wait for sphinx moths.

28   I first heard a soft muffled fluttering. Then, looking like a small hummingbird, a *Hyles* sphinx moth hovered in front of me. It dipped into a flower, backed out, and went on to the next flower. In another instant the moth was fluttering wildly in my net. I grabbed it and stabbed it with the thermocouple probe: 42.5°C (108°F), or 32.5°C above air temperature! I remembered having seen *Hyles* flying near Los Angeles on a warm day, at 25°C. If the moth's body temperature is a simple passive phenomenon of the flight metabolism, as my flight mill experiments had suggested, then the Los Angeles moths should have heated up to 57.5°C (136°F). That was clearly impossible. They would have been cooked. There was something funny going on. They probably *do thermoregulate* in flight, at least when they are in the field. Why didn't the *Manduca* sphinx moths do it on my flight mill? Was it a species difference?

29   Back in the lab at UCLA I abandoned the flight mill. I simply allowed the moths to fly freely in a temperature-controlled room. After they had been in continuous free flight for two minutes (to simulate activity under field conditions), I grabbed them out of the air and stabbed them with the thermocouple as I had done in the desert. The results were entirely different: now their thoracic temperatures were high, close to 40°C (104°F) and sometimes up to 43°C. Furthermore, the moths were hot even when air temperature varied from 15°C to 34°C. They were thermoregulating!

30   Should I pick up the moths again and continue the study, or would I get beaten out in the race with Heath's lab, where students had been working on the moth problem for a long time? I had better

find out what had already been done, so I wrote Heath about my results. He answered in December 1969 and told me that in five years of working with *Manduca sexta* his lab had never recorded a moth's temperature higher than 40°C. Of course, he added, their animals were never "forced" to fly. Were my results screwy, then? "Forced?" All this time I had thought the point was to make sure the moths I took data from were in continuous flight. I felt some apprehension, but I knew I had been careful. Maybe *they* had missed something. I decided to continue with the problem, sensing that it involved some profound complexities that none of us was yet aware of.

31   As a first step in my decision to proceed, I spent a few months in the library reading about insect physiology in general and everything about sphinx moths in particular. Something in the known physiology and morphology might provide a clue. It would be necessary to collect more and more details on the problem until I could visualize it as closely as if it were a rock sitting in the palm of my hand: I wanted to find out *how* the moths were thermoregulating. Adams and Heath thought they did it by varying heat production, but their explanation didn't make sense to me. The heat produced by the moths during flight could *all* be an inevitable by-product of the flight metabolism. I needed to design an experiment that would separate out heat that might be produced for temperature regulation from heat unavoidably produced as an unwanted by-product of the flight metabolism. Upon some reflection I realized that one such experiment had already been done. The moths held aloft on my flight mill had a lower thoracic temperature (less heat production?) than those working harder in free flight. If the moths on the flight mill had produced heat specifically for temperature regulation, they should have been as hot as those in free flight.

32   Increases in temperature, however, are no proof of increased metabolism, or heat production. Metabolism had to be measured directly (most conveniently by determining the rate of oxygen

consumption). *Manduca sexta* are reluctant flyers, and I had trouble getting them to fly nonstop in the huge pickle jar I used as a respirometer. But some did fly, and the moths had nearly the same oxygen consumption, wingbeat frequencies, and amplitudes at all air temperatures, as long as they remained in continuous free flight. When I suspended them from a tether (like the one on the flight mill), wingbeat amplitude and metabolic rate was immediately reduced by one half. They worked less to fly. This explained why they had lower thoracic temperatures than when in free flight; they produced half as much heat. Heat production did not vary at all with the moth's cooling rate or with air temperature, but only with the effort they made to stay aloft and flying. The inescapable conclusion was that they were thermoregulating in free flight by regulating the rate of heat loss, with heat production remaining constant. The moths on the flight mill did not thermoregulate simply because, with lower flight effort, they never produced enough heat to call for the dissipation response.

33   My conclusion was now almost precisely the opposite of what Heath and his co-workers had published. They said the mechanism of thoracic temperature stabilization involved the regulation of heat *production.* I said it was the regulation of heat *loss.* One of us was wrong. I could hardly claim to be right, however, unless I could prove a mechanism whereby heat is dissipated.

34   There are three ways vertebrate homeotherms may increase heat loss: by varying their insulation, by panting or sweating, or by increasing blood flow to the capillaries in the skin. But the moths could not vary their insulation like a bird or a hairy mammal. Their scales are fixed solidly in the hard exterior skeleton. Insects do not pant or sweat. They have only a single large circulatory vessel, the "heart" that traverses the abdomen and extends into the thorax as the "aorta." They do not have capillaries with which to direct blood to or away from the body surface. Furthermore, Norman Church, a student of Francis Wigglesworth, the father of insect physiology, had examined avenues of heat gain and loss in insects

and had concluded that neither blood circulation nor evaporative water loss was a significant factor in an insect's heat balance. Whatever it was that the moths might do to thermoregulate, it would probably be a discovery.

35 I came across an obscure French paper of 1919 by Franck Brocher on the anatomy of the blood circulatory system of sphinx moths. The odd thing about these moths is that the aorta makes a loop through their thoracic muscles. In many or most other insects, it passes *underneath* these muscles before terminating in the head. Why should evolution introduce such a wrinkle unless there was some selective pressure for it? Brocher gave no speculations on the functional anatomy. But given my results I wondered if the selective pressure for the evolution of the loop might have been heat dissipation—could the loop be a cooling coil for the muscles? In insects the blood is pumped from the abdomen into the thorax, and the abdomen of the moths remains relatively cool in flight. The blood entering the thorax from the abdomen must be cool, too, and common sense dictated that the anatomy of the sphinx moth was arranged so that cooling of the thorax would be enhanced during blood flow.

36 My problem was now specific: Is heat loss regulated by way of the circulatory system? I couldn't stay away from the lab for more than a few hours at a time. Once I went to camp out for a weekend in the Sierras, but my mind was in the lab and I didn't see the birds or flowers. My measurements of heat production (oxygen consumption rate) and thoracic temperature showed that the moths thermoregulated by as much as tripling their rate of heat loss during flight at high air temperatures. But how could you measure heat loss facilitated by blood flow in a flying moth? Sphinx moths are extremely fast. You can't trail them in flight with instruments attached. I decided to mimic the overheating that normally occurs in flight and to control it myself.

37 Moths were tied down and heat was focused by a narrow beam of light from a heatlamp directly onto the thorax. Meanwhile,

thermocouples in the thorax, as well as several placed in the abdomen, were used to record body temperature simultaneously with heart pulsations on a polygraph machine. Would the moth tell me the "truth"? The results made all the efforts and waiting worthwhile. The new pieces of the puzzle fit, and provided attachment places for other pieces.

38   A captive moth heated on its thorax with a focused beam of light stabilized thoracic temperature (at about 42°C, 108°F), while the temperature of the abdomen continued to increase! Further experiments showed that heat transfer into the abdomen (and thoracic temperature stabilization) was correlated with strong pumping action of the heart. This was clear proof that temperature stabilization of the thorax involved variations of heat transfer and not necessarily of heat production. My thesis advisers were not all that convinced, though.

39   Franz Englemann said that I needed to eliminate the circulatory system to prove my point. I had thought of that, too, but dismissed it as an impossibility. Now I thought about it again and had an idea: I would do heart surgery. I'd take a surgeon's needle, thread it with a fine human hair, loop it around the heart where it empties into the thorax, and tie the knot to stop the pumping action of the heart. This would eliminate all possibility of the blood's acting as a potential coolant. But would the moths with extirpated hearts fly at all?

40   They did indeed, but soon stopped with heat prostration at high air temperatures. Even air temperatures of 24°C were too high for them, as their thoracic temperature approached the lethal limit of 46°C (115°F). With their heat-dissipation mechanism totally gone, but with the insulating scales removed from the thorax, they could fly at air temperatures several degrees higher. This was frosting on the cake. To see what had never been seen before and to have it confirmed is an indescribable feeling. At this point I published a short report in *Science* to foreshadow a more detailed account where the full evidence could be given.

41   If I thought that the moth problem had been settled, however, I was sadly mistaken. I need not have worried about getting scooped. The other papers did come out on thermoregulation in *Manduca sexta,* but none of the workers had deciphered the mechanism of thermoregulation in flight. One of Heath's students showed that the moths' temperature sensitivity resides in the thoracic ganglion, adjacent to the thoracic muscles. Heath and his colleagues made numerous calculations to construct hypothetically derived relationships and models. Drawing from earlier work in the same lab, they now claimed (as before) that "measured rates of oxygen consumption in flying animals increase as air temperature decreases," causing them to conclude that flying moths thermoregulate in the manner of known endotherms generally measured at rest (by varying heat production). Their measured metabolic rates closely matched the calculated rates of how much heat the moths "should" produce.

42   Later I learned through correspondence that their flying moths had their wings amputated; the researchers assumed that wing-stub movements corresponded to actual flight. It was a detail that made all the difference, but they had not deemed it important enough to state in their published methods. I had already suspected that their supposedly flying moths had not been in flight at all; using their own data I was able to show that some of their moths "flying" at high air temperatures had rates of heat production identical to those of torpid moths at the same temperature. Perhaps these workers were blinded by their preconceptions based on higher vertebrate endotherms. It is easy to see what you are looking for, as any intent deerhunter can testify when he sees a big buck in every arrangement of brown ferns and branches.

43   After I left UCLA for the summer to go back to Maine, I stopped off at a symposium in Bloomington, Indiana, where Heath was scheduled to speak on the regulation of heat production in moths. It was a large new auditorium, well filled with people. Heath was a forceful speaker, and he presented his evidence for thermoregula-

tion. Questions were pounding in my head: "What was your chart speed when you measured warm-up rates?" "Are you certain that your flying moths did not, even for a fraction of a second, stop beating their wings?" The questions had to be asked, and I put up my hand. The dean of comparative physiology, who was presiding, called on me, but hardly had I opened my mouth when he asked me to sit down. He suggested that I should see Heath afterwards.

44   So I did: "Look, we obviously have drastically different conceptions of this problem . . ." Our moth discussion was short. We wandered over to a room where a large group was having an informal get-together over beer. Heath talked about the hypothalamus of birds. There was no indication that he had any interest in discussing the moth problem. I was frustrated. One of the people in the group said to me, "I suspect that your moths and Heath's moths will, with time, become more and more alike." Perhaps, I thought. But how and by whom would that be decided? Which moth would the scientific community "see"? The experimental evidence had already been published. I couldn't provide better proof—if this didn't do it, what would?

45   It seems that it is not always the force of the experiment or the evidence that wins the day. It is also the force of the argument and prestige of the person presenting it. I would at least have to write a visible article to guide readers into the principles of insect thermo-regulation so that they would want to delve into the details. I would have to offer a broad theoretical perspective. Only then could the results fit into a rational pattern and no longer be ignored simply out of convenience. With these thoughts in mind, I wrote a review article. After a rejection, I protested that the criticisms of the anonymous referee were not valid. The journal reconsidered, and the paper was published in 1974.

46   Six years later I overheard two students. Their conversation went something like this:

47   "Did you get that exam question on thermoregulation in big flying insects?"

48   "Sure. The insects stabilize thoracic temperature by shunting heat by the blood to the abdomen."

49   "How did they prove that?"

50   "Easy. They just tied off the blood vessel to the thorax."

51   "Oh! And what about the other question on . . . ?"

52   As in so many discoveries, any reasonably capable person could have performed the conclusive experiment. But what makes the experiment possible is the long struggle of ideas that leads up to it.

Index

Index

Movies, citing, 237

N

"Naked," (China Forbes), 44–48
Narration, 27
Neffinger, Gian, "House of Cards,"
 93–96
Newspaper articles, citing, 236
Notes, 243–244

O

"Old Mrs. Grey," (Virginia Woolf),
 353–354
"*Onamaewa* (What is your name?),"
 (Leon Yen), 12, 255–259
Order
 ideas and, 136–145
 imposing, 22–28

P

"Painful (in)Justice?," (Simon Pole),
 149–153
Parenthetical documentation, 228–238
Pattern, 132–135
Periodicals, articles in, citing, 235–236
Persona, 123–132
Personal experience, 28–30
Personal style, 78–85
Peters, Barbara, "Another Light,"
 155–157
Pickering, Samuel F., Jr., "Being
 Familiar," 130–132, 269–279
Plagiarism, 77
Plays, citing, 238
Poems, citing, 37
Pole, Simon, "Painful (in)Justice?,"
 149–153
Preliminary research, 172–180
Preparation, manuscript, 247–248
Primary texts, 168–169

Punctuation marks in quotation marks,
 248

Q

Question, restricted topic (RTQ),
 175–176
Quotation marks
 with block quotations, 239
 punctuation marks in, 248
Quotations
 block, 76, 145, 239, 245
 from secondary sources, 246
Quoted evidence, 146–147

R

Reading, 2–3
 additional, 83
 essays for, 249–404
 to find controversial issues, 172–180
Reading and Writing Essays, 1–4
Recordings, citing, 236–237
Reed, Roy, "Spring Comes to
 Hogeye," 16–20, 259–263
"Report from the Bahamas, 1982,"
 (June Jordan), 306–319
Reports versus essays, 178–180
Research
 future, guidelines for, 223–225
 preliminary, 172–180
Research essays, 2
 short, *see* Short research essays
Restricted topic question (RTQ),
 175–176
Revision, 160–164
Rhetorical considerations, 241–243
RTQ (restricted topic question),
 175–176

S

Sanders, Scott Russell, "The Men We
 Carry in Our Minds," 263–269